IFIP Advances in Information and Communication Technology 737

Editor-in-Chief

Kai Rannenberg, Goethe University Frankfurt, Germany

Editorial Board Members

IFIP Advances in Information and Communication Technology

The IFIP AICT series publishes state-of-the-art results in the sciences and technologies of information and communication. The scope of the series includes: foundations of computer science; software theory and practice; education; computer applications in technology; communication systems; systems modeling and optimization; information systems; ICT and society; computer systems technology; security and protection in information processing systems; artificial intelligence; and human-computer interaction.

Edited volumes and proceedings of refereed international conferences in computer science and interdisciplinary fields are featured. These results often precede journal publication and represent the most current research.

The principal aim of the IFIP AICT series is to encourage education and the dissemination and exchange of information about all aspects of computing.

More information about this series at https://link.springer.com/bookseries/6102

Gaëtan Rey · Jean-Yves Tigli ·
Erwin Franquet
Editors

Internet of Things

7th IFIP WG 5.5 International Cross-Domain Conference, IFIPIoT 2024
Nice, France, November 6–8, 2024
Proceedings

 Springer

Editors
Gaëtan Rey 🅾
Université Côte d'Azur, CNRS, I3S
Sophia Antipolis, France

Jean-Yves Tigli 🅾
Université Côte d'Azur, CNRS, I3S
Sophia Antipolis, France

Erwin Franquet 🅾
Université Côte d'Azur, Polytech'Lab
Sophia Antipolis, France

ISSN 1868-4238   ISSN 1868-422X   (electronic)
IFIP Advances in Information and Communication Technology
ISBN 978-3-031-81899-8   ISBN 978-3-031-81900-1   (eBook)
https://doi.org/10.1007/978-3-031-81900-1

This Springer imprint is published by the registered company Springer Nature Switzerland AG
The registered company address is: Gewerbestrasse 11, 6330 Cham, Switzerland

If disposing of this product, please recycle the paper.

Preface

The rapid evolution of technology has led to the development of the Internet of Things (IoT), a network of physical objects that are embedded with sensors, software, and network connectivity, enabling them to collect and exchange data. The IoT is transforming our digital landscape, and the IFIP Internet of Things (IFIP-IoT) 2024 conference was a crucial platform for scholars, researchers, and practitioners to come together, share ideas, and advance this transformative field.

This edited book is a compilation of cutting-edge research and developments presented at the IFIP-IoT conference. The conference serves as a dynamic hub where experts from diverse backgrounds come together to explore the multifaceted aspects of IoT, from its technological foundations to its far-reaching implications for society, industry, and beyond.

The chapters in this book are a testament to the collaborative spirit of the IFIP-IoT community. They offer insights into the latest innovations, challenges, and opportunities in IoT, covering a wide array of topics, including IoT architectures, security and privacy, data analytics, edge computing, and applications in various domains. These contributions not only reflect the state of the art in IoT research but also provide valuable perspectives that pave the way for future breakthroughs.

The IFIP-IoT Conference is an annual IFIP event dedicated to IoT research, innovation, and applications, emphasizing the multidisciplinary nature of IoT. IoT encompasses topics from network protocols and embedded systems to analytics, machine learning, and social, legal, ethical, and economic considerations, enabling services in e-health, mobility, energy, manufacturing, smart cities, agriculture, and more. Security, privacy, and societal aspects are essential in IoT deployment. IFIP-IoT covers these diverse areas, seeking papers showcasing technical advancements, research, innovation, pilot results, and policy discussions. Contributors include researchers, users, organizations, ICT industry experts, authorities, and regulators.

IFIP-IoT 2024 welcomed full and short paper submissions, with full papers being original and unpublished elsewhere. The conference program featured keynotes, plenary talks, tutorials, technical sessions, special sessions, and expert panels. Two new workshops were added to the conference this year: STAND4IoT on various aspects of IoT standards and GRAAL4IoT on design, verification, and validation of IoT systems. A session was dedicated to the presentation of several Horizon Europe projects all contributing to IoT system security, design, and management. This session was initiated and organized by the DYNABIC EU project.

The conference, including the workshops, received a total of 33 submissions. 13 full papers and 4 short papers were accepted out of 28 submissions for the main conference. In addition 5 workshop papers and 3 poster papers were accepted for publication. The paper submission guidelines included an 18-page limit for full papers, which applied to both regular and workshop sessions, as well as a 12-page limit for short papers, applicable to any session. To ensure a thorough review process, we implemented a two-tier review mechanism within EasyChair, consisting of TPC Chairs, and TPC members as reviewers. Reviews were single-blind, with each submission receiving at least three reviews. We took measures to address conflicts of interest by appointing multiple TPC Chairs and multiple Track Chairs for each track. Additionally, we imposed a limit of 2 papers maximum for PC members. Furthermore, our conference included Regular Tracks/Sessions that accepted submissions from any authors, as well as Special Sessions/Tracks proposed by established researchers, with submissions received by invitation.

The IFIP-IoT conference had six regular tracks, each focusing on a different aspect of IoT:

- **Hardware/Software Solutions for IoT and CPS**: This track focused on the integration of hardware and software technologies to enable the development of efficient and scalable systems for the IoT and CPS. This track explored topics such as system architecture, energy-efficient hardware design, low-power communication protocols, software optimization for resource-constrained devices, and security and privacy issues. Additionally, this track highlighted recent advancements and future research directions in the field of IoT and CPS, including machine learning and artificial intelligence techniques, edge computing, and cloud-based systems.
- **Electronics and Signal Processing for IoT**: This track focused on the design and development of electronic devices and signal processing techniques for IoT applications. This track covered a broad range of topics, including sensor design, low-power electronics, wireless communication, and embedded systems. The track also explored signal processing techniques such as signal acquisition, filtering, compression, and analysis.
- **Networking and Communications Technology for IoT**: This track focused on the latest advancements and innovations in the field of IoT, in particular on IoT networking, wireless and wired communication technologies, protocols, standards, and applications.
- **Artificial Intelligence and Machine Learning Technologies for IoT**: This track focused on the integration of AI and ML techniques for IoT applications. This track covered a broad range of topics including the development of intelligent algorithms, big data analytics, and decision-making frameworks for IoT systems. The track also explored the use of AI and ML for predictive maintenance, anomaly detection, and optimization of IoT systems. The AI and ML track highlighted advancements and challenges in the field of IoT systems and their integration with AI and ML techniques.
- **Cyber Security/Privacy/Trust for IoT and CPS**: This track focused on the security and privacy challenges of IoT and CPS systems. This track covered a broad range of topics including cyber threats, privacy breaches, data breaches, and unauthorized access to IoT and CPS systems. The track also explored solutions for securing IoT and CPS systems, including cryptographic techniques, security protocols, intrusion detection, and prevention mechanisms. Additionally, this track discussed the challenges of maintaining trust and privacy in IoT and CPS systems and the importance of ethical considerations.

- **IoT or CPS Applications and Use Cases**: This track focused on exploring the real-world applications and use cases of IoT and CPS technology. The track brought together experts and professionals from various industries to discuss the challenges, opportunities, and innovative solutions for utilizing IoT and CPS to improve various domains such as healthcare, transportation, energy, agriculture, and others.

In addition to the session papers, the IFIP-IoT 2024 conference featured 2 workshops, 2 poster sessions, and 3 invited presentations. We are pleased to announce that all of these sessions took place and contributed to the IFIP-IoT 2024 conference:

- **GRAAL4IoT Workshop**: The GRAAL4IoT International Workshop was one of the most appropriate venues to discuss and advance all topics related to the design, verification, and validation of IoT systems, with a special focus on security. The main goals of the workshop were: (1) to encourage work on novel topics covering both fundamental and applied research in the design, verification, and validation of IoT systems, (2) to bring together researchers from the software development and IoT communities, and to foster discussions between theorists and practitioners.
- **STAND4IoT Workshop**: The international workshop Standards4IoT was the place to discuss all topics related to the standardization of IoT systems with different focuses. More specifically, the objectives of Standards4IoT were: (1) to gain a better understanding of the field of standardization and to demonstrate the concrete actions of this work; (2) to promote work on novel topics covering standardization research and/or education; (3) to bring together the IoT communities of industry, developers, and researchers to foster discussions on current common issues such as security, efficiency, and sustainability.
- **Invited Talks:**

  - **AI Detects and Mitigates Cyber-Attacks by Erol Gelenbe**: Simple cyber-attacks can disrupt networks for hours or days, compromise data security and cause unpredictable effects through malware. This underscores the importance of early detection and effective response. The presentation focused on the use of the Random Neural Network for cyber-attack detection, describing the mathematical model, deep learning algorithms, and concrete examples with low false alarm rates. Experiments with active mitigation strategies were also presented.
  - **Privacy in the IoT: Evolution and Expectations by Maryline Laurent**: Faced with the need to track the activity of objects, manage them flexibly and securely, detect anomalies, and make the best possible economic use of the data collected, it is imperative to preserve privacy in the IoT environment. The presentation identified the scientific challenges of IoT privacy with categories of solutions and then identified several emerging research topics in support of privacy preservation in the IOT.
  - **DEVS as a language for IoT System Design by Bernard P. Zeigler**: As IoT applications evolve, adaptive behaviours become essential. Although complex adaptive systems have existed in theory for some time, their implementation in operational IoT systems is still evolving. The DEVS formalism enables modular,

adaptive modelling, facilitating verification and the transition between design and implementation of IoT systems.

We are grateful to the authors who contributed their expertise to these volumes, and we commend their dedication to advancing the field of IoT. We would also like to acknowledge the reviewers whose insightful feedback ensured the quality and rigor of the included chapters.

We hope that these edited books will serve as a valuable resource for researchers, educators, policymakers, and industry professionals alike, fostering a deeper understanding of IoT and inspiring further innovation in this transformative domain. As the IFIP-IoT conference continues to evolve and grow, we look forward to witnessing the continued impact of this vibrant community on the ever-expanding Internet of Things.

November 2024

Gaëtan Rey
Jean-Yves Tigli
Erwin Franquet

Organization

General Chairs

Gaëtan Rey   Université Côte d'Azur, France
Jean-Yves Tigli   Université Côte d'Azur, France
Erwin Franquet   Université Côte d'Azur, France

Technical Program Chairs

Ana Rosa Cavalli   Institut Polytechnique de Paris, France
Bidyadhar Subudhi   Indian Institute of Technology Goa, India
Lei Chen   Georgia Southern University, USA
Leonardo Lizzi   University of Trento, Italy
Phu Nguyen   SINTEF, Norway
Srinivas Katkoori   University of South Florida, USA
Te-Chuan Chiu   National Tsing Hua University, Taiwan

Workshops Chairs

Nicolas Ferry   Université Côte d'Azur, France
Marie-Agnès Peraldi-Frati   Université Côte d'Azur, France

Technical Program Committee

Mike Borowczak   University of Central Florida, USA
Karima Boudaoud   Université Côte d'Azur, France
Laurent Capocchi   Université de Corse, France
Sibi Chakkaravarthy S.   VIT-AP University, India
Lei Chen   Georgia Southern University, USA
Te-Chuan Chiu   National Tsing Hua University, Taiwan
Jiban Das   Georgia Southern University, USA
Kaustubh Dhondge   Glaukes Labs, USA
Fabien Ferrero   Université Côte d'Azur, France
Nicolas Ferry   Université Côte d'Azur, France
Erwin Franquet   Université Côte d'Azur, France
Agbotiname Imoize   University of Lagos, Nigeria
Dheryta Jaisinghani   University of Northern Iowa, USA
Jongyeop Kim   Georgia Southern University, USA
Ashok Kumar   IBM, USA
Stéphane Lavirotte   Université Côte d'Azur, France
Leonardo Lizzi   University of Trento, Italy
Dino Lopez   Université Côte d'Azur, France

Contents

Artificial Intelligence and Machine Learning Technologies for IoT

Cyber Security/Privacy/Trust for IoT and CPS

IoT or CPS Applications and Use Cases

Hardware/Software Solutions for IoT and CPS

Relocation of Container-Based Services in a MEC-NFV Orchestrated Environment

Cristina Bernad[1]([✉])(iD), Vojdan Kjorveziroski[2](iD), Pedro Roig[1](iD),
Salvador Alcaraz[1](iD), Katja Gilly[1](iD), and Sonja Filiposka[2](iD)

[1] Department of Computer Engineering, Miguel Hernández University, Elche
(Alicante), Spain
{cbernad,proig,salcaraz,katya}@umh.es
[2] Faculty of Computer Science and Engineering, Ss. Cyril and Methodius University,
Skopje, North Macedonia
{vojdan.kjorveziroski,sonja.filiposka}@finki.ukim.mk

Abstract. With the rapid growth of real-time next-generation mobile services, it has become necessary to work towards holistic orchestration of the benefits promised with edge computing based on bringing the computing infrastructure closer to the end user. While the concept of Multi-access Edge Computing (MEC) integrated with Network Function Virtualisation (NFV) is being standardised, there is still a lot of work to be done to orchestrate the relocation of edge applications integrated in 5G and beyond systems in a smooth and efficient manner. In this paper, we document the current status of the transparent relocation of edge services in an experimentally deployed MEC-NFV environment based on OSM. Working towards gathering monitoring training datasets necessary for the development of proactive MEC application orchestrators that will implement seamless follow-me behaviour for MEC services, we provide benchmark results for the service downtime of three potential MEC services hosted in lightweight containers. Our analysis of results shows that containers exhibit improved performance over that of virtual machines, but there are still some issues that require improvement in both the orchestration implementation as well at the relocation process for containers.

Keywords: Edge Computing · Optimisation · Standardisation · Migration · Mobile nodes · Containers

1 Introduction

Dynamic online services have an important role in people's daily lives worldwide. With the promised specifications of 5G [1], which include ultra-low latency (less than 1 ms), high data rates (over 10 Gbps), and high reliability (99.999%), the design and implementation of real-time services for mobile users that make use of the increased bandwidth and reduced latency times has been accelerated, promoting applications such as 4K video, autonomous cars, augmented reality,

© IFIP International Federation for Information Processing 2025
Published by Springer Nature Switzerland AG 2025
G. Rey et al. (Eds.): IFIPIoT 2024, IFIP AICT 737, pp. 3–20, 2025.
https://doi.org/10.1007/978-3-031-81900-1_1

telemedicine, or IoT devices. This explosion of services with a wide variation in flexible resource requirements in terms of networking and computing needs to be addressed by taking advantage of several complementary technologies.

The self-organisation of networking systems emerges as an important challenge that requires to be taken into consideration so as to provide the network with the necessary capabilities to readjust resource management and network configurations in real-time based on the highly changing service demands. Technological advances such as Software Defined Networking (SDN) technologies, which define and adapt network topologies programmatically and Network Function Virtualisation (NFV), which enables the virtualisation of network services and functions such as firewalls, routers, etc.; provide the ability to build agile networks with on-the-fly configurations [2].

To fully support the next-generation users of highly demanding applications, the computation facilities need to be brought closer to data sources thus reducing the user-perceived latency. In other words, 5G and beyond services need to be integrated with edge computing solutions such as the Multi-access Edge Computing (MEC) initiative promoted by the European Telecommunications Standards Institute (ETSI), which has spent years working on standardising the edge architecture for mobile users (MEC) [3]. Moreover, the union of 5G and MEC facilitates an optimal result when dealing with the requirements of real-time applications (high bandwidth, ultra-low delay and intense computational effort), requirements that the cloud cannot fully cover. Recognising that the marriage of MEC and 5G will pave the way for a holistic approach to developing a unified system based on mutual benefits, ETSI has released a new version of the MEC architecture standardisation that focuses on implementing the MEC system as a part of an NFV architecture, thus effectively incorporating MEC into 5G [4]. This view provides a way to manage the lifecycle of MEC applications alongside other virtual network functions (VNFs), while recognising the need to orchestrate the MEC services in a specific way that enables the implementation of placement and migration policies based on the quality of service (QoS) and user location. The overall VNF orchestrator in the system is managed by an NFV Management and Orchestration (MANO) orchestrator [5].

Using servers co-located with 5G base stations at the edge, as close to the end user as possible, MEC applications are released from the computational load, delay is reduced and bandwidth is gained. To ensure a sustained high-performing edge system, efficient implementation of the edge facilities and their highly dynamic resource management is a must. The increased complexity in this scenario is due to the fact that mobility is implicit in online mobile services. Thus, continuous ultra-low latency requires that the MEC application 'follows' the user's trajectory [6]. Therefore, taking into consideration a changing ecosystem, MEC applications may be instantiated in the currently optimal computing node, but as users move to a different geographical area, i.e. the user is being handed off from one 5G base station to another, the allocated MEC service needs to be moved to a 'closer' computing node. It is strictly necessary for the MEC-NFV system to be able to manage and orchestrate this 'follow me' practice, that permits MEC applications to be migrated between geographically dispersed computing nodes.

The brains for this operation in the MEC-NFV architecture fall on the shoulders of the MEC application orchestrator [7]. This component is vital when it comes to the decision-making on optimal placement of new MEC services as well as maintaining high QoS during the MEC service use by smartly migrating the MEC service using the follow-me paradigm. The decisions made by the MEC orchestrator can trigger adjustments in the MEC-NFV system via the NFV orchestrator. A proactive decision-making implementation of the MEC orchestrator can take advantage of the current and past knowledge about the system to forecast future service migrations and thus improve the overall system performance. This is the reason why the attention in MEC orchestration and decision-making has been focused on proactive approaches, mostly based on Artificial Intelligence (AI) [8]. However, to be able to take full advantage of the potential of AI forecasting the model needs to be fed with a lot of information regarding the users and services status.

To address the challenge of online services live migrations in a MEC architecture, we have developed a testbed environment based on ETSI MEC-NFV [4] using the Open Source MANO (OSM) orchestrator. Considering the functions that each element of the architecture must perform [9], we have carried out tests with different types of potential MEC applications according to their computational load. Traditionally in the ETSI MEC ecosystems, virtual machines (VMs) are considered as the virtualisation technology used to host MEC services. Observing the increasing use of containers in virtual computing environments, we have developed an experimental MEC implementation using containers to host MEC services aiming to verify the behaviour of the MEC orchestrator when performing on-demand service migrations. This has also enabled us to analyse the current possibilities to implement seamless container relocation in a MEC-NFV architecture implemented using OSM as the NFV orchestrator. While application instantiation benchmark results exist using the old version of OSM, to the best of the authors' knowledge, there is no study that provides benchmark results regarding the relocation of standalone containers in an OSM-based MEC-NFV experimental environment.

We summarise the contributions of this paper as follows:

– investigate the ability to implement 'follow-me' relocation functionality in the current OSM release while using standalone containers to host MEC services,
– comparative performance analysis of migrating Kubernetes containers and Microstack virtual machines in an MEC-NFV environment,
– gather benchmark migration data that can be used for training proactive MEC orchestrator resource management algorithms.

The rest of the document is structured as follows: In Sect. 2, we address the background and motivation of our tests. We analyse the current state of using OSM to implement a MEC-NFV system based on standalone containers that will support seamless follow-me behaviour in Sect. 3. In Sect. 4 we discuss the developed experimental environment. In Sect. 5 we present the results obtained and finally we conclude the article and comment on future work.

2   Background and Motivation

The problem of optimal placement of MEC services that needs to be solved by the MEC orchestrator has been a very active field of research in recent years. Different approaches have been proposed to correctly identify the 'correct' node where the MEC service should be instantiated so as to achieve maximum performance. In [10] the authors propose a Markov approximation algorithm to optimise the placement of shared VMs taking into account the price of implementing MEC systems. In [11] they focus on minimising the average response time using a latency-aware heuristic placement algorithm for VM placement, while the topic of energy-aware resource placement using trees social relations algorithm is the topic of interest in [12].

In contrast to the typical reactive approach, where the optimal placement is decided upon receiving a service request, lately, there is a growing number of proactive approaches that are attempting to forecast an optimal placement before the actual request comes in. Most of these approaches are based on the implementation of Machine Learning (ML) techniques such as [13, 14], including deep learning [15]. In addition, recent research has also focused on the need to relocate the once-instantiated MEC services in order to preserve optimal QoS. The study in [16] proposes a Deep Reinforcement Learning to estimate optimal policy that jointly minimises migration cost, transaction cost, and consumed energy. It also provides a very good overview of the different approaches to MEC service migration both conventional and learning-based.

Typically, the performance of the proposed approaches is based on numerical analysis or simulation frameworks that enable the analysis of what-if scenarios as is the case with [16] for one example. To ensure that the perceived performance will be attainable in real-life implementations, it is essential that the work is also tried and tested in an experimental testbed that will provide the opportunity to ascertain how all components of the 5G-MEC system are orchestrated by the MEC orchestrator. For these purposes, a well-defined, validated and benchmarked testbed needs to be established, which not only incurs cost and resources but also requires experience in setting up and managing virtualised infrastructures and MANO solutions. Another problem that arises is that the current development of MEC orchestration functionalities mostly focuses on using VMs to host MEC services, while real-life implementations are starting to move away from VMs and turn towards containers as their lightweight cloud-native counterparts due to optimised performances and pricing.

To help close this gap of MEC orchestration analysis in an experimental environment, researchers have proposed new edge orchestration architectures such as [17] that serves as a MEC platform where MEC services can be hosted in containers and is compliant with the main ETSI MEC architecture. The authors in [18] propose their own orchestration architecture that is loosely based on ETSI

NFV and MEC aiming to provide multi-layered orchestration. However, having in mind that the ETSI NFV architecture is closely followed in the 5G implementations, and the ETSI MEC-NFV [4] provides a multi-layer orchestration for this scenario, using open-source solutions that implement the NFV MANO functionalities will enable building an experimental scenario that can be very close to real-life implementations. Towards this goal, the authors in [19] validate and benchmark a test-bed implementation of the ETSI-compliant Open Source MANO (OSM) [20] in combination with Kubernetes containers as the main virtualisation technology. The authors in this work focus on the placement of container-based network functions as the newly available feature in OSM release 7. OSM is one of the most popular open source NFV MANO solutions [21] and is therefore the solution of choice when building experimental testbeds as is the case with [22,23]. In both works the focus is on relocation of containers managed by OSM and hosted inside an OpenStack virtual infrastructure. While [23] uses OpenNESS as the edge management platform for the containers inside OpenStack, [22] builds an additional layer with the MEC orchestrator in accordance with the ETSI MEC-NFV proposed architecture. The focus of both is the implementation of application context switching for container migration and its incurring delay in the system that has been found to be increasing linearly with its size.

As the current research focus is put mostly on placement-only for MEC services together combined with experimental environments that are implemented with containers inside VMs, we aim our research on the topic of validating and benchmarking relocation of containers deployed using a standalone Kubernetes platform in an ETSI MEC-NFV environment using OSM. Thus we complement and build upon the work discussed previously while using a newer release of OSM compared to previous efforts. By analysing the latency incurred when relocating several different MEC applications as both VMs and containers, we are able to produce additional monitoring data that can be of further use to the deep learning MEC orchestration algorithms that currently mostly focus on data related to the user and base station.

3   Container Relocation in a MEC-NFV Environment Using OSM

The ETSI's MEC initiative is promoting a standardisation effort that periodically provides enhanced versions of its open environment framework and reference architecture for edge computing in mobile environments. The latest release [3] includes a variant for MEC deployment in an NFV environment given in Fig. 1 wherein the role of the MEC Orchestrator which is the management heart of the MEC ecosystem is split between the 'Mobile Edge Application Orchestrator' (MEAO) and the 'Network Functions Virtualisation Orchestrator' (NFVO).

This division of functionalities enables the integration of the ETSI NFV high-level functional architectural framework and design philosophy of virtualised network functions in the edge reference model. When handling MEC applications,

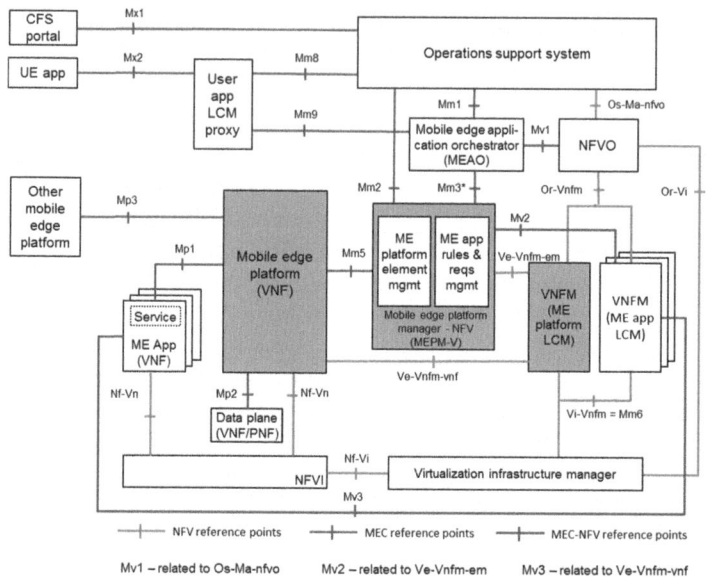

Fig. 1. NFV-based MEC generic architecture [3].

the MEAO module is the high-level orchestrator that decides when and where to put/move a virtualised instance based on user information, monitoring information, available resources and topology. The actual actions of management of the lifecycle of a MEC application are left to the NFVO which translates the MEAO orchestration decisions to Virtual Network Functions (VNF) language and executes them. The ETSI NFV special interest group has issued a standard NFV Management and Orchestration (MANO) framework [5] that covers the functionality of the NFVO module defined in the MEC-NFV architecture and with OSM developed as an open source implementation of this framework [20].

Within the MEC-NFV architecture from the perspective of NFVO the MEC application is considered as just another type of Virtual Network Function (VNF). The typical implementation of VNFs supported by existing MANO frameworks is in the form of a VM. In recent years, interest in containers as an alternative virtualisation technology has grown significantly. ETSI is putting more effort into integrating CNFs (Containerised Network Functions) in the reference system [24] as the range of implemented services as containers is constantly increasing. Applications running in containers can be deployed faster by downloading from many public repositories and simply executing, which not only saves time for the development teams but also enables a straightforward expansion of the MEC service portfolio with a large number of third-party applications.

The key difference between VMs and containers is that VMs virtualise the entire machine down to the hardware (hardware-level virtualisation), and containers only virtualise the software layers above the operating system (OS) level.

In hardware-level virtualisation, the hypervisor (also called virtual machine monitor) emulates server hardware resources to the different deployed VMs. Each VM runs its OS and applications in a way that several instances of virtualised applications effectively share the same physical server. On the other hand, virtualisation at the OS encapsulates dependencies such as libraries and OS processes to create containers. Containers are deployed using a lightweight virtualisation layer that leads to obtaining an improved performance at a lower cost. Both virtualisation systems can be deployed in the 5G and MEC ecosystem.

In accordance with this move towards containers, in its release 7, the feature to manage CNFs has been added to OSM. However, even with the regular new releases of OSM with the current latest being 14, it still doesn't offer full support for CNFs. Instead, OSM MEC applications are implemented as VNFs considering the MEC-NFV architecture in Fig. 1. The use of containers in the OSM context is still not straightforward and mostly stays in the same status as in release 7 [19]. From an MEAO point of view, this creates a complicated situation, as the MEC orchestrator expects to be able to fully control the location of placement and relocation of containers and get real-time info about their status. In this section, we aim to describe how container relocation can be implemented in OSM and what are the lessons learnt while implementing our experimental testbed.

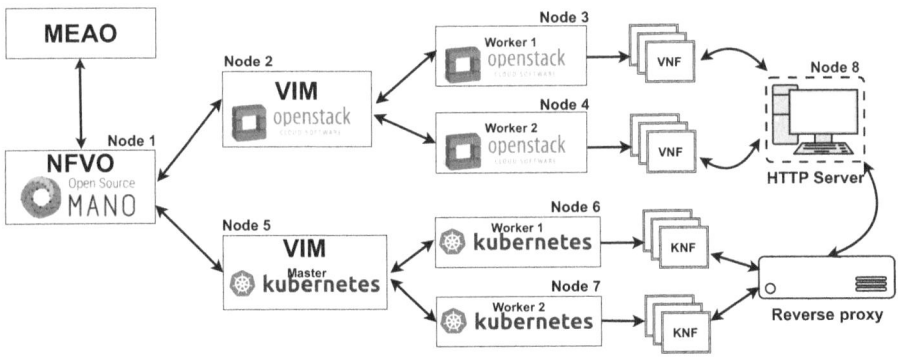

Fig. 2. Configuration used in our experimental deployment from Kubernetes perspective

In alignment with the ETSI NFV MANO specification, the management of the underlying virtualised infrastructure is performed by the Virtualisation Infrastructure Manager (VIM) that prepares the infrastructure to boot the software image and reports information about it. It also is the one that should execute a relocation of any application when commanded by the NFVO.

In the OSM case, if the VIM is implemented based on VMs, using OpenStack or MicroStack for managing VMs, for example, then the addition of the MEAO in the overall system is quite straightforward. OSM supports the ability to control the destination node for a network service placement, and it offers the ability to migrate a service from the source node to the destination node, while at the same time reporting on the current status and progress. This means that the MEAO components only need to call the OSM Northbound API to be able to effectuate the decision made using its smart follow-me algorithms.

When it comes to using containers, the situation is much more complicated. As already mentioned, OSM supports network functions based on Kubernetes in the form of Kubernetes-based VNFs (KNFs) since version 7. Ever since the features regarding managing KNFs with OSM have not improved much. To be able to run KNFs, required to create a Kubernetes cluster and link it to a VIM network [25] so that it can be used for MEC services deployment via OSM. In this way, the Kubernetes cluster should behave as expected even when the pod management commands come from a higher entity such as OSM.

To build the test environment, we have followed the requirements described in the OSM documentation that include installing a load balancer (used for automated instantiation of containers based on current performance) and the storage class that includes the non-SQL database system MongoDB [26]. It is important to note that there are two different options to connect OSM with a Kubernetes (K8s) cluster:

- the cluster can be deployed inside a VM that is running in the OSM's registered VIM, where all VMs are connected to the VIM network; or
- a standalone K8s cluster (bare-metal or virtualised) can be physically connected to the VIM network.

All previous research related to the relocation of containers that are known to the authors is implemented using the first option: inside a VM. The reason behind this is that currently, this is the only way to use the OSM Northbound API to control the placement of the KNFs indirectly, by controlling the VMs on which the worker nodes are placed, requiring a distributed work nodes approach as in [22]. This scenario is however not desirable when it comes to performances and, more importantly, direct use and management of containers.

In this paper, we opted to choose the second configuration of standalone containers for our environment. As we chose to implement the K8s cluster outside the OSM's VIM, we have defined a controller node and two separate worker nodes that implement Network Services (NS) using Kubernetes containers. In this way, we can gain the maximum performance of the worker nodes unlike [19] wherein the worker nodes are co-located with the controller which is not recommended for production environments. The details of setting up standalone containers are fully documented in [19]. In this text, we only highlight the most important steps to emphasise that the need for clear distinction and improved handling of CNFs still persists.

The definition of an edge service in OSM is provided in a network service descriptor (NSD) that is defined in YAML and includes a description of the service format and requirements. Although similar to what is used to deploy VMs, it needs to be adapted for use with Kubernetes containers and linked to the external Kubernetes cluster. We provide the adapted NSD that can then be deployed as a KNF in Fig. 3(a). As the structure of the definition is exactly the same as the one used to define network services for VMs, the container-based NSD is relatively simple to develop. The adapted NSD defines a virtual link descriptor (VLD) that is provided where it can be observed that the 'ClusterIP' is the label used to identify the OSM's internal IP address that connects to the Kubernetes cluster. This label is also defined in the Kubernetes cluster as an external IP address. The ClusterIP service, default in Kubernetes, offers specific communication within the cluster, with access restricted to other applications or internal services. To boost Internet access, the Kubernetes proxy is used. In contrast, Ingress Controller is not classified as some kind of service in itself, but rather as a vital substance that sits before numerous services, acting as the highest passing point for our cluster. This device is especially cost-effective when you want to present different services over the same IP address, offering a perfect solution for test and development situations. We chose to use Nginx, which is one of the most common and versatile solutions for this purpose.

Finally, Fig. 3(b) defines the adapted virtual network function descriptor (VNFD) that is now used as a KNFD with a single Kubernetes deployment unit (KDU) that links to the K8s repository in OSM using a 'helm-chart' from where the image of the application is downloaded to be immediately instantiated in a Kubernetes pod. A K8s repository is defined in OSM where a large number of edge applications can be directly downloaded and instantiated. Note that typically for VMs the hardware resources that constitute the VNF are defined in the VNFD wherein you can define the location of the VNF. On the other hand, in KNFs this is not possible.

In essence, for the standalone K8s option in OSM this translates to the inability to use the OSM Northbound API to control the placement and relocation of the KNFs, leaving this to the Kubernetes controller that will place the containers, re-instantiate them in another pod or scale them based on the monitoring feedback received. This makes the development of a MEAO that will control standalone KNFs via OSM not possible at the moment.

Another important difference when considering containers instead of VMs, is that the concept of container migration is quite different and significantly more difficult to perform [27]. While for VMs the process of live migration is fully implemented and documented in many available VIMs today, to migrate a service for containers such as Kubernetes, it is required to first move a pod from one edge node to another by creating an identical container on the destination node and then deleting the container on the source node (leaving it to the SDN implementation to seamlessly move the network connection for the user). Because of the complexities when it comes to container migration, there is no single command to migrate a container available in OSM nor in the underlying Kubernetes infrastructure as is the case with VMs. As a showcase example of these complexities, in [28] the challenges of performing a live migration of containers made up of one or more pods (the minimum unit in Kubernetes) is discussed. The authors focus their efforts on extending the capabilities of K8s to perform a live migration using the CRIU tool that provides the ability to transfer the container checkpoint states on the destination node. However, as

```
vld :
- name: external
  vim-network-name: external
  additionalParamsForVnf :
- member-vnf-index : lang_detec_knf
  additionalParamsForKdu :
  - kdu_name : lang_detec_knf
    additionalParams :
      ingress :
        enabled : true
        className : nginx
        url : lang-detec.test.local
      service :
        type : ClusterIP
      name : knf_packets_received
      performance-metric : packets_received
```

a) Additional parameters for the NSD defined in OSM

```
vnfd :
  description : KNF with single KDU using helm-chart
  df :
  - id : default-df
  ext-cpd :
  - id : mgmt-ext
    k8s-cluster-net : external
  id : lang_detec_knf
  k8s-cluster :
    nets :
    - id : external
  kdu :
  - name : lang_detec_knf
    helm-chart : lang-detect-KNF/flask-lang-detect
    mgmt-cp : mgmt-ext
  product-name : lang_detec_knf
  provider : test
  version : 1.0
```

b) KNFD links with the K8s cluster and repository

Fig. 3. YAML definitions of container-based network services in OSM

the source pod is deleted and another one is created on the destination during the migration, it is not possible to maintain smooth IP/TCP connections as the pod IP changes on the destination host. This is where SDN comes into play to ensure transparent networking from the user perspective. In addition, note that if the MEC services are stateful and require context switching during the container migration procedure then this must be performed manually by following the process described in [22].

To circumvent the problem of no existing readily available Northbound API in OSM for fine control of the KNF placement for standalone containers, we have developed an additional software module that relocates an existing MEC service from the source to the destination worker node. This module is used by our MEAO to be able to implement the follow-me behaviour on-demand. In order to be able to monitor the relocation process (as this action is not reflected in the MEC service status in OSM) we have also implemented an HTTP benchmark that can inform us of the down/up status of the container in question. In this way, the MEAO can get its information regarding the process of relocation.

Overall the lessons learnt from our investigation and implementation can be summarised as follows:

– support for CNFs has not advanced much since its first release in version 7, including the use of VNFD
– fine grain control for the positioning and relocation of VMs via GUI and Northbound API is available
– positioning control of containers in a standalone scenario is not available, load balancing is used, service status is reported
– relocation control of containers in a standalone scenario is not available, must be custom developed, the service status is not recognised and if needed must also be custom implemented
– interaction between OSM and KNFs can present interoperability challenges. Components must integrate properly which usually requires extra effort, especially when it comes to choosing compatible versions
– lack of detailed error messages can significantly complicate the identification and resolution of problems related to the deployment of KNFs in the container infrastructure

In the next section, we provide the technical details of our experimental setup and the MEC applications used for benchmarking.

4   MEC-NFV Testbed Setup Details

To aid in the development of the tests and facilitate their performance testing, a set of 8 hosts was used, all connected to the same physical switch, providing 1Gbps connectivity. The nodes were placed on the same local network to eliminate any unforeseen impacts that could jeopardise the validity of the results, such as jitter or packet drops. No other workloads or tasks were running on them, other than those required for testing.

One host was dedicated to hosting OSM which assumes the NFVO role. The MEAO has been implemented as a separate component that performs API calls to start, migrate, and terminate edge services, and receives status and monitoring information. Two independent VIMs have been implemented to compare VM and container implementations: first VIM is set in a second node using a multi-node Microstack that controls two separate compute nodes in two additional nodes, and the second dummy VIM is connected to standalone a Kubernetes master with two Kubernetes nodes in three separate nodes as in Fig. 2. The external Kubernetes cluster was deployed using the K3s lightweight Kubernetes distribution since existing research has shown that it is the preferred option for resource-constrained environments, such as the edge [29].

For the VMs case, all actions including monitoring are performed using the OSM Northbound AP. In the case of containers, an additional software layer has been developed to perform the process of container relocation and receive status information. The last node was dedicated to the configuration of an HTTP server to where we direct the HTTP requests for the tests in order to obtain the external performance measurements of the relocation operation.

Table 1 summarises the software versions and hardware specifications used in the complete experimental setup. Note that the software versions of the Kubernetes cluster and the OSM must be compatible for the system to work as a whole. In other words, careful combing through the documentation must be done to ensure that the version of your Kubernetes cluster is supported by the OSM release in question.

Table 1. Host role and Hardware specifications for the experimental setup.

Name	Role	Software version	GB RAM	CPU cores
Node 1	OSM	OSM 12	16	8
Node 2	MicroStack control plane	microstack (beta) ussuri	8	4
Node 3–4	2 x MicroStack compute nodes	microstack (beta) ussuri	8	4
Node 5	Kubernetes master	v1.22.17+k3s	8	4
Node 6–7	2 x Kubernetes workers	v1.22.17+k3s	8	4
Node 8	HTTP server	Ubuntu 20.04.3 LTS	8	4

In order to obtain a sufficiently wide range of results, we have considered different application sizes to be relocated in a VM and container environment that we identify as small (S), medium (M) and large (L). All chosen applications are such that they do not require context transfer during the migration process so as to be able to measure the performance in a clean, fast scenario. The price of context switching can then be added according to the findings in [22] as the particular Kubernetes setup does not have a significant impact on the context switching functionality. Table 2 summarises the chosen applications for the VMs and containers scenarios. Note that the applications can not be the same for both cases as the size of the same application for VM and container differs greatly. The goal of this performance analysis is on the other hand to test different types of applications and check how their sizes impact the service downtime due to relocation. Care has been taken that all chosen container-based MEC apps expose a REST API that can be called via the HTTP server so as to implement the external service monitoring system using the hey benchmark.

The procedure to install the chosen apps starts with adding the repository to OSM. VNF, KNF and NS packages are developed and uploaded to OSM. Then, OSM is called to start the deployment of a VNF or KNF depending on the scenario, allowing the VIM control plane to decide on which node the

Table 2. Example MEC applications in three sizes S, M and L

Designation	Container MEC Applications		VM MEC Applications	
	App. Type	Compressed Img. Size	App. Type	Image Size
S	Owntracks location tracker	20.2MB	Cirros	12.13 MB
M	Flask language detection	178MB	Xenial server	300.75 MB
L	R studio plumber	996 MB	bitnami ELK	1.17 GB

service will be instantiated based on load balancing. If an error occurs during the deployment of a KNF, it is essential to have precise and specific information about the problem in order to take corrective measures. However, in some cases, the error messages provided by OSM may be generic or lack sufficient detail to understand the root cause of the problem.

5   Results

Using the prepared experimental testbed, we have carried out a number of tests aimed at monitoring the performance of relocation for both VMs and containers.

In the VM migration scenarios, the process of live migration is triggered by the MEAO with simple API calls to OSM. The measurements done in this case are based on the monitoring and status information available in OSM, we also refer to these as external measurements. These measurements have been augmented with the corresponding information that can be found in the NOVA module and instance logs of Microstack. We refer to the latter as internal measurements As our investigations have shown that OSM uses a period pull mechanism to query the status of a started migration operation with a default period of 10 s, in order to obtain more granular and precise results we have changed this behaviour by enabling pull requests every 1 s.

To monitor the performance of the relocation operation in containers we have carried out two types of tests

– external - we take measurements using an Apache HTTP server in order to mimic the OSM pulling for monitoring and obtain the latencies as they would be perceived by the NFVO. We measure how long a service is unavailable during its migration by continuously sending requests from an HTTP benchmark to the container
– internal - we consider measurements taken from inside the Kubernetes cluster itself. We measure the time it takes for the new container to start after it is removed as it is reported in the Kubernetes logs

For each MEC application, we carry out a set of 10 tests, covering both internal and external evaluations. In each of these tests, more than 10,000 samples were collected and analysed to ensure thorough evaluation and validation of our approach.

In Fig. 4 we can observe the delay boxplots of the relocation operation as perceived with the internal and external measurements for both VMs and containers hosting the chosen MEC applications. The results show that the relocation

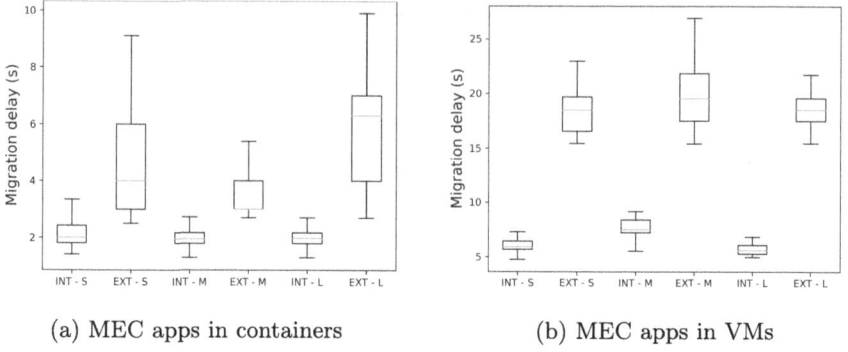

(a) MEC apps in containers (b) MEC apps in VMs

Fig. 4. External and internal relocation latencies for different MEC app sizes

latency is not necessarily dependent on the application image size, which can be spotted for the S application in the case of Kubernetes, or the M applications in both the VM case. This leads to the conclusion that the image size has a smaller significance when compared to the complexity of the application itself, i.e. number of internal services that need to be configured and started. We have also computed the 95% confidence intervals that increase with the size of the edge service as the variance increases during the relocation process, which should be taken into account as an important parameter by the proactive MEAO.

A very interesting result is presented when comparing the external and the internal measurements in Fig. 4. It seems that the time spent on relocation is quite short, in the range of 5 s to 9 s for VMs, and expectedly lower 1 s to 3 s for containers. However, the time reported with the external measurements is quite higher reaching 15 s to 25 s for VMs and 3 s to 9 s for containers. This means that there is a significant delay from the moment the NFVI decided the relocation has terminated to acknowledging this process by OSM and the HTTP server correspondingly. This discrepancy is of vital importance when aiming to build a proactive MEAO that is aware of the real-time status of relocations in progress. In addition, when comparing these values with the results obtained in [22] where the instantiation of MEC app in OpenNESS is reported to be in the range of 50 s to 55 s it can be concluded that the results obtained are several times lower leading to the conclusion that the implementation of a standalone Kubernetes cluster can provide much-improved performances when compared to the deployment inside a VIM solution.

Figure 5a represents the internal and external delay metrics of relocation are presented one against the other. Internal measurements without outliers show a range of 1 s to 10 s, while external measurements show 2 s to 8 s high variability. This variability re-exposes the importance of considering more than just the size regarding service performance for efficient service relocation management since there may be cases in which the S application takes a considerably longer time.

Figure 5b shows the combination of the obtained internal and external measurements and we can observe that internal values range from 3 s up to 10 s while external values go up to a range between 14 s and 28 s. It is obvious that the image sizes of these applications are considerably larger compared to the containers case and, hence, migration delays increase accordingly. We can observe that there is no clear location differentiation of the measurements corresponding to the three application sizes as in the case of the containers test. However, with these results, we can state that the overhead of OSM is considerably higher when considering applications deployed as VMs instead of as containers.

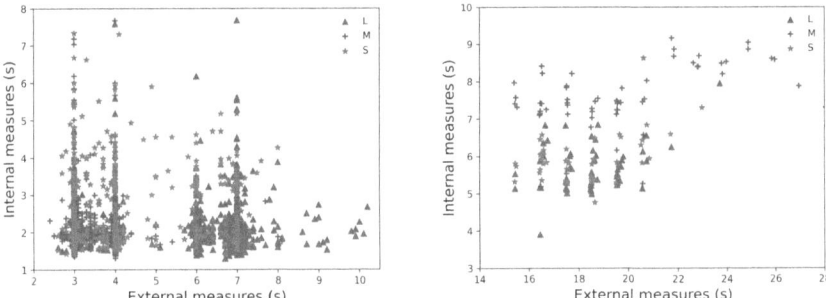

(a) Kubernetes containers relocation oper-(b) Microstack VMs live migration opera-
ations   tions

Fig. 5. Internal vs external measures

Performing these measurements is the first step to optimising the migration process of service hosting containers in complex environments such as MEC-NFV. It is essential that one primarily analyses the obtained data and understands the dependencies and relationships that are present in the collected dataset. The next step is to use the gathered data as one of the inputs for training proactive algorithms that improve the orchestrator's resource management during migration, making better decisions, reducing latency and improving real-time resource management. The main idea is to use the latency data, along with other contextual features such as container size, application type, network conditions, and resource availability, as input features for an AI-based model. When training the model historical latency data can be used to capture patterns and trends that help predict future migration needs. In addition, the data can be labelled with optimal migration times or decisions based on past successful migrations with minimal disruption. Labelling can also be performed for instances where resource allocation is suboptimal, thus helping the algorithm learn to predict and avoid such situations. In this way, an algorithm can be developed so that it learns to predict the best times to migrate containers based on the current and predicted future state of the network and resources, minimising latency and optimising resource use. Finally, the model can be integrated with the real-time monitoring environment to make proactive decisions. The model can also be continuously updated with new latency measurements, which will allow it to adapt and improve over time.

6   Discussion and Conclusions

The commitment to join 5G and MEC technologies based on NFV seems to be a winner in solving the requirements of applications in real-time. With containers gaining prominence in application virtualisation with ultra-low latency requirements, in this work, we analysed the performance of the procedure of relocation of containers in an OSM-based MEC-NFV system with a standalone cluster versus the traditional OSM setup that uses virtual machines.

While OSM has continued to be improved in its new releases, the implementation of standalone Kubernetes cluster for MEC applications based on KNFs lags behind especially when it comes to seamless support for container relocation. Our performance results and comparison however show that the performances of standalone containers are significantly improved when compared to VMs, but also inside a VM container implementations. With the research activities being focused on the development of intelligent MEAOs with proactive capabilities for optimal placement and relocation of cloud-native container-based MEC applications, the ability to perform these functionalities and supply the MEAO with real-time status and monitoring updates becomes crucial.

Adapting to online services changing demands and improving the end-user experience underscores this importance in modern network architectures. To address the challenges while designing for maximum gain we will continue our efforts towards the development of full support for CNFs in an ETSI MEC NFV-compliant architecture with the aim to support the implementation of proactive service relocation.

References

1. Attar, H., et al.: 5g system overview for ongoing smart applications: structure, requirements, and specifications. Comput. Intell. Neurosci. **2022**, 1–11 (2022)
2. Barakabitze, A.A., Ahmad, A., Mijumbi, R., Hines, A.: 5g network slicing using SDN and NFV: a survey of taxonomy, architectures and future challenges. Comput. Netw. **167**, 106984 (2020)
3. ETSI Gs MEC. V2. 1.1. multi-access edge computing (MEC); framework and reference architecture (2022)
4. Mobile Edge Computing: Deployment of mobile edge computing in an NFV environment. ETSI Group Report MEC **17**, V1 (2018)
5. Network Functions Virtualisation ETSI: Network functions virtualisation (NFV). Manag. Orchestr. **1**, V1 (2014)
6. Ouyang, T., Zhou, Z., Chen, X.: Follow me at the edge: mobility-aware dynamic service placement for mobile edge computing. IEEE J. Sel. Areas Commun. **36**(10), 2333–2345 (2018)
7. Svorobej, S., Bendechache, M., Griesinger, F., Domaschka, J.: Orchestration from the cloud to the edge. In: The Cloud-to-Thing Continuum: Opportunities and Challenges in Cloud, Fog and Edge Computing, vol. 4, pp. 61–77 (2020)
8. Faraji-Mehmandar, M., Jabbehdari, S., Javadi, H.H.S.: A self-learning approach for proactive resource and service provisioning in fog environment. J. Supercomput. **78**(15), 16997–17026 (2022)

Relocation of Container-Based Services in a MEC-NFV Orchestrated Env.   19

9. Bernad, C., Kjorveziroski, V., Roig, P.J., Alcaraz, S., Gilly, K., Filiposka, S.: Multi-access edge computing smart relocation approach from an NFV perspective. In: Zdravkova, K., Basnarkov, L. (eds.) ICT Innovations 2022. CCIS, vol. 1740, pp. 38–48. Springer, Cham (2022). https://doi.org/10.1007/978-3-031-22792-9_4
10. Siew, M., Guo, K., Cai, D., Li, L., Quek, T.Q.S.: Let's share VMS: optimal placement and pricing across base stations in MEC systems. In: IEEE INFOCOM 2021-IEEE Conference on Computer Communications, pp. 1–10. IEEE, New York, NY (2021)
11. Zhao, L., Liu, J.: Optimal placement of virtual machines for supporting multiple applications in mobile edge networks. IEEE Trans. Veh. Technol. **67**(7), 6533–6545 (2018)
12. Asghari, A., Azgomi, H., Zoraghchian, A.A., Barzegarinezhad, A.: Energy-aware server placement in mobile edge computing using trees social relations optimization algorithm. J. Supercomput. **1**(1), 1–29 (2023)
13. Nguyen, T.-V., Dao, N.-N., Noh, W., Cho, S., et al.: User-aware and flexible proactive caching using LSTM and ensemble learning in IoT-MEC networks. IEEE Internet Things J. **9**(5), 3251–3269 (2021)
14. Mazloomi, A., Sami, H., Bentahar, J., Otrok, H., Mourad, A.: Reinforcement learning framework for server placement and workload allocation in multiaccess edge computing. IEEE Internet Things J. **10**(2), 1376–1390 (2022)
15. Jiang, X., Hou, P., Zhu, H., Li, B., Wang, Z., Ding, H.: Dynamic and intelligent edge server placement based on deep reinforcement learning in mobile edge computing. Ad Hoc Netw. **145**, 103172 (2023)
16. Boukerche, A., et al.: A comparative study on service migration for mobile edge computing based on deep learning. Ph.D. thesis, Université d'Ottawa/University of Ottawa (2023)
17. Ferreira, V., et al.: Netedge MEP: a CNF-based multi-access edge computing platform. In: 2023 IEEE Symposium on Computers and Communications (ISCC), pp. 1–6. IEEE, New York, NY (2023)
18. Sonkoly, B., et al.: Scalable edge cloud platforms for IoT services. J. Netw. Comput. Appl. **170**, 102785 (2020)
19. Pino, A., Khodashenas, P., Hesselbach, X., Coronado, E., Siddiqui, S.: Validation and benchmarking of CNFs in OSM for pure cloud native applications in 5g and beyond. In: 2021 International Conference on Computer Communications and Networks (ICCCN), pp. 1–9. IEEE, New York, NY (2021)
20. ETSI. Open source MANO (OSM) project, December 2023
21. Yilma, G.M., Yousaf, Z.F., Sciancalepore, V., Costa-Perez, X., Osm and onap: Benchmarking open source NFV MANO systems. Comput. Commun. **161**, 86–98 (2020)
22. Fondo-Ferreiro, P., et al.: Seamless multi-access edge computing application handover experiments. In: 2021 IEEE 22nd International Conference on High Performance Switching and Routing (HPSR), pp. 1–6. IEEE, New York, NY (2021)
23. Hathibelagal, M.A., Garroppo, R.G., Nencioni, G.: Experimental comparison of migration strategies for MEC-assisted 5g-v2x applications. Comput. Commun. **197**, 1–11 (2023)
24. Arora, S., Ksentini, A., Bonnet, C.: Cloud native lightweight slice orchestration (CLISO) framework. Comput. Commun. **213**, 1–12 (2024)
25. Kaur, K., Mangat, V., Kumar, K.: A review on virtualized infrastructure managers with management and orchestration features in NFV architecture. Comput. Netw. **217**, 109281 (2022)

26. ETSI. Using kubernetes-based VNFs (KNFs), December 2023
27. Canto, C.B., Roig, P.J., Filiposka, S., Carrasco, S.A., Gilly, K.: Challenges of implementing NFV-based multi-access edge computing environments. In: 2021 29th Telecommunications Forum (TELFOR), pp. 1–4. IEEE, New York, NY (2021)
28. Tsourdinis, T., Makris, N., Fdida, S., Korakis, T.: DRL-based service migration for MEC cloud-native 5g and beyond networks. In: 2023 IEEE 9th International Conference on Network Softwarization (NetSoft), pp. 62–70 (2023)
29. Kjorveziroski, V., Filiposka, S.: Kubernetes distributions for the edge: serverless performance evaluation. J. Supercomput. **78**(11), 13728–13755 (2022)

The Good, the Bad and the Ugly: Investigating the Effectiveness of Graph Deep Neural Networks for Anomaly Detection in Industrial Control Systems

Martin Nahalka$^{(\boxtimes)}$ ⓘ, Marco M. Cook ⓘ, and Dimitrios Pezaros ⓘ

University of Glasgow, Glasgow, Scotland
m.nahalka.1@research.gla.ac.uk,
{marco.cook,dimitrios.pezaros}@glasgow.ac.uk

Abstract. Industrial Control Systems (ICS) are paramount to the efficient operation of Critical National Infrastructure (CNI) ranging from electricity generation and distribution to manufacturing. However, the growing convergence of ICS with Information Technology (IT) systems renders CNI vulnerable to a range of cyber threats. Graph neural networks are being increasingly used for anomaly detection by adding granularity to the detection process. In this paper, we present a comparative study of graph-based deep learning models for ICS anomaly detection. Through the evaluation of four models using three multivariate industrial datasets, we aim to discern the effectiveness of prediction and reconstruction-based graph models in the ICS domain. We investigate data reduction techniques to minimise features needed to represent the window size and examine the representation of sliding window in terms of feature size for time-series analysis. Additionally, we assess the impact of the length of a context window on anomaly detection performance. Our results show that using feature reduction techniques on a longer context window produces better results while having the computational advantages of a shorter window size. Graph autoencoder is the most resilient to feature size reduction by maintaining similar F1 and AUC-PR score regardless of the number of features used to represent a context window. The results also provide insight to the suitability of graph-based models in this domain and offer recommendations for their optimal usage, paving the way for enhanced security and resilience in ICS.

Keywords: Anomaly detection · Industrial Control Systems · Deep Learning · Graph Neural Networks · Machine Learning

1 Introduction

With the advent of modern digital paradigms such as Industry 4.0 and the Industrial Internet of Things (IIoT), Operational Technology (OT) and Industrial

ⓒ IFIP International Federation for Information Processing 2025
Published by Springer Nature Switzerland AG 2025
G. Rey et al. (Eds.): IFIPIoT 2024, IFIP AICT 737, pp. 21–36, 2025.
https://doi.org/10.1007/978-3-031-81900-1_2

Control Systems (ICS) that control physical processes are no longer isolated environments. Instead, they are becoming increasingly interconnected with enterprise networks and cloud platforms. This integration of ICS into IIoT enables real-time data exchange enhancing operational efficiency and improving decision-making. However, revealing ICS to the internet also exposes it to a wide range of cyber threats [19]. Such threats have been realised through attacks conducted by Advanced Persistent Threat (APT) groups with significant resources, targeting industrial components and underlying physical processes within CNI environments [6]. The detection of these attacks is challenging due to the lack of integrated security controls within industrial networks and its components. Hence, retrofitting anomaly detection mechanisms is vital to enable digital resilience within modern OT environments, with machine learning techniques such as deep learning, now often being used to improve detection accuracy and efficiency.

The majority of deep learning anomaly detection models can be categorised into two types: prediction-based models [23] or reconstruction-based methods [15]. Recently, graph neural networks (GNNs) have emerged as a promising approach for anomaly detection in ICS, offering a different way of representing data through nodes (vertices) and edges, in contrast to traditional convolutional and recurrent methods. GNNs have been leveraged for both forecasting [5] and reconstruction [7] tasks, demonstrating their versatility in handling different aspects of time-series data. The use of GNNs in ICS anomaly detection is particularly intriguing due to their ability to capture complex relationships between industrial networks and physical measurements over time. Both forecasting and reconstruction using GNNs have reported high detection scores [5,7,11]. Hence, GNNs can offer an alternative approach to traditional prediction and reconstruction models, potentially overcoming limitations such as handling more complex non-linear data. While forecasting and reconstruction with GNNs have shown promise, there is limited work empirically evaluating the performance of prediction-based and reconstruction-based alongside GNNs within the context of ICS anomaly detection. Studies such as [3] or [23] have examined the application of prediction and reconstruction based models in ICS but they do not provide a comparison with alternative approaches on a plurality of datasets. Some studies focused on the comparison of anomaly detection techniques in ICS [13], however they are limited in terms of data type and mostly focus on sensor data. Furthermore, time series data analysis is computationally expensive [21] and it is important to examine how these models perform when feature reduction techniques are applied to reduce the size of the data within time-series window to be potentially applicable over resource-constrained environments at the edge [2].

In this paper, we present an empirical evaluation on the efficacy of three graph-based deep learning models for ICS anomaly detection. We examine their comparative performance and selected baseline benchmarking through three different ICS datasets. ICS data is inherently different from other types of data due to the multi-modal nature of the environments. ICS data commonly represents time-series features, alongside graph based system dependencies and data values representing sensor data as well as network traffic between specific components in the network. Comparing these models in the context of ICS data is necessary in order to explore how machine learning approaches perform on various ICS datasets in terms of prediction quality and computational performance considering inference time, training time and scalability of the models.

The contributions of this paper are as follows:

1. Provides a comparative evaluation of graph-based deep machine learning models, in two configurations: reconstruction and prediction against baseline models on multiple ICS datasets containing varied data types.
2. Investigates the effects of applying data reduction techniques to context window representation and assess their impact on the performance of models.
3. Examines the effects of utilising various context window lengths on the quality of predictions.

The rest of this paper is organised as follows: Sect. 2 provides an overview of the related work in the field of anomaly detection with a focus on ICS data. Section 3 discusses the models used for the experiments. In Sect. 4, we present the experimental results and analyse the findings. Finally, Sect. 5 concludes the paper, summarises the key findings and outlines the future directions.

2   Related Work

ICS anomalies are generally detected using two types of data: industrial network traffic or physical measurements extracted from sensors and actuators. Due to the heterogeneity of the data and the overhead associated with designing a model able to handle both data types in a single graph network, most anomaly detection approaches focus on the properties of one type [29]. Many previous studies have explored the use of sensor and actuator data to detect anomalies that manifest in the underlying physical processes [16,17,25]. Measurements from sensor and actuators represent the physical parameters within the processes and reflect the real-time state of the components within the system and is inherently multivariate at each timestep. Similarly, there are studies [10,22] attempting to perform anomaly detection on network datasets. Network data is commonly parsed into flows and recorded as a series of timestamps, creating multivariate time series data. Such time series data is complex and cannot be easily represented by traditional machine learning models such as SVM [18] or logistic regression [24] due to their inability to capture temporal dependencies. Deep Learning techniques have demonstrated greater effectiveness for this type of data [17]. Normal profile learning techniques are commonly used for anomaly detection. The model learns the behaviour of the system under normal conditions and then attempts to distinguish such conditions from anomalous ones. To learn the normal profile of a system, prediction and reconstruction-based approaches are typically used in an unsupervised manner. This is driven by the limitations of supervised learning, which is constrained by the scarcity of labelled attack data and is confined to recognizing known or seen attacks. Prediction-based methods tend to utilise Recurrent Neural Networks (RNNs), Long Short-Term Memory (LSTM) networks, or more recently Graph Neural Networks (GNNs). [9] uses a series of timestamped data to predict the next timestamp utilising LSTM networks, which is then compared with the genuine data observed at the timestamp. The resulting loss is compared to a threshold to classify this instance as an anomaly or genuine data. Unlike traditional sequence-to-sequence LSTM that takes one sequence as input and produces another one as an output, ClozeLSTM [25] uses a single LSTM to encode the data and multiple decoders, based on the number of features to be processed to decode the data, and the output is then concatenated to produce a single prediction. This prediction model is able to predict not only the immediate subsequent values but also values further in the future. An approach with multiple decoders is also used in [1], however here it is used for reconstruction.

Reconstruction-based approaches such as autoencoders are trained to learn a representation of data in a low-dimensional latent representation and then decode this representation into the same number of dimensions as the original input. The resulting reconstruction error is compared to the threshold to determine an anomaly. Work conducted in [31] expands on ConvLSTM [27] by incorporating an attention mechanism to capture temporal patterns within layers. Another approach [15] uses hierarchical variational autoencoder with 2 latent representations to individually capture the inner and temporal embeddings.

A recent study used graph networks to predict the next sequence and compared it to the genuine data sequence to calculate the difference between them [5]. This results in a list of differences for each sensor's expected and actual value per timestamp. The highest value of which is then used as the anomaly score for the whole sequence. Previous work has focused on comparing anomaly detection methods [13]. However, these studies typically compare single datasets or data types, such as sensor measurements. In the context of ICS, the data generated extends beyond sensor values to encompass network-related information such as packets and various time-related elements associated with data transmitted across different nodes in the ICS network. Additionally, the prevalent practice involves mostly using only F1 scores to demonstrate model performance. Nonetheless, this metric is not all-encompassing, particularly when dealing with highly imbalanced datasets, a common characteristic of anomaly detection datasets [30]. In such cases, the Area Under the Precision-Recall curve (AUC-PR) emerges as a more indicative metric [12], particularly at identifying the rare events, since it provides a comprehensive summary of a model's ability to trade off precision and recall across various decision thresholds.

3   Methodology

In this section, we discuss the models chosen to explore our research objectives, explain the rationale behind their selection and show how they process the data.

3.1   Model Selection

In line with state-of-the-art approaches in anomaly detection highlighted in Sect. 2, we examined both predictive and reconstruction-based models. The models we selected to best represent the use of GNN models for anomaly detection are presented and summarised in Table 1. We used GNNs for both reconstruction and forecasting based normal behaviour profiling.

Table 1. Models Comparison

Model	Type	Loss	Layers
RGCN	Prediction	Smooth L1	GCNConv, DCRNN, FC
State RGCN	Prediction	Smooth L1	GCNConv, DCRNN, FC
GAE	Reconstruction	Smooth L1	GCNConv, ReLU, dropout

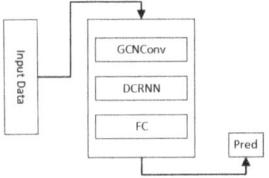

Fig. 1. Recurrent Graph Convolutional Network

Recurrent Graph Convolutional Network (RGCN). RGCN is based on a sequence prediction architecture where the input to the model is a sequence, and a subsequent sequence is the output. For this project we use a configuration where context window size - 1 timestamps serve as the input and the model learns to predict the last timestamp of the context window, see Fig. 1. Traditionally, Recurrent Neural Networks (RNNs) are used for sequence-to-sequence prediction because they can maintain hidden states to retain information from previous timesteps and use this context for prediction. This makes them very suitable for time series data analysis. Our RGCN implementation utilises graph network framework [26] and is inspired by [32] as we use recurrent graph layers for inference. The predicted instance is then compared to the true instance at the timestamp, where the difference between the two instances is then compared against a threshold to determine anomaly status. To examine the performance of GNNs for this use case, we decided to use a combination of graph convolutional layers and graph diffusion convolutional gated recurrent unit (DCRNN) [14] to perform predictions. DCRNN uses diffusion convolution to capture spatial dependency and GRU to capture long-term dependency in data which is necessary for anomaly prediction tasks. Each node in the graph comprises the value of a column at a given time and the n number of values a particular column was in, where n is the window size. The prediction is the new value for each node.

State RGCN. State RGCN utilises the same logic as RGCN but uses a different approach to representing the data. One node in the graph network is a "state" of the network at a given time, that is the row of the data representing all the values the dataset has for a corresponding timestamp. The graph is hence a collection of n number of nodes, where n is the window size. The prediction produced is the next node on the graph.

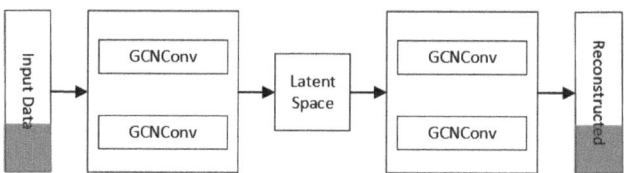

Fig. 2. Graph Autoencoder

Graph Autoencoder (GAE). The reconstruction-based model we used is a graph autoencoder consisting of three parts: an encoder, the latent representation, and a decoder. In the GAE implementation, the encoder comprises of two normalised graph convolutional layers and one dropout layer which is applied between the two convolutional layers. GCConv layers aggregate the information from neighbouring nodes within the graph, making the condensed information more representative of the overall graph. Convolutional layers can aggregate local information to retain important parts of it, which can then be used for anomaly detection as anomalies can be identified by comparing the original data with the reconstructed input. The second convolutional layer reduces the size of the data to two dimensions. This representation is deconvoluted by one normalised convolutional layer, one dropout layer and a second normalised convolutional layer in the decoder which returns a reconstructed input, see Fig. 2. To recognise an anomaly threshold was applied to the loss function at the testing phase. The nodes within the GAE model represent the data values at a given timestamp and window, resulting in n number of graphs, where $n = len(dataset) - w$, and w is the window size.

Baselines. We used the Unsupervised Anomaly Detection (USAD) model [1] as the baseline. It is an unsupervised reconstruction-based model designed to work well on multivariate series and utilises the autoencoder architecture, with two decoder units. One of which is used for the reconstruction of the data, and the second one for recognising the reconstructed data from the original data. The overall anomaly score is then obtained by multiplying the results of the outputs from the two decoders. The structure of both decoders is constant. This model was chosen for its design tailored for anomaly detection in ICS and favourable performance across multiple ICS datasets during evaluation by the authors. Isolation forest is the second baseline model and was chosen due to its general effectiveness and efficiency for anomaly detection tasks.

4   Evaluation

4.1   Datasets and Pre-processing

To evaluate the models presented in the previous section, we selected three ICS datasets from emulated testbeds: SWaT [8], HAI [28], and ICS-flow [4]. Due to the general unavailability of real-world ICS data, particularly data points containing attack traces caused by security concerns, data from emulated environments is commonly used for anomaly detection research [20]. These datasets were chosen as they represent the intricacies and variety present within the ICS data. Despite being of a smaller scale, these datasets are generally considered representative of real-world systems. To evaluate the generalisability of the models on the data we use different datasets with varying numbers of features and feature types (Table 2).

SWaT Dataset. The SWaT dataset represents a scaled-down industrial water treatment plant producing filtered water, comprising 51 sensors and actuators. The data was collected over 11 days, the first seven days were operated under normal conditions and the last four days included attacks on the treatment plant. 51 measurement readings were provided at each timestamp, which we filtered by removing constant features and the timestamp field.

HAI Dataset. The HAI datasets comprises three physical control processes (boiler process, turbine process and water treatment process) and a hardware-in-the-loop simulator that enhances the dependencies between the other three processes. HAI contains ten days of normal training data and 5.5 days of test data including 38 attacks. A total of 59 sensor and actuator values were measured every second. We filtered these values by the impact on the resulting attack label, hence static values were removed to reduce the parameter space.

ICS-Flow Dataset. Unlike the SWAT and HAI datasets, the ICS-flow dataset [4] contains industrial network data including packet flow and TCP features. The dataset was generated using an ICS emulation environment consisting of two PLCs and three HMIs to control a bottle-filling process. The network protocol used within the testbed is Modbus, and the dataset contains five types of attack:

man-in-the-middle, network scanning, port-scanning, Denial of Service (DoS), and replay attacks. From the total 46 features, we used twenty-three features selected using the MRMR (Maximum Relevance, Minimum Redundancy) feature selection as suggested by [4]. Furthermore, categorical values were assigned a number value corresponding to their category and empty values were replaced with 0.

Normalisation. Values within all datasets were normalised using min-max scaling to ensure consistent scale and achieve numerical stability, this is important due to the sensitivity of gradient-based optimisation methods.

4.2 Data Representation

For the SWaT/HAI datasets, a node is represented by the value of the sensor at a given timestamp and the values of the sensor at window number of times in the past. For the ICS-Flow dataset, a node is represented by the value of the flow characteristic at a given timestamp and the values of it at window number of times in the past. The edges were extracted manually from the flowcharts represented in the documentation of the testbeds. They are static and do not vary over the duration of the dataset. In the case of ICS-Flow the edges were generated from dependencies, such as the relationships between send and received data items within a flow of data-points as presented in [4].

Table 2. Dataset splits

Dataset	Types of attack	Attack Flows	Data Splits		
			Train	Val	Test
ICS Flow	DDoS, MitM, Replay, IP-Scan, Port-Scan	9012	27694	9012	9012
SWaT	False Data Injection	174915	480712	174915	174916
HAI	False Data Injection	49955	240335	49955	49956

4.3 Environment

The training environment used an NVIDIA RTX 2080TI GPU, 32 GB of System RAM and an Intel i7-6700K CPU. Further optimisation was performed using the CUDA toolkit[1] and cuDNN library[2], which enhance GPU acceleration capabilities for deep learning frameworks.

---

[1] https://developer.nvidia.com/cuda-toolkit.
[2] https://developer.nvidia.com/cudnn.

4.4   Results

90 Context Window Length. Initially, we selected a sliding context window length of 90 for the experiment. This choice was made to capture a sufficiently large temporal context to model dependencies presented within the data and is based on the characteristics of the datasets. To investigate the performance of the models proposed in the previous section we evaluated their performance using F1 and AUC-PR metrics, presented in Table 3. In the ICS-Flow network dataset, all models achieved high F1 and AUC-PR scores. Conversely, there was a noticeable performance difference between the SWaT and HAI physical measurement datasets, particularly in the case of Isolation forest. The graph-based models demonstrated consistent scores with the F1 score being slightly higher than AUC-PR, indicating that all the models perform best at maximising the precision compared to recall. Maximising precision is desirable within anomaly detection models since false flagging of anomalies may lead to unnecessary resources being expended on investigating benign behaviour. High precision score indicates high degree of confidence that a true anomaly has been detected. The performance of the remaining models is very similar, with the predictive models performing slightly better than the reconstruction ones on HAI and SWaT. The overall trend remained similar with all models demonstrating high precision with the recall reaching approximately 70%.

Table 3. Prediction performance of all models with different ICS dataset using a context window size of 90. Measurements in bold highlight the best performing model per dataset and metric.

Model	Dataset	Metric				
		F1	AUC	AUC-PR	Recall	Precision
GAE	ICS-Flow	**0.9998**	**0.9984**	**0.9970**	0.9995	**0.9973**
	HAI	0.8014	0.9509	0.7073	0.7019	0.9337
	SWaT	0.8169	0.8691	0.7228	**0.6998**	0.9810
RGCN	ICS-Flow	0.9701	0.9798	0.9510	0.9447	0.9969
	HAI	**0.8240**	**0.9550**	0.7021	0.7131	**0.9756**
	SWaT	0.8156	**0.8697**	0.7351	0.6921	**0.9928**
State RGCN	ICS-Flow	0.9345	0.9850	0.9418	0.9772	0.9349
	HAI	0.8096	0.9511	**0.7117**	0.7151	0.9327
	SWaT	**0.8203**	0.8694	**0.7352**	0.6694	0.9917
Isolation Forest	ICS-Flow	0.9031	0.0497	0.8971	0.8721	0.9365
	HAI	0.1280	0.4105	0.0672	**0.8226**	0.0694
	SWaT	0.2436	0.8162	0.1387	0.9998	0.1387
USAD	ICS-Flow	0.9949	0.9948	0.9901	**0.9996**	0.9903
	HAI	0.7988	0.8489	0.6677	0.7010	0.9282
	SWaT	0.8138	0.8472	0.7236	0.6970	0.9778

In addition to detection performance, we evaluated the time cost required for inference which are presented in Table 4. We observed that the GAE takes the longest amount of time for all three datasets implying that the process of reconstruction using a graph convolutional network takes substantially longer when compared to the forecasting models and the USAD reconstruction model. This is due to the GAE requiring to reconstruct the entire time series to calculate the loss function $window * NumberOfNodes$, whereas the prediction models only need to process the time series and then predict the next timestamp, which is significantly less resource-exhaustive. Comparing across the datasets, as expected the size of the dataset is the most significant factor influencing the time taken by the models. To determine the consistency of the results, we downsampled the datasets to be the same number of samples to examine to what extend does the nature of a particular dataset influence the training and inference time. We identified that there is a negligible difference across the three datasets as shown in Tables 6 and 7. This is somewhat surprising since the number of graph nodes varies across the datasets (25 for SWat, 28 for HAI and 23 for ICS-Flow) suggesting the variety in number of nodes is not significantly influencing the processing time.

Another interesting observation is between RGCN and State RGCN, as they take a similar amount of time for the inference across all three datasets despite their graph representation being different. When using 90 features to represent the context window both RGCN models require the same time for inference. In terms of the time required to train per epoch presented in Table 5, RGCN takes more time to train then State RGCN, despite having a lower quantity of nodes. We assess that this is likely due to the recurrent layer which needs to process additional historical data in the RGCN configuration, recall Sect. 3.1. When comparing the GAE and RGCN models which both use the same graph representation, GAE required more time when using 90 features due to the reconstruction process, which does not exist in RGCN. Note that we do not provide the training time for isolation forest because it cannot be configured to run for multiple epochs, nor can we specify the batch size.

Table 4. Inference times in seconds, the change factor in time decrease from 90 features to 5 features represented in % as Chg. Change factor in bold indicates the largest time reduction per model.

Model	SWaT			HAI			ICS-Flow		
	90 feat	5 feat	Chg	90 feat	5 feat	Chg	90 feat	5 feat	Chg
GAE	48.3221	23.6240	**51.35**	14.0610	7.0333	49.92	2.4140	1.2039	50.21
RGCN	24.8341	24.7700	0.26	7.6301	7.4561	2.28	1.1653	1.1275	**3.25**
State RGCN	24.7201	12.6599	**48.77**	7.0540	3.7878	46.13	1.2179	0.6580	45.92
IF	2.2525	0.0620	**97.26**	0.2407	0.0201	91.69	0.0386	0.0037	90.57
USAD	30.855	5.5489	**81.92**	8.2321	1.6001	80.56	1.5211	0.2983	80.44

Table 5. Training times in seconds, the change factor in time decrease from 90 features to 5 features represented in % as Chg. Change factor in bold indicates the largest time reduction per model.

Model	SWaT			HAI			ICS-Flow		
	90 feat	5 feat	Chg	90 feat	5 feat	Chg	90 feat	5 feat	Chg
GAE	127.1551	59.4570	**53.17**	64.9099	30.7220	52.72	7.6984	3.8859	49.57
RGCN	87.1233	85.8977	1.41	46.6211	46.3988	0.48	5.5345	5.2256	**5.59**
State RGCN	79.3133	41.0002	**48.31**	39.9369	23.2745	41.59	4.9148	3.0646	37.63
USAD	139.2899	61.3100	**55.97**	63.9500	31.3350	50.94	7.6288	3.7009	51.65

Table 6. Inference times when the length of all datasets are the same.

Model	SWaT		HAI		ICS-Flow	
	90 feat	5 feat	90 feat	5 feat	90 feat	5 feat
GAE	2.5072	1.2233	2.4498	1.2283	2.4140	1.2039
RGCN	1.2552	1.2361	1.3091	1.2846	1.1653	1.1275
State RGCN	1.2293	0.6498	1.2394	0.6540	1.2179	0.6580
USAD	1.5225	0.2926	1.4632	0.2827	1.5211	0.2983

Table 7. Training times when the length of all datasets are the same.

Model	SWaT		HAI		ICS-Flow	
	90 feat	5 feat	90 feat	5 feat	90 feat	5 feat
GAE	8.0838	3.9668	7.7603	3.9351	7.6984	3.8859
RGCN	5.5382	5.4303	5.8225	5.7008	5.3453	5.2256
State RGCN	5.0302	2.9934	5.0036	2.9381	4.9148	3.0646
USAD	7.3868	3.7945	7.4171	3.7511	7.6288	3.7009

Examining Shorter Context Window Lengths. As shown in the previous section, decreasing the number of features correlates with a decrease in training and testing time. As reducing the number of features can be addressed by decreasing the context window, we further investigate the impact on detection performance when reducing the context window size. Examining different window sizes enables us to understand how detection models respond to variations in the amount of historical information used to make predictions. Utilising a larger context window entails processing more features requiring greater computational resources, while a window that is too short may not provide sufficient context to identify an anomaly accurately. As demonstrated by the results in Table 8, we deduce that the context window length is more important for some datasets than others. The most apparent is the change in HAI dataset, where a shorter context window drastically reduced the effectiveness of all the models at identifying anomalous events. This is likely due to the duration of the attacks present in the data. For instance, if an attack takes 47 s it may be difficult to observe it using a context window size of five. A less substantial decrease was observed in the remaining two datasets, but it still represents a decrease of tens and hundreds of anomalous events that were not identified.

Table 8. F1 scores according to context window size, the change factor in F1 decrease from 90 to 5 represented in % as Chg. Measurements in bold indicate the best score per dataset.

Model	Dataset	Context Window Length					Chg
		90	45	20	10	5	
GAE	SWaT	0.8169	0.8151	0.8138	0.8136	0.7995	4.7
	HAI	0.8014	0.4863	0.4863	0.4419	0.4147	63.5
	ICS-Flow	**0.9998**	0.9909	0.9947	0.9956	0.9759	2.4
RGCN	SWaT	0.8156	0.8203	0.8211	0.8198	0.8191	0.4
	HAI	**0.8240**	0.678	0.6825	0.6964	0.6592	22.2
	ICS-Flow	0.9701	0.9491	0.9655	0.9407	0.9160	5.7
State RGCN	SWaT	**0.8203**	0.8202	0.8200	0.8199	0.8056	1.8
	HAI	0.8096	0.6859	0.6997	0.6752	0.6176	26.9
	ICS-Flow	0.9345	0.8856	0.9655	0.8923	0.8784	6.2
USAD	SWaT	0.8138	0.8151	0.8196	0.8197	0.7961	2.2
	HAI	0.7988	0.7127	0.7074	0.7067	0.6788	16.2
	ICS-Flow	0.9949	0.9973	0.9968	0.9952	0.9851	1

Computational Performance. While results using smaller window sizes were generally inferior to the ones using a window size of 90, there is a noticeable improvement in training and inference times. In light of this, we reduced the number of features used to represent the larger context window to keep shorter training and inference times and increase the detection performance. We first examined the computational performance and observed that decreasing the number of features has minimal impact on RGCN inference and training times, presented in Tables 4 and 5, respectively. The time decrease is within 5% for each of the datasets. In comparison to the GAE model, which shares the same graph representation as RGCN, the main difference appears to be the reconstruction element in GAE and the recurrent layer in RGCN. Both of these take a similar amount of time whether 90 features or 5 features represent the graph node. All other models observed a noticeable decrease in the time difference highlighting that reducing the number of features does lead to a decrease in both training and inference time. Examining the training and testing time for GAE, we see an overall decrease of about 25 s for inference and 68 s for training, further illustrating that decreasing the number of features to be reconstructed results in substantial saving in computational savings. State RGCN has significant time savings due to the number of nodes being reduced from 90 to 5, keeping the number of features per node constant shows that reducing the number of nodes has a greater impact on time reduction than reducing the dimensionality of the nodes by the same factor. The USAD baseline model achieves the greatest time decrease of about 80% for inference. Since this model does not use graph structures in its architecture, the primary factor contributing to the expected considerable decrease is the number of features to be processed via linear layers in the USAD model.

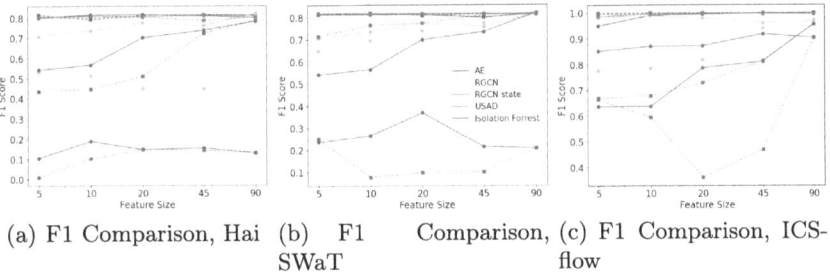

(a) F1 Comparison, Hai   (b)   F1   Comparison,   (c) F1 Comparison, ICS-
                          SWaT   flow

Fig. 3. Comparison of F1 Scores and Feature size. Solid line with • scatter point represents Random Sampling and dashed line with ■ scatter points represents PCA.

Prediction Quality. To complement time evaluation, we examined the changes in detection performance according to the number of features. Figure 3 presents the results on the reduced feature sizes with the same window. This experiment explored two feature reduction techniques: Principal Component Analysis (PCA) and random subsampling. Each technique was applied to the window of data considered within the data loader when creating batches. Generally, random subsampling was shown to outperform PCA, particularly in the case of Isolation Forest and its performance using the ICS-Flow dataset. When PCA was used, the prediction performance notably declines as the number of features decreases before rising slightly as the feature size approaches five. Random subsampling produced noticeably improved results for all models across most of the feature sizes. This implies that using the real data points rather than the synthetic features created through PCA enables the models to better represent and learn patterns within the datasets. Using PCA for dimensionality reduction removes the noise preserved when using randomly subsampled data which appears to improve the prediction performance. The most significant variation was noted in the performance of the forecasting models. We found that decreasing the number of features adversely impacts prediction quality. This is attributed to the forecasting models striving to predict the next timestamp, which becomes more challenging when the models only have partial data points from the past and lack the complete context window. In contrast to the reconstruction models that observe the whole context window in an attempt to reconstruct it.

5 Conclusion

In this paper, we have evaluated three graph deep learning models using physical process data and network data for anomaly detection in ICS environments. Our results demonstrated that the performances of prediction and reconstruction graph models exceed the performance of the baseline models. The prediction models are more sensitive to feature size reduction than the reconstruction models and generally perform better with a reduced context window. The graph autoencoder model retains consistent detection performance across reduced feature sets and datasets, hence enabling the model to perform well regardless of the data type and attack length, making it the most generalisable approach. Regarding computational performance, the prediction-based graph models are shown to be less expensive than reconstruction models. The reconstruction element was identified as the most resource-intensive element with both graph and non-graph approaches. Graph neural networks perform well at identifying anomalous events and add a level of granularity that is not possible in non-graph approaches. Leveraging graph-based representations and incorporating edges holds promise for enhancing the robustness of critical infrastructure systems. In the future, we will examine how graph-based anomaly detection models handle dynamic graph representation by modifying the graph topology throughout the duration of a dataset to capture the evolution of systems.

Acknowledgements. This work has been supported in part by the Royal Academy of Engineering under grant number RCSRF2223-1645, Dstl under order number DSTL0000014002, EDF under order number 4840659490, and UK Research and Innovation (UKRI) under reference number 10091225.

References

1. Audibert, J., Guyard, F., Marti, S., Zuluaga, M.: USAD: UnSupervised Anomaly Detection on Multivariate Time Series (2020). https://doi.org/10.1145/3394486.3403392
2. Cziva, R., Pezaros, D.P.: On the latency benefits of edge NFV. In: 2017 ACM/IEEE Symposium on Architectures for Networking and Communications Systems (ANCS), pp. 105–106. IEEE (2017)
3. de Riberolles, T., Zou, Y., Silvestre, G., Lochin, E., Song, J.: Anomaly detection for ICS based on deep learning: a use case for aeronautical radar data. Ann. Telecommun. 1–13 (2022). https://doi.org/10.1007/s12243-021-00902-7
4. Dehlaghi-Ghadim, A., Helali Moghadam, M., Balador, A., Hansson, H.: Anomaly detection dataset for industrial control systems. IEEE Access 1 (2023). https://doi.org/10.1109/ACCESS.2023.3320928
5. Deng, A., Hooi, B.: Graph neural network-based anomaly detection in multivariate time series. In: Proceedings of the AAAI Conference on Artificial Intelligence, vol. 35, no. 5, pp. 4027–4035 (2021). https://doi.org/10.1609/aaai.v35i5.16523
6. Dragos: ICS/OT Cybersecurity: Year in review 2022 (2022). https://www.dragos.com/year-in-review/

7. Du, X., Yu, J., Chu, Z., Jin, L., Chen, J.: Graph autoencoder-based unsupervised outlier detection. Inf. Sci. **608**, 532–550 (2022). https://doi.org/10.1016/j.ins.2022.06.039

8. Goh, J., Adepu, S., Junejo, K.N., Mathur, A.: A dataset to support research in the design of secure water treatment systems. In: Havarneanu, G., Setola, R., Nassopoulos, H., Wolthusen, S. (eds.) CRITIS 2016. LNCS, vol. 10242, pp. 88–99. Springer, Cham (2017). https://doi.org/10.1007/978-3-319-71368-7_8

9. Goh, J., Adepu, S., Tan, M., Lee, Z.S.: Anomaly detection in cyber physical systems using recurrent neural networks. In: 2017 IEEE 18th International Symposium on High Assurance Systems Engineering (HASE), pp. 140–145. IEEE, Singapore (2017). https://doi.org/10.1109/HASE.2017.36

10. Jiang, J.R., Chen, Y.T.: Industrial control system anomaly detection and classification based on network traffic. IEEE Access **10**, 41874–41888 (2022). https://doi.org/10.1109/ACCESS.2022.3167814

11. Jin, M., et al.: A survey on graph neural networks for time series: forecasting, classification, imputation, and anomaly detection. arXiv abs/2307.03759 (2023). https://api.semanticscholar.org/CorpusID:259501265

12. Khan, S.A., Ali Rana, Z.: Evaluating performance of software defect prediction models using area under precision-recall curve (AUC-PR). In: 2019 2nd International Conference on Advancements in Computational Sciences (ICACS), pp. 1–6 (2019). https://doi.org/10.23919/ICACS.2019.8689135

13. Kim, B., Alawami, M.A., Kim, E., Oh, S., Park, J., Kim, H.: A comparative study of time series anomaly detection models for industrial control systems. Sensors **23**(3), 1310 (2023). https://doi.org/10.3390/s23031310

14. Li, Y., Yu, R., Shahabi, C., Liu, Y.: Graph convolutional recurrent neural network: data-driven traffic forecasting. CoRR abs/1707.01926 (2017). http://arxiv.org/abs/1707.01926

15. Li, Z., et al.: Multivariate time series anomaly detection and interpretation using hierarchical inter-metric and temporal embedding. In: Proceedings of the 27th ACM SIGKDD Conference on Knowledge Discovery and Data Mining, pp. 3220–3230. ACM, Virtual Event Singapore (2021). https://doi.org/10.1145/3447548.3467075

16. Lin, Q., Adepu, S., Verwer, S., Mathur, A.: TABOR: A Graphical Model-based Approach for Anomaly Detection in Industrial Control Systems (2018). https://doi.org/10.1145/3196494.3196546

17. Luo, Y., Xiao, Y., Cheng, L., Peng, G., Yao, D.D.: Deep learning-based anomaly detection in cyber-physical systems: progress and opportunities. ACM Comput. Surv. **54**(5) (2021). https://doi.org/10.1145/3453155

18. Manevitz, L., Yousef, M.: One-class SVMs for document classification. J. Mach. Learn. Res. **2**, 139–154 (2001). https://doi.org/10.1162/15324430260185574

19. Miller, T., Staves, A., Maesschalck, S., Sturdee, M., Green, B.: Looking back to look forward: lessons learnt from cyber-attacks on industrial control systems. Int. J. Crit. Infrastruct. Prot. **35**, 100464 (2021)

20. Mitseva, A., Thierse, P., Hoffmann, H., Er, D., Panchenko, A.: Challenges and pitfalls in generating representative ICS datasets in cyber security research. In: Katsikas, S., et al. (eds.) ESORICS 2022. LNCS, vol. 13785, pp. 379–397. Springer, Cham (2023). https://doi.org/10.1007/978-3-031-25460-4_22

21. Nguyen, T.P.Q., et al.: Time-series anomaly detection using dynamic programming based longest common subsequence on sensor data. Expert Syst. Appl. **213**, 118902 (2023). https://doi.org/10.1016/j.eswa.2022.118902

22. Ortega-Fernandez, I., Sestelo, M., Burguillo, J.C., Piñón-Blanco, C.: Network intrusion detection system for DDoS attacks in ICS using deep autoencoders. Wirel. Netw. (2023). https://doi.org/10.1007/s11276-022-03214-3

23. Perales Gómez, Á.L., Fernández Maimó, L., Huertas Celdrán, A., García Clemente, F.J.: MADICS: a methodology for anomaly detection in industrial control systems. Symmetry **12**(10), 1583 (2020). https://doi.org/10.3390/sym12101583

24. Ranganathan, P., Pramesh, C.S., Aggarwal, R.: Common pitfalls in statistical analysis: logistic regression. Perspect. Clin. Res. **8**, 148–151 (2017). https://api.semanticscholar.org/CorpusID:39844737

25. Rao, S., Ghaderi, M., Zhang, H.: CloudPAD: managed anomaly detection for ICS. In: Proceedings of the 4th Workshop on CPS and IoT Security and Privacy, pp. 55–61. ACM, Los Angeles CA USA (2022). https://doi.org/10.1145/3560826.3563383

26. Rozemberczki, B., et al.: PyTorch geometric temporal: spatiotemporal signal processing with neural machine learning models. In: Proceedings of the 30th ACM International Conference on Information and Knowledge Management, pp. 4564–4573 (2021)

27. Shi, X., Chen, Z., Wang, H., Yeung, D.Y., Wong, W.K., WOO, W.C.: Convolutional LSTM network: a machine learning approach for precipitation nowcasting. In: Advances in Neural Information Processing Systems, vol. 28. Curran Associates, Inc. (2015)

28. Shin, H.K., Lee, W., Yun, J.H., Kim, H.: HAI 1.0: HIL-based augmented ICS security dataset. In: 13th USENIX Workshop on Cyber Security Experimentation and Test (CSET 20). USENIX Association (2020). https://www.usenix.org/conference/cset20/presentation/shin

29. Umer, M.A., Junejo, K.N., Jilani, M.T., Mathur, A.P.: Machine learning for intrusion detection in industrial control systems: applications, challenges, and recommendations. Int. J. Crit. Infrastruct. Prot. **38**, 100516 (2022). https://doi.org/10.1016/j.ijcip.2022.100516

30. Wardhani, N.W.S., Rochayani, M.Y., Iriany, A., Sulistyono, A.D., Lestantyo, P.: Cross-validation metrics for evaluating classification performance on imbalanced data. In: 2019 International Conference on Computer, Control, Informatics and Its Applications (IC3INA), pp. 14–18 (2019). https://doi.org/10.1109/IC3INA48034.2019.8949568

31. Zhang, C., et al.: A deep neural network for unsupervised anomaly detection and diagnosis in multivariate time series data. In: Proceedings of the AAAI Conference on Artificial Intelligence, vol. 33, no. 01, pp. 1409–1416 (2019). https://doi.org/10.1609/aaai.v33i01.33011409

32. Zhou, J., et al.: Graph neural networks: a review of methods and applications. AI Open **1**, 57–81 (2020). https://doi.org/10.1016/j.aiopen.2021.01.001

Programmable and Scalable Bit-Sliced VLSI Architecture for Decision Tree-Based Machine Learning Edge Inference

Raaga Sai Somesula$^{(\boxtimes)}$ (ID), Sibi Rajagopal Sivakumar (ID),
and Srinivas Katkoori (ID)

University of South Florida, Tampa, FL 33620, USA
{raagasai,sibi,katkoori}@usf.edu

Abstract. As the volume and diversity of Internet of Things (IoT) data continues to grow, traditional cloud-based processing methods face significant challenges, including latency, bandwidth constraints, and privacy concerns. Our research focuses on employing decision trees (DTs) [1] as an intelligent filtering mechanism on the edge. We propose a novel programmable and scalable custom ASIC architecture designed for decision tree based Machine Learning (ML) inference. Each bit-slice incorporates two 8-bit SISO input registers connected to an 8-bit comparator for data processing, the output of the comparator drives the select line of Mux, which selects the respective true and false paths. Each bit-slice can be programmed into either a leaf node or a regular node. A leaf node stores classification labels. A regular node compares a feature value with a weight value to decide between true and false paths. Given a DT model, the decision tree can be pre-programmed to store the model weights in respective tree nodes. In the inference phase, feature values are sequentially fed into the DT nodes. After the feature values are loaded the DT tree performs an inference with the classification value generated in the root node. We have implemented and validated the architecture at the layout level using Cadence Virtuoso in 0.5 μm CMOS technology node. A 5-level DT occupies roughly 90 mm^2 area with 22.58 mW of power consumption at a maximum clock speed of 12.8 MHz.

Keywords: Decision Tree · Edge-AI · IoT · ASIC · VLSI

1 Introduction

The term "Internet of Things" (IoT) describes how everyday objects and machinery, such as buildings, cars, and furniture, are connected to the internet or to one another. The drive behind IoT stems from its potential to streamline operations, increase automation, and facilitate data-driven decision-making in various sectors. It's ability to connect physical devices to the internet offers advantages such as more efficient processes, reduced operational expenses, the gathering of extensive data for predictive maintenance, improved resource utilization, and enhanced safety and security. It offers opportunities to reduce environmental

© IFIP International Federation for Information Processing 2025
Published by Springer Nature Switzerland AG 2025
G. Rey et al. (Eds.): IFIPIoT 2024, IFIP AICT 737, pp. 37–54, 2025.
https://doi.org/10.1007/978-3-031-81900-1_3

impact through optimized resource management. Despite the transformative potential of the IoT, it presents a myriad of challenges. One significant hurdle is the issue of latency, where delays in data processing can hinder the real-time responsiveness expected from IoT applications. Coping with the rapid increase in connected devices requires a robust infrastructure. Bandwidth constraints pose another challenge, particularly as the volume of data generated by IoT devices at the edge (by sensors) increases.

Edge computing is the practice of gathering, analyzing, and processing data at or near its point of generation to support local decision-making, reduce network traffic and congestion, and enable quicker and more efficient data transport. It arises as a strategic approach to address the difficulties encountered by conventional cloud-based processing in the context of IoT. It reduces latency, improves real-time processing, and mitigates bandwidth limitations by dispersing computing capacity across the network.

As the volume and diversity of data generated by IoT devices continue to grow, there is a compelling need for intelligent data processing at the edge. ML plays a pivotal role in this context by providing the capability for data filtering and informed decision-making. The idea of "ML on edge" implies an approach that enables the direct application of ML models to edge devices. By deploying ML algorithms on edge devices as in Fig. 1, data can be analyzed locally, reducing the need for extensive data transfers to centralized servers. This not only addresses the challenges of latency and bandwidth but also enables swift and context-aware decision-making directly at the source. Because edge machine learning can filter out irrelevant data and make decisions based on the relevant data that is accessible, it is particularly useful when network bandwidth is limited. For example, wearable technology may use edge machine learning to identify certain activities while eliminating noise. TensorFlow Lite [3] and other machine learning frameworks can aid in the efficient deployment of machine learning models on edge devices. It is becoming more and more important to implement ML models directly on specialized hardware, such as Application Specific Integrated Circuits (ASICs), to guarantee quick answers in real-time applications.

The design of classifiers that can be embedded in a chip and need extremely little computational and memory resources is crucial for edge computing in cutting-edge industries such as smart agriculture and medical devices. Besides, to comply with strict power constraints, ML capabilities must be included in integrated circuits rather than depending on power-hungry FPGA-based microprocessors in mobile or implantable devices. This work aims to provide a custom ASIC architecture for DT model implementation on edge hardware.

The novelty and contributions of this work are:

- To the best of our knowledge, this is **the first work** to propose a programmable custom VLSI ASIC for decision trees.
- The architecture is bit-sliced hence, users can generate decision tree of any height automatically with a parameterized layout generator.
- The proposed architecture is re-programmable such that any DT model can be deployed and thus agnostic to the end user IoT application. Further, this enables model updates on the edge nodes in the field.

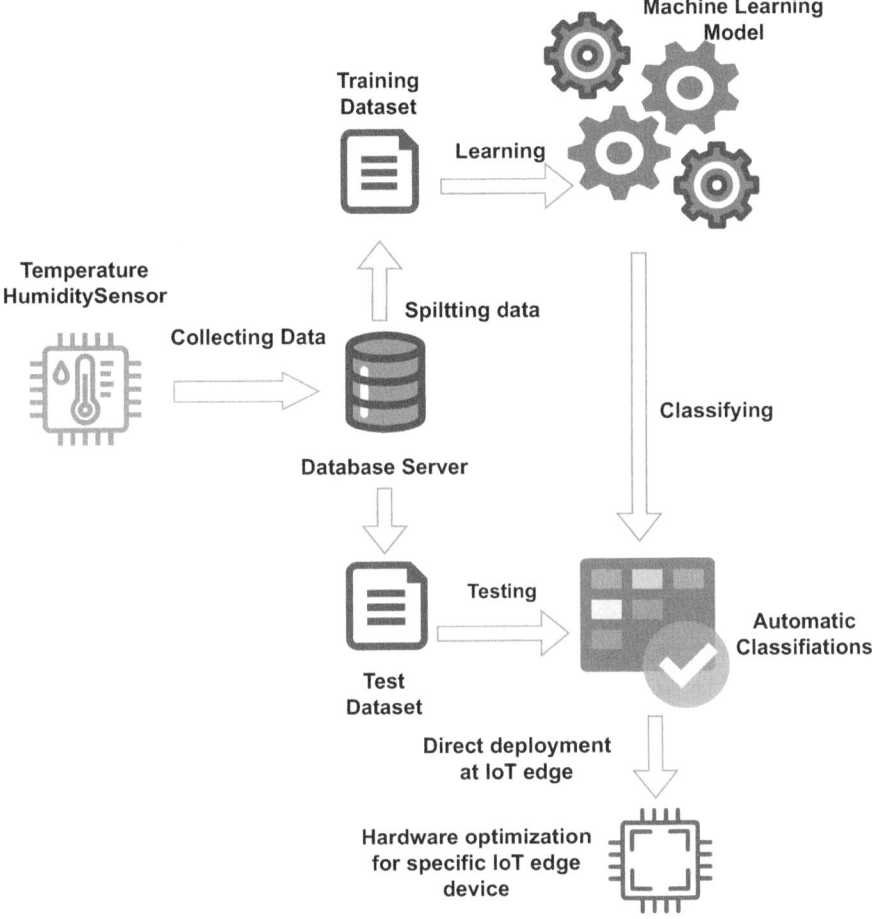

Fig. 1. Deploying Machine Learning Model on an IoT Edge Device

The rest of the paper is organized as follows: Sect. 2 provides an introduction to DTs, their hardware implementations, and an overview of related research. Section 4 presents the proposed bit-slice architecture in detail with an illustrative example of DT model mapping. Section 5 presents the results of our experiments, comparative analysis, and in-depth discussions on the outcomes. Section 6 concludes and illustrates possible future perspectives.

2   Background

2.1   Decision Trees

Decision trees, originally described by Breiman [1], are a flexible supervised learning technique that may be applied to both classification and regression applications. Their structure is evident and follows a definite hierarchy. Figure 2 provides an example of the decision-making process which is clearer and more a visual representation. These models operate by iteratively partitioning datasets into homogenous subgroups based on various criteria, such as information gain or gini impurity. This procedure generates a model that is capable of managing nonlinear interactions without the need for feature scaling. However, machine learning models are susceptible to overfitting and can exhibit strong sensitivity to even little variations in data. To solve these difficulties, one might utilize pruning processes or implement ensemble approaches like random forests. Decision trees are widely employed in several industries, including banking, healthcare, and retail, because of their efficient management of both numerical and categorical data.

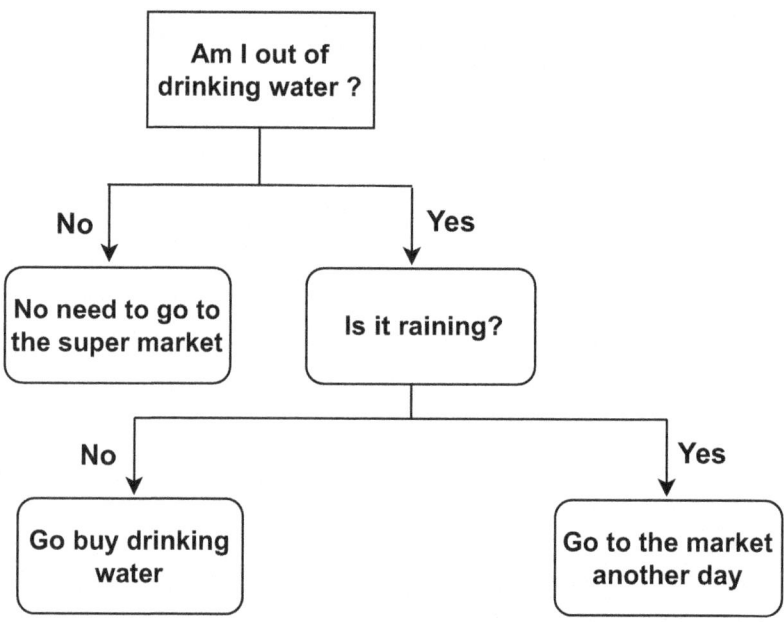

Fig. 2. Example of a Decision Tree

2.2 Decision Tree Training

During the training [5] of a decision tree, every node, including the root and internal nodes, is split into two paths: a left-hand path and a right-hand path. The division is dependent upon a distinct discrete function that is derived from the attributes of the input data. Labels are exclusively assigned to the leaf nodes only based on information derived from the original training data. An essential component of training decision trees is determining the most effective splitting measure function for each internal node, excluding the leaf nodes. Within our specific framework, we establish the optimal splitting function based on the concept of information gain (IG).

$$IG(E, A) = H(E) - H(E|A), \tag{1}$$

$H(E)$ represents the entropy of dataset E, while $H(E|A)$ signifies the conditional entropy of dataset E with respect to the attribute A.

Entropy estimates the level of uncertainty associated with the label values in the samples in a dataset. Increased entropy is directly proportional with higher uncertainty. The CART algorithm utilizes the concept of Gini Index (GI), which has parallels to the concept of entropy. Similar to entropy, GI is positively correlated with the degree of uncertainty. We employed the CART technique to train the datasets.

2.3 Decision Tree Classification

Initially, the input data and its attributes are introduced at the root node, where the splitting condition is assessed. If the condition is met, the data proceeds to the left node with a '1' result; otherwise, it's directed to the right node with a '0' result, concluding the evaluation at depth 0. This process recurs at subsequent levels, with results being combined and passed along the target path. The sequence continues until it reaches a leaf node, where the data's label is retrieved to finalize the Decision Tree classification [5].

3 Related Work

In this section, we explore recent developments and research in the hardware implementation of DTs. Hardware implementations of Decision Trees (DTs) have been reported in the literature and shown to be effective in various practical applications. Most of the existing work is targeting to FPGA platform.

Lopez [4] presented an architecture utilizing field-programmable gate arrays (FPGAs) to categorize sea states based on texture analysis. The main objective was to enhance the selection of constant false alarm rate (CFAR) algorithms in radar systems. The classification process employed GLCM characteristics extracted from radar data to improve target recognition in the presence of marine clutter. The architecture demonstrated remarkable precision in analyzing both simulated and actual data, marking a substantial advancement in maritime surveillance technology. However, it recognized the constraints of managing a wide range of sea state fluctuations and suggested potential improvements for the future.

Choudhury [2] proposed a hybrid decision tree (HDT) method specifically designed for FPGA implementation. The technique aimed to minimize complexity and improve training time. The results showcased an 8-fold enhancement in execution speed and notable hardware efficiency when compared to conventional decision tree techniques. The work emphasized the need for optimization in managing different node configurations and enhancing accuracy.

Struharik et al. [10], presented IP core proposals and architectural solutions for the hardware-based implementation of decision tree inference, emphasizing an evolutionary optimization approach. The paper introduced serial and parallel hardware designs for single decision trees using the Here Boy evolutionary algorithm.

Struharik [9], proposed decision tree hardware implementations using universal nodes, reducing hardware resources by 56% while maintaining throughput. They also explored an alternative architecture with a single universal node module for scenarios where classification speed was less critical. Struharik [8], presented four hardware acceleration architectures for diverse decision tree ensemble classifiers. They performed a comparative evaluation of FPGA-based oblique DT ensemble classifier implementations against software implementations on MicroBlaze and ARM processors.

Sayed [6] developed an automated framework to transform datasets into machine learning classifier-integrated circuits, generating verilog designs for ASIC implementations tailored for real-time applications. The author showcased the whole process, from raw dataset to ASIC design, highlighting the automation of Verilog code generation and the challenges encountered, particularly in data binarization and overfitting prevention. Even though the classifier worked well, the study suggested that binarization techniques and entropy conditions could be improved in the future to make the framework more useful and the models more accurate.

Shih and Chiu presented [7] an ASIC chip design for online Decision Tree (DT) training and classification, incorporating innovative techniques to eliminate division in Gini Impurity calculations, enhance learning functions, and accelerate classification through a double-root tree topology. Their architecture was focused on maximizing hardware implementation efficiency and minimizing delay. However, the experimental results of their study were constrained by a maximum tree depth of 8 and only 10 attributes, with each attribute represented by an 8-bit wordlength. Additionally, their training was conducted on a dataset of 1024 instances. While their work demonstrated notable advancements in speed and hardware resource utilization, the limited tree depth and attribute count suggest that there is potential for further exploration and development, particularly in adapting the architecture for more complex datasets and enhancing computing efficiency. These limitations highlight opportunities for advancing DT hardware implementations, especially for applications in IoT edge nodes where more extensive and intricate data processing might be required.

DTs were commonly deployed on IoT devices via FPGAs, which are inferior to ASICs in terms of power, performance and area (PPA). Although ASIC DT implementations are superior in PPA they fall short in terms of programmability and flexibility. The mentioned limitations serves as a guide for the creation of a proposed design that seeks to achieve a balance among these elements for IoT edge devices. This proposed bit-sliced VLSI architecture aims to provide programmability and flexibility for any variety of datasets targeting IoT edge applications without compromising PPA.

4   Proposed Work

In designing our custom ASIC architecture, we have strategically placed the bit-slices in an H structure, drawing inspiration from its widespread use in clock topology. This configuration, where bit-slices represent the nodes of the H-tree structure, was specifically chosen for its proven efficacy in minimizing skew and latency. By adopting this structure, we aim to achieve efficient and reliable data propagation to each node within our ASIC.

4.1   Bit Slice Architecture

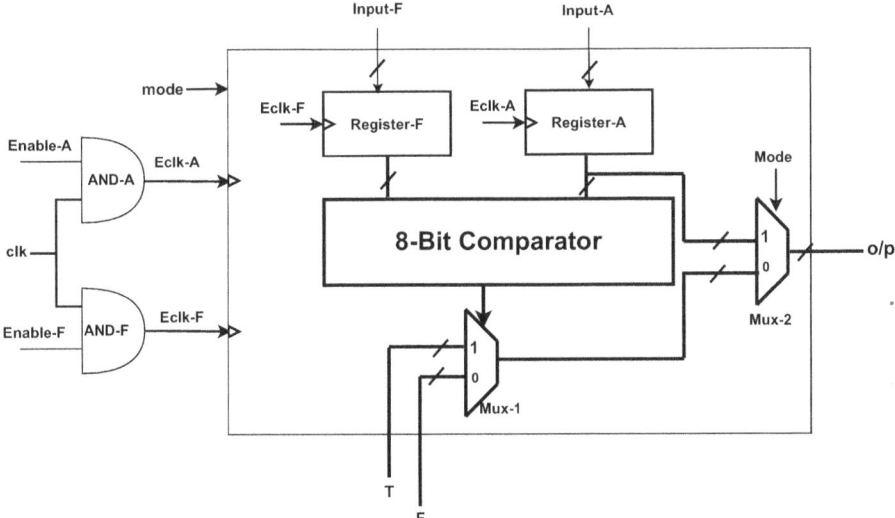

Fig. 3. Bit-Slice Architecture

The bit-slice architecture Fig. 3 consists of two 8-bit shift registers (F, A), an 8-bit Comparator, two 8-bit Mux ('Mux-1' and 'Mux-2') and two 2-input AND gates ('AND-F','AND-A') for the enabled clock connection, which governs the loading of inputs to the shift registers. The clock signal is given as a common input to both AND gates, with the second input being 'Enable A' and 'Enable F', respectively. 'Enable A' is kept high for the clock input to propagate to shift register A until all the attribute and classification values are loaded into respective bit-slices, and then 'Enable A' is turned low. Similarly, 'Enable F' is kept low until all attribute values are loaded, and then we make it high for the feature values to be loaded to each bit slice. After loading is done, the 8-bit comparator, compares the A and F values, resulting in an output that drives the select line of 'Mux-1', which selects the respective true and false paths.

The 'Mux-2' has two modes of operation controlled by asserting mode signals. When the mode is asserted high, the circuit behaves as a leaf node, and we can store classification label values in it, whereas when the mode is asserted low, it behaves as a normal comparator, which takes the input from the Mux-1 output and decides true and false paths.

Figure 4 shows the layout designed and implemented in the Cadence Virtuoso Layout editor in 0.5 μm CMOS technology node. It consists of the device layers with the interconnects required to work as a stand-alone bit-slice circuit. The components are strategically placed w.r.t internal connections and further integration of slices. Here, we have two multiplexers on top, followed by a comparator sandwiched between the two serial in and serial out input registers. We have routed the buses to carry inputs and outputs. Our IO interface bus system consists of 7 different buses. Three are used for interfacing with neighboring bit-slices, of which two are the outputs of Mux-1 that connect the true and false paths to the neighboring bit-slices, and the other one is the output bus. Four others are the dedicated global buses for transferring the serial inputs (attribute and feature) values and the enabled clock connections (Eclk-A, Eclk-F) to each register. The buffer circuitry is responsible for buffering the global signals. We have used a pair of inverters as buffers within our layout at each stage to increase the signal strength. The strategic placement of the bit-slices and buffer circuits makes this an area-optimized design.

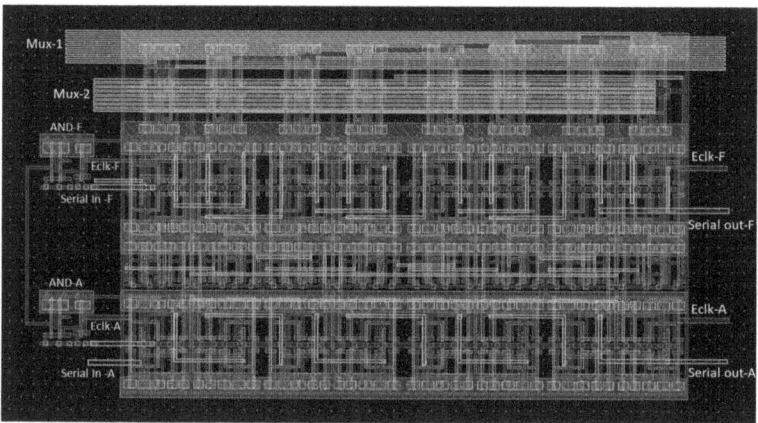

Fig. 4. Layout of Bit-Slice with I/O

We show the floorplan of a 2-level DT in Fig. 5, consisting of 7 nodes with 7 bit-slices interconnected w.r.t. true and false paths in an H structure minimizing timing violations. The two vacant places in the first and third rows are used for buffer circuits. Figure 6 shows the layout of the 2-level H architecture for the above DT model. The design's functionality is verified using the ADEL (Analog Design Environment) simulation tool.

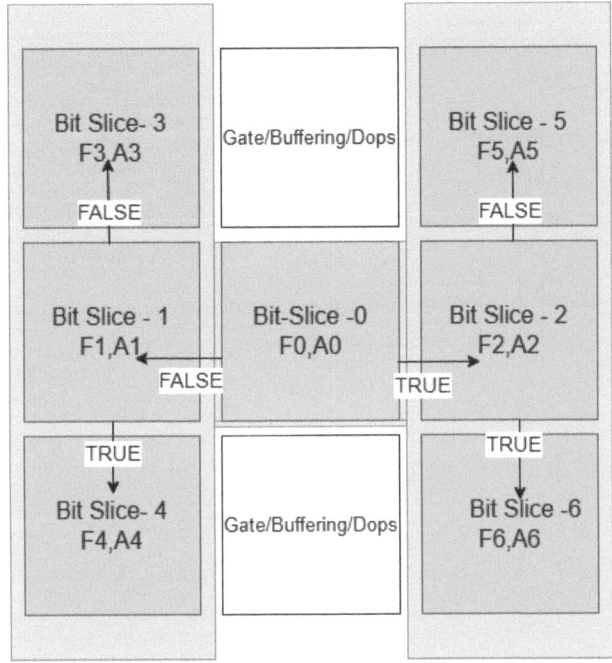

Fig. 5. H-Architecture for 2-Level DT Model

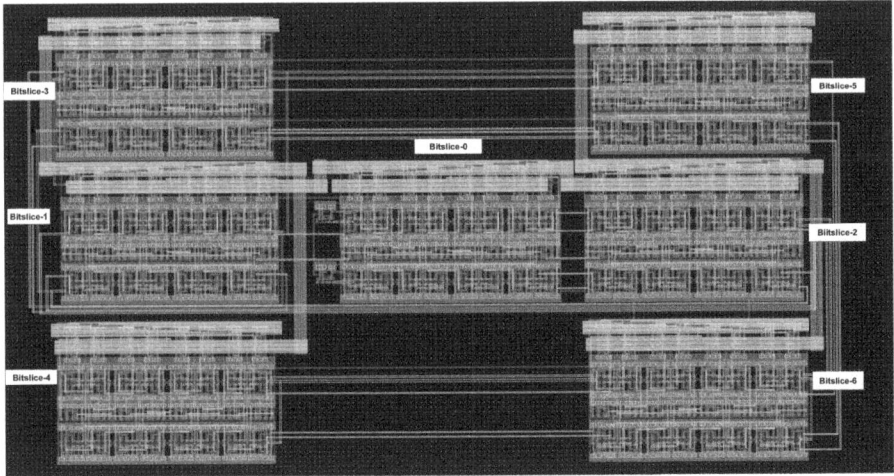

Fig. 6. Layout of H-Architecture for 2-Level DT Model

4.2 Programming and Operation

In our custom bit-sliced architecture, each bit-slice has two modes of operation, which can be controlled by asserting mode signals. When the mode is asserted

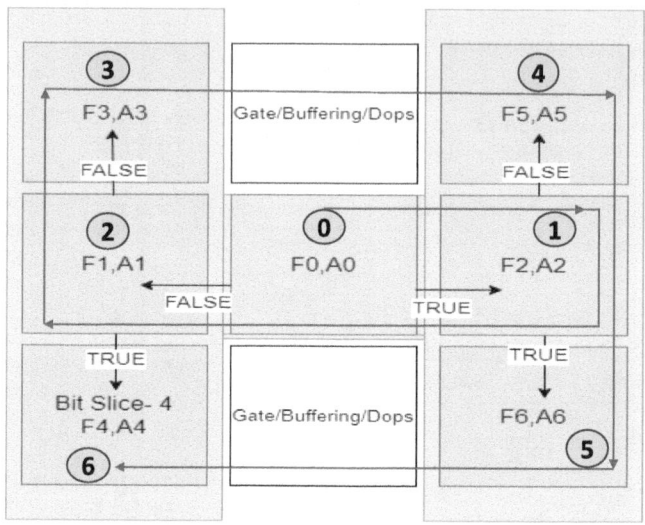

Fig. 7. Order Sequence for Loading Inputs to Bit-Slices

high, the circuit behaves as a leaf node, and we can store classification label values in it, whereas when the mode is asserted low, it behaves as a normal comparator, which decides true and false paths. Our design processes the trained datasets for classification through two operational phases. Initially, in the programming phase, attribute values are assigned to bit slices along with leaf classification values. In the inference phase, the feature values are loaded serially for comparison at each bit slice, resulting in a final classification label at the root node.

At first, when the enable input of the AND gate connected to the Register-A (Enable-A) is set to high, the clock propagates through the register for the values to be loaded to each bit-slice until all the attribute and classification values are loaded at their respective bit-slices in the order starting from (F0, A0) following the path from '0' along the blue line, until '6' (F4, A4), as shown in Fig. 7. Then, it is triggered low to cut the clock to the attribute register. During the real-time phase, the enabled input (Enable -F) is triggered high for the clock to propagate through 'Register -F'. Subsequently, inferencing takes place by loading the feature values for comparison at each bit slice, resulting in classification at the output Mux-2.

Depending on the comparison result, the output is determined; if the comparison is true, then it follows the true path, which connects bitslice-0 and bitslice-2 resulting in bitslice-2 output at Mux-2 at bitslice-0. Similarly, when the comparison is false, it follows the false path, which connects bitslice-0 and bitslice-3 with bitslice-3 output at Mux-2 at bitslice-0. This process of comparison continues up to the leaf node, with the final results being observed at Mux-2 in bitslice-0.

4.3 Illustrative Example: Mapping of Iris DT Model to H-Architecture

Figure 8 shows the mapping of Iris DT model with a max depth of 3 to a 3-Level H-structure. The nodes of the Iris tree model, from the root node until the leaf classification, are mapped to bit-slices in the H-structure, starting from the centre of the H-tree and moving along the vertical lines w.r.t. true and false paths. For ease of understanding, each bit-slice in the H-structure has been color-matched with corresponding nodes in the Iris DT model. The feature values i.e., Petal Length (PL) and Petal Width (PW), are compared with the attribute values (0.8, 4.75, etc.) in the respective nodes at each level to determine the traversal of the tree to result in the classification values (Setosa, Versicolor, and Virginica) at the leaf nodes. For our 3-level H-structure the attribute registers enable input is set high for 3600 ns (number of bit-slices * register bitwidth * clock period). In this model, the number of bit-slices is 15, the bitwidth is 8, and the clock period is 30 ns. Thus, 15 * 8 * 30 = 3600 ns is required to load the attribute and classification label values.

Following this, the feature register's enable input is toggled high for the next 3600 ns for all the feature inputs to load and compared at each bit-slice, leading to the output of a classification label from mux2 in bit-slice-0 with a propagation delay of 78 ns, operating at 33.33 MHz and consuming 14.30 mW of power.

Figure 8 is a 3-level H-Architecture that is mapped to the 3-level Iris DT model. Here, only 9 bit-slices are used during the computation, as the 3-level Iris DT model consists of only 9 nodes, which are colored-matched, and the remaining nodes, with no color, are unused for this DT model and thus waste power. To alleviate this, we have introduced a power gating circuit for each bit-slice to pass the global clock only through the bit-slices that are active during the computation.

This was achieved by using Fig. 9, which receives the global VDD and common clock. Each power gating circuit is responsible for propagating the Vdd to the respective bit slices. The control is given through the input to the flip-flop, which is kept high until we load all the inputs and then make it low during computation. Each bit-slice will have a power gating circuit that can be accommodated within the cell allocated for the gates and buffers on the first and third rows within the H-structure.

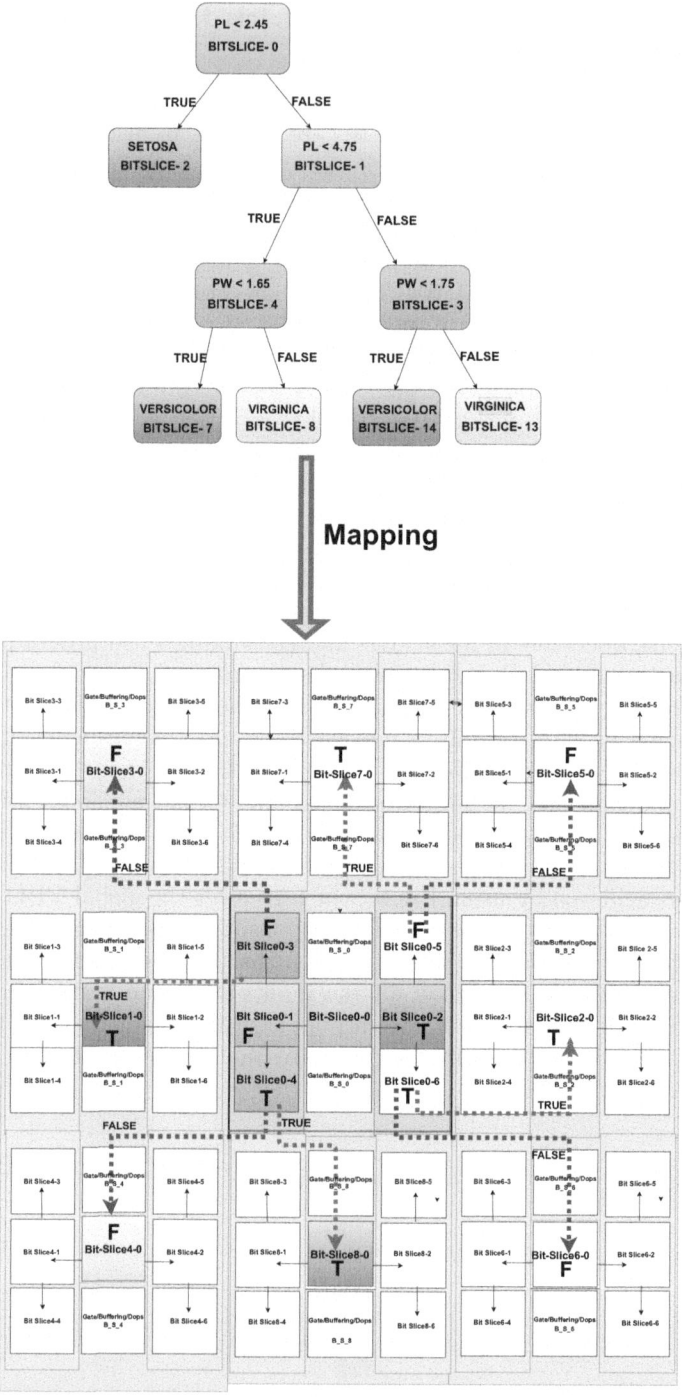

Fig. 8. An Illustrative Example: Mapping Iris DT Model to a 3-Level H-Architecture

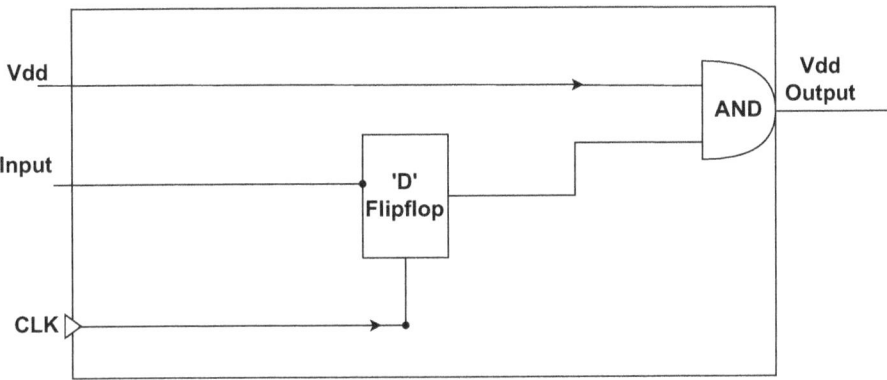

Fig. 9. Power gating

4.4 Scalable Architecture

The scaling is done by connecting the 2-Level Integrated Slice in the N x N array, with the primary input being given to the i = j location. In Fig. 10, the scaling of the '5-Level DT' is shown with the primary input given to the '2-Level Integrated Slice' located at the center. Here, we map the root node of the tree to bit slice-0 and the programming is done similar to a 2-level H-structure. It is further connected to neighboring 2-level bit slices in a clock-wise manner, with the end nodes (bit slice 0-(3, 5, 6, 4)) connected to the center node of bit-slices (1, 3, 7, 5, 2, 6, 8, 4) respectively according to true and false paths denoted by blue and red arrows in the figure. From there, the traversal is with respect to the 2-level H-structure. It can be further scaled to 8, 11, 14 levels, and so on using the same technique.

5   Experimental Results

The layout implementations for the DT model are created with the Cadence Virtuoso Layout Editor in 0.5 μm CMOS technology node. On a DRC (Design Rule Check) clean layout, we perform Parasitic Extraction (PEX) using the Mentor Calibre tool. The extracted netlist was then converted into Hspice format, allowing us to evaluate the design's performance comprehensively. For functional verification of the design, we used the Analog Design Environment Tool (ADEL), where transient analysis is carried out to inspect the outputs in the generated waveforms. Synopsys HSPICE simulator is used to measure the average power consumption and the worst-case delay.

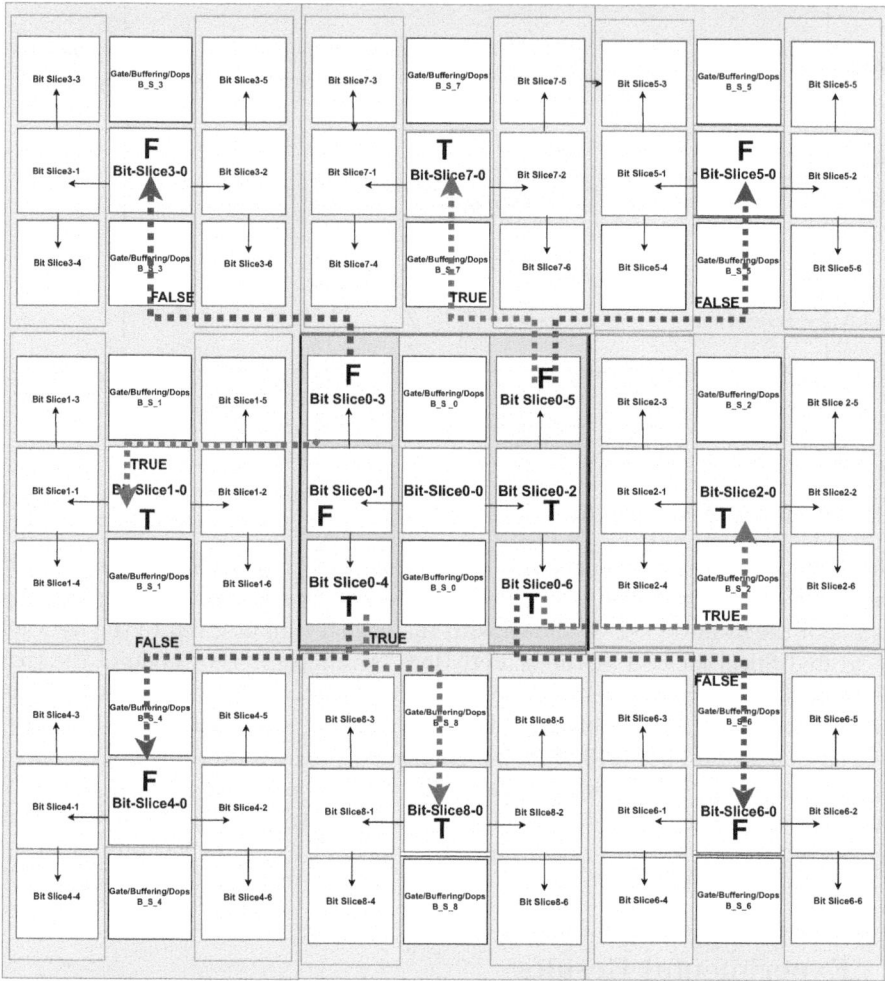

Fig. 10. H-Architecture for the 5-Level DT Model

5.1   Performance Metrics of Custom ASIC

Table 1 outlines the design specifications of a custom ASIC tailored for machine
learning applications across five levels, emphasizing scalability and efficiency.
At the initial level 0, the ASIC design is compact, comprising 4,860 transistors
within an area of 40,299 μm^2, and it achieves power efficiency with an average
consumption of just 3.18 mW, alongside a worst-case delay of 14 ns. As the
number of levels increase, the number of transistors and the area increase non-
linearly. Level 1 DT uses 14,364 transistors and level 3 uses 71,028 transistors,
with corresponding areas of 121,242 μm^2 and 934,241 μm^2, respectively. Power
consumption rises modestly in correlation with complexity, from 7.10 mW in level

Table 1. Hardware Design Attributes of Custom ASIC

Levels	No. of Transistors	Area (μm^2)	Avg.Power (mW)	Worst-case delay (ns)
0	4,860	40,299	3.18	14
1	14,364	121,242	7.10	29
2	33,372	384,319	10.16	60
3	71,028	934,241	14.30	78
5	107,034	1,400,740	22.58	123

1 to 14.30 mW in level 3. This ASIC's design evolution demonstrates significant area and power savings potential, making it well-suited for a range of machine learning datasets where resource efficiency is paramount.

Table 2 compares the performance of our custom ASIC on multiple datasets. These datasets, which vary in the quantity of features and instances, include Iris, Breast Cancer, Credit Card, Heart Disease, Raisin, Fetal Health, and Liver Diagnostic. For each data set, we evaluated the average power consumption and inference time. The Iris dataset, has 150 instances and 4 features. The average power usage was 10.7 mW, and the inference delay was 1,080 µs. Similarly, in the Breast Cancer dataset with 11 features and 569 instances, the average power consumption was 14.83 mW, with an inference delay of 72,000 µs. We found that the average power consumption across all datasets was between 10.7 and 16.28 mW, and the related inference delays were between 1,080 µs and 72,000 µs. These results highlight how crucial it is to take accuracy and computational economy into account when implementing machine learning models in contexts with limited resources.

Level 2 exhibits a precise rise of 4.20% in transistor count and a significant decrease of 18.8% in power consumption. On the other hand, level 3 demonstrates a little increase of 4.61% with the most considerable power optimization of 27.97%. The results in Fig. 13 highlight the effectiveness of power gating. The amount of power saved depends on the number of unused nodes in the decision tree.

Figures 11 and 12 provide a concise overview of the impact of power gating on five levels of hierarchical design. It presents a comparative study of the power consumption used and the efficiency of power consumption. Before using power gating, level 1 has 14,364 transistors. After implementing power gating, there is a 3.25% increase in the number of transistors, resulting in a total of 14,824 transistors. However, this increase in transistor count leads to an 18.3% improvement in power efficiency. The average power consumption is reduced from 7.101 mW to 5.8 mW. The pattern of increasing transistor count and decreasing power consumption continues in levels 2,3 and 5.

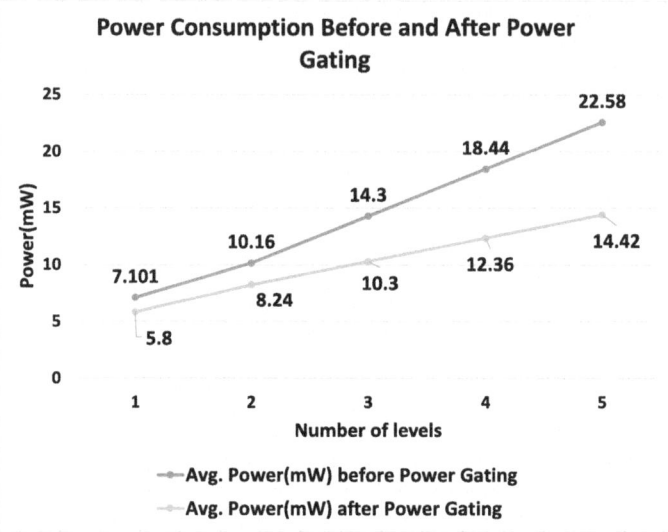

Fig. 11. Power Consumption before and after Power Gating

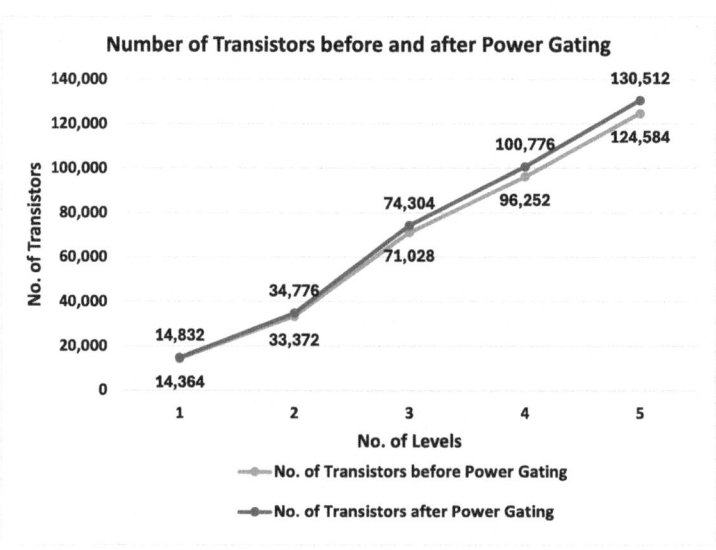

Fig. 12. No. of Transistors before and after Power Gating

Table 2. Performance Metrics for 3-Level Architecture

Dataset	Input Features	ML Dataset Size	Avg. Power (mW)	Inference time delay (ns)
Iris	4	150	10.7	7200
Breast Cancer	11	569	38.18	14,400
Credit Card	28	30,000	38.07	14,400
Heart Disease	13	303	38.20	14,400
Raisin	7	900	38.00	14,400
Fetal Health	21	2,126	16.03	7,653
Liver Diagnostic	11	583	16.28	2,098

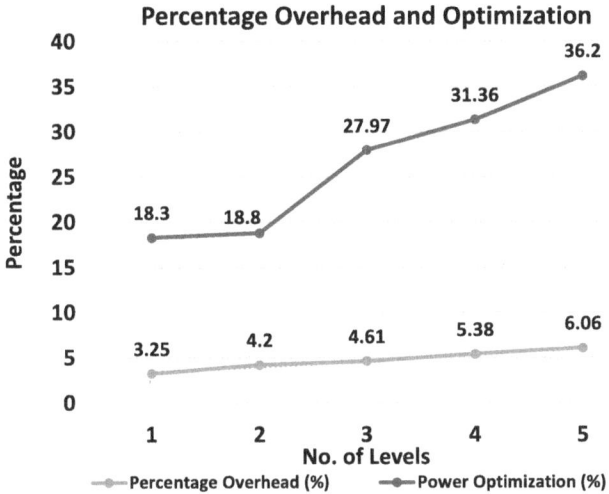

Fig. 13. Power Savings and Overhead with Power Gating

6   Conclusions

We present a scalable and programmable bit-sliced VLSI architecture for decision tree-based machine learning inference that is area- and power-efficient. By using the H-Tree structure, we were able to place the slices strategically and minimize timing and routing-related issues. Our proposed bit-sliced VLSI architecture has demonstrated significant power savings; the 5-level design consumes 22.58 mW with 36% power optimization and a minimal overhead of 6.06% attributed to the in-house power gate circuitry incorporated into the design. The bit-sliced design optimized for area efficiency occupies 90 mm^2 and is estimated to occupy only 2.69 mm^2 when implemented in a 15 nm technology node operating at a frequency of 0.271 GHz. The flexibility and scalability of the architecture suggest its potential for use in various IoT edge devices, where efficient power consumption and low-latency processing are important. Future directions for this work include adding support for floating-point weights and attribute values, and automating the design generation process based on the input tree height.

References

1. Breiman, L., Friedman, J., Olshen, R.A., Stone, C.J.: Classification and Regression Trees, 1st edn. Routledge (1984). https://doi.org/10.1201/9781315139470
2. Choudhury, R., et al.: FPGA implementation of low complexity hybrid decision tree training accelerator. In: 2021 IEEE International Midwest Symposium on Circuits and Systems (MWSCAS), pp. 511–514 (2021). https://doi.org/10.1109/MWSCAS47672.2021.9531848
3. Guillame-Bert, M., Bruch, S., Gordon, J., Pfeifer, J.: Introducing tensorflow decision forests (2021). https://blog.tensorflow.org/2021/05/introducing-tensorflow-decision-forests.html. Accessed 27 Aug 2024
4. Lopez-Estrada, S., Cumplido, R.: Decision tree based FPGA-architecture for texture sea state classification. In: 2006 IEEE International Conference on Reconfigurable Computing and FPGA's (ReConFig 2006), pp. 1–7 (2006). https://doi.org/10.1109/RECONF.2006.307770
5. Quinlan, J.R.: Induction of decision trees. Mach. Learn. **1**, 81–106 (1986)
6. Sayed, R., Azmi, H., Nassar, A.M., Shawkey, H.: Design automation and implementation of machine learning classifier chips. IEEE Access **8**, 192155–192164 (2020). https://doi.org/10.1109/ACCESS.2020.3032658
7. Shih, X.Y., Chiu, Y., Wu, H.E.: Design and implementation of decision-tree (DT) online training hardware using divider-free GI calculation and speeding-up double-root classifier. IEEE Trans. Circuits Syst. I Regul. Pap. **70**(2), 759–771 (2023). https://doi.org/10.1109/TCSI.2022.3222515
8. Struharik, J.: Implementing decision trees in hardware. In: 2011 IEEE 9th International Symposium on Intelligent Systems and Informatics, pp. 41–46 (2011). https://doi.org/10.1109/SISY.2011.6034358
9. Struharik, R.: Decision tree ensemble hardware accelerators for embedded applications. In: 2015 IEEE 13th International Symposium on Intelligent Systems and Informatics (SISY), pp. 101–106 (2015). https://doi.org/10.1109/SISY.2015.7325359
10. Struharik, R., V.V., Vukobratovic, B.: IP cores for hardware evolution of decision trees. In: 2012 IEEE 10th Jubilee International Symposium on Intelligent Systems and Informatics, pp. 407–412 (2012). https://doi.org/10.1109/SISY.2012.6339554

Electronics and Signal Processing
for IoT

Efficient Implementation of Authenticated Encryption on 16-bit MSP430 Microcontrollers

Christian Franck and Johann Großschädl$^{(\boxtimes)}$

DCS and SnT, University of Luxembourg, 6, Avenue de la Fonte,
4364 Esch-sur-Alzette, Luxembourg
{christian.franck,johann.groszschaedl}@uni.lu

Abstract. Algorithms for Authenticated Encryption with Associated Data (AEAD) extend the normal functionality of authenticated encryption schemes by the ability to process data that is only authenticated but not encrypted. Such algorithms have attracted much interest in the past few years, especially the question of how they can be designed and implemented efficiently to perform well in resource-constrained devices like miniature sensor nodes or RFID tags. In this paper, we analyze the performance of the lightweight AEAD schemes ELEPHANT V2, GRAIN-128AEADv2, ISAP v2.0, PHOTON-BEETLE, and ROMULUS v1.3 on the MSP430 family of 16-bit ultra-low-power microcontrollers. All five have in common that they offer large security margins and made it into the last round of the Lightweight Cryptography (LWC) standardization project of the U.S. National Institute of Standards and Technology. We describe how these AEAD algorithms can be implemented efficiently in software and introduce Assembly-level optimization techniques for the underlying primitives, which include three permutations, one tweakable block cipher, and one stream cipher. Furthermore, we present numerous detailed benchmarking results (i.e., execution time and code size) for the primitives as well as for the full AEAD algorithms for different lengths of plaintext and associated data. Our benchmarks clearly show that all five AEAD algorithms are much more efficient (up to almost two orders of magnitude) on MSP430 than indicated by results in the literature.

Keywords: Lightweight cryptography · AEAD algorithm ·
Permutation · Block cipher · MSP430 architecture

1 Introduction

Algorithms for authenticated encryption do not only produce ciphertext from plaintext (or vice versa), but also generate or verify a so-called authentication tag using the secret key. In this way, they are capable to simultaneously ensure the confidentiality and authenticity/integrity of data. *Authenticated Encryption with Associated Data (AEAD)* is a special variant of authenticated encryption

© IFIP International Federation for Information Processing 2025
Published by Springer Nature Switzerland AG 2025
G. Rey et al. (Eds.): IFIPIoT 2024, IFIP AICT 737, pp. 57–73, 2025.
https://doi.org/10.1007/978-3-031-81900-1_4

that supports auxiliary, non-confidential data, which is authenticated but does not get encrypted. The canonical use case for AEAD schemes is the protection of network packets where the payload is encrypted and authenticated, but the header containing the destination address must remain in the clear (yet should be authenticated) to enable routers to forward the packet. Historically, authenticated encryption schemes were based on generic composition of a symmetric encryption algorithm, commonly a block cipher, and a message-authentication algorithm such as HMAC or CBC-MAC [28]. However, generic composition is not ideal in terms of efficiency because the obtained authenticated encryption schemes need two different algorithms and make two separate passes over the data. Furthermore, generically-composed authenticated encryption is prone to (accidental) misuse since, for example, it can be extremely difficult to analyze whether MAC-then-Encrypt is secure in a certain context. These shortcomings have led to the construction of single-pass combined schemes for authenticated encryption, which are based on a single cryptographic primitive (in most cases either a block cipher or an unkeyed permutation).

AEAD schemes attracted a lot of attention in the past five years due to the Lightweight Cryptography (LWC) standardization project of the U.S. National Institute of Standards and Technology (NIST) [21]. This project had the form of a public, competition-like process with the goal of developing new standards for AEAD as well as hashing that perform "significantly better in constrained environments" compared to existing NIST standards, most notably AES-GCM and SHA-2 [24]. In August 2018, the NIST released a request for nominations for lightweight cryptographic schemes and also published detailed submission requirements [23]. A total of 57 candidates were submitted by the (extended) deadline of March 25, 2019, of which 56 satisfied the acceptance criteria and were considered as "proper and complete." These 56 proposals entered a multi-round evaluation procedure that took almost four years altogether. By the end of the first round the number of candidates was reduced to 32 and then, in the second round, an additional 22 algorithms were eliminated. The remaining ten candidates made it to the third and final round, in which they were scrutinized for security and efficiency over a period of 1.5 years. On February 7, 2023, the NIST declared the candidate ASCON [10] as the sole winner of the competition and to become the new standard for lightweight cryptography.

Besides security, the evaluation of submitted algorithm proposals took into account the efficiency in restricted environments, e.g., hardware and embedded software platforms. The NIST document describing evaluation criteria for the submissions mentions that performance on "a wide range of 8-bit, 16-bit, and 32-bit microcontroller architectures" is desirable [24]. NIST's evaluation of the software efficiency (i.e., execution time and binary code size) of the candidates largely relied on three major benchmarking initiatives. First and foremost, the NIST LWC team developed a benchmarking toolsuite and collected results on five 8-bit and 32-bit architectures: AVR, ARMv6-M (Cortex-M0+), ARMv7-M (Cortex-M3/M4), MIPS32 (PIC32), and Xtensa (LX6) [25]. The benchmarked implementations were contributed by the designer teams or by volunteers and independent researchers. The majority of designer teams developed optimized implementations for (at least) AVR and ARMv7-M, whereby most final-round submissions even included carefully-tuned Assembly code for the performance-critical parts (e.g., the underlying primitive of the AEAD algorithm). A second source of benchmarking results were the implementations and execution times of the final-round candidates contributed by Rhys Weatherley [32]. He focused on AVR, ARM Cortex-M3, and ESP32 microcontrollers, the latter of which are based on the 32-bit Xtensa LX6 architecture (i.e., his evaluation platforms are a subset of the NIST platforms). Finally, also a team of researchers from OTH Regensburg collected benchmarking results of the AEAD candidates on various microcontrollers [26,27]. They developed their own benchmarking toolset from scratch, which is capable to determine the execution time, code size, and RAM footprint of AEAD algorithms (i.e., hash functions are not supported). Besides AVR, Cortex-M3, Cortex-M7, and ESP32, they also generated benchmarks on a development board equipped with a 64-bit RISC-V processor [26].

NIST's recommendation for algorithm designers to consider "a wide range of 8-bit, 16-bit, and 32-bit microcontroller architectures" [24] hints at a highly-desirable property of lightweight cryptosystems, namely that of multi-platform (resp., cross-platform) efficiency. However, achieving this property is not trivial because the architectural and micro-architectural characteristics and features of modern microcontrollers differ significantly, even among architectures of the same word size. Consider, for example, Ascon, the winner of the NIST LWC competition and future standard for lightweight AEAD and hashing. Ascon is a permutation-based design that performs a lot of rotations of 64-bit words in its linear diffusion layer, whereby the rotation distances are fixed and have the following values: 1, 6, 7, 10, 17, 19, 28, 39, 41, 61 (see [10] for details). All these rotations can be executed in a single clock cycle on a 64-bit ARM processor; in many cases they can even be combined with some other arithmetic or logical instruction, making them basically free. On the other hand, the rotations take three instructions on a simple 64-bit RISC-V (i.e., RV64I) processor since the base instruction set is relatively minimalist and does not include explicit rotate instructions, i.e., a rotation has to be composed of two shifts and a XOR. The cycle count of 64-bit rotations further increases on 32-bit microcontrollers like the ARM Cortex-M3, though they support rotate instructions. However, these instructions can only rotate a 32-bit register but not a 64-bit word, i.e., a 64-bit rotation has to be emulated by four 32-bit shifts and two other instructions (costing six clock cycles in total). The situation becomes even worse on small 8/16-bit microcontrollers since most of them lack a barrel shifter, which means a multi-bit shift or multi-bit rotation has to be performed through a sequence of 1-bit shift (resp., 1-bit rotate) instructions [2,8]. Depending on the rotation distance, rotating a 64-bit word can take more than 30 clock cycles.

Multi-platform efficiency is particularly important for lightweight cryptosystems targeting the Internet of Things (IoT) and its billions of resource-limited devices. These devices are highly diverse and heterogeneous, and they come in all shapes and sizes. Consequently, it is not surprising that there exist dozens of different microcontroller platforms, operating systems, and communication standards for the IoT, many of which are optimized to serve a niche domain with specific requirements and constraints. This heterogeneity of IoT devices is the main reason why all benchmarking initiatives for lightweight cryptosystems carried out during the NIST LWC competition collected results (e.g., execution time, binary code size) on a number of different microcontrollers architectures instead of one. However, when looking at the target architectures summarized above, one could argue that 32-bit platforms are over-represented, 8-bit platforms under-represented, and 16-bit platforms completely lacking. Indeed, none of the three main benchmarking toolsuites (NIST, Weatherley, OTH) supports a 16-bit microcontroller. Nonetheless, there exist a few benchmarking results of second and third-round LWC candidates on 16-bit MSP430 microcontrollers from Texas Instruments. For example, Blanc et al. [6] analyze and compare the execution time of 18 of the 32 s-round candidates (which includes all ten finalists) on a MSP430F1611 microcontroller [31]. However, their results stem from C implementations (in most cases the reference C code of the designers) and lack Assembly-level optimizations for the performance-critical components (e.g., the underlying primitive). Alsahli et al. [2] implemented the permutation of four permutation-based LWC finalists, which are ASCON, SPARKLE, TINY-JAMBU, and XOODYAK, in MSP430 Assembly and also evaluated the execution time of the permutations and full AEAD algorithms using a MSP430F1611 as target platform. In an extended version of [2] (not yet publicly available), the final-round candidate GIFT-COFB was included in the evaluation.

Table 1. Basic properties of the AEAD algorithms (according to [29, Table 5]).

AEAD algorithm	Primitive	Mode	Key size	N. size	Tag size
Elephant v2	Spongent-π[160]	Enc-then-MAC	128	96	64
Grain-128AEADv2	Grain-128A	Enc-and-MAC	128	96	64
ISAP v2.0	Ascon P	Enc-then-MAC	128	128	128
PHOTON-Beetle	PHOTON$_{256}$	Sponge/COFB	128	128	128
Romulus v1.3	Skinny-128-384+	COFB	128	128	128

This paper introduces Assembly-optimized MSP430 implementations of the five final-round candidates ELEPHANT V2 [5], GRAIN-128AEADv2 [15], ISAP V2.0 [9], PHOTON-BEETLE [3], and ROMULUS V1.3 [12]. Some of the basic characteristics of these five AEAD algorithms, including the primitive they are based on, are summarized in Table 1. We developed Assembly implementations of the underlying primitive of each algorithm, while the rest (i.e., the mode) is written in portable C. Our optimized implementations shed some new light on the efficiency of these five AEAD algorithms on the MSP430 platform since all execution times reported in the literature were determined without Assembly-level optimizations. Our work aims to contribute to a better understanding on how lightweight AEAD algorithms can be optimized for small microcontrollers and what performance they can reach on the MSP430 platform, all of which is important for the progress of the field of lightweight cryptography. Finally, we point out that (variants of) four of the primitives we implemented, namely the stream cipher GRAIN-128A, the (tweakable) block cipher SKINNY, and the two permutations PHOTON and SPONGENT, are ISO standards [17–19].

2   MSP430 Architecture and Development Tools

MSP430 is a popular architecture for 16-bit microcontrollers designed by Texas Instruments with the goal of very low power dissipation [30]. Modern MSP430 microcontrollers have up to seven low-power modes and draw less than 1 μA in standby mode, making them an excellent choice for IoT applications that need high energy-efficiency. Even though the MSP430 is described as a 16-bit RISC architecture in [31], it provides some features that are more CISC-like, such as memory-to-memory operations without an intermediate register holding of the operand(s). The MSP430 architecture has 16 registers, each of which is 16 bits long, whereby registers r0–r3 serve a special purpose (program counter, stack pointer, status register, constant generator) and the remaining 12 are available for general use. The instruction set includes 27 core instructions and additional 24 emulated instructions to facilitate Assembly programming. There are seven addressing modes in total; depending on the used mode(s), one and the same instruction can be either 2, 4, or 6 bytes long. The instruction set is orthogonal and allows every instruction to be used with every combination of source and destination addressing mode(s). Memory management is relatively simple since the MSP430 is a "von-Neumann" architecture, i.e., instructions and data share the same address space and are accessed through a single bus. This means, in particular, that every memory read access anywhere in the address space takes one cycle, regardless of whether it targets flash or RAM. Consequently, static look-up tables do not necessarily need to be in RAM to reach top performance (this contrasts with, e.g., Harvard-based ARM microcontrollers where tables in RAM can be accessed faster than tables in flash, even with 0 wait states).

The latency of MSP430 instructions depends on the instruction format and the used addressing mode(s). More concretely, execution time of an instruction is determined by the number of memory accesses needed to fetch the complete instruction and to subsequently read/write the data being processed from/to flash or RAM. For example, an instruction that operates only on registers (and requires only one single memory access to read the instruction itself), such as mov r5, r8, executes in a single cycle. An instruction of a length of four bytes whose operands require a read and a write access to memory needs four cycles to execute. For example, xor r8, 0x1234 takes one cycle to fetch the opcode for xor, one cycle to read the value 0x1234, a further cycle to read the operand stored at the address 0x1234, and finally one cycle to write the result back to the address 0x1234. In general, the number of cycles corresponds to the overall number of memory accesses to be performed. There are only a few exceptions to this simple rule; for example using the `dadd` instruction or using the program counter as destination register costs an additional cycle.

IAR Embedded Workbench for MSP430 is a (proprietary). Integrated Development Environment (IDE) for which a free trial version exists that is limited to a code size of 8 kB [16]. Besides a modern graphical user interface, it comes with a range of tools, including a C++ compiler, a feature-rich debugger, and a cycle-accurate instruction-set simulator. We used the latter to optimize the Assembly code of the underlying primitives and to evaluate the execution time of the complete AEAD algorithms on a MSP430F1611 microcontroller [31]. In addition, we developed a special simulation script to gain further insights into code execution on our target device. By using snapshots of the memory of the MSP430 and its register state at two different breakpoints, both exported from the Embedded Workbench debugger, our script generates statistics about the instructions that are executed in between those breakpoints. The output of the script provides, for instance, detailed information on:

- Memory usage, e.g., how many different RAM or flash memory addresses have been accessed overall, or how many read accesses and how many write accesses have been performed;
- Instruction execution, e.g., how many times a certain instruction has been executed, how often each addressing mode has been used, how many of the executed instructions are register-to-register, register-to-memory, etc.
- A number of other events, like how many times a certain macro has been executed, or how much stack memory has been used.

This enables us to analyze our implementations of the primitives and to assess to what extent computations are performed locally (i.e., all operands are held in registers), how much memory is occupied by static look-up tables, how many accesses are made to these look-up tables, and so on.

3   Overview of Algorithms and Their Implementation

In this section, we describe our implementation of ELEPHANT v2 (the instance DUMBO [5]), GRAIN128-AEADv2 [15], ISAP v2.0 (concretely ISAP-A-128A) [9], the 128-bit instance of PHOTON-BEETLE [3], and ROMULUS-N [12].

3.1   Elephant V2 (Dumbo)

ELEPHANT [5] is a family of Encrypt-then-MAC constructions whose members use a permutation masked with a Linear-Feedback Shift Register (LFSR) in an Even-Mansour-like way [11] instead of a block cipher. Encryption/decryption is performed via counter mode, while message authentication was originally done with a Wegman-Carter-Shoup MAC. However, in the final round, the designers decided to replace this MAC by a variant of the protected counter-sum MAC function, which has the advantage of guaranteeing authenticity in nonce-reuse scenarios. All three ELEPHANT members have a small state size of between 160 and 200 bits, thereby enabling lightweight hardware implementations, and are parallelizable by design. The primary instance for the NIST LWC competition was DUMBO; it is based on the SPONGENT-π permutation [7], provides 112 bits of security, and is particularly well-suited for hardware implementation.

The SPONGENT variant used by DUMBO has state of 160 bits and executes 80 rounds. In each round, the following three operations are carried out [7].

- *lCounter:* a 7-bit LFSR defined by the polynomial $p(x) = x^7 + x^6 + 1$.
- *sBoxLayer:* a 4-bit S-box applied 40 times in parallel.
- *pLayer:* a fixed bit-level permutation over the 160-bit state.

To reduce the execution time, we merged the S-box and fixed permutation into a single Assembly macro, so that the values this macro operates on can be kept in a register-set as long as possible and unnecessary memory accesses are avoided. There are several different steps that all require the same operations with respect to rotation and S-box, but there are also some operations that are specific to each step. As illustrated in Fig. 1, the *pLayer* permutation is quite regular, making it possible to sequentially go through the 160 bits and fill up four blocks of 40 bits. This operation is expensive to perform in C, but can be implemented very efficiently in Assembly language, since one can roll the bits one by one from the source register to the carry flag and then successively roll them into four destination registers. In order to keep the binary code size small without compromising performance by using subroutines that are expensive to call (because of operands placed on the stack), we used a technique of dynamic branching, i.e., the execution of the program is controlled by successive loadings of address values directly from a table into the program-counter register r0.

bit 0 → bit 0	bit 1 → bit 40	bit 2 → bit 80	bit 3 → bit 120
bit 4 → bit 1	bit 5 → bit 41	bit 6 → bit 81	bit 7 → bit 121
bit 8 → bit 2	bit 9 → bit 42	bit 10 → bit 82	bit 11 → bit 122
...	...	...	...
bit 156 → bit 39	bit 157 → bit 79	bit 158 → bit 119	bit 159 → bit 159

Fig. 1. Illustration of the *pLayer* permutation of Spongent.

Despite our optimization efforts, SPONGENT is the by far slowest of the five considered primitives (see Sect. 4), partly because its design is everything else than "software-friendly" and partly due to the large number of rounds.

3.2   Grain-128AEADv2

GRAIN-128AEAD was the only candidate of the NIST competition that used a stream cipher, namely GRAIN-128A, as its low-level primitive [15]. The initial design was submitted to the eStream project[1] and then tweaked to prevent an attack based on linear approximation (GRAIN v1). Furthermore, the designers proposed a variant (GRAIN-128) with an extended key size of 128 instead of 80 bits and an initialization vector of 96 bits. The GRAIN family made it into the final eStream portfolio for Profile 2 ("stream ciphers for hardware applications with restricted resources") [14]. After the end of the eStream project, it turned out that the 128-bit version has a security flaw, which was fixed in a revision (known as GRAIN-128A) that is not only more secure, but features also native support for authentication with tag sizes up to 32 bits [1].

The stream cipher on which GRAIN-128AEAD is based on is (essentially) GRAIN-128A with some small modifications to allow for a larger authentication tag and to support AEAD. Due to a weakness discovered in the second round of the NIST competition, the initialization of the stream cipher was modified (resulting in GRAIN-128AEADv2) to better protect against key recovery from a known internal state. This stream cipher is bit-oriented and consists of two major components, namely a so-called *Pre-Output Generator (POGen)* and an *Authenticator Generator (AUGen)*. The former itself is composed of: (i) a 128-bit Linear Feedback Shift Register (LFSR) whose (linear) feedback polynomial and state at time t is denoted $f(x)$ and $S_t = [s_0^t, s_1^t, \ldots, s_{127}^t]$, respectively, (ii) a 128-bit Non-linear Feedback Shift Register (NFSR) with polynomial $g(x)$ and state at time t referred to as $B_t = [b_0^t, b_1^t, \ldots, b_{127}^t]$, and (iii) a simple Boolean function $h(x)$ that takes as input seven bits from the LFSR and two bits from the NFSR. Using these components, the *POGen* generates es a pseudo-random stream of bits through the pre-output function $y_t = h(x) + s_{93}^t + \sum b_j^t$, where $j = \{2, 15, 36, 45, 64, 73, 89\}$. On the other hand, the *AUGen* computes the 64-bit authentication tag and comprises a simple 64-bit shift Register (R) and an Accumulator register (A) of the same length. After initialization, register R is shifted one bit per clock and always contains the 64 most recent *odd bits* from the pre-output bit-stream (more details below). Furthermore, in each clock, the 64 bits of R are ANDed with a single message bit m_i and the 64-bit result is XORed to the content of the accumulator register A.

We developed a variant of the *POGen* in Assembly language that produces 16 bits of pre-output stream following the approach proposed in [20]. Both the LFSR and NFSR are shifted 16 bits in 1-bit steps since the shift instructions of the MSP430 do not support any distances beyond a single bit. We first load the 128-bit LFSR into eight registers and compute (intermediate results of) the terms that form the feedback functions $f(x)$, $g(x)$, and the Boolean function $h(x)$. Thereafter, we load the NFSR and again compute terms of $f(x)$, $g(x)$, as well as $h(x)$. Due to the limited register space, some of the intermediate results have to be stored in RAM, but thanks to the multitude of addressing modes they can be updated very efficiently. While the execution time of the *POGen* is relatively small (just 589 cycles), it has to be considered that only eight of the 16

---

[1] The eStream project was run by the ECRYPT Network of Excellence from 2004 to 2008 with the goal to identify new stream ciphers suitable for widespread adoption.

pre-output bits, namely the eight *even bits*, are actually used for encryption or decryption since the other eight bits are fed into the *AUGen*.

3.3   Isap v2.0

The ISAP family of AEAD algorithms [9] is somewhat special amongst the ten LWC finalists in the sense that the main design goal was not efficiency in hardware or software, but to offer strong protection against various implementation attacks such as Differential Power Analysis (DPA) and fault analysis. ISAP can be characterized as a family of permutation-based MAC-then-Encrypt schemes consisting of four instances. The primary instance is ISAP-A-128A and uses the ASCON-p permutation [10] with 1, 6, or 12 rounds as underlying primitive. All ISAP instances feature a mode-level protection against implementation attacks based on the *fresh re-keying* technique [22], which means encryption/decryption and authentication do not directly process the provided secret key but are performed with session keys that are unique for distinct input data. These session keys are derived from the provided secret key and some public data (either the nonce or a hash of the nonce, associated data, and ciphertext) by a duplex-like re-keying function named *IsapRk*. After initialization with the secret key, the *IsapRk* function absorbs the public data at a rate of only one bit, which limits the number of possible inputs to the permutation's inner part to two per call of the permutation. This, in turn, limits the input data complexity exploitable in DPA such that classical DPA attacks become impractical. Since *IsapRk* uses a very small rate, the number of rounds of ASCON-p was reduced to one. The other two main functions of ISAP, namely *IsapEnc* (for encryption/decryption) and *Isap-Mac* (authentication), operate with higher rates than *IsapRk*, but also execute a larger number of rounds (either six or 12).

An Assembly implementation of the ASCON-p permutation for the MSP430 platform was presented in our previous paper [2]. We used this implementation to determine the execution times of ISAP-A-128A given in Sect. 4. A detailed description of our optimizations for ASCON-p can be found in [2].

3.4   Photon-Beetle

PHOTON-BEETLE is a family of AEAD and hash algorithms whose members are all based on PHOTON$_{256}$, a 256-bit permutation designed for efficiency in hardware [3]. The main AEAD instance uses the so-called BEETLE mode and operates on top of this permutation with a rate of 128 bits, i.e., the capacity is also 128 bits. In contrast to a conventional duplex construction, where the rate-part of the next input for the permutation is a block of ciphertext (obtained as the direct result of XORing a plaintext-block to the rate), the BEETLE mode produces the next input "indirectly" by a COmbined FeedBack (COFB) of the current state and ciphertext-block. More concretely, PHOTON-BEETLE uses a linear function ρ, performing a 1-bit right-rotation of a 128-bit word and an XOR, to update the state and encrypt a block of plaintext [3]. In this way, the BEETLE mode achieves a security level of $c - \log_2(r)$ bits where c and r denote the size of capacity and rate, respectively (i.e., the security level is only a little below the capacity in bits). Thus, the primary instance of PHOTON-BEETLE offers 121-bit security for plaintext confidentiality and ciphertext integrity.

The PHOTON permutation, introduced at CRYPTO 2011 [13], shows some similarities with the AES, though its columns mixing layer can be computed in a serial way, thereby reducing area cost in hardware. PHOTON$_{256}$ represents its internal state in the form of 64 elements of four bits, which are arranged as an 8×8 matrix of cells. Each of the 12 rounds performs four basic operations:

- *AddConstants* adds a fixed constant to each cell of the first column.
- *SubCells* applies a 4-bit S-box to each cell of the state.
- *ShiftRows* rotates the cells within each row.
- *MixColumnsSerial* mixes the columns using matrix multiplication.

We used a number of techniques to optimize our Assembly implementation of PHOTON$_{256}$ for the MSP430. A naive implementation of the four operations is quite slow, but as the designer's reference implementation already shows, the three expensive computations *SubCells*, *ShiftRows*, and *MixColumnsSerial* can be significantly accelerated using a pre-computed look-up table (referred to as SCShRMCS table). We use a table of $8 \times 12 = 96$ bytes for the round constants and a table of $16 \times 8 \times 8 = 1024$ bytes for the other three operations. Since the look-ups into the SCShRMCS table require a multiplication of the state values by 8, it is possible to achieve a speed-up by pre-multiplying the state by 8 and adapting the operations accordingly (e.g., all the round constants are also pre-multiplied by 8 and so on). Only at the very end of the permutation, the state values are divided by 8 so as to bring them back to the expected range. At the beginning of each of the 12 rounds, we copy the state to a temporary area in RAM, and we combine this copying with the round-key addition to reduce the number of loads and stores. Our general optimization strategy was to minimize the number of memory accesses by keeping state-values as much as possible in the 12 (unrestricted) MSP430 registers. During the execution of the main loop of the permutation, one line of the matrix (containing eight values) is kept in four registers, which are successively updated. We use another four registers to store pointers to the tables and the state matrix, respectively. Two out of the four remaining registers serve as counters and as temporary variable, while the other two hold constants that are frequently used.

3.5   Romulus v1.3

ROMULUS [12] is a family of AEAD algorithms based on the Tweakable Block Cipher (TBC) SKINNY, which was introduced at CRYPTO 2016 [4]. The main instance, ROMULUS-N, uses a rate-1 TBC-based COmbined FeedBack (COFB) mode of operation. It encrypts a 16-byte block of plaintext with one invocation of the TBC and also needs just one TBC-call for a 32-byte block of associated data. However, the processing of associated data involves a relatively expensive tweakey-schedule per block. The main benefits of ROMULUS-N are efficiency in hardware and extremely low overhead for short messages since there is no pre-processing TBC-call. For example, authenticating 16 bytes associated data and encrypting/decrypting 16 bytes plaintext/ciphertext can be done with just two TBC-calls altogether. Plaintext is added to the cipher-state via a state-update function ρ performing a multiplication by a binary matrix, which boils down to a 1-bit right-rotation of each state-byte and an XOR. The computation of the tweak mainly consists of updating a 56-bit counter (initially set to 0) by means of an LFSR with polynomial $f(x) = x^{56} + x^7 + x^4 + x^2 + 1$.

The SKINNY variant used by ROMULUS-N is SKINNY-128-384+; it has, as indicated by its name, a block size of 128 bits, a tweakey size of 384 bits, and iterates its round function 40 times. This round function represents the cipher-state as a 4×4 array of 8-bit cells and performs five relatively simple AES-like operations: *SubCells* applies an 8-bit S-box to every cell, *AddConstants* XORs round-dependent constants (generated using a 6-bit LFSR) to the first column of the state-array, *AddTweakey* XORs the first two rows of the tweakey arrays to the state and then updates the tweakeys (see below), *ShiftRows* rotates the second, third, and fourth row of the state cell-wise, and *MixColumns* multiplies each column of the state-array by a binary matrix [4]. SKINNY-128-384+ uses three 128-bit tweakeys, which are represented through three 4×4 arrays of cells (referred to as *TK1*, *TK2*, and *TK3*). The three tweakey-states are updated in every round via a cell-permutation (i.e., the 16 cells of the tweakey-matrix are re-ordered) and, thereafter, the cells of the first two rows of *TK2* and *TK3* are individually manipulated, treating them as 8-bit LFSRs.

The designer team provided some optimized implementations of ROMULUS-N, among these is a version using a 256-byte S-box table and one based on the so-called fixed-slicing method [12]. Our implementation for MSP430 follows the former approach and comprises four functions altogether; three to pre-compute the round-tweakeyes, and one for the encryption of a 16-byte block, which gets the three expanded tweakeys as input. We developed optimized Assembly code for the block-encryption and the tweakey schedule for *TK2*, the latter to speed up the processing of associated data. We did not implement the *TK1* schedule in Assembly since it is very light (the last 64 bits of *TK1* are always 0 and the tweakeys repeat after 16 rounds) and relatively fast in C. Also the *TK3* schedule exists only in C because it is executed just once. Our Assembly implementation of the encryption function keeps the full 16-byte state in registers and merges *SubCells* and *ShiftRows* to a single macro, taking advantage of the swap-bytes (`swpb`) instruction. On the other hand, our *TK2*-schedule function utilizes the bit-test (`bit`) instruction to efficiently execute the 8-bit LFSR.

4   Performance Evaluation and Comparison

As explained in Sect. 2, we used IAR Embedded Workbench 7.2 to develop the Assembly implementations of the underlying primitives of the AEAD schemes and determined execution times (and other results) using IAR's cycle-accurate instruction set simulator and our specifically developed Python script.

Table 2. Implementation results for the underlying primitives of (in this order) Elephant (Dumbo), Grain-128AEADv2, ISAP v2.0, PHOTON-Beetle and Romulus-N.

Underlying primitive in Assembly	Asm function (s)		Throughput		Static table look-ups	
	Size (bytes)	Time (cycles)	Encr. bytes	Cycles per byte	Table size (bytes)	Look-ups (cycles)
Spongent-π[160]	822	40495	20	2025	428 (52%)	2562 (6%)
Grain-128A	916+144	584+287	1	871	0	0
Ascon-p^6	710	3520	8	440	0	0
PHOTON$_{256}$	1612	17034	16	1065	1120 (69%)	6240 (37%)
Skinny-128-384+	782	5490	16	343	256 (33%)	1280 (23%)

Table 2 summarizes some basic size and performance characteristics of the Assembly functions of the five primitives, assuming that they are used for the processing of plaintext, i.e., encryption. The Assembly component of the three permutation-based AEAD schemes (ELEPHANT, ISAP, PHOTON-BEETLE) is simply the function for permuting the state. ISAP is somewhat special because it executes ASCON-p with either one, six, or even 12 rounds, but *IsapEnc* calls the permutation-function with six rounds only. GRAIN-128A has two functions written in Assembly language, namely the *POGen* and *AUGen*. The execution time of both is given in Table 2, whereby the cycle-count for the former refers to the generation of a 16-bit pre-output stream and the cycles for the latter to the authentication of eight bits. Finally, for SKINNY, the table lists the results of the function for encrypting a 16-byte block, which receives the three round-tweakeys as input. This function, as well as the *TK2*-schedule, are written in Assembly language, but the latter is only used for the processing of associated data and, therefore, omitted from Table 2. Also not included in the table is the *TK1*-schedule, even though it is part of the main encryption loop, since it takes only 521 clock cycles in C and so we did not bother to write it in Assembly.

The results in Table 2 show that four of the five implemented primitives are very compact and have a binary code size of only about 1 kB (including static look-up tables). PHOTON$_{256}$ is a bit larger, but roughly two thirds of its code space are occupied by static tables. The execution time of the primitives varies by a much greater extent than their code size. GRAIN-128A has an execution time of less than 1000 clock cycles (sum of the cycle counts of the *POGen* and *AUGen*), whereas SPONGENT, which is at the other end of the spectrum, needs more than 40000 cycles for a single permutation. However, the number of bytes processed by each primitive while encrypting plaintext varies significantly too and ranges from one byte to 20 bytes. Consequently, it makes sense to compare the (inverse) throughput values, obtained by dividing each cycle-count by the corresponding number of bytes. The resulting cycles per byte, included in the table, indicate that ROMULUS is the fastest AEAD scheme for encryption since its underlying primitive has the best (i.e., smallest) cycle-per-byte value.

Table 3. Execution time (in cycles) of the AEAD algorithms for authentication only (dlen = 0), encryption only (adlen = 0), and authenticated encryption (adlen = dlen).

adlen	dlen	Elephant	Grain	ISAP	PHOTON	Romulus
16	0	166795	36044	157330	35494	25793
128	0	417230	142203	269556	157254	70171
1024	0	2254717	984501	1167124	1131094	381894
0	16	167203	36140	277555	36212	26064
0	128	668652	142007	448833	162830	71706
0	1024	4430480	988727	1818817	1175534	436601
16	16	208684	51165	293583	53676	26127
128	128	958893	263164	577058	302025	116118
1024	1024	6545252	1952182	2844610	2288569	792736

Table 3 contains the execution times of the five AEAD algorithms in three different case studies: (i) authentication of associated data (without encryption of plaintext, i.e., dlen = 0), (ii) encryption of plaintext (without authentication of associated data, i.e., adlen = 0), (iii) authenticated encryption (associated data and plaintext of the same size are processed). For each use case, we give the execution time for short (i.e., 16-byte), medium (i.e., 128-byte) and large (i.e., 1024-byte) amounts of associated data and plaintext, respectively. When inspecting the results of each algorithm individually, it turns out that GRAIN-128AEAD and PHOTON-BEETLE have roughly the same execution times in the "authentication-only" and "encryption-only" scenario, respectively. On the other hand, ELEPHANT and ISAP-A-128A process plaintext much slower than associated data, which is due to the Encrypt-then-MAC mode. Namely, when using this mode, a plaintext block requires two executions of the primitive, one to produce the ciphertext block and the other to authenticate it. ROMULUS is slightly slower in the "encryption-only" scenario since it needs one invocation of the block-encryption function for 16 plaintext bytes, while authenticating 32 bytes of associated data requires also one call of the block-encryption function and one call of the *TK2*-schedule, the latter being 670 cycles faster. When we compare the five schemes with each other, ROMULUS is the clear winner since it reaches the best execution times in all three use cases and across all operand lengths, which is not surprising given the throughput of SKINNY. ROMULUS is even faster than the LWC winner ASCON; for example, when adlen = dlen = 1024, ASCON has, according to [2], an execution time of 941924 clock cycles on a MSP430F1611, i.e., almost 150000 cycles more than ROMULUS. ELEPHANT is the worst of the five schemes, partly because of the poor software performance of SPONGENT and partly due to its relatively inefficient mode.

Table 4. Execution times of the reference and optimized C implementations from [6] and our mixed C-and-Assembly implementations of the five AEAD algorithms for 16 bytes of associated data and 16 bytes of plaintext.

AEAD Algorithm	Ref. C [6] (cycles)	Opt. C [6] (cycles)	Our impl. (cycles)	Speed-up factor for our impl.
Elephant (Dumbo)	17073111	–	208684	81.81×
Grain-128AEAD	3601170	244766	51165	70.38× / 4.78×
ISAP-A-128A	8109430	–	293583	27.62×
PHOTON-Beetle	1125425	–	53676	20.97×
Romulus-N	187504	–	26127	7.17×

Table 4 compares the execution time of our five Assembly-optimized AEAD schemes with that of the "plain" C implementations benchmarked in [6]. These timings are for an authenticated encryption of 16 bytes of associated data and 16 bytes of plaintext. Even though we optimized only the underlying primitive at the Assembly level, all five AEAD algorithms experienced a massive speed-up (e.g., nearly two orders of magnitude for ELEPHANT). These results confirm that reference C implementations are not suitable to evaluate the performance of an AEAD algorithm. They also show that the performance of the algorithms depends heavily on the efficient implementation of the underlying primitive.

5 Concluding Remarks

The recently concluded LWC standardization project of the NIST has spurred a large body of research on "lightweight" AEAD algorithms that are suitable for resource-restricted devices. However, since the NIST focussed their software benchmarking primarily on 8 and 32-bit architectures, many questions related to the efficiency of the final-round candidates on 16-bit microcontrollers have remained largely unexplored. We contributed to fill this gap by developing and benchmarking optimized implementations of the final-round LWC candidates ELEPHANT (i.e., DUMBO), GRAIN-128AEAD, ISAP, PHOTON-BEETLE, and ROMULUS for 16-bit MSP430 microcontrollers. More concretely, we developed highly-tuned MSP430 Assembly implementations of the underlying primitives of these five AEAD schemes and analyzed their efficiency with a cycle-accurate simulator as well as a special Python tool. Our results show that SKINNY-128-384+ (part of ROMULUS-N) has the best throughput of all five primitives. The outstanding efficiency of SKINNY contributes to the superior execution times of ROMULUS-N, which outperforms its competitors by a factor of at least two when the length of the input(s) exceeds 128 bytes. Remarkably, ROMULUS-N is even faster than the LWC winner ASCON, despite the fact that software speed was not the main objective of the designers. Our work also shows that the five AEAD algorithms are much faster (by a factor of between 4.78 and 81.81) on MSP430 microcontrollers than indicated by previously-published results.

Acknowledgments. The second author was supported, in part, by the Luxembourg National Research Fund (FNR) under CORE grant C19/IS/13641232 (APLICA).

References

1. Ågren, M., Hell, M., Johansson, T., Meier, W.: A new version of Grain-128 with authentication. In: Leander, G., Thomsen, S.S. (eds.) Proceedings of the 6th ECRYPT Workshop on Symmetric Encryption (SKEW 2011) (2011). http://skew2011.mat.dtu.dk/proceedings/A%20New%20Version%20of%20Grain-128%20with%20Authentication.pdf
2. Alsahli, M., Borgognoni, A., Cardoso dos Santos, L., Cheng, H., Franck, C., Großschädl, J.: Lightweight permutation-based cryptography for the ultra-low-power internet of things. In: Bella, G., Doinea, M., Janicke, H. (eds.) SecITC 2022. LNCS, vol. 13809, pp. 17–36. Springer, Cham (2022). https://doi.org/10.1007/978-3-031-32636-3_2
3. Bao, Z., et al.: PHOTON-Beetle authenticated encryption and hash family. Specification (2021). http://csrc.nist.gov/CSRC/media/Projects/lightweight-cryptography/documents/finalist-round/updated-spec-doc/photon-beetle-spec-final.pdf
4. Beierle, C., et al.: The SKINNY family of block ciphers and its low-latency variant MANTIS. In: Robshaw, M., Katz, J. (eds.) CRYPTO 2016. LNCS, vol. 9815, pp. 123–153. Springer, Heidelberg (2016). https://doi.org/10.1007/978-3-662-53008-5_5
5. Beyne, T., Chen, Y.L., Dobraunig, C., Mennink, B.: Dumbo, Jumbo, and Delirium: parallel authenticated encryption for the lightweight circus. IACR Trans. Symmetr. Cryptol. **2020**(S1), 5–30 (2020)
6. Blanc, S., Lahmadi, A., Le Gouguec, K., Minier, M., Sleem, L.: Benchmarking of lightweight cryptographic algorithms for wireless IoT networks. Wirel. Netw. **28**(8), 3453–3476 (2022)
7. Bogdanov, A., Knežević, M., Leander, G., Toz, D., Varıcı, K., Verbauwhede, I.: SPONGENT: A lightweight hash function. In: Preneel, B., Takagi, T. (eds.) CHES 2011. LNCS, vol. 6917, pp. 312–325. Springer, Heidelberg (2011). https://doi.org/10.1007/978-3-642-23951-9_21
8. Cardoso dos Santos, L., Großschädl, J.: An Evaluation of the multi-platform efficiency of lightweight cryptographic permutations. In: Ryan, P.Y., Toma, C. (eds.) SecITC 2021. LNCS, vol. 13195, pp. 75–90. Springer, Cham (2022). https://doi.org/10.1007/978-3-031-17510-7_6
9. Dobraunig, C., et al.: ISAP v2.0. IACR Trans. Symmetr. Cryptol. (S1), 390–416 (2020)
10. Dobraunig, C., Eichlseder, M., Mendel, F., Schläffer, M.: Ascon v1.2: lightweight authenticated encryption and hashing. J. Cryptol. **34**(3), 33 (2021)
11. Granger, R., Jovanovic, P., Mennink, B., Neves, S.: Improved masking for tweakable blockciphers with applications to authenticated encryption. In: Fischlin, M., Coron, J.-S. (eds.) EUROCRYPT 2016. LNCS, vol. 9665, pp. 263–293. Springer, Heidelberg (2016). https://doi.org/10.1007/978-3-662-49890-3_11

12. Guo, C., Iwata, T., Khairallah, M., Minematsu, K., Peyrin, T.: Romulus v1.3. Specification (2021). http://csrc.nist.gov/CSRC/media/Projects/lightweight-cryptography/documents/finalist-round/updated-spec-doc/romulus-spec-final.pdf

13. Guo, J., Peyrin, T., Poschmann, A.: The PHOTON family of lightweight hash functions. In: Rogaway, P. (ed.) CRYPTO 2011. LNCS, vol. 6841, pp. 222–239. Springer, Heidelberg (2011). https://doi.org/10.1007/978-3-642-22792-9_13

14. Hell, M., Johansson, T., Maximov, A., Meier, W.: The grain family of stream ciphers. In: Robshaw, M., Billet, O. (eds.) New Stream Cipher Designs. LNCS, vol. 4986, pp. 179–190. Springer, Heidelberg (2008). https://doi.org/10.1007/978-3-540-68351-3_14

15. Hell, M., Johansson, T., Maximov, A., Meier, W., Sönnerup, J., Yoshida, H.: Grain-128AEADv2 – a lightweight AEAD stream cipher. Specification (2021). http://csrc.nist.gov/CSRC/media/Projects/lightweight-cryptography/documents/finalist-round/updated-spec-doc/grain-128aead-spec-final.pdf, 2021

16. IAR Systems AB. IAR Embedded Workbench for MSP430. Product description (2023). http://www.iar.com/iar-embedded-workbench/msp430

17. International Organization for Standardization (ISO). ISO/IEC 29167-13:2015 Information technology—automatic identification and data capture techniques—Part 13: Crypto suite Grain-128A security services for air interface communications (2015)

18. International Organization for Standardization (ISO). ISO/IEC 29192-5:2016 Information technology—Security techniques Lightweight cryptography—Part 5: Hash-functions (2016)

19. International Organization for Standardization (ISO). ISO/IEC 18033-7:2022 Information technology—Encryption algorithms—Part 7: Tweakable block ciphers (2022)

20. Maximov, A., Hell, M.: Software evaluation of Grain-128AEAD for embedded platforms. Cryptology ePrint Archive, Report 2020/659 (2020). http://eprint.iacr.org

21. McKay, K.A., Bassham, L., Turan, M.S., Mouha, N.: Report on lightweight cryptography. Technical report IR 8114, National Institute of Standards and Technology (NIST), Gaithersburg, MD, USA (2017). http://nvlpubs.nist.gov/nistpubs/ir/2017/NIST.IR.8114.pdf

22. Medwed, M., Standaert, F.-X., Großschädl, J., Regazzoni, F.: Fresh re-keying: security against side-channel and fault attacks for low-cost devices. In: Bernstein, D.J., Lange, T. (eds.) AFRICACRYPT 2010. LNCS, vol. 6055, pp. 279–296. Springer, Heidelberg (2010). https://doi.org/10.1007/978-3-642-12678-9_17

23. National Institute of Standards and Technology (NIST). Announcing request for nominations for lightweight cryptographic algorithms. Federal register notice (2018). http://csrc.nist.gov/news/2018/requesting-nominations-for-lightweight-crypto-algs

24. National Institute of Standards and Technology (NIST). Submission Requirements and Evaluation Criteria for the Lightweight Cryptography Standardization Process (2018). http://csrc.nist.gov/CSRC/media/Projects/Lightweight-Cryptography/documents/final-lwc-submission-requirements-august2018.pdf

25. National Institute of Standards and Technology (NIST). Benchmarking of lightweight cryptographic algorithms on microcontrollers (2023). http://github.com/usnistgov/Lightweight-Cryptography-Benchmarking

26. Renner, S., Pozzobon, E., Mottok, J.: The final round: benchmarking NIST LWC ciphers on microcontrollers. In: Li, W., Furnell, S., Meng, W. (eds.) ADIoT 2022.

LNCS, vol. 13745, pp. 1–20. Springer, Cham (2022). https://doi.org/10.1007/978-3-031-21311-3_1

27. Renner, S., Pozzobon, E., Mottok, J.: NIST LWC software performance benchmarks on microcontrollers (2022). http://lwc.las3.de

28. Rogaway, P.: Authenticated-encryption with associated-data. In: Atluri, V. (ed.) Proceedings of the 9th ACM Conference on Computer and Communications Security (CCS 2002), pp. 98–107. ACM Press (2002)

29. Turan, M.S., et al.: Status report on the final round of the NIST lightweight cryptography standardization process. In: Internal Report IR 8454, National Institute of Standards and Technology (NIST), Gaithersburg, MD, USA (2023). http://nvlpubs.nist.gov/nistpubs/ir/2023/NIST.IR.8454.pdf

30. Texas Instruments Inc. MSP430 Family Architecture Guide and Module Library. TI literature number SLAUE10B (1996). http://www.ti.com/sc/docs/products/micro/msp430/userguid/ag_01.pdf

31. Texas Instruments, Inc. MSP430x1xx Family User's Guide (Rev. F). Manual (2006). http://www.ti.com/lit/ug/slau049f/slau049f.pdf

32. Weatherley, R.: Lightweight cryptography primitives documentation (2021). http://rweather.github.io/lwc-finalists/index.html

Networking and Communications Technology for IoT

Multi-layered Model for Performance Evaluation of oneM2M-Based IoT Solution

Samir Medjhah[1]($\boxtimes$), Thierry Monteil[2]($\boxtimes$), Marie-Agnès Peraldi-Frati[3]($\boxtimes$), and Luigi Liquori[3]($\boxtimes$)

[1] Université de Toulouse, Université Paul Sabatier, LAAS-CNRS, Toulouse, France
`medjiah@laas.fr`
[2] Université de Toulouse, INSA, IRIT, Toulouse, France
`thierry.monteil@irit.fr`
[3] Université Côte d'Azur, Inria, Nice, France
`marie-agnes.peraldi@univ-cotedazur.fr`, `luigi.liquori@inria.fr`

Abstract. In this paper we evaluate the impact of standards in terms of performance and their applicability in the field of IoT system design and deployment. We focus on the global IoT oneM2M standard. Our objective is to evaluate a oneM2M-based IoT solution regarding different relevant Key Performance Indicators. We propose a multi layered-model of an IoT standardized solution, able to tackle applicative, infrastructure and deployment aspects. Based on this model, we are able to globally evaluate and analyze, through simulation, the adequacy of a deployment with respect to the initial applicative constraints and the chosen oneM2M standard implementation. In our case, the constraints are mix-critical coming from the e-Health remote monitoring of patient by their physician but also the management of the patient in case of vital emergency situation. By tuning the system configuration and parameters of the proposed applicative scenario, we evaluate, by simulation, the KPIs of a oneM2M-based IoT solution by exploiting (1) the different features of the standard, (2) the capabilities of the underlying infrastructure, and (3) the performance of the oneM2M stacks used in the solution. The simulation and performance evaluation are based on two tools developed by the authors. One is a specific profiler for oneM2M open-source stack, whereas the simulation and performance evaluation is build on top of the OMNeT++ discrete event simulator.

Keywords: ETSI · oneM2M Consortium · IoT Use Cases · Performance Evaluation · Meta-Modeling

1 Introduction

In the IoT system design, there is a need for rationalizing and dimensioning the devices-edge-cloud computing infrastructure and deployments, according to different criteria ranging from the amount of data and their velocity by the devices, to their analysis or the decision making located on the edge or the cloud computing parts. This design is highly dependent on the application domain and the

ⓒ IFIP International Federation for Information Processing 2025
Published by Springer Nature Switzerland AG 2025
G. Rey et al. (Eds.): IFIPIoT 2024, IFIP AICT 737, pp. 77–95, 2025.
https://doi.org/10.1007/978-3-031-81900-1_5

specific extra-functional requirements (time, energy, sustainability, scalability, etc.) of the applications. Associated with these constraints, and to move away from siloed IoT application design, an additional strategic constraint is the need for interoperability. This requires the integration of standards in the design process and consequently, the additional choices and possible strategies in the use of these standards and their impact on the infrastructure deployments choices.

IoT standard such as oneM2M [3] provides a communication architecture and associated services that bring together devices, communications networks and IoT applications. This standardizes links between connected devices, gateways, communications networks and cloud infrastructure. oneM2M is highly supported by telecom operators, ICT solution companies, SMEs hardware designer and IoT stakeholders. There is a real need from these parties for methodologies and tools to support the design and planning phase of IoT networks, infrastructures, and behaviours. The ETSI SmartM2M Technical Committee, engaged in IoT standards, is highly supporting work that illustrates the different uses of the oneM2M standard in the different fields, but until now, there has been few work that addresses the problem of evaluating implementations (stacks) of oneM2M standard, from the point of view of performance in these different uses. This subject is not fully covered by standardization bodies, and can constitutes an obstacle for new IoT customers who desire to explore the potential of oneM2M for their specific use cases. The initiative by ETSI SmartM2M TC of a building a specific "task force" on performance evaluation, is a first step for an evaluation of the deployment scenarios of oneM2M-based IoT solutions.

This paper conducted inside the ETSI SmartM2M Technical Committee and hand-to-hand with oneM2M Consortium aims at proposing an assistance in the specification and the design of IoT-standardized systems, taking into account the application edge cloud continuum down to the deployment on a oneM2M infrastructure. We propose a multi layered-model of an IoT standardized system, able to tackle applicative, infrastructure, performance and deployment aspects of the system. Each layer of the model provide the concepts and artefacts that closely matches the specific needs of the different engineering aspects i.e.: the application development, oneM2M logical infrastructure, and the hardware deployment infrastructure. In addition, we propose a tooled-methodology able to discern between different oneM2M stacks and to assist the specification and the design of IoT systems. First, the objective is to measure, through a *profiler*, the relevant Key Performance Indicators (KPI) values resulting on a oneM2M stack execution, that will be injected in an *adhoc simulation library* to globally evaluate and analyze, the conformance of a deployment with respect to the initial applicative constraints and the chosen standard implementation. The detailed description of this model, their different artifacts, and the different performance indicators, are presented in [10–12].

Concerning the application domain, we put a special emphasis on the eHealth IoT domain because it gives us the possibility to envisage concrete scenarios characterizing either mix-critical constraints from the applications side but also CPU time and memory space constraints from the oneM2M infrastructure side. All of these constraints are important, sometimes essential to be verified for a conform deployment of an IoT application using oneM2M. We choose ACME [2] as a open-source oneM2M implementation stack, written in Python. By tuning the system configuration and parameters of the proposed applicative scenario, we evaluate, by simulation, the KPIs of an oneM2M-based IoT solution by exploiting (1) the different features of the standard, (2) the capabilities of the underlying infrastructure, and (3) the performance of the oneM2M used stacks.

The paper is organized as follows. Section 2 provides a necessary reminder of interesting works and results in the field of oneM2M standard, network simulation and IoT deployment principles. Section 3 presents our contribution in the specification of oneM2M standardized infrastructure with a multi-layered model that takes into account application, infrastructure, performance and deployment aspects. Section 4 implements the multi-layered model into the OMNeT++ [6], a discrete event network simulator. Section 5 presents an experimental proof of concept of one realistic scenario, using the scalability features of OMNeT++. Finally, Sect. 6 shows conclusions and future perspectives of this work.

2 Context and State of Art

This section explore works in the different fields of IoT standardization, network simulation, as well as current trends and issues in the computing deployment and data storage on the continuum device, edge, cloud w.r.t. applications domains.

2.1 The oneM2M IoT Standard

oneM2M [3] is a Consortium including five standardization organizations, bringing over 200 industrial partners and laboratories. This standardization initiative aims to delineate a suite of services, communication patterns and resource structures that enable the establishment of a network of interconnected objects. All technical specifications of the associated functional architecture and the associated services are available online [9]. By doing so, oneM2M facilitates uniform access across different hardware, infrastructures, and datasets.

Several implementations are currently available by private companies and academic laboratories, but only few of them are currently available in the open-source ecosystem: as example, OM2M [1] in Java, ACME [2] in Python, Ocean-Mobius [7] in Javascript and TinyIoT [8] in C, just to mention a few.

oneM2M entities. The standard delineates various kind of nodes, each of one running on the equipment that participates in an IoT solution. These nodes are interconnected in a tree-based topology. Starting from the leaves of the tree, these nodes are:

- the **Application Dedicated Node (ADN):** hosts the sensors and actuators of an IoT system and the associated application known as the Application Entity (AE).

- the **Application Service Node (ASN):** is an ADN endowed with the oneM2M Common Service Layer (CSE). It is deployed on objects with robust processing capabilities.
- the **Middle Node (MN):** acts as a gateway that collect from the ADN and ASN the IoT data. A MN hosts the common service entities that allows to collect these data. From a communication point of view, an MN acts as a bridge between local sensor/actuator networks and long-distance networks. Several levels of MN can be connected for scalability and security with the physical systems.
- the **Infrastructure Node (IN):** can be considered as the root of the tree, it serves as a hub for connecting different middle nodes, enabling high-level user applications to interact with all nodes. Typically deployed in the cloud, the IN node hosts the Common Service Entity (CSE) defined below.

OneM2M Resources. The oneM2M service layer operates on the RESTful [15] software architectural style, where data and services are structured within a resource tree topology. Within oneM2M, this structure begins with the creation of a Common Service Entity (CSE), serving as the root of the tree. Resources within the tree can encompass various types, with the primary ones including:

- **Application Entity (AE):** This resource signifies a sensor, an actuator, a connected object, or an application. Within an AE resource, data and executable actions are stored.
- **Containers (CNT):** Positioned beneath an AE resource, containers group multiple other resources for storage and organization.
- **Content Instance (CIN):** Typically housed within containers, content instances predominantly represent sensor-collected values or descriptions of potential actions on an actuator.
- **Subscriptions (SUB):** Primarily situated within containers, subscriptions delineate actions to be executed, such as when a content instance is added to the same container. In a broader sense, they enable subscription to any modification within the resource where they are established by implementing a notification mechanism.

A typical operational procedure unfolds as follows for the resources management:

- The Infrastructure Node (IN) is started on the cloud, it creates its representation in own resources tree by the creation of an IN-CSE.
- The Middle Node (MN) is running on a gateway and initiates its registration on the Infrastructure Node (IN), establishing reciprocal links within their respective databases (remote IN/MN CSE).
- The Application Node (AN) hosting the different sensors, actuators and application parts complete their registration on the different MN, generating an Application Entity (AE) that encapsulates application descriptions. Sensor and actuators data are instantiated in the resource tree of this AE but creating Containers (CNT). Each sensor's new value create a new Content Instance (CIN).

– The end-user applications, like a smartphone app or a supervision center, are hosted by ASN nodes and gains access to the IoT application via a call to the different oneM2M services. These accesses can make a request to get the last value of a CIN or the subscription to certain data to receive notifications upon updates. The majority of accesses occur at the IN level. The internal mechanism of re-targeting inside oneM2M architecture allows to access to all CSE running and their resource tree on all equipment through an unique access to the IN node. CSE are able to transmit the request to an other CSE if the resource asked is not on their resources tree.

2.2 IoT Systems Simulation and Performance Evaluation

IoT systems have specific characteristics such as the numerous and multiform nature of their communications, different data exchange protocols along with the number of nodes participating in the system and their network topology. Their modeling and simulation requires a rich environment to capture different protocols, but also a high performance simulation engine able to specify and run large-scale topologies and system's behaviour. In addition and depending on the fine or coarse grain modeling-level of the system under evaluation, the environment must be open to programming, to enable a certain level of accuracy of the behavior of nodes, their interconnections, as well as the performance parameters to be measured. Finally, simulation results must be easily exploitable, which requires open environments for accessing simulation results and, ideally, a open source environment for their comprehension and exhaustive analysis.

Among the many discrete event network simulators, some of them cover partially the previous requirements, NS3 [4] is highly adopted by the network performance evaluation community. As NS3 is network-dedicated, it has some weaknesses in the tuning of nodes behaviors and scalability. SimGrid [5] is also highly network-oriented, with a distributed Grid simulation engine that makes it difficult to get to grips with.

The chosen simulator is OMNeT++ [6], an extensible and modular, component-based C++ simulation library and framework, well-suited for a generic description of node processing and a programmatic style for network description via its NEtwork Description language (NED). Its large open source community has enabled the development of numerous APIs for protocols and interesting features for distributed simulation. We intensively use the component architecture capabilities of OMNeT++ i.e.: the definition components/nodes of the IoT network into C++ specific classes, their assembling into larger components or via their interconnection described in the NED. With such a decomposition, the re-usability is an inner characteristics. The simulation kernel (and models) and the associated simulation results can be extracted from events traces, output vector and/or output scalar files to be analysed or plotted in a simulation interface, sequence diagrams or simple text-based files.

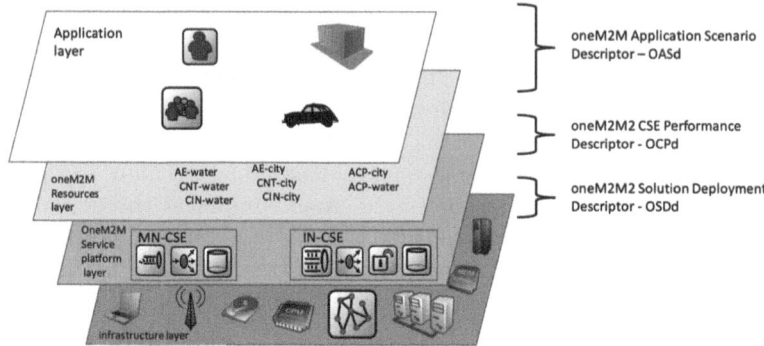

Fig. 1. Multi-layer model for an Standardized-IoT system

2.3 Applications/Edge Cloud

In IoT systems, the data collection protocols, the data storage locations, their analysis, their computing and the associated algorithms making decisions, are dependent on the real time and of the amount of data and the application concerns in terms of energy, time-sensitivity, security and privacy. A number of studies have been carried on the criteria for distributing and allocating the computational and collection parts of IoT systems according to application constraints.

In particular, the paper [13] proposes a coarse-grained classification of the distribution of computational and storage parts on fog and cloud parts according to application situations as well as their constraints. Authors compare the different computing paradigms of edge, Fog, Cloud Computing in Multi-access Edge-Computing (MEC) according to the features (heterogeneity, distribution, mobility, real-time support, ultra low latency ...) however, if it raises awareness the designer to the different pros and cons of these paradigms, it does not enable a precise reasoning on the scenario under development.

Additional research works, more specific to e-Health applications highlights the essential features of services and infrastructure in the domain of remote healthcare services. In [14], authors analyses such systems in terms of their essential features of scalability, bandwidth supposed to be high as the QoS, latency supposed to be low as the energy consumption. They choose 5G network as their communications medium and they provide an architecture (Cloud-RAN for 5G slicing, Fog, and Cloud Computing Data centers) and a queue-based model and the associated analytical equations for a performance analysis and simulation of KPIs. In their solution, the various aspects of a IoT system, present intricate connections. In their solution, there is a strong intricacy between the different aspects of the system, i.e.: the applicative parts, the communication and hardware infrastructure, intricacy visible on the analytical models, which reveals a *ad hoc* character. Nevertheless, and for this particular use case, interesting results are presented which have fed our own reflection, in particular the application aspects as well as the KPIs evaluated during the performance analysis.

3   Modeling Approach for a oneM2M IoT System

We propose a multi layered-model of an oneM2M-based standardized IoT system, able to tackle applicative, infrastructure, and deployment aspects of the system. The detailed description of this model, their different artifacts, and the different performance indicators, are presented in [11]. The model view proposed on Fig. 1 facilitates the decomposition of all the physical, hardware, software, and human elements involved in a IoT system. Each layer interacts with the others, ultimately forming the IoT system and its usage environment.

3.1   A Layered Vision

The initial top layer on Fig. 1, termed broadly the "application layer", communicates with the physical realm with which the IoT system interacts. This layer encompasses human and environmental interactions with sensors and actuators, as well as the constraints and requirements articulated by application domains for actions in the physical world.

The next layer, termed the "resource layer", embodies the mapping of the IoT system and its specific use case onto resources (in the context of oneM2M). This layer delineates the relationships among its resources and their ownership, articulating the business logic on the application side. The environment and resource layers will be detailed in a model referred to as the oneM2M Application Scenario descriptor (OASd).

The next layer, termed the "oneM2M service platform layer", represents the software or middleware system necessary to support the requirements of the above layers. In the oneM2M framework, it embodies the Common Service Entities (CSEs) and their interconnections, as well as modeling the behavior and performance of CSEs based on their configuration and the projection of the above layers onto this service platform layer. This layer will be instantiated in a model known as the oneM2M2 CSE Performance descriptor (OCPd).

The lower layer, termed the "infrastructure layer", encompasses the hardware infrastructure that hosts all preceding layers. It defines the equipment, communication links, and hardware characteristics. The oneM2M Solution Deployment descriptor (OSDd) model will describe this layer.

This framework allows for the dissection and understanding of the complexity of an IoT system, leveraging specialized expertise in each layer. Designing and deploying an IoT system entails implementing and integrating all these layers. From a performance analysis perspective, it enables the characterization of the requirements, parameters, and behavior of each layer, elucidating the connections between them through models.

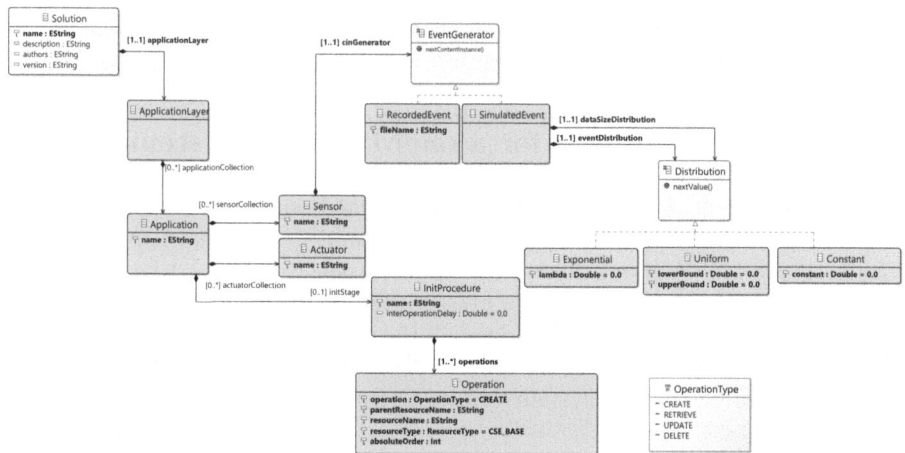

Fig. 2. Eclipse Ecore model for a oneM2M application Scenario Descriptor

3.2   A oneM2M Eclipse Ecore Meta Model

In this subsection we present the implementation in the Eclipse Ecore format [16], of our oneM2M system layered-model. The Ecore representation is at the hearth of the Eclipse Modeling Framework (EMF) and describes, through an object-oriented syntax and associated relations, the different concepts to be handle in a modeling project. In our case, these concepts are more or less the one described in the proposed multi-layered model for a oneM2M infrastructure.

From the Ecore representation, multiple models can be instantiated by manipulating the Ecore inner defined elements. The advantage of such a representation is first to visualize in a standardized format, our reasoning framework, second to play quite easily and for free with the model, and last but not least, to explore the serialization capacity in EMF and to navigate into the modeling elements and to generate code.

The oneM2M Ecore meta model is divided into three parts. The first one, presented in Fig. 2, is dedicated to the IoT application and the capture of its behaviour. The objective of the OASd model is to represent the behavior of the IoT application. We consider a high-level modeling of an IoT application as a set of sensors and actuators endowed with a behavior modelled by event generation (for the sensors). The policy for the generation of sensor data is based on different distribution profiles i.e. constant (equivalent to periodic) or sporadic with different laws. Sensors and actuators have at an initial stage a transient behavior that corresponds to the creation of standardised oneM2M resources.

The second part of the meta model, called OCPd (oneM2M CSE Performance descriptor), is presented on Fig. 3. The OCPd refers to the underlying oneM2M platform and services. It describes the CSEs (IN-CSE, MN-CSE, ASN) and their interconnection onto a tree-based topology. The meta model also considers performance aspects i.e. the impact of the implementation choices of a CSE by a supplier such as the services call and the execution costs in terms of memory and processor, the interconnection protocols characteristics such as the bandwidth, the latency, and all additional costs generated by the data persistence of resources creation, storing and retrieving.

The last part of the meta model called OSDd (oneM2M Solution Deployment descriptor). The associated meta model is presented on Fig. 4. The deployment refers to the allocation of CSEs onto a physical architecture. This hardware platform is composed of servers nodes, gateway nodes, IoT nodes and communication links that hosts the IoT application. This infrastructure is made of multiple nodes of different types, interconnected by a network. The meta model quantifies the capacities (memory storage, processing capabilities, location) of the physical nodes and the underlying communication networks.

4   Implementation of the Meta Model in OMNeT++

OMNeT++ is an extensible, component-based C++ simulation library and framework IDE, dedicated to the simulation of distributed/networked systems. The OMNeT++ environment is open source and thus, federates a large community who develops different features and libraries for specifying, editing, programming, and simulating networked systems. The simulation engine is a discrete event simulator that can handle multiple nodes and their network topology. Depending on the fine or coarse grain modelling-level of the system under evaluation, the environment can provide either predefined libraries that implements

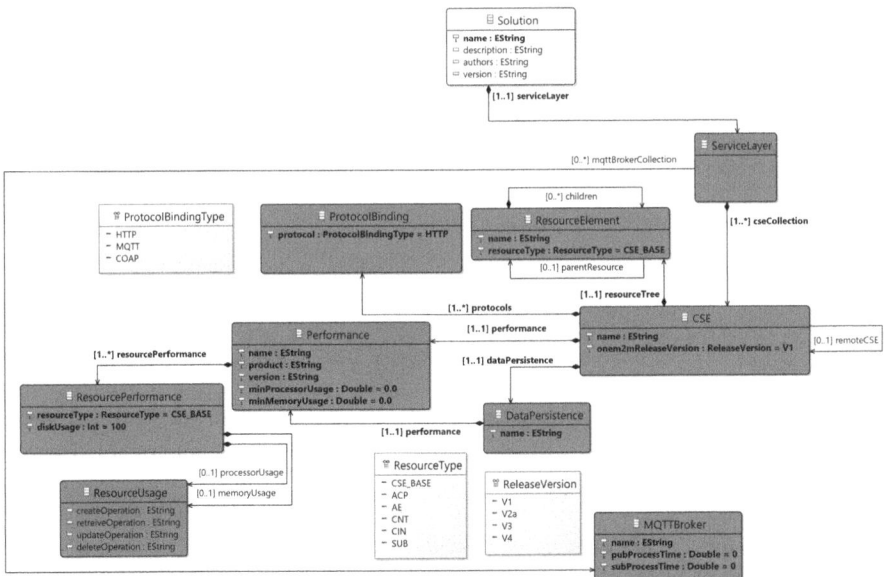

Fig. 3. Eclipse ECore model for a oneM2M CSE Performance Descriptor

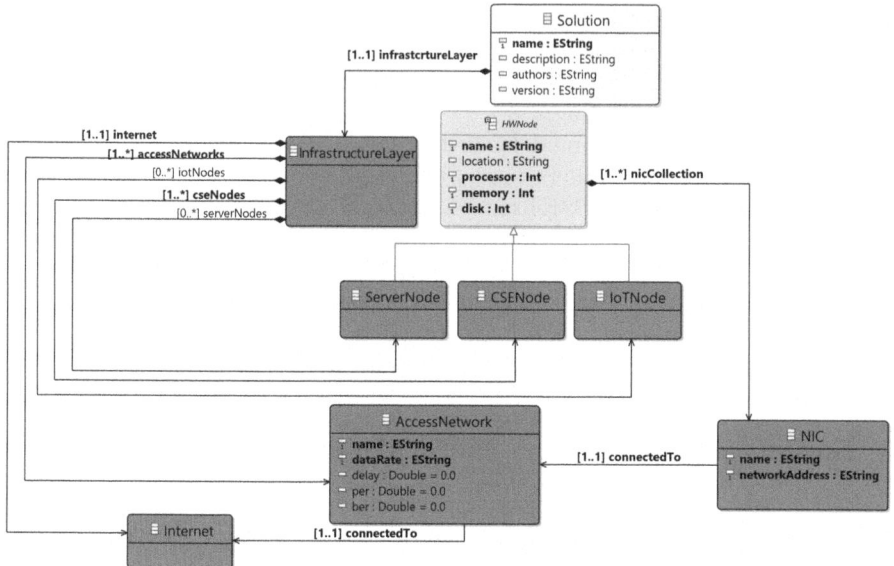

Fig. 4. Eclipse Ecore model for a oneM2M Solution Deployment Descriptor

full protocol stacks such as TCP/IP, MQTT, or enables a more or less accurate programming of the communication protocols and nodes behaviour, their interconnections, as well as the performance parameters to be measured. The integrated discrete event simulation engine also supports parallel distributed simulation to run large-scale topologies and system's behaviour. We use intensively the programming features of the IDE for the development of a oneM2M system simulator. The notions of modules (simple or compound), gates, channels, networks, interfaces are the inner elements of an OMNeT++ specification. Each element is associated with a `C++` class with the associated properties, attributes, variables, and behaviour. The element behaviour is developed in two `C++` methods namely: `initialize()` and `handleMessage()`. The method `initialize()` is called at the initial/transitional phase where OMNeT++ elements of these different types are instantiated whereas the `handleMessage()` method is called every simulation step and covers the permanent behaviour of the element.

The `<project-name>.ini` and `<project-name>.ned` files participate in the definition of the network. The `<project-name>.ini` file contains the parameters and variables initialization values for a current simulation whereas in the `<project-name>.ned file`, written with the NED language, allows the description of the topology of an OMNeT++ system. The NED language has a programming syntax closed to an imperative language to define graph topologies of different shapes, such as, e.g. tree, ring, mesh, and their size. This is a real advantage of OMNeT++ over its direct competitor NS-3. The OMNeT++ simulator of our oneM2M-standardized IoT system is organized into multiple modules either simple or compound with respect to the meta model presented in

Sect. 3 and fully defined in [11]. The modules are organized into three categories: `ApplicationLayer` (OASd in the meta model), `ServiceLayer` (OCPd in the meta model), and `InfrastructureLayer` (OSDd in the meta model).

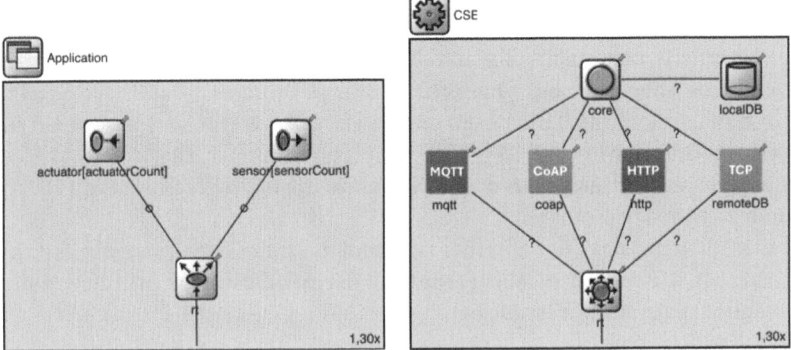

Fig. 5. Application Layer modules and Service layer modules

4.1 Application Layer

The application layer is represented by a compound module named Application that hosts 3 types of sub-modules as shown in Fig. 5.

- `actuator:Actuator [0..N]`: an *Actuator* is a simple module that receives messages from a remote CSE.
- `sensor:Sensor [0..N]`: a *Sensor* is a simple module that sends messages to a remote CSE. One of the main parameters of this module is a JSON object representing a *CinGenerator* as defined in [11]. The *CinGenerator* is a description of how oneM2M Content Instances (CIN) messages are being generated by the sensor. The *CinGenerator* includes informations about its generation and its size. Concerning the event generation, the simulator supports periodic generation, stochastic generation (uniform & exponential distribution), and generation following a time-series provided in an external file. Concerning the size of the message, the simulator supports constant size, stochastic size (uniform & normal distributions), and generation following a time-series provided in an external file.
- `rt:AppRouter[1..1]`: an *rt* is a simple module that handles messages routing between sensors/actuators and the underlying communications services. Both `sensor` and `actuator` modules have a parameter `InitializationProcedure` that contains the internal actions and messages sent to the remote CSE at start-up. Examples of these messages include the creation of oneM2M resources such as *ApplicationEntity* (AE), *Containers* (CNT), *Subscription* (SUB) or initial *ContentInstances* (CIN).

Finally, an *Application* can host multiple *Sensor* and *Actuator* modules.

4.2   Service Layer

The service layer is represented by the compound module *CSE* as shown in Fig. 5. Depending on its parameters, the CSE compound module hosts multiple simple modules that implement a feature of a oneM2M CSE. These modules are:

- `core:Core [1..1]`: refers to the oneM2M common services. This mandatory module is responsible for handling CRUD operations received by a CSE through message passing. One of its main parameter is a JSON object that represents a oneM2M CSE Performance Descriptor (OCPd) as defined in [11]. Based on this parameter, the CSE core can simulate the processing cost of a message and its associated operations in terms of computing (CPU) and memory (RAM) resources.
- `mqtt:MQTTBinding [0..1]`: this optional module is responsible for managing the MQTT protocol encapsulation/decapsulation of primitive oneM2M messages (requests & responses).
- `coap:COAPBinding [0..1]`: this optional module is responsible for managing the CoAP protocol encapsulation/decapsulation of primitive oneM2M messages (requests & responses).
- `http:HTTPBinding [0..1]`: this optional module is responsible for managing the HTTP protocol encapsulation/decapsulation of primitive oneM2M messages (requests & responses).
- `remoteDB:TCPBinding [0..1]`: this optional module represents a data persistence service that is available in a remote host, and that needs a TCP communication. It is suitable for representing CSEs that use remote databases.
- `localDB:DataStorage [0..1]`: this optional module represents a data persistence service that is embedded within the CSE. It is suitable for representing CSEs that use embedded databases (either file-based or in-memory database).
- `rt:CSERouter [1..1]`: this is a simple module that handles messages routing between different components of the CSE and the underlying communication services.

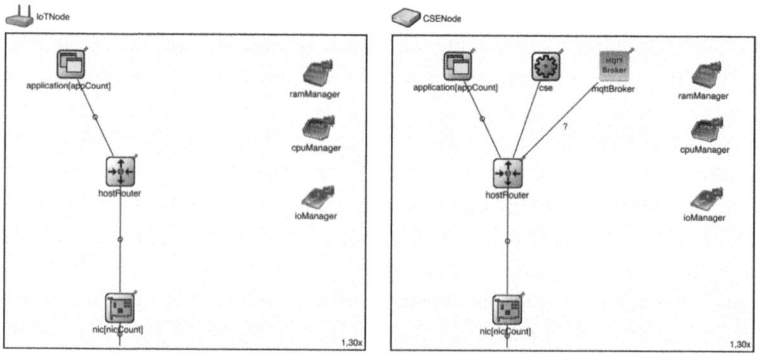

Fig. 6. Infrastructure Hardware nodes

4.3   Infrastructure Layer

The infrastructure layer is represented by modules related to hosting nodes (IoTNode, CSENode, ServerNode) and to networking (WiFiLink, LoRaLink, CellularLink, FiberLink, NetworkElement, InternetNode). First, all hosting nodes derive from one generic node: the HWNode one. This compound module hosts the following modules, as shown in Fig. 6.

- IoTNode: hosts only IoT applications, manages sensors and/or actuators.
- CSENode: extends the generic HWNode and hosts one CSE. It can also host an MQTT brooker alongside the CSE.
- ServerNode: extends the HWNode by hosting an MQTT Broker and/or a database. This node is suitable for representing nodes acting as remote databases for a CSE, an independent MQTT Broker, or any application logic such as a monitoring application.

Inside these 3 nodes, operate different sub modules:

- application:Application [0..N]: this compound module represents the IoT applications (cf. Application Layer) that run on the hosting node.
- hostRouter:HostRouter [1..1]: this is a simple module that handles messages routing between different applications/services running on the hosting nodes and the underlying communication services (NICs).
- ramManager:RAMManager [1..1]: this is a simple module that tracks the overall usage of the processing power of the hosting node (i.e. CPU).
- cpuManager:CPUManager [1..1]: this is a simple module that tracks the overall usage of the memory of the hosting node (i.e. RAM).
- ioManager:IOManager [1..1]: this is a simple module that tracks the overall usage of the disk usage of the hosting node.
- nic:NIC [1..N]: this simple module representing a networking interface available on the hosting node. The networking aspect is represented by two simple modules and four specific channels.

NetworkElement: This simple module represents a network router with basic IPv4 routing logic. It can be connected to any hosting node using a specific network channel.

- Internet: This is a simple module that is similar to the NetworkElement module since it acts as second hop router and connects all the network elements present in the IoT solution. It could be seen as the core network of telecommunication operators.

Four channels are defined in the simulator. These channels represent the common communication links found in IoT solutions. Each channel defines its own data rate, latency, bit error rate (BER) and packet error rate (PER).

4.4   Simulation of an OneM2M-Based Iot Solution

A simulation of our IoT solution following the Meta Model is composed by two main files: first, the physical topology (Infrastructure Layer) of the IoT solution must be defined in a file compliant with the syntax and semantics of OMNeT++'s description language (NED) describing the topology such a graph where vertices are one of the following: `IoTNode`, `CSENode`, `ServerNode`, `NetworkElement`, and `Internet`. Vertices are connected using one of the links defined in the simulator: `WiFiLink`, `CellularLink`, `LoRaLink`, and `Fiber-Link`. The topology can be seen as a tree with 3 levels: Level 0 (root element): `Internet` node, Level 1: nodes of type `NetworkElement`, and Level 2: nodes of type: `IoTNode`, `CSENode`, or `ServerNode`. A second file is the `omnetpp.ini` that contains values for the relevant parameters of the modules present in the topology file. All these parameters are of basic types such as `String`, `IPAddress`, and `Integer`. Two specific parameters use structured data that can also be references to external files. These parameters are the following (in C++):

- **Event Generator:** this is a parameter of the Sensor module. It is provisioned in JSON format. It implements the oneM2M Application Scenario descriptor (OASd) as defined in [11]. It contains information about how a sensor generates oneM2M messages (i.e. CREATE operation of `ContentInstance` resource on the remote CSE) in terms of time instant and message data size.
- **Performance Descriptor:** this is a parameter of both CSE and Storage modules. It is provisioned in JSON format. It implements the oneM2M CSE Performance Descriptor (OCPd) defined in [11]. It contains information about system resources usage in terms of processing, memory, and disk usages for each CRUD operation per resource type.

Measurement probes have been integrated in the source code of the simulator to build KPIs and evaluate the performance of the IoT system based on multiple simulation runs. These indicators include measures such as runtime, memory utilization, volume of data transferred, as well as specific metrics for each CRUD operations in the context of oneM2M resource creation on oneM2M objects. The associated KPIs are defined and described in Clause 5 of [11].

5   Experiments

This section reports on the experimental work carried out to simulate an oneM2M-based IoT solution following the multi-layered model proposed in this paper. It presents the simulation procedure as well as the performance indicators obtained from the simulation. The chosen case study is the deployment of e-Health services for patient monitoring, requiring varying levels of quality of services. Thanks to the multi-layered model, we are able to offer a high-level specification of these services. Once these specifications are instantiated in the proposed OMNeT++ based simulator, application layer, service layer, and infrastructure layer designers are able to assess, by simulation, the relevance of their choices at a very early stage in the design cycle.

5.1   Use Case Description

The deployment of e-Health services for a remote monitoring of patients with chronic health disease, have led to a powerful transformation of the traditional medical practices. Due to the inner characteristics of these services, the underlying IoT solution should be capable, at any time, of collecting and storing patient data in real time, identifying abnormal patient situations before they become emergencies, and of course reacting to any emergencies that do occur. The chosen use case illustrates these different situations by considering three main types of actors namely:

- the *patient* with a chronic health disease that uses sensor devices for medical status measurements (heart rate, glycemia, ...).
- the *physician* that follows remotely the pathology of its patient through an application that is able to access patient medical measures.
- the *emergency physician* or *cardiologist* at the hospital who is called in urgency to treat an acute episode (heart attack, diabetic coma,...), who needs near-real-time access to the patient constants to stabilize the patient.

The oneM2M logical infrastructure that will instantiate the various elements of the e-Health monitoring system is shown on Fig. 7. The different sensors devices and applications appear as oneM2M logical entities such as ANs (Application Nodes) for the sensors, ASNs for the patient applications which collects the sensors data and carries the Patient Application Service (PLA). Middle MN-CSE nodes host the collection and detection services associated with the monitoring application from the Physician side and act as a gateway able to manage multiple patients. Finally, an infrastructure IN-CSE node is the root node of the oneM2M e-Health infrastructure, able to interact with practitioners or directly with patients in case of emergency situations. The different use case application flows are represented in plain or dashed lines according to the three situations:

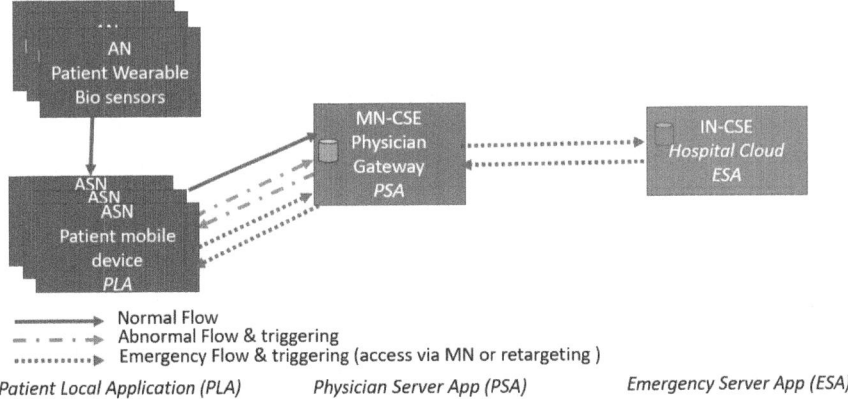

Fig. 7. oneM2M logical e-health monitoring application

– *Normal flow.* Every X minutes, sensors measure the patient biological constants and send them when possible to the *Patient Local Application (PLA).* Periodically (e.g. every week) or in case of presential or remote consultation, the last data are deposited on the Physician Data Space and processed.
– *Abnormal flow* with triggering. In case of a abnormal evolution of data detected by the *Physician Server App (PSA)*, an alert with the associated data is sent to the Physician. The Physician triggers an adequate action for a future consultation or new directives in the medical treatment of the patient.
– *Emergency flow.* In case on critical data threshold or value detected by the Patient Local App, an emergency alarm is sent to the hospital emergency service. The emergency doctor need a real-time access to the health data constants of the patient through a *Emergency Server App (ESA).*

5.2 Simulator Parameters

The OMNeT++ topology of the use case is pictured on Fig. 8. In order to instantiate this use case, the oneM2M-based IoT solution considers a patient with his/her medical sensor connected to his smartphone or a medical device acting as oneM2M ASN node. This device is connected to the internet through the internet gateway (i.e. Internet Box). Within the patient's home, these devices are assumed to be connected through a WiFi network (green dashed links). The practitioner has data management software connected to an oneM2M CSE (mnNode) that is connected to the Internet. Finally, the emergency physician (at the hospital) has access to a data management software connected to an oneM2M CSE (inNode). At the practitioner's office or at the hospitals, devices are assumed to be connected through wired links such as Fiber (solid black links). The corresponding NED topology file for this use case as well as the corresponding configuration .ini file can be found in the git repository [17].

5.3 Simulation Results

Multiple parameters can be considered for tuning the simulation. By changing these parameters it is possible to adjust the numbers of devices to be managed by nodes or the quantity of data to be collected and/or to check the need to reinforce the processing and communication infrastructure to absorb the application load. In this way, by simulation, it is possible to dimension and/or verify an IoT system deployment at an early stage of the design. These parameters characterize the application's load (number of devices, rate of data production, etc.) in relation to the infrastructure on which the application will be deployed (networks and their bandwidth, computing capacity, RAM on the edge or on the cloud). The parameter we are considering are :

– the numerosity of the applicative elements (sensors, actuators) and their velocity to produce/consume data that characterize the applications' generated traffic (initially expressed through the application descriptor). In the OMNeT++ tool, the sizing and the structure are instanciated in the .ned file whereas the velocity of sensors are stated in the `omnetpp.ini` file.

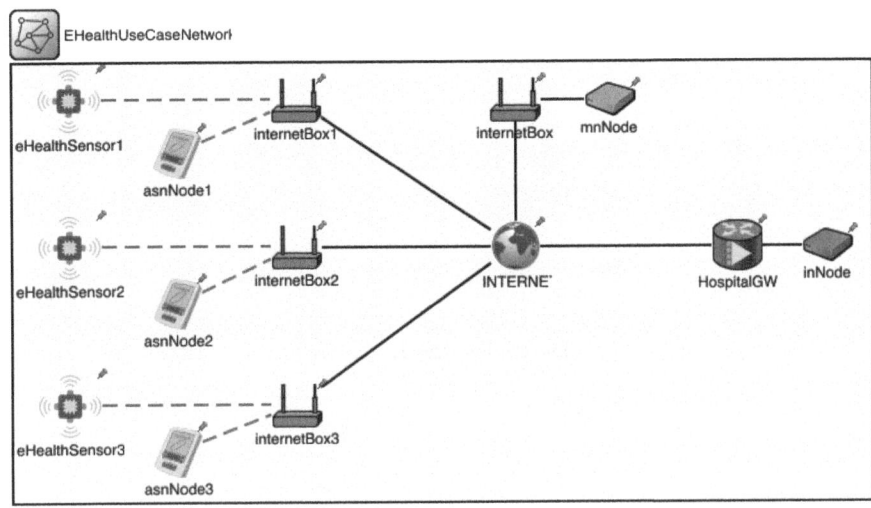

Fig. 8. Topology view of the E-Health Use Case in OMNeT++

- the available hardware resources on CSE nodes (amount of RAM in bytes & processing power in terms of instructions per seconds). These information are collected from the performance descriptor of the hardware node, and defined in the `omnetpp.ini` file.
- the characteristics of the communications links (bandwidth, latency, packet/bit error rates) take also part of the `omnetpp.ini` file.
- the performance characteristics of the CSE nodes (expressed through the performance descriptor generated by the oneM2M stack profiler). Here again this information is in the `omnetpp.ini` file.

Thanks to the instrumented code placed inside the simulation modules, multiple KPIs are measured during the simulation. Figure 9 draws the results of the normal flow simulation and its associated RTT. In this demonstration simulation, ASN nodes are given different processing capabilities (asnNode3 > asnNode2 > asNode1) but IoT sensors attached to these nodes generate similar traffic (periodic messages for the normal flow and exponential traffic for the alternative flow). Also, the IN Node is deliberately under-provisioned in terms of CPU and RAM given the overall traffic it manages.

Due to the different resources available at the ASN nodes, the application layer RTT grows during the simulation. The random peaks correspond to the messages that are sent to the IN nodes (alternative data flow) where this node is always saturated due to its poor resources.

These KPI include information such as (1) application-layer RTT representing time difference between message sending time and acknowledgement reception, (2) the message processing time in a CSE, and (3) the message queue occupancy in a CSE.

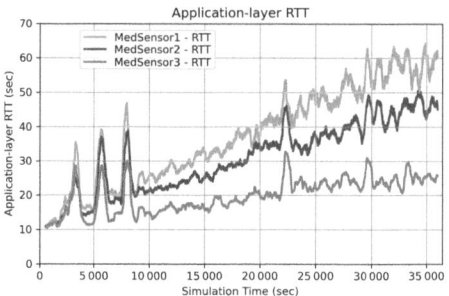

Fig. 9. Application-Layer RTT

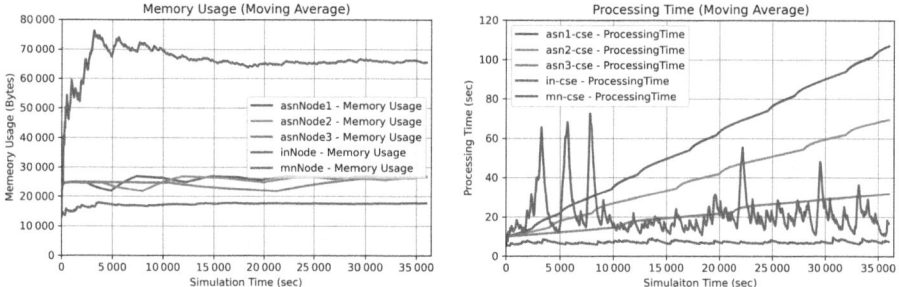

Fig. 10. CSE Memory usage and Processing Time

Figure 10 shows examples of these two KPIs generated at the end of the simulation. In the left part the (simulated) RAM occupancy grows on ASN Node as messages are queued before being processed by the CSE (as it happens in real CSEs). The right part shows the impact of this phenomenon on the processing time since it is the sum of the waiting time in the queue and the actual processing time (provided in the performance descriptor of the CSE). This figure also shows how the memory usage and the processing time of messages in the case of the IN Node are always high. It is also worth noticing that the MN node is behaving well since the node is well provisioned. These experiments clearly show that the resources allocated to the IN Node are undersized to handle the overall traffic. Therefore, our simulator can be used in order to seek the best deployment plan by tuning the configuration parameters (in particular nodes resources).

6   Conclusions and Further Work

The objective of this paper is to evaluate the impact of standards and more precisely oneM2M in terms of performance and its applicability in the field of IoT system design and deployment. We first proposed a multi-layered meta model that facilitates the decomposition of all the physical, hardware, software, and human elements involved in an IoT-standardized solution. From this meta model and results of the effective performance profiling of oneM2M stacks, we are able to generate an OMNeT++ simulator of a full oneM2M-based IoT solution. By tuning the system configuration and parameters, we evaluate the KPIs of this system and compare these KPIs with the real-time constraints of an application.

A first original contribution of this work is the possibility to include in the simulation, the effective performance values of oneM2M stacks.

A second interesting contribution is the flexible design of the simulator that can be used to simulate any other use case. Thanks to the modularity of the simulator, it is possible to capture other application scenarios. IoT system designers or deployment engineers, interested in experimenting with these tools can access them from the ETSI lab repository [17].

Some extensions of this work have already been identified such as improving the scalability of simulated systems to large realistic simulations, firstly by developing a adhoc domain specific language and associated automatic OMNeT++ code generation tools to speed up the description phase of the IoT system in all its aspects, and automatically produce the associated simulator. A second enhancement is to explore OMNeT++'s parallel computing features to address the processing limitation of current simulations on a single server for grid-based computing simulations.

References

1. Eclipse OM2M platform M2M communication. https://eclipse.dev/om2m
2. ACME. https://github.com/ankraft/ACME-oneM2M-CSE
3. The global oneM2M IoT standard. https://www.onem2m.org
4. Ns-3 network simulator. https://www.nsnam.org
5. Simulation of distributed computer systems. https://simgrid.org
6. OMNeT++ Discrete Event Simulator. https://omnetpp.org
7. Mobius oneM2M IoT Server Platform. https://github.com/IoTKETI/Mobius
8. TinyIoT. A oneM2M implementation. https://onem2m.org/technical/published-specifications/release-4
9. oneM2M Functional Architecture. Technical Specification TS-0001-V4.20.0. https://onem2m.org/technical/published-specifications/release-4
10. Flynn, B., Liquori, L., Peraldi-Frati, M.A., Medjiah, S., Monteil, T.: SmartM2M: scenarios for evaluation of oneM2M deployments, ETSI TS 103839 (2023)
11. Medjiah, S., Monteil, T., Liquori, L., Peraldi-Frati, M.A., Flynn, B.: SmartM2M; Model for oneM2M Performance Evaluation, ETSI TS 103840 (2023)
12. Medjiah, S., Monteil, T., Liquori, L., Peraldi-Frati, M.-A., Flynn, B.: SmartM2M: oneM2M Performances Evaluation Tool, ETSI TS 103841 (2024)
13. Yousef, A., et al.: All one needs to know about fog computing and related edge computing. J. Syst. **98**, 289–330 (2019)
14. AlQahtani, S.A.: An evaluation of e-health service performance through the integration of 5G IoT, fog, and cloud computing. Sensors **23**, 5006 (2023)
15. Fielding, R.T.: Chapt 5 of Architectural Styles and the Design of Network-based Software Architectures (Ph.D.). University of California (2000)
16. The Eclipse meta model. https://wiki.eclipse.org/Ecore
17. oneM2M Performance Evaluation Tools: Profiler & Simulator. https://labs.etsi.org/rep/iot/smartm2m-onem2m-performance-evaluation

An Information-Theoretic Approach for Anomaly Detection in RPL-Based Internet of Things

Vinh Hoa La[(✉)][iD], Edgardo Montes de Oca[iD], and Ana Cavalli[iD]

Montimage, 39 rue Bobillot, 75013 Paris, France
vinh_hoa.la@montimage.com

Abstract. In recent years, cyber-attacks have increased significantly in both volume and sophistication, making the detection of security violations a crucial feature in computer systems. This is particularly true in the Internet of Things (IoT), where devices are vulnerable to failures and malicious attacks due to their resource-constrained nature. Given the proliferation of new security threats, anomaly-based detection approaches are essential for intrusion detection and prevention systems to effectively defend against attackers. This paper proposes an information-theoretic approach based on entropy to establish an anomaly detection model. A real case study in IoT networks based on Routing Over Low power and Lossy networks (RPL) illustrates the application of the proposed approach. Preliminary experimental results demonstrate that our method is both practical and extendable.

Keywords: Intrusion Detection · Anomaly Detection · 6LoWPAN · Wireless Sensor Networks · IoT · Security Monitoring

1 Introduction

Computer security, also known as cybersecurity or IT security, has been a critical and evolving topic for decades. It continues to attract significant attention due to the increasing reliance on computer systems in virtually every aspect of modern life. These systems are not limited to traditional desktops or laptops but also encompass smart devices such as smartphones, connected objects, and sensor devices.

Despite advancements in security measures, cyber-attacks are growing in both volume and sophistication. According to a 2015 study by *Symantec*[1], nearly one million new malware threats are released every day. Additionally, two-thirds of Internet users have been victims of cyber-crime, with more than 1.5 million new victims emerging daily. These statistics underscore the urgent need for robust cybersecurity measures.

Furthermore, the remarkable growth of the Internet and wireless networks such as Bluetooth and Wi-Fi, along with the concept of the *Internet of Things*

---

[1] https://www.symantec.com/security-center/threat-report.

© IFIP International Federation for Information Processing 2025
Published by Springer Nature Switzerland AG 2025
G. Rey et al. (Eds.): IFIPIoT 2024, IFIP AICT 737, pp. 96–111, 2025.
https://doi.org/10.1007/978-3-031-81900-1_6

(IoT), promises to transform future networks into the *Internet of Every Things*. As of 2024, there are approximately 17.08 billion connected Internet of Things (IoT) devices globally. This number is projected to nearly double by 2030, reaching around 29.42 billion. The significant growth in IoT devices highlights their increasing integration into various sectors and everyday life, according to a report by IoT Analytics[2].

Wireless Sensor Networks (WSNs) serve as a prominent example of the expanding IoT landscape, attracting significant interest from both the research community and the public. However, the resource-constrained nature of physical objects in these networks presents substantial challenges for the design and development of security protocols. Moreover, sensor nodes, which often operate in unattended and harsh environments, are particularly susceptible to failures and malicious attacks.

In the last years, the research on IoT/WSNs was mainly focused on how to make the concept of IoT realistic and practical. In the other words, most of the IoT research projects have been trying to qualify this technology by standardizing the communication protocols, ameliorating the performance of the IoT systems, optimizing the resource consumption, etc. Security is always considered as an important issue but difficult to achieve thoroughly because it seems contradictory with the system's performance due to the resource constraints of IoT devices.

To date, a substantial body of research has been dedicated to the security of IoT systems. However, much of this work primarily focuses on **designing** secure communication protocols, lightweight encryption methods, authentication mechanisms, and ensuring data freshness to prevent packet injection. Recently, there has been an increasing interest in monitoring and intrusion detection for IoT and Wireless Sensor Networks (WSNs). Nonetheless, many existing approaches remain theoretical and have yet to be implemented practically.

In the realm of intrusion detection, there are two principal approaches: signature-based detection and anomaly-based detection. Signature-based detection relies on a database of known attack signatures to identify security threats. In contrast, anomaly-based detection establishes profiles of expected behaviors and identifies deviations from these norms as potential threats. While signature-based methods require frequent updates to remain effective against new attacks, anomaly-based detection is crucial for identifying novel threats, given the rapid evolution and increasing complexity of cyber-attacks.

In this paper, we propose an anomaly detection approach based on Information Theory. We present a general methodology and a specific framework tailored for IoT environments using the RPL (Routing Over Low power and Lossy networks) protocol. A key focus of our approach is to avoid generating additional network traffic, which is especially important in RPL-based WSNs where resources are limited. We validate our proposed method through experiments conducted on a real testbed, demonstrating its practicality and effectiveness.

The rest of this paper is organized as follows: Sect. 2 provides an overview of information-theoretic measures applicable to anomaly-based detec-

---

[2] https://iot-analytics.com/number-connected-iot-devices/.

tion approaches. Our general methodology is described in Sect. 3. A concrete case study and framework specific to RPL in IoT networks are described in Sect. 4. Experimental validation is presented in Sect. 5, followed by a discussion of related works in Sect. 6. Finally, we conclude our study and suggest directions for future research in Sect. 7.

2   Information Theory Preliminaries

This section aims to incorporate Information Theory into the foundational framework of our learning phase (Sect. 3). Information-theoretic measures are calculated from extracted attributes and serve multiple purposes: describing the characteristics of an audit dataset, defining a suitable detection model, and evaluating the model's performance.

In Information Theory, entropy [11] is the most important concept measuring the uncertainty or impurity of a collection of data items. Suppose X is a collection comprising N classes of data items x_i (i = 1, 2, ..., N). The entropy of X is defined as follows:

$$H(X) = H(x_1, x_2, ..., x_N) = -\sum_{i=1}^{N} P(x_i) * log P(x_i) \qquad (1)$$

where $P(x_i)$ is the probability of x_i in X for i = 1, 2, ..., N. The "purer" dataset has a smaller entropy, meaning that the class distribution is more skewed. The smallest possible value of entropy is 0, which occurs when the dataset consists of only one class of items. In this scenario, there is no uncertainty because we know for sure that every item belongs to this unique class. As the dataset becomes more "impure" and diverse, the uncertainty increases, resulting in a higher entropy value.

In the context of this paper on anomaly detection, we use entropy to measure the regularity of the data input. For example, a trace file can be translated into a set of events $E = \{e_1, e_2, ..., e_N\}$, where each event represents a specific action or occurrence within the system. By calculating the entropy of these events, we can determine how predictable or random the sequence of events is. The concept of high regularity underscores the recurrence of events, suggesting their likelihood to reoccur in the future. Moreover, in systems operating on a duty cycle basis, such as Wireless Sensor Networks (WSNs) where sensors periodically transmit sensed data, the regularity appears stable. This assumption will be evaluated in detail in the experimental section.

In addition, the conditional entropy [11], as defined by Shannon entropy, can serve as a useful metric for assessing the temporal or sequential patterns within complex audit datasets, which encompass temporal user behaviors, program executions, and network activities. From an intrusion detection perspective, this metric is particularly valuable for identifying sophisticated attacks that require the correlation of diverse events. The conditional entropy of dataset X given dataset Y is defined as follows:

$$H(X|Y) = - \sum_{\substack{i=\overline{1,N} \\ j=\overline{1,M}}} P(x_i, y_j) * logP(x_i|y_j) \tag{2}$$

where x_i, y_j are classes of data items of X and Y respectively ($i = \overline{1,N}, j = \overline{1,M}$), $P(x_i, y_j)$ is the joint probability of x_i and y_j and $P(x_i|y_j)$ is the conditional probability of x_i given y_j.

Furthermore, in addition to the two aforementioned measures, several other concepts warrant consideration, namely, *relative conditional entropy, information gain and classification, and information cost*, as outlined in [11]. These concepts can prove valuable in both constructing and assessing an anomaly detection model.

3   Methodology

The general approach to monitoring a computer system involves observing the behavior of specific entities (such as a user, a program, or a network element) through the available audit data logs. We aim to incorporate "entropy" as a potential metric for defining an anomaly detection model. The methodology comprises two phases: first, learning the normal characteristics of the data, and then constructing a suitable detection model.

In most computing environments, the behavior of these entities is monitored using available audit data logs. The fundamental assumption in anomaly detection is that there exists an intrinsic characteristic or regularity in audit data that aligns with normal behavior and is distinct from abnormal behavior. Therefore, the process of building an anomaly detection model involves initially examining the characteristics of the data and subsequently selecting a model that effectively leverages these characteristics.

3.1   Learning Phase

The Fig. 1 illustrates the high-level diagram of the training/learning phase. The main objective of this phase is to establish a set of expected normal behaviors based on entropy and/or a database of signatures related to malicious activities. Normal behaviors can be represented by an expected interval of a variable, while a signature can vary in complexity depending on the abnormal behavior it refers to. In the context of this paper, we primarily focus on the former approach, which is anomaly detection.

During this phase, the input consists of training data captured by the monitoring tool or provided by a third party. Optionally, *dimension reduction* can be performed depending on the complexity of the audit data. Valuable attributes essential for the learning algorithm are then extracted. In this study, we exclusively use labeled data, indicating supervised machine learning, where we know whether the input is normal or related to attacks prior to the learning process.

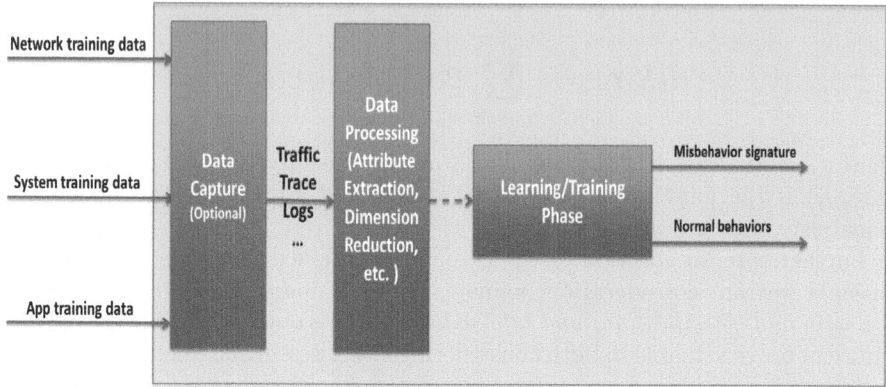

Fig. 1. Training/Learning phase diagram

3.2 Monitoring Phase

Following the conclusion of the learning phase, the set of entropy-based mis-behavior signatures as well as normal behaviors are saved for reference in the monitoring phase (Fig. 2). Additionally, signatures from third parties are encouraged, as a more extensive signature database increases the likelihood of detecting malicious intruders or attacks.

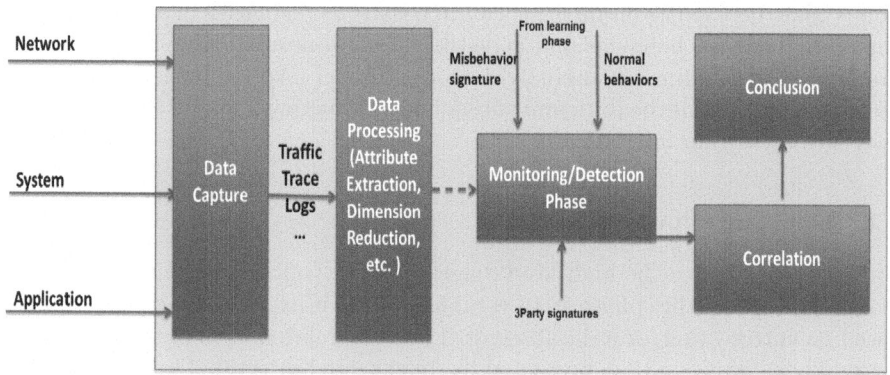

Fig. 2. Detection/Monitoring phase diagram

During this phase, the input consists of live data captured from the environment or offline data stored for analysis. Operations such as dimension reduction, attribute extraction, and variable calculations are performed similarly to those in the learning phase. Subsequently, we reference the signature database and the expected zone of normal behaviors to ascertain whether an observed activity is legitimate or malicious. In some cases, *event correlation* is necessary to detect complicated attacks.

4   RPL-Based IoT Case Study

4.1   Routing with RPL

RPL (Routing Protocol for Low power and Lossy Networks) [12] is proposed by the Routing Over Low-power and Lossy Networks (ROLL) working group of the IETF, which was established to design routing solutions for IoT applications using IPv6. RPL is a distance-vector routing protocol, but instead of offering a generic approach, it offers different variations tailored to specific classes of applications (such as urban low-power applications, industrial applications, home automation applications, etc.). In a network running RPL as the routing protocol, multiple RPL instances can be combined, each consisting of multiple DODAGs (Destination-Oriented Directed Acyclic Graphs). A DODAG comprises a root node (e.g., sink node, base stations, border router) responsible for data collection and coordination, and a number of leaf nodes forming a tree topology. Communications in an RPL network can be point-to-multipoint (P2MP) from the root to leaves using downward routes, multipoint-to-point (MP2P) from leaves to the root via upward routes, and point-to-point (P2P) using both up and downward routes.

A DODAG is constructed using various types of control messages encapsulated in ICMPv6 (Internet Control Message Protocol version 6) packets, namely DIO (DODAG Information Object), DIS (DODAG Information Solicitation), and DAO (Destination Advertisement Object). Initially, a DIO message is broadcasted by the root and forwarded by the leaf nodes to discover their parents, their rank value in the graph, and thus the network topology. The DIS message is utilized when a new node joins an existing network. On the other hand, DAO messages are employed for building downward routes.

4.2   Anomaly Detection Framework

In RPL, DODAGs are typically updated periodically or each time a new node joins the network. In many scenarios, such as smart agriculture, smart parking, and smart home applications, sensor nodes are relatively static and operate on a duty cycle. Intuitively, the distribution of RPL control messages in the network should follow a periodic pattern that determines the normal state. Building upon this concept, we aim to monitor the routing processes to develop an anomaly detection model.

For each packet, we extracted the set of attribute consisting of *source's MAC address, destination's MAC address, timestamp, type of routing packet*. Specifically, we defined five different routing packet types: *RPL DIS, RPL DIO, RPL DAO, Neighbor solicitation* and *Router Advertisement*. An event e_i is defined by a triplet <source's MAC address, destination's MAC address, type of routing

packet>. In summary, we analyzed the traffic and recorded the received events. Then, we calculated the entropy of the set of all received events as a temporal variable. Monitoring this variable provided us with several interesting results (Sect. 5).

5 Experimental Results

5.1 Testbed Description and Dataset

To validate our framework, we deployed a real 6LoWPAN-based WSN using the open platform provided by FIT-IoT lab[3] Fig. 3 depicts the hierarchical architecture of our network, serving as the proof-of-concept. In this setup, each Border Router (BR) acted as the sink node equipped with a sniffer, enabling the capture of live traffic. For our implementation, we utilized A8 and M3 nodes for deploying BR nodes, while M3 and WSN430 nodes[4] were used for sensor nodes. All nodes ran Contiki as the operating system. The sniffers were integrated with BRs to capture and pass the network traffic to the Montimage Monitoring Tool (MMT). In our study, we adapted MMT, originally a monitoring tool designed for traditional TCP/IP(v4) networks [7,14], to support 6LoWPAN (IPv6) traffic [4,5]. The extracted attributes were stored in a local database, and further computations were performed to detect any anomalies or problems.

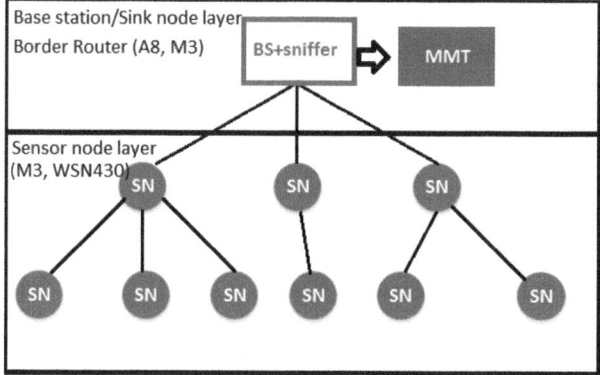

Fig. 3. Hierarchical architecture of the 6LoWPAN-based WSN in our experiment

The network deployment was conducted in the following step-by-step process:

– Selection of Available Sensor Nodes: We selected M3/A8 nodes to act as BR nodes and M3/WSN430 nodes to serve as sensor nodes from the FIT-IoT test-bed for our experiments.

---

[3] FIT IoT Lab: https://www.iot-lab.info/.
[4] Hardware info: https://www.iot-lab.info/hardware/.

– Loading Suitable Firmware: We loaded suitable firmware onto each node. The
BR firmware included an integrated sniffer, while the sensor node firmware
contained HTTP server code.
– Booting Nodes and Starting Experiments: After loading the firmware, we
booted the nodes and initiated the experiments. Sensor nodes periodically
sent sensed data to their corresponding BR nodes. The Montimage Monitoring Tool (MMT) captured the traffic collected by the sniffers as input.

5.2 MMT-IoT for Monitoring IoT Networks

Montimage has developed an extensible monitoring framework called Montimage
Monitoring Tool (MMT) [7,14]. It has been conceived as a modular approach
to analyse security properties of conventional networks (both wired and wireless) by means of extracting statistical information from the network protocols
and feeding it to an engine to perform a temporal logic-based analysis. Montimage has adapted this technology to, respectively, the Cyber Physical Systems
(CPS/IoT) and 5G networks, considering the particular requirements of these
networks.

The MMT-IoT [4,5] has thus been developed to be used with the MMT-
Probe software. In general, the main goal of the MMT-IoT solution is designed
to avoid performing heavy operations on the IoT devices, leaving the security
analysis for the traditional MMT-Probe solution. Since the latter is a Linux-
based tool, it is implicitly constrained to the protocols that the Linux kernel
is capable of handling. In particular, the IEEE 802.15.4 Protocol (IoT-specific
Layer 2 protocol) is not natively supported by the Linux kernel. In this case, when
Linux protocol stack tries to identify the layer 2 protocol, it will not understand
the frame format and, in consequence, discard the packets they reach the Linux
network drivers. To avoid this, an abstraction layer needs to be inserted between
the IoT traffic and MMT-Probe, so the latter will be able to capture the traffic
from any traditional Linux interface.

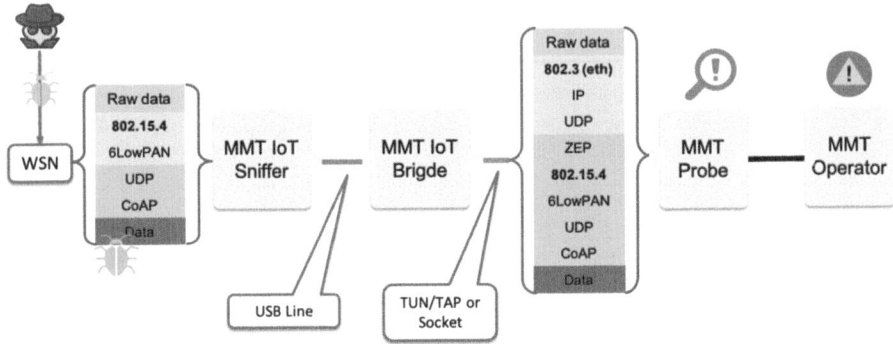

Fig. 4. MMT-IoT general architecture

Figure 4 shows how the MMT-IoT technology is capable of extracting the information from the IoT protocols. In order to correctly adapt this approach (designed initially for traditional Ethernet networks) it was required to split the network extractor (sniffer) in two parts: the MMT-IoT Sniffer and the MMT-IoT Bridge. The former is the IoT endpoint that is in charge of sniffing the packets and forwarding them to a more powerful machine through a USB line. The latter recovers the transferred packets from the USB line and injects them (encapsulated using the ZEP protocol) in the loopback interface of the machine, making the packets ready to be analysed by MMT-Probe (in charge of parsing the protocol communications and analysing them) and visualised by the MMT-Operator (in charge of collecting the information provided by the probes and visualising statistics and alarms).

The described technology is the core of the proposed IoT framework, that is tested in the context of this paper to determine its performance and scalability, as well as to evaluate the effectiveness of the anomaly detection on IoT networks.

5.3   Experimental Results

The primary objective of these experiments is to monitor the entropy value of the system (6LoWPAN-based WSNs) under normal conditions and during incidents to determine if it can be useful in designing an anomaly detection model. We

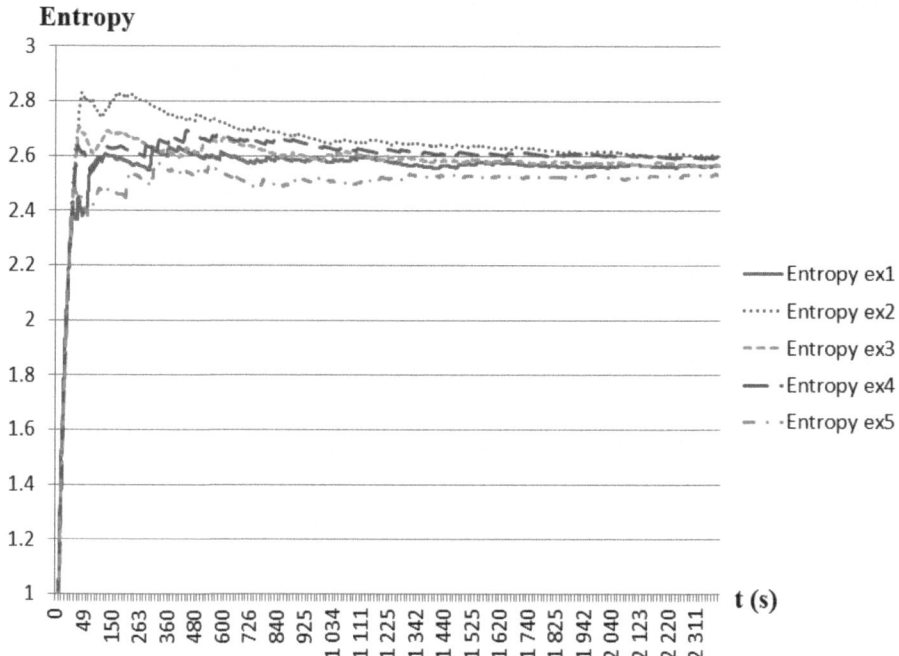

Fig. 5. Entropy monitoring of 10 nodes under normal condition

focused solely on routing packets, as mentioned in Sect. 4.2. For each packet, we extracted a set of attributes, including the source's MAC address, destination's MAC address, timestamp, and type of routing packet (RPL DIS, RPL DIO, RPL DAO, Neighbor solicitation, Router Advertisement). An event e_i is defined by a triplet <source's MAC address, destination's MAC address, type of routing packet>. During the traffic monitoring, we recorded these events, calculated the entropy of the set of all received events, and statistically analyzed it as a temporal variable.

Fig. 6. Entropy monitoring of 30 nodes under normal condition

In the initial phase, we conducted five experiments on networks consisting of 10 nodes each. We monitored the entropy of the set of received events over approximately 40 min, starting from the booting of sensor nodes. The network topology remained fixed throughout the five experiments, but we loaded BR firmware onto five different nodes. The sniffer was consistently positioned in the BR node.

As displayed in the Fig. 5, after the first two or three minutes, the entropy increased rapidly before stabilizing and oscillating around a convergence value. This pattern was consistent across all five experiments, although the specific convergence values varied slightly between the cases. We also observed that when the BR node was positioned closer to the center of the network (resulting in a more symmetric topology), the entropy tended to decrease, indicating a purer set of events.

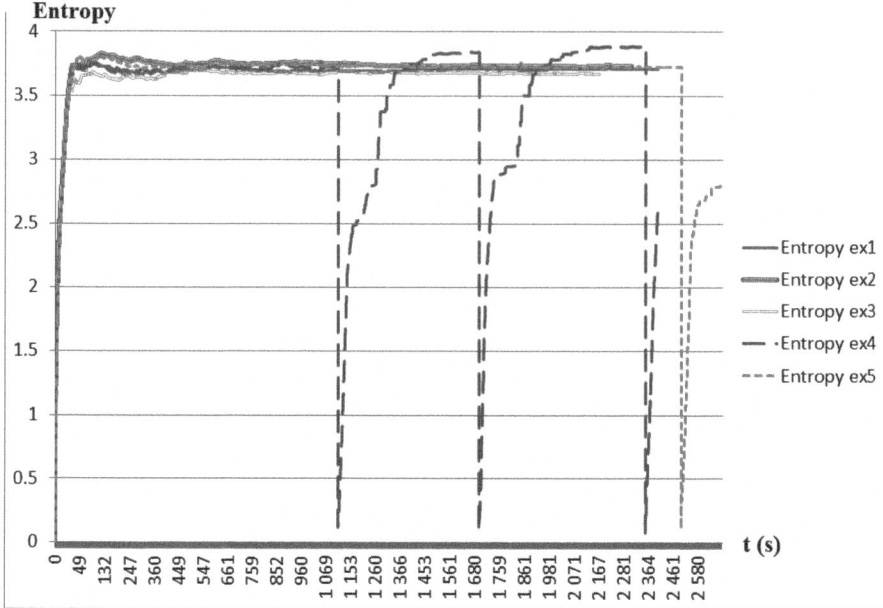

Fig. 7. Entropy monitoring of 30 nodes under rebooting

Next, to observe potential changes on larger networks, we conducted the experiments three more times, this time on networks consisting of 30 nodes each. On one hand, we obtained similar results (Fig. 6), with the entropy quickly increasing during the booting duration until reaching a relatively stable value. On the other hand, we noticed that the entropy for the 30-node networks was higher compared to the 10-node networks. This is understandable, as larger systems with a greater number of entities are likely to be less pure compared to smaller systems.

In the third phase, we conducted two additional experiments on networks consisting of 30 nodes. However, in these experiments, we rebooted the BR several times to observe how the entropy variable reacted. As depicted in Fig. 7), the behavior of the entropy variable resembled that of a fresh experiment (ex4 and ex5). However, the stable point was slightly higher than before the reboot. This is because the reboot event and the necessary routing events performed after the reboot introduce additional impurity to the set of captured events.

Lastly, we injected some routing attacks into the networks. Figure 8 (ex6) illustrates the results when we forced some nodes to perform a flooding attack (attack 1) and a selective forwarding attack (attack 2) [3]. An almost immediate increase in entropy is observed at the moment of the attack. When the attack is terminated, the entropy returns to a stable state, albeit at a point higher than before the attack. This can be explained by the fact that our model also takes the attack into account, resulting in a set of events that is impurer. Indeed,

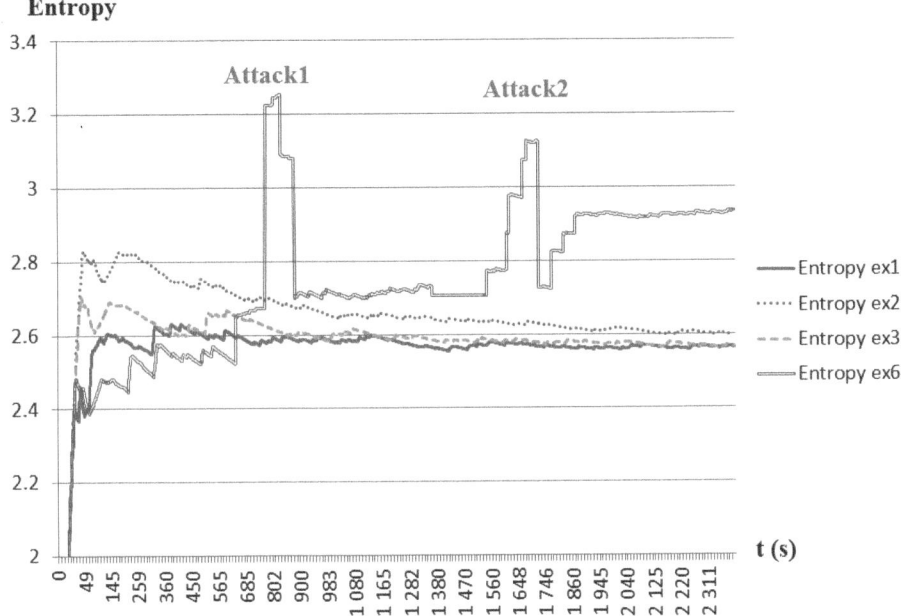

Fig. 8. Entropy monitoring of 10 nodes under attacks

any routing attack that significantly disrupts the normal routing process of the network can trigger a sudden change in the entropy value.

In summary, we have recognized the utility of entropy as a metric for monitoring 6LoWPAN-based WSNs. We have developed a simple entropy-based rule within the Montimage Monitoring Tool (MMT-Security) to automatically detect abnormal changes in the entropy value and subsequently identify potential attacks. The main idea can be summarized as follows: (i)- Monitor the network and learn the normal expected zone for the entropy value $(e - \varepsilon, e + \varepsilon)$; (ii)- Keep monitoring the network and raise an alert if the temporal entropy value fall outside the pre-learned normal zone. The learning phase, including the determination of the expectation e and the threshold ε, is repeated up to the network administrators. The larger threshold can result in a higher rate of false negatives, while a smaller one can increase the rate of false positives. Table 1 presents the performance of our solution in various networks consisting of different numbers of sensor nodes, where we defined $\varepsilon = 5\% * e$. Clearly, as more nodes are added to the network, more traffic is generated, and MMT-IoT requires more processing time (PT) to handle the data. However, MMT-IoT has demonstrated a promising processing rate, consistently around 420 Mbps. The processing rate is calculated as follows:

$$PR(Mbps) = \frac{traffic\_volume(kB) * 8}{1024 * PT} \qquad (3)$$

Indeed, the processing rate (PR) demonstrates that MMT-IoT is a viable candidate for monitoring even large networks consisting of hundreds or thousands of connected objects. With a consistent processing rate of around 420 Mbps, MMT-IoT exhibits the capability to efficiently handle the data generated by extensive networks, making it suitable for real-time monitoring and analysis.

Table 1. Traffic volume, processing time and processing rate depending on the size of network

Nb of nodes	Traffic (kB)	PT (mS)	PR (Mbps)
5	47	0.86	424
10	118	2.19	420
15	235	4.38	419
20	393	7.33	418
25	648	12.16	417
30	1038	19.34	419
35	1334	24.83	419
40	2096	39.06	419

In conclusion, alongside other usable metrics, entropy proves to be a strong candidate for systems where defining normal states is crucial. Specifically, in the context of RPL-based WSNs, we believe that link weight can serve as another valuable metric, offering a local view of the network, as illustrated in our previous work [4]. In contrast, entropy can provide a global view of the entire system, enabling comprehensive monitoring and analysis. Together, these metrics can provide a holistic understanding of the network's behavior, facilitating effective anomaly detection and network management.

6   Related Work

The idea of utilizing Information Theoretic measures for detecting security violations has been explored in both theoretical and practical works. A foundational analysis of the usability of these measures is presented in [6], where the authors investigate the theoretical significance of each measure and their potential applicability in different case studies. Additionally, in works such as [1,10], entropy is employed as the core of the analysis to detect attacks and anomalies. However, as far as our research is concerned, there has not been a formalized methodology or a specific Information-Theoretic proposition tailored for IoT applications. These are the primary objectives of our paper.

Regarding Intrusion Detection System (IDS) solutions for IoT in general and for 6LoWPAN-based WSNs in particular, SVELTE [9] stands out as one of the most well-known among very few intrusion detection tools designed for such small devices. SVELTE comprises three main centralized modules, including lightweight modules and mini-firewalls deployed in sensor nodes (SNs), and central modules called 6Mapper located in Border Routers (BRs). 6Mapper collects routing information with the help of its "little" collaborators located in SNs. In comparison with our approach, SVELTE is more active and creates additional traffic to achieve its goal. On the other hand, our solution aims to passively monitor the network based on the network's existing traffic to avoid incurring additional costs, which might impede the efficiency of 6LoWPAN.

In the context of Intrusion Detection Systems (IDS) for Wireless Sensor Networks (WSNs) that are not specifically based on 6LoWPAN technology, there are several notable solutions discussed in the literature. As studied in [2], many IDS implementations share a common issue: the IDS modules installed in the nodes use the same wireless medium for communication. This reliance on the shared medium can lead to significant additional costs, particularly in the event of Denial of Service (DoS) attacks such as jamming or flooding. Consequently, the fundamental task of an IDS, which is to detect and mitigate attacks, becomes inefficient or unachievable under these conditions.

The authors of [13] addressed the threat of COPYCAT attacks in RPL-based IoT networks by employing machine learning techniques for detection. Their approach utilizes supervised learning algorithms to analyze traffic patterns and identify deviations indicative of COPYCAT attacks. The study identifies effective features for detection, such as packet loss rates, route changes, and inconsistencies in node behavior. It presents a practical framework for implementing these methods in real-world IoT environments, addressing the challenge of accurately detecting sophisticated attacks while maintaining the resource efficiency required by IoT devices. The proposed machine learning-based detection system offers a balance between detection accuracy and computational efficiency, ensuring its effectiveness and feasibility for implementation in resource-constrained IoT networks. By focusing on supervised learning, the research demonstrates the potential to reliably distinguish between normal and malicious traffic, thus enhancing the security and reliability of IoT deployments using RPL as their routing protocol.

Another notable development in the field is the advancement of Intrusion Detection Systems (IDS) tailored for 6LoWPAN networks, as demonstrated in [8]. This research integrates reinforcement learning to augment the detection capabilities of IDS in IoT networks. The reinforcement learning approach enables the system to dynamically learn and recognize anomalous behaviors by continuously interacting with the network environment. This approach has been demonstrated to enhance the detection rate of complex and evolving threats, thus bolstering the overall security posture of IoT networks. The study underscores the effectiveness of reinforcement learning in addressing the dynamic nature of IoT environments and its capacity to offer robust security solutions.

In short, recent studies have also explored the integration of machine learning with information-theoretic approaches to improve anomaly detection. By combining entropy-based metrics with machine learning algorithms, researchers aim to create hybrid models that benefit from the strengths of both techniques. For instance, entropy measures can help reduce the feature space and highlight significant deviations, which can then be further analyzed by machine learning models for accurate classification of anomalies. This synergy is particularly useful in RPL-based IoT networks where resource constraints and the need for real-time detection are critical considerations.

7   Conclusion

In this paper, we have presented an Information-Theoretic methodology for building anomaly detection systems. As a demonstration, we conducted a case study in RPL-based Wireless Sensor Networks (WSNs). The experimental results have illustrated the usability of the entropy metric to passively monitor such networks without generating additional traffic. In addition to the link-weight, which provides a local view as presented in our previous work [4], the entropy variable offers a global view of the network.

We implemented a complete entropy monitoring solution based on the Montimage Monitoring Tool for IoT (MMT-IoT) to report in real-time the current value of the network's entropy and automatically raise an alert in case of sudden changes. This alert can be sent to the network administrators to trigger further investigations aimed at identifying potential security or safety violations.

Due to the lack of material, we were unable to conduct experiments to verify the performance of our solution on a larger network consisting of hundreds or thousands of nodes. In the future, we plan to address this by simulating such scenarios using Cooja[5]. We also intend to evaluate the false positive and negative rates.

Furthermore, another potential future direction is to apply other supervised machine learning algorithms, such as neural networks, support vector machines, and decision trees, to automatically learn valuable metrics. Additionally, we will consider unsupervised learning approaches if labeled training data is not available. These efforts will help enhance the effectiveness and scalability of our anomaly detection system for RPL-based WSNs.

Acknowledgments. This research was partially supported by the ResilMesh project, funded by the European Union's Horizon Europe Framework Programme (HORIZON) under grant agreement 101119681.

References

1. Cuadra-Sánchez, A., Aracil, J.: Proposal of a new information-theory based technique and analysis of traffic anomaly detection (2014)
2. Farooqi, A.H., Khan, F.A.: Intrusion detection systems for wireless sensor networks: a survey. In: Ślęzak, D., Kim, T., Chang, A.C.-C., Vasilakos, T., Li, M.C., Sakurai, K. (eds.) FGCN 2009. CCIS, vol. 56, pp. 234–241. Springer, Heidelberg (2009). https://doi.org/10.1007/978-3-642-10844-0_29

---

[5] https://github.com/contiki-os/contiki/wiki/An-Introduction-to-Cooja.

3. Mayzaud, A., Badonnel, R., Chrisment, I.: A taxonomy of attacks in RPL-based internet of things. Int. J. Netw. Secur. **18**(3), 459–473 (2016)
4. La, V.H., Cavalli, A.R.: A misbehavior node detection algorithm for 6LoWPAN wireless sensor networks. In: Proceedings of 36th IEEE International Conference on Distributed Computing Systems (ICDCS 2016), Second IEEE International Workshop on Security Testing and Monitoring (STAM 2016) (2016)
5. La, V.H., Fuentes, R., Cavalli, A.R.: A novel monitoring solution for 6LoWPAN-based wireless sensor networks. In: Proceedings of 22nd Asia-Pacific Conference on Communications (APCC 2016) (2016)
6. Lee, W., Xiang, D.: Information-theoretic measures for anomaly detection. In: Proceedings 2001 IEEE Symposium on Security and Privacy. S&P 2001, pp. 130–143 (2001)
7. Mallouli, W., Wehbi, B., de Oca, E.M.: Online network traffic security inspection using MMT tool. In: Systems Testing and Validation Workshop 2012, pp. 23–31 (2012)
8. Pasikhani, A.M., Clark, J.A., Gope, P.: Reinforcement-learning-based ids for 6LoWPAN. In: 2021 IEEE 20th International Conference on Trust, Security and Privacy in Computing and Communications (TrustCom), pp. 1049–1060 (2021)
9. Raza, S., Wallgren, L., Voigt, T.: SVELTE: real-time intrusion detection in the internet of things. Ad Hoc Netw. **11**(8), 2661–2674 (2013)
10. Shahriar, H., Zulkernine, M.: Information-theoretic detection of SQL injection attacks. In: 2012 IEEE 14th International Symposium on High-Assurance Systems Engineering, pp. 40–47 (2012)
11. Shannon, C.E.: A mathematical theory of communication. SIGMOBILE Mob. Comput. Commun. Rev. **5**(1), 3–55 (2001)
12. Vasseur, J.P., Agarwal, N., Hui, J., Shelby, Z., Bertrand, P., Chauvenet, C.: RPL: the IP routing protocol designed for low power and lossy networks. In: Internet Protocol for Smart Objects (IPSO) Alliance, (April):20 (2011)
13. Verma, A., Ranga, V.: Cosec-RPL: detection of copycat attacks in RPL based 6lowpans using outlier analysis. Telecommun. Syst. **75**(1), 43–61 (2020)
14. Wehbi, B., de Oca, E.M., Bourdelles, M.: Events-based security monitoring using MMT tool. In: IEEE Fifth International Conference on Software Testing, Verification and Validation (ICST), 2012, pp. 860–863 (2012)

Formal Development of a Delay-Tolerant Multicast Protocol for Wireless Sensors

Emil Sekerinski$^{(\boxtimes)}$ and Tianyu Zhou

Department of Computing and Software, McMaster University, Hamilton, ON, Canada
{emil,zhout34}@mcmaster.ca

Abstract. We consider environmental monitoring in a remote area with limited connectivity where motes can join and leave the network arbitrarily, the topology is dynamic, transmission is highly unreliable, power is restricted, data points are sampled in large intervals, the data volume is low, a delay of the reception of data points can be tolerated, and motes have large memory. We propose a new protocol with blind multicasting of data points, blind multicasting of acknowledgements, and caching of data points and acknowledgements. This paper presents the protocol by stepwise refinement with Event-B. The unreliability of transmissions is modelled by finitary fairness. Rodin is used to prove the correctness and an upper bound for the transmission delay. The protocol has been implemented using LoRa for the physical layer.

Keywords: Wireless sensor networks · Water quality monitoring · Modelling · Stepwise refinement · Event-B · Termination

1 Introduction

This paper formally develops a protocol for transmitting sensor data within a sparse sensor network in remote areas.

While the original motivation comes from monitoring water quality in Indigenous communities in Canada, the protocol is applicable in other network-limited settings. Water insecurity is a global issue, particularly for Indigenous peoples [25]. Monitoring water quality is essential to ensure the health and safety of ecosystems and human populations. Traditional monitoring by analyzing samples in a lab is not only labour-intensive and costly but also does not provide real-time data crucial for timely drinking water and health advisories. Motes equipped with probes for indicators like pH, temperature, dissolved oxygen, conductivity, and turbidity can transmit the readings in real time. To detect the spread of pollutants, multiple motes are needed. In remote areas, 3G/4G connectivity is not guaranteed. Equipping each mote with satellite connections is not feasible as satellites require a direct line of sight, have substantial power requirements, and have high operational and deployment costs. Drone-enabled monitoring allows a

© IFIP International Federation for Information Processing 2025
Published by Springer Nature Switzerland AG 2025
G. Rey et al. (Eds.): IFIPIoT 2024, IFIP AICT 737, pp. 112–128, 2025.
https://doi.org/10.1007/978-3-031-81900-1_7

large area to be covered but is weather-dependent and requires the motes to be on standby, which increases power consumption [28]. Drones still require human supervision and require a complex permission process. Our solution is to connect the motes with a long-range wireless network. Routers, which are motes without probes, can physically extend the network to an area like a road or the top of a hill where there is at least intermittent 3G/4G or satellite connectivity and where a gateway is placed, see Fig. 1.

The author's group developed motes that can be used with off-the-shelf commercial water quality probes and research prototypes that have been developed in the GWF project[1], see Fig. 2. The motes use inexpensive hardware consisting of Arduino boards with LoRa and GPS cards. Depending on the configuration, each mote costs between C$ 600 and C$ 1,400. The low cost helps with affordability and minimizes the impact of motes lost in remote areas. The motes can be self-assembled with parts from hardware stores[2]. The motes have been used for STEM outreach.

The characteristics of the sensor network are that motes may become unavailable at any time, that new motes may be introduced, that the network topology may change by motes moving or being relocated, that sampling occurs in "large" intervals of about an hour, that the data volume is low, and that delays in transmission can be mostly tolerated. The LoRa (low-power, long-range) protocol is well-suited as it allows transmissions of up to 10 km in ideal circumstances at low bit rates. However, there is no routing of packets, necessitating a star topology. Field experiments revealed that the range is typically 300 m, which necessitates routers, and transmissions are unreliable, necessitating retransmissions.

The implemented solution uses a novel protocol on top of LoRa's physical layer. The protocol transmits data and acknowledgements in large intervals, allowing the motes to sleep in between; all motes have an RTC (real-time clock) that is programmed to wake up the motes at the same time and exchange messages for a short period. The protocol is based on *blind multicast with blind acknowledgements*. Event-B is used as it allows a protocol to be specified abstractly as an assignment of sender data to receiver variables and then refined by correctness-preserving steps [1]. The correctness of the protocol does not depend on timing, although the implementation uses timed sleeping for power conservation and random delays to minimize collisions. Event-B supports relations as data types, which are used to model the states of the motes. Since Event-B has no notion of fairness, a difficulty is expressing eventual successful transmission. For this, we use *finitary fairness* as it can be expressed with the existing Event-B proof rules [23]. We show how, with finitary fairness, an upper bound on the transmission delay can be verified. This use of finitary fairness is applicable to other protocols.

Section 2 discusses related wireless sensor protocols. Section 3 discusses related formalizations of protocols in Event-B. Section 4 develops the protocol in four refinement steps. We conclude in Sect. 5.

---

[1] https://gwf.usask.ca/.

[2] https://github.com/re-mote-sensing/re-mote/blob/master/Documentation/Water_Sensor/Build_a_Water_Sensor_Portal.md.

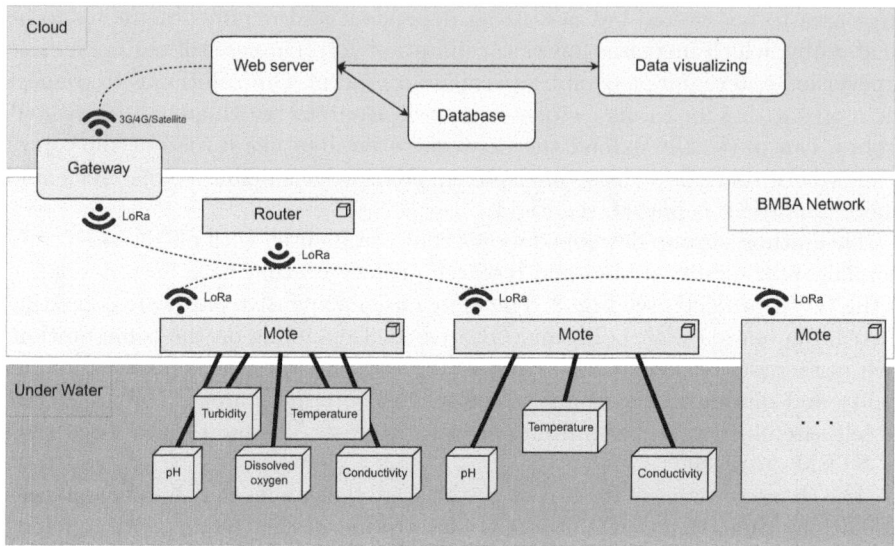

Fig. 1. Sensing network architecture. The routers and the gateway may have probes for air temperature, humidity, etc.

2   Wireless Sensor Network Protocols

The LoRa protocol uses a modulation that makes it particularly suitable for low-power, wide-area networks (LPWANs) without direct line-of-sight. It operates on an unlicensed spectrum. Compared to WiFi, Bluetooth, and ZigBee, the range is longer. Compared to cellular data, the power consumption is lower. However, the data rate and the size of the data packages are smaller [26]. LoRa allows point-to-point and mesh communication. LoRaWAN adds a medium access control (MAC) layer on top of LoRa, including security and device authentication.

Miao et al. use LoRaWAN for environmental monitoring with battery-powered motes, e.g. [19]. As LoRaWAN uses a star topology, and the gateway must be powered all the time, LoRaWAN is unsuitable for our application [26].

Michalik et al. propose LoRaLitE as an alternative to LoRaWAN for energy-efficient environments: the gateway can enter sleep phases [20]. To make the sensor network more robust, if a gateway fails, another mote with a cellular connection can take over. LoRaLitE has been employed for monitoring remote areas. However, it also uses a star topology, making it unsuitable for our application.

Lee and Ke study environmental monitoring using a LoRa mesh network within a university campus [17]. The gateway acts as a beacon and advertises its presence. As other nodes join the network, they become beacons as well. The gateway maintains the network topology and polls each node periodically. For this, all nodes and the gateway are wall-powered. The authors report a better packet delivery ratio than with a star topology. In our application, the

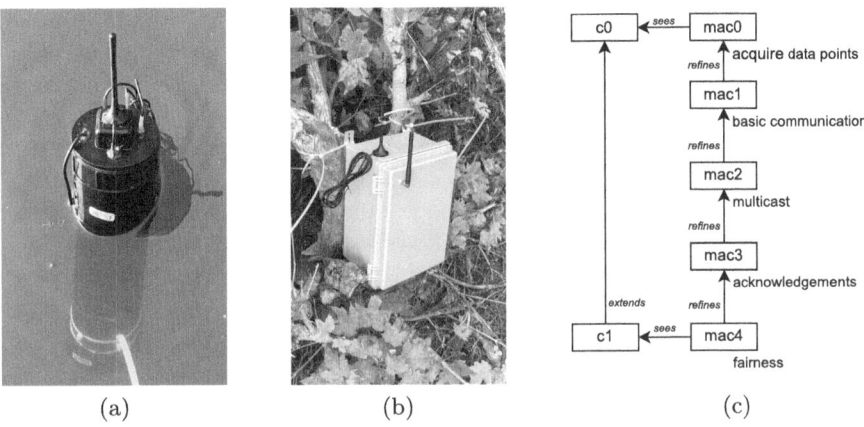

Fig. 2. (a) A deployed mote secured with an anchor. The probes are attached at the top and dangling at the bottom. The (black) antenna is close to the water surface, making cell tower connections difficult. (b) A gateway with LoRa and cell connection antennae. The enclosure houses larger batteries. (c) Event-B refinement steps.

network topology can change, and the nodes are battery-powered, hence cannot continuously listen to polling requests.

Aranzazu-Suescun and Cardei propose a routing protocol with *reactive routing* for detecting composite events [5]. Unlike with *proactive routing*, messages are sent only when needed. For example, having temperature, light, and smoke sensors reporting values over their thresholds is a composite event that may indicate a fire. The proposed protocol addresses the issue of how to maintain routing information in that setting. Our application involves the periodic sampling of data, so requires proactive routing. The unreliability of the transmission makes it difficult to maintain routing information.

Flooding protocols have been used for *information diffusion* with dynamic topology, e.g. recently for underwater acoustic sensor networks [22]. By comparison, the application is here for *information collection*. Here, *flooding with a barrier* is used: a data point floods the network until it arrives at the gateway; then, an acknowledgement of that data point floods the network to stop the further spread of the data point.

Remote monitoring of water environments with LoRa has also been studied by Ceclio [7]. The author dismisses LoRaWAN because of its star topology in favour of a mesh network with a custom time-division multiple-access (TDMA) mechanism for node-to-node communication. The proposed protocol allows nodes to leave and join without manual reconfiguration and uses flooding. To prevent cycles when flooding, the message header maintains the path from the source, which allows a node to detect that a message has already been received. Each node builds a local routing table using RSSI values as a reference. The LoRa gateway broadcasts a hello message, and every node that receives the hello message will rebroadcast it. The hello message includes the information of the sender and the shortest distance from the sender to the gateway. If a node fails, the gateway detects a failure, and the gateway will issue a reset beacon message and flood it to all nodes. In our application, the transmission between nodes is too unreliable to send beacons and maintain routing information. Also, the message header increases with each retransmission, which we avoid here.

Flooding protocols are related to *gossip protocols* for the dissemination of information: in gossip protocols, each node randomly selects nodes to whom to send a message; the random selection allows a probabilistic analysis, e.g. [3,15] In our application, the selection of receivers of a message is nondeterministic, and nodes are not "aware" of each other.

3   Modelling Wireless Sensor Protocols with Event-B

Event-B is a formal proof-based development method based on set theory and first-order logic. The development starts with a model of the system under development that is so abstract that it is "obviously" correct. Details are added in a sequence of refinement steps. The models or *machines* are built with *variables* and *events*. The events are guarded commands that describe the progress of the computation. Variables are constrained by *invariants*. Machines can use *constants* that are declared in *contexts* and are constrained by *axioms*. The following models of a file transfer protocol are adopted from [1]. Context c0 declares constant f, the file to be transmitted, as a total function from 1 .. n to D, without specifying what D is and only assuming that n is positive. Machine mac0 declares variable g, the file to be received, as a partial function from 1 .. n to D.

```
context c0
sets
   D
constants
   n, f
axioms
   0 < n
   f ∈ 1 .. n → D
```

```
machine mac0
variables
   g, b
invariants
   g ∈ 1 .. n ⇸ D
   b = FALSE ⇒ g = ∅
   b = TRUE ⇒ g = f
initialisations
   g := ∅
   b := FALSE
event final
   when
      b = FALSE
   then
      g := f
      b := TRUE
   end
```

```
machine mac1
refines mac0
variables
   b, h, r
invariants
   r ∈ 1 .. n + 1
   h = (1 .. r − 1) ◁ f
   b = TRUE ⇒ r = n + 1
variants
   n + 1 − r
initialisations
   b := FALSE
   h := ∅
   r := 1
event receive ⟨convergent⟩
   when
      r ≤ n
   then
      h := h ∪ {r ↦ f(r)}
      r := r + 1
   end
event final
   when
      r = n + 1
      b = FALSE
   then
      b := TRUE
   end
```

The invariant states that if Boolean variable b is false, g is the empty function, and if b is true, g is the same as f. The initialisation models that the file is not yet transmitted. Event final models the transmission as a one-shot event that disables itself once executed. The proof obligations require that the initialisation establishes the invariants and event final preserves the invariants. Machine mac1 models the successive transmission of the elements of f by introducing integer r for the number of elements received plus one. The received elements are stored in h. The invariant states that in the refinement of mac0 by mac1, function h is the first $r - 1$ elements of f; the operator $\lhd$ stands for domain restriction. A new event, receive, models the transmission of the elements of f in order. Its *convergence*, i.e. eventual *termination* is shown through a *variant* that has to be decreased and, once it reaches zero, disables the event. The variant here is $n + 1 - r$. Event final of mac1 has to refine final of mac0 through their joint invariants and event receive has to refine skip.

While Event-B allows proving the eventual termination of events, there is no notion of *fairness*, which is relevant for modelling unreliable communication in a distributed system like a wireless sensor network (WSN).

Mery and Poppleton address fairness in Event-B by combining it with Lamport's Temporal Logic of Actions [16]. This involves reasoning about the *always*, *eventually*, and *leads to* temporal operators [21]. Mery and Poppleton also address the preservation of temporal properties in refinement steps and consider weak and strong fairness. Zhu et al. [29] propose to strengthen or replace the Event-B proof conditions for specifying and preserving Linear Temporal Logic properties. This is illustrated with an example of transmitting packets over an unreliable channel. Here, the generality of TLA and LTL is not needed: since the events in question are always enabled, weak and strong fairness coincide. Fairness is only introduced in the last refinement step. Instead of standard fairness of TLA and LTL, we use *finitary fairness* as it gives a bound on the number of steps needed to transmit all sensor data. We do not employ temporal operators but express fairness by a counter. This allows us to be more specific than stating that the event for successful transmission is fair: instead, we specify that the set of recipients of multicasting is not always empty.

Mery and Poppleton [21] consider *population protocols*, which represent networks of sensors that have unpredictable mobility. While similar techniques apply, it is worth noting that in population protocols *agents* are simple and can be described by a finite state machine. By contrast, our protocol makes use of the "infinite" memory of nodes. Agents have no unique identity. By contrast, nodes have an identity to enable tracing the provenance of data for legal reasons. Agents communicate in pairs. By contrast, nodes multicast.

It is common in Event-B to specify a protocol as a one-shot event that assigns the source data to target variables. Bechar et al. instead use Colored Petri Nets to first validate and analyze each of the four layers of a WSN protocol and then verify each layer in Event-B [6]. Fairness can be dealt with by the CPN tool. Here, we start with a one-shot specification.

The approaches to modelling a WSN with Event-B of Taktak et al. [27], Intana et al. [11], Kamali and Petre [14], Hariche et al. [10], Singh and Yadav [24], Gawanmeh [9], Fu and Zheng [8], and Kamali et al. [13] do not cover network layers that need fairness to guarantee eventual transmission, which is the concern here.

4   Finitary Fairness

Alur and Henzinger propose finitary fairness as a stronger notion of fairness [4]. Whereas fairness of an event requires that it will eventually be taken, finitary fairness puts a bound on how often it can be neglected before taken. In a concurrent system, finitary fairness means that a scheduler has finite memory for counting how often an event is delayed. In a distributed system, finitary fairness implies that the difference in the speed of processors cannot diverge indefinitely. Sekerinski and Zhang show how to encode finitary fairness in event (transition) systems in two different ways [23]. The following example illustrates the translation of with a regular event L and a fair event R. Without R being fair, the event system on the left is not guaranteed to terminate. The event system on the right introduces *fairness counter* C and uses B as the bound.

```
variables                    variables
    x                            x, C
invariants                   invariants
    x ∈ N                        x ∈ N
initialisations                  C ∈ 1..B
    x :∈ N                   initialisations
event L                          x :∈ N
    when                         C := B
        x > 0                event L
    then                         when
        skip                         x > 0
    end                              C > 1
fair event R                     then
    when                             C := C − 1
        x > 0                    end
    then                     event R
        x := x − 1               when
    end                              x > 0
                             then
                                 x := x − 1
                                 C := B
                             end
```

In general, a *fair event system* P is a structure (Q, I, E, F, T) where Q is the set of states, I is the set of initial states with $I \subseteq Q$, E is set of all events, F is the set of fair events such that $F \subseteq E$, and T is the set of transitions, which are relations over $Q \times Q$ indexed by E. A computation *comp* of P is a finite or infinite maximal sequence of states and events alternating, written

$$comp = \sigma_0 \xrightarrow{\tau_0} \sigma_1 \xrightarrow{\tau_1} \sigma_2 \xrightarrow{\tau_2} \cdots$$

such that $\sigma_0 \in I$ and $\forall i \cdot i \in \mathbb{N} \Rightarrow \tau_i \in E \wedge \sigma_i \mapsto \sigma_{i+1} \in T(\tau_i)$. That is, states σ_i and σ_{i+1} must be in relation $T(\tau_i)$. A computation is *terminating* if it ends with a state σ_n, for some $n \in \mathbb{N}$, that is not in the domain of any transition relation, i.e. $\forall e \cdot e \in E \Rightarrow \sigma_n \notin dom(T(e))$. Otherwise, it is *nonterminating*. The *schedule* of a computation *comp* is its projection to the events, $\tau_0 \tau_1 \tau_2 \ldots$ The *trace* of *comp* is its projection to the states, $\sigma_0 \sigma_1 \sigma_2 \ldots$

The *guard* of an event is the domain of its relation, $grd(e) = dom(T(e))$; an event is *enabled* in a state if the state is in its guard, otherwise *disabled*. A computation *comp* is *bounded* if it is finite or if for some $k \in \mathbb{N}$, any fair event e_f, for $f \in F$, cannot be enabled for more than k consecutive states without being taken, formally:

$$\forall i, f \cdot i \in \mathbb{N} \wedge f \in F \Rightarrow \exists j \cdot j \in i \mathrel{..} i + k \wedge (\tau_j = e_f \vee \sigma_j \notin grd(e_f))$$

The translation of a k-bounded fair event system to an equivalent without fair events is more involved if there are multiple fair events, and the events can become disabled and enabled [23]. That generality is not needed here. Finitary fairness is used here in a novel way to not only ensure the eventual termination of message delivery but to derive an upper bound of the delay of messages with unreliable transmission.

5   The Blind Multicast with Blind Acknowledgements Protocol

We propose a mesh protocol where (1) motes can join and leave the network arbitrarily, (2) the topology is dynamic, (3) transmission is highly unreliable due to environmental influences, (4) power is restricted (typically by a battery that has to last for a whole season), (5) data points are sampled in large intervals, (5) the data volume is low, and (6) a delay of the reception of data points can be tolerated, as long as they are eventually received.

Points (1) and (2) make routing tables unreliable. Points (3) and (6) imply that resending a data point can be delayed. The key observations are that (a) when multicasting, all nodes within the range of a sender receive the sent message anyway, without additional power consumption, and (b) all nodes have sufficient memory to buffer all data points and their acknowledgements during the lifetime of the network.

The protocol is implemented on top of the LoRa physical layer, though the only assumption about the underlying layer is that if a message is multicast, it is either correctly received or not received. LoRa is not explicitly modelled. The motes operate by waking up in intervals, typically of an hour, and exchanging acknowledgements and data points for a couple of minutes before sleeping again. This timing affects the power consumption. The model is more general and does not make any assumptions about timing.

Initial Model. There is a finite set of nodes, which are either motes (including routers) or the gateway. Event `acquire` models a mote sending a data point directly to the gateway. Each data point includes the probe readings, the GPS coordinates, and a unique time stamp from the RTC. For the purpose of modelling the protocol, it is sufficient to consider a data point as a pair n ↦ s with node n and unique sequence numbers s. As, later, data points may overtake each other in transmission, event acquire selects an arbitrary sequence number that has not yet been considered. There are finitely many sequence numbers 1 .. maxSeq. Because there are finitely many nodes and sequence numbers, the stated variant ensures that acquire is convergent, i.e. eventually terminates.

```
CONTEXT c0
SETS Nodes
CONSTANTS gateway, maxSeq
AXIOMS
  axm1 :  gateway ∈ Nodes
  axm2 :  finite(Nodes)
  axm3 :  maxSeq > 1
END
```

```
MACHINE mac0
SEES c0
VARIABLES gateway_data
INVARIANTS
  inv1 :  gateway_data ∈ Nodes ↔ 1..maxSeq
VARIANTS
  vrn1 :  card(Nodes) ∗ maxSeq − card(gateway_data)
EVENTS
  Initialisation ⟨ ordinary ⟩
    begin
      act1 :  gateway_data := ∅
    end

  acquire ⟨ convergent ⟩
    any mote, s
    where
      grd1 :  mote ↦ s ∉ gateway_data
      grd2 :  s ∈ 1..maxSeq
    then
      act1 :  gateway_data := gateway_data ∪ {mote ↦ s}
    end
END
```

First Refinement. The state of the nodes is introduced. Each node gets its own variable with the sequence number of its next data point, which is modelled by variable seqnum ∈ Nodes → 1..maxSeq. Event acquire is split into event sample, which stores the next data point in its sending buffer, and transmit, which transfers a data point from a mote's sending buffer to the gateway. Thus, sample refines skip and transmit refines acquire. Function sum, defined in context sum_ctx, sums the elements of a set. This is used in the variant to prove that sample is convergent: as the maximal number of data points is maxSeq ∗ card(Nodes), each execution of sample decreases the variant and sample is disabled when the variant reaches zero.

```
MACHINE mac1
REFINES mac0
SEES c0, sum_ctx
VARIABLES gateway_data, seqnum, sending_buffer
INVARIANTS
  inv1 :  sending_buffer ∈ Nodes ↔ 1..maxSeq
  inv2 :  seqnum ∈ Nodes → 1..maxSeq
  inv3 :  ∀ n · n ∈ Nodes ⇒ seqnum(n) = max(sending_buffer[{n}] ∪ {0}) + 1
```

VARIANTS
  vrn1 : $\text{maxSeq} * \text{card}(\text{Nodes}) - \text{sum}(\{n \cdot n \in \text{Nodes} \mid \text{seqnum}(n)\})$
EVENTS
  Initialisation ⟨ extended ⟩
    begin
      act1 : $\text{gateway\_data} := \varnothing$
      act2 : $\text{sending\_buffer} := \varnothing$
      act3 : $\text{seqnum} := (\lambda n \cdot n \in \text{Nodes} \mid 1)$
    end

  sample ⟨ convergent ⟩
    any mote
    where
      grd1 : $\text{seqnum}(\text{mote}) < \text{maxSeq}$
    then
      act1 : $\text{sending\_buffer} := \text{sending\_buffer} \cup \{\text{mote} \mapsto \text{seqnum}(\text{mote})\}$
      act2 : $\text{seqnum}(\text{mote}) := \text{seqnum}(\text{mote}) + 1$
    end

  transmit ⟨ convergent ⟩
    refines acquire
    any mote, s
    where
      grd1 : $\text{mote} \mapsto s \notin \text{gateway\_data}$
      grd2 : $\text{mote} \mapsto s \in \text{sending\_buffer}$
    then
      act1 : $\text{gateway\_data} := \text{gateway\_data} \cup \{\text{mote} \mapsto s\}$
    end
END

Second Refinement. The mesh network is introduced. Rather than modelling the connectivity as a graph, which would require events for changing topology, the connectivity is modelled by nondeterministically selecting the receivers of a multicast. Variable sending_buffer is refined by forwarding_buffer such that forwarding_buffer(n) for node n is the set of all the received data points and the node at which they originate. Event sample places a new data point into its own forwarding_buffer. Event multicast models that a mote sends a data point of its forwarding buffer to other nodes. Event multicast is anticipated, meaning that the convergence proof is postponed. Event gatewayReceive copies a data point from its forwarding buffer to gateway_data, thus refining transmit.

MACHINE mac2
REFINES mac1
SEES c0, sum_ctx
VARIABLES gateway_data, seqnum, forwarding_buffer
INVARIANTS
  inv1 : $\text{forwarding\_buffer} \in \text{Nodes} \rightarrow (\text{Nodes} \leftrightarrow 1..\text{maxSeq})$
  inv2 : $\text{union}(\text{ran}(\text{forwarding\_buffer})) = \text{sending\_buffer}$
  inv3 : $\forall n1, n2 \cdot n1 \in \text{Nodes} \land n2 \in \text{Nodes} \Rightarrow \text{seqnum}(n1) = \max(\text{forwarding\_buffer}(n1)[\{n1\}] \cup$
    $\{0\}) + 1$
EVENTS
  Initialisation ⟨ ordinary ⟩
    begin
      act1 : $\text{gateway\_data} := \varnothing$
      act2 : $\text{seqnum} := (\lambda n \cdot n \in \text{Nodes} \mid 1)$
      act3 : $\text{forwarding\_buffer} := (\lambda n \cdot n \in \text{Nodes} \mid \varnothing)$
    end

  sample ⟨ convergent ⟩
    refines sample
    any mote
    where

```
        grd1  :  seqnum(mote) < maxSeq
      then
        act1  :  forwarding_buffer(mote) := forwarding_buffer(mote) ∪ {mote ↦ seqnum(mote)}
        act2  :  seqnum(mote) := seqnum(mote) + 1
      end

  gatewayReceive ⟨ convergent ⟩
    refines transmit
    any mote, s
    where
      grd1  :  mote ↦ s ∉ gateway_data
      grd2  :  mote ↦ s ∈ forwarding_buffer(gateway)
    then
      act1  :  gateway_data := gateway_data ∪ {mote ↦ s}
    end

  multicast ⟨ anticipated ⟩
    any mote, n, s, to
    where
      grd1  :  n ↦ s ∈ forwarding_buffer(mote)
      grd2  :  mote ≠ gateway
      grd3  :  s < maxSeq
      grd4  :  to ⊆ Nodes
      grd5  :  mote ∉ to
    then
      act1  :  forwarding_buffer := forwarding_buffer ∪ {a · a ∈ to | a ↦ {n ↦ s}}
    end

END
```

Third Refinement. Acknowledgement messages are introduced. Each mote keeps transmitting sampled and received data points until it receives an acknowledgement for that data point. Variable forwarding_buffer is refined by buffer, which stores both data points and their acknowledgements. Event gatewayReceive, on receiving n ↦ s, sends out the acknowledgement of that data point, represented as the pair n ↦ −s, by placing it in its own buffer.

```
MACHINE mac3
REFINES mac2
SEES c0, sum_ctx
VARIABLES gateway_data, seqnum, buffer
INVARIANTS
  inv1  :  buffer ∈ Nodes → (Nodes ↔ −maxSeq..maxSeq)
  inv2  :  union(ran(forwarding_buffer)) = (union(ran(buffer)) ∪ gateway_data) \ {n, nn, s · nn ↦ s ∈
           buffer(n) ∧ s < 0 | nn ↦ s}
  inv3  :  ∀ n, nn, s · nn ↦ s ∈ buffer(n) ⇒ s ≠ 0
EVENTS
  Initialisation ⟨ ordinary ⟩
    begin
      act1  :  gateway_data := ∅
      act2  :  seqnum := (λn·n ∈ Nodes | 1)
      act3  :  buffer := (λn·n ∈ Nodes | ∅)
    end

  sample ⟨ convergent ⟩
    refines sample
    any mote
    where
      grd1  :  mote ≠ gateway
      grd2  :  seqnum(mote) < maxSeq
    then
      act1  :  buffer(mote) := buffer(mote) ∪ {mote ↦ seqnum(mote)}
      act2  :  seqnum(mote) := seqnum(mote) + 1
    end
```

```
gatewayReceive ⟨ convergent ⟩
  refines gatewayReceive
  any mote, s
  where
    grd1  :   mote ↦ s ∈ buffer(gateway)
    grd2  :   mote ↦ s ∉ gateway_data
    grd3  :   s > 0
  then
    act1  :   gateway_data := gateway_data ∪ {mote ↦ s}
    act2  :   buffer(gateway) := buffer(gateway) ∪ {mote ↦ −s}
  end

multicast ⟨ anticipated ⟩
  refines multicast
  any mote, n, s, to
  where
    grd1  :   n ↦ s ∈ buffer(mote)
    grd2  :   n ↦ −s ∉ buffer(mote)
    grd3  :   s > 0
    grd4  :   to ⊆ Nodes
    grd5  :   mote ∉ to
    grd6  :   mote ≠ gateway
  then
    act1  :   buffer := (buffer ⩤ {mm · mm ∈ to | mm ↦ buffer(mm) ∪ {n ↦ s}})
  end

multicastAck ⟨ anticipated ⟩
  any mote, n, s, to
  where
    grd1  :   n ↦ s ∈ buffer(mote)
    grd2  :   n ↦ −s ∈ buffer(mote)
    grd3  :   s > 0
    grd4  :   to ⊆ Nodes
    grd5  :   mote ∉ to
    grd6  :   ∀ nn · nn ∈ to ⇒ n ↦ −s ∉ buffer(nn)
  then
    act1  :   buffer := (buffer ⩤ {mm · mm ∈ to | mm ↦ buffer(mm) ∪ {n ↦ −s}}) ⩤ {mote ↦
              buffer(mote) \ {n ↦ s}}
  end

END
```

Fourth Refinement. The (un-) reliability of transmission is modelled. Above, in multicast and multicastAck, the set to of recipients could be empty each time the event occurs, which means that transmission never succeeds. We now assume that, after some time, one data point or one acknowledgement will be sent to at least one recipient. That is, we do not assume how often a specific message is retransmitted or how long motes have to retry. Environmental factors like weather or physical obstruction may put a specific mote out of range for some time. We only assume that some message in the network will eventually be transmitted. That is the weakest possible assumption for all data points to eventually reach the gateway. A fairness counter, C, is introduced that forces the set to of recipients in multicast and multicastAck not to be empty after B attempts.

```
MACHINE mac4
REFINES mac3
SEES c1, sum_ctx
VARIABLES gateway_data, seqnum, buffer, C
INVARIANTS
  inv1  :   C ∈ 1..B
VARIANTS
```

vrn1 : card(Nodes) * maxSeq * (B − 1) * card(Nodes) * 2 − sum({n · n ∈ Nodes | card(buffer(n))}) *
(B − 1) + C

EVENTS

Initialisation ⟨ ordinary ⟩
  begin
    act1 : gateway_data := ∅
    act2 : seqnum := (λn·n ∈ Nodes | 1)
    act3 : buffer := (λn·n ∈ Nodes | ∅)
    act4 : C := B
  end

sample ⟨ convergent ⟩
  extends sample
  any mote
  where
    grd1 : mote ≠ gateway
    grd2 : seqnum(mote) < maxSeq
  then
    act1 : buffer(mote) := buffer(mote) ∪ {mote ↦ seqnum(mote)}
    act2 : seqnum(mote) := seqnum(mote) + 1
  end

gatewayReceive ⟨ convergent ⟩
  extends gatewayReceive
  any mote, s
  where
    grd1 : mote ↦ s ∈ buffer(gateway)
    grd2 : mote ↦ s ∉ gateway_data
    grd3 : s > 0
  then
    act1 : gateway_data := gateway_data ∪ {mote ↦ s}   // move dp to gateway_data
    act2 : buffer(gateway) := buffer(gateway) ∪ {mote ↦ −s} // add ack to buffer
  end

multicast ⟨ convergent ⟩
  extends multicast
  any mote, n, s, to
  where
    grd1 : (n ↦ s) ∈ buffer(mote)
    grd2 : (n ↦ −s) ∉ buffer(mote)
    grd3 : s > 0
    grd4 : to ⊆ Nodes
    grd5 : mote ∉ to
    grd6 : mote ≠ gateway
    grd7 : C = 1 ⇒ card(to) > 0
  then
    act1 : buffer := (buffer ⊰ {mm · mm ∈ to | mm ↦ buffer(mm) ∪ {n ↦ s}})
    act2 : C :| (C' ∈ 2..B ⇒ C' = C − 1) ∧ (C' = 1 ⇒ C' = B)
  end

multicastAck ⟨ convergent ⟩
  extends multicastAck
  any mote, n, s, to
  where
    grd1 : n ↦ s ∈ buffer(mote)
    grd2 : n ↦ −s ∈ buffer(mote)
    grd3 : s > 0
    grd4 : to ⊆ Nodes
    grd5 : mote ∉ to
    grd6 : ∀ nn · nn ∈ to ⇒ n ↦ −s ∉ buffer(nn)
    grd7 : C = 1 ⇒ card(to) > 0
  then
    act1 : buffer := (buffer ⊰ {mm · mm ∈ to | mm ↦ buffer(mm) ∪ {n ↦ −s}}) ⊰ {mote ↦
    buffer(mote) \ {n ↦ s}}
    act2 : C :| (C' ∈ 2..B ⇒ C' = C − 1) ∧ (C' = 1 ⇒ C' = B)
  end

END

Table 1. Proof obligation statistics

Event-B Model	Number of proof obligation	Automatically proved	Need interactive proofs	Number of lines
mac0	7	3	4	29
mac1	16	7	9	50
mac2	22	11	11	68
mac3	35	16	19	90
mac4	14	2	12	98
Total	94	39	55	335

The variant provides an upper bound on the number of multicast and multicastAck events: card(Nodes) * maxSeq * (B − 1) * card(Nodes) * 2. There are card(Nodes) * maxSeq data points. In the worst case, each of these will reach all nodes before the acknowledgements reach these nodes, hence card(Nodes) * 2. Each data point and acknowledgement needs B - 1 transmissions.

6   Conclusions

This work presents the formal development of a protocol for wireless sensor networks where motes can join and leave the network arbitrarily, the topology is dynamic, transmission is highly unreliable, power is restricted, data points are sampled in large intervals, the data volume is low, and a delay in the reception of data points can be tolerated. The protocol uses a limited form of flooding based on the observation that all receivers in the range of a sender are listening to incoming messages anyway have the capacity to store them: each probe reading requires 4 bytes plus 1 byte for the probe type; for all probes read by a mote, there are additionally 8 bytes for the GPS coordinates, 4 bytes for the time stamp and 1 byte for the mote number. For five probes, that makes 38 bytes per reading, or 912 bytes per day if sampled hourly. Assuming that additional indexing information brings that to 1KB per day, with the 32 GB SD cards that the motes use and a network with 100 motes whose data is stored in all motes allows the data of 320,000 days to be stored. Even if the sampling frequency is increased to every minute, that would be sufficient for 14 years of data. The common application is for monitoring one season, as the motes, particularly their probes, require maintenance. The formal development covers only the correctness, including termination, of data transmission. Timing is not formalized as that affects only the power consumption. Our experience is that power consumption is better determined experimentally than analytically.

This project did not start with the goal of using a formal development approach. After observing in the field that existing protocols were too unreliable, Event-B was instrumental in the development; it was not clear if a protocol with the stated goals could be developed and what guarantees could be made. The final Event-B development is pleasingly compact. First, ProB was used to debug the models before the Rodin interactive prover was used [2]. Table 1 provides some statistics of the development.

The routing protocol of Jain et al. addresses the issue that nodes closer to the gateway (sink) have a higher power consumption due to the forwarding of packets. The approach is to distinguish some nodes as *ring nodes*. This approach is meant for "dense" networks [12]. In our application, the power consumption of obtaining the GPS position and sampling the probes is of the same order as the power consumption of receiving acknowledgements and multicasting data. We plan to conduct field experiments to determine if, in our "sparse" network, the battery of motes and repeaters closer to the gateway drains significantly faster.

Flooding in LoRa networks is also used for *concurrent transmission*, where collisions of the same message are used to amplify the signal [18]. Here, we try to avoid collisions in the implementation: all motes wake up at the same time and listen to acknowledgements that the gateway initiates and multicast them. In the second phase, the motes multicast data points for which they have not received acknowledgements. Currently, multicasting of data points and acknowledgements involves a random delay. Since the network is sparse, collisions are less likely. We leave an experimental evaluation of the benefits of a concurrent transmission of data points or acknowledgements as future work.

The Delay-Tolerant Multicast Protocol was implemented with ESP32 for evaluation[3]. In a preliminary experiment, two nodes and a gateway were deployed in a forested area with a 100-meter distance between the nodes, no line of sight, and no external antenna attached. The change of environmental influences was simulated by moving the gateway within a 50-meter radius. Despite about half of the packets not being correctly received, the protocol was able to successfully retransmit all data points.

Acknowledgement. Generous funding was provided by the Global Water Futures project, subproject Co-Creation of Indigenous Water Quality Tools. We like to thank our collaborators of the GWF project for providing a stimulating application of WSN under the leadership of Dawn Martin-Hill. We like to thank in particular Charles de Lannoy and Erik Frechette for their work in deploying the sensors. Comments by the reviews lead to improvements of the paper.

References

1. Abrial, J.R.: Modeling in Event-B: System and Software Engineering. Cambridge University Press, Cambridge (2010)
2. Abrial, J.R., Butler, M., Hallerstede, S., Hoang, T.S., Mehta, F., Voisin, L.: Rodin: an open toolset for modelling and reasoning in Event-B. Int. J. Softw. Tools Technol. Transfer **12**(6), 447–466 (2010). https://doi.org/10.1007/s10009-010-0145-y
3. Allavena, A., Demers, A., Hopcroft, J.E.: Correctness of a gossip based membership protocol. In: Proceedings of the Twenty-Fourth Annual ACM Symposium on Principles of Distributed Computing, pp. 292–301. PODC 2005: ACM Symposium on Principles of Distributed Computing, Las Vegas, Nevada, USA. ACM (2005). https://doi.org/10.1145/1073814.1073871

---

[3] The protocol was implemented with the Arduino IDE. The project files are available at https://github.com/KrunkZhou/DTMP-Protocol.

4. Alur, R., Henzinger, T.A.: Finitary fairness. ACM Trans. Program. Lang. Syst. **20**(6), 1171–1194 (1998). https://doi.org/10.1145/295656.295659

5. Aranzazu-Suescun, C., Cardei, M.: Reactive routing protocol for event reporting in mobile-sink wireless sensor networks. In: Proceedings of the 13th ACM Symposium on QoS and Security for Wireless and Mobile Networks, pp. 43–50. ACM, Miami Florida USA (2017). https://doi.org/10.1145/3132114.3132116

6. Bechar, R., Tahar Abbes, M., Mezzoudj, F., Bellatreche, L.: On formal modeling and validation of wireless sensor network protocols. Wireless Pers. Commun. **114**(4), 2855–2888 (2020). https://doi.org/10.1007/s11277-020-07507-8

7. Cecílio, J.: AQUAMesh: a low-power wide-area mesh network protocol for remote monitoring applications in water environments. In: IECON 2021: 47th Annual Conference of the IEEE Industrial Electronics Society, pp. 1–6. IEEE, Toronto, Canada (2021). https://doi.org/10.1109/IECON48115.2021.9589117

8. Fu, C., Zheng, K.: Formal modeling and analysis of ad hoc Zone Routing Protocol in Event-B. Int. J. Softw. Tools Technol. Transfer **21**(2), 165–181 (2017). https://doi.org/10.1007/s10009-017-0463-4

9. Gawanmeh, A.: Embedding and verification of ZigBee protocol stack in event-B. Procedia Comput. Sci. **5**, 736–741 (2011). https://doi.org/10.1016/j.procs.2011.07.097

10. Hariche, A., Belarbi, M., Chouarfia, A.: Embedded systems design using event-B theories. Int. J. Comput. Digit. Syst. **05**(02), 173–188 (2016). https://doi.org/10.12785/IJCDS/050207

11. Intana, A., Poppleton, M.R., Merrett, G.V.: A formal co-simulation approach for wireless sensor network development. Electron. Commun. EASST **70** (2014). https://doi.org/10.14279/tuj.eceasst.70.969.970

12. Jain, S., Pattanaik, K.K., Verma, R.K., Bharti, S., Shukla, A.: Delay-aware green routing for mobile-sink-based wireless sensor networks. IEEE Internet Things J. **8**(6), 4882–4892 (2021). https://doi.org/10.1109/JIOT.2020.3030120

13. Kamali, M., Laibinis, L., Petre, L., Sere, K.: Formal development of wireless sensor-actor networks. Sci. Comput. Program. **80**, 25–49 (2014). https://doi.org/10.1016/j.scico.2012.03.002

14. Kamali, M., Petre, L.: Modelling link state routing in Event-B. In: 21st International Conference on Engineering of Complex Computer Systems (ICECCS), pp. 207–210 (2016). https://doi.org/10.1109/ICECCS.2016.035

15. Kwiatkowska, M., Norman, G., Parker, D.: Analysis of a gossip protocol in PRISM. ACM SIGMETRICS Perform. Eval. Rev. **36**(3), 17–22 (2008). https://doi.org/10.1145/1481506.1481511

16. Lamport, L.: The temporal logic of actions. ACM Trans. Program. Lang. Syst. **16**(3), 872–923 (1994). https://doi.org/10.1145/177492.177726

17. Lee, H.C., Ke, K.H.: Monitoring of large-area IoT sensors using a LoRa wireless mesh network system: Design and evaluation. IEEE Trans. Instrum. Meas. **67**(9), 2177–2187 (2018). https://doi.org/10.1109/TIM.2018.2814082

18. Liao, C.H., Zhu, G., Kuwabara, D., Suzuki, M., Morikawa, H.: Multi-hop LoRa networks enabled by concurrent transmission. IEEE Access **5**, 21430–21446 (2017). https://doi.org/10.1109/ACCESS.2017.2755858

19. Miao, H.Y., Yang, C.T., Kristiani, E., Fathoni, H., Lin, Y.S., Chen, C.Y.: On construction of a campus outdoor air and water quality monitoring system using LoRaWAN. Appl. Sci. **12**(10), 5018 (2022). https://doi.org/10.3390/app12105018

20. Michalik, L.S., Guegan, L., Raïs, I., Anshus, O., Bjørndalen, J.M.: LoRaLitE: LoRa protocol for energy-limited environments. In: 30th International Symposium on Modeling, Analysis, and Simulation of Computer and Telecommunication Systems (MASCOTS), pp. 73–80. IEEE, Nice, France (2022). https://doi.org/10.1109/MASCOTS56607.2022.00018

21. Méry, D., Poppleton, M.: Towards an integrated formal method for verification of liveness properties in distributed systems: with application to population protocols. Softw. Syst. Model. **16**(4), 1083–1115 (2015). https://doi.org/10.1007/s10270-015-0504-y

22. Porretta, S.F., Barbeau, M., Blouin, S., Kranakis, E., Webstey, A.: A novel underwater packet flooding protocol. In: IEEE Canadian Conference on Electrical and Computer Engineering (CCECE), pp. 438–443. IEEE, Regina, Saskatchewan (2023). https://doi.org/10.1109/CCECE58730.2023.10288842

23. Sekerinski, E., Zhang, T.: Finitary fairness in action systems. In: Liu, Z., Woodcock, J., Zhu, H. (eds.) ICTAC 2013. LNCS, vol. 8049, pp. 319–336. Springer, Heidelberg (2013). https://doi.org/10.1007/978-3-642-39718-9_19

24. Singh, A., Yadav, D.: Formal specification and verification of total order broadcast through destination agreement using event-b. Int. J. Comput. Sci. Inf. Technol. **7**, 85–95 (2015). https://doi.org/10.5121/ijcsit.2015.7506

25. Sultana, A., Wilson, J., Martin-Hill, D., Davis-Hill, L., Homer, J.: Assessing the impact of water insecurity on maternal mental health at Six Nations of the Grand River. Front. Water **4** (2022). https://doi.org/10.3389/frwa.2022.834080

26. Sun, Y., Hu, J., Liu, Y., Tian, Z.: Theoretical analysis and performance testing of LoRa technology. In: ICCTEC 2017: International Conference on Computer Technology, Electronics and Communication, pp. 686–690. IEEE, Kolkata WB India (2017). https://doi.org/10.1109/ICCTEC.2017.00153

27. Taktak, E., Tounsi, M., Mosbah, M., Hadj Kacem, A.: Proving distributed algorithms for wireless sensor networks by combining refinement and local computations. In: IEEE 27th International Conference on Enabling Technologies: Infrastructure for Collaborative Enterprises (WETICE), pp. 217–222 (2018). https://doi.org/10.1109/WETICE.2018.00049

28. Zhang, M., Li, X.: Drone-enabled internet-of-things relay for environmental monitoring in remote areas without public networks. IEEE Internet Things J. **7**(8), 7648–7662 (2020). https://doi.org/10.1109/JIOT.2020.2988249

29. Zhu, C., Butler, M., Cirstea, C., Hoang, T.S.: A fairness-based refinement strategy to transform liveness properties in Event-B models. Sci. Comput. Program. **225**, 102907 (2023). https://doi.org/10.1016/j.scico.2022.102907

Artificial Intelligence and Machine Learning Technologies for IoT

Graph-Based Classification of IoT Malware Families Enhanced by Fuzzy Hashing

Nastaran Mahmoudyar$^{(\boxtimes)}$, Ali A. Ghorbani, and Arash Habibi Lashkari

University of New Brunswick, Fredericton, NB, Canada
{n.mahyar,ghorbani,a.habibi.l}@unb.ca

Abstract. The proliferation of Internet of Things (IoT) devices has led to an increase in IoT malware, posing a significant cybersecurity threat. Detecting and mitigating this threat is challenging due to the diverse CPU architectures in IoT malware families and the limited resources of IoT devices. Specialized detection methods are needed to identify malware across different platforms, while lightweight mechanisms are required to minimize resource strain. This paper introduces a novel graph-based framework, Aggregated Weighted Graph of Hashes (AWGH), to tackle the CPU diversity challenge. The framework leverages Function Call Graphs (FCGs) and fuzzy hashing to capture the structural and code characteristics of IoT malware. By utilizing static analysis techniques, the framework can efficiently group new malware samples and identify similarities with existing families, even in the case of unknown malware to mitigate potential risks before they cause significant damage. FCGs are generated using IDA Pro [1], and fuzzy hashes are calculated using *ssdeep* [2]. The framework is implemented in Python and evaluated using a dataset from VirusTotal [3] through 10-fold cross-validation. The experimental results demonstrate the effectiveness of the proposed framework in accurately classifying the IoT malware into IoT malware families across various CPU architectures (MIPS, ARM, i386, PowerPC, and AMD64).

Keywords: IoT Malware Family · Function Call Graph · Fuzzy Hashing · Graph-based Malware Classification

1 Introduction

The Internet of Things (IoT) is a network of connected devices that communicate through standard methods such as RFID, Zigbee, WiFi, Bluetooth, and 3G/4G/5G, including sensors, software, and actuators with various CPU architectures. IoT devices are particularly vulnerable to malware attacks due to inadequate security mechanisms and their persistent internet connectivity. Malware poses a severe threat, as it can compromise and control devices without the

© IFIP International Federation for Information Processing 2025
Published by Springer Nature Switzerland AG 2025
G. Rey et al. (Eds.): IFIPIoT 2024, IFIP AICT 737, pp. 131–148, 2025.
https://doi.org/10.1007/978-3-031-81900-1_8

owner's awareness or consent. The growth of IoT devices has led to a rise in malware targeting these systems, making IoT malware a significant cybersecurity threat that requires efficient detection mechanisms to overcome several obstacles. Firstly, the diverse CPU architectures, including MIPS, i386, ARM, and Motorola, supported by IoT malware families, demand tailored detection methods capable of identifying malware across different platforms. Additionally, the limited resources of IoT devices necessitate the development of efficient and resource-friendly detection mechanisms to avoid excessive strain on these devices. Traditional techniques used for analyzing Windows or Android malware are not practical when applied to IoT malware due to the unique behavioural, structural, and contextual characteristics that require a different approach.

In this research, we conducted a comprehensive review of existing approaches in IoT malware detection based on the features and methodologies. We identified a research gap concerning the underutilization of graph-based methods, which have the capacity to capture the distinctive attributes of IoT malware. To address the aforementioned limitations, we present a method that combines graph-based similarities and fuzzy hashing by comparing hash values of functions in low-level of assembly code. This approach is designed to capture the structural patterns of IoT malware, distinguishing similarities and differences among malware codes from various families across different CPU architectures. This enables us to determine the percentage of similarity between an unknown malware and a well-known family, facilitating a deeper understanding of the tactics used by threat actors. Consequently, this allows for the implementation of effective countermeasures, examination of Indications of Compromise (IoCs), and recommendations for remediation.

The study offers several contributions, including the development of an Aggregated Weighted Graph of Hashes (AWGH) to identify similarities and differences between IoT malware families, and an automated system that uses Function Call Graphs (FCGs) and fuzzy hashing to classify IoT malware families with vary CPU architecture. The research also provides a comprehensive review of previous studies on various IoT malware analysis and detection techniques, which offers valuable insights for future research opportunities.

2   Literature Review

This section provides an overview of non-graph-based and graph-based approaches for IoT malware detection. Non-graph-based methods include network-based, honeypot-based, statistical-based, string-based, sensor-based, energy patterns, and runtime-based techniques. Graph-based studies are divided into two categories: analysis and detection.

2.1   Non-graph-Based Related Work

Network-Based Approaches. Network-based approaches in IoT malware detection involve analyzing network traffic at the flow-level granularity to identify abnormal patterns. This analysis can include features like lightweight statistics and protocol-agnostic characteristics found in all types of packets. Machine learning and deep learning algorithms can also be employed to identify patterns and anomalies in network traffic that indicate the presence of IoT malware. In [4], Gopal et al. analyzed Mirai malware and provided a whitelist to prevent IoT botnets from expanding by scanning all router applications to capture their hashes and store them in a database. If a hash does not match, the application is blocked. Similarly, [5] discussed Mirai and other similar worms in a comprehensive review of the IoT botnet domain. In another study [6], the authors designed a network-based algorithm to detect IoT Mirai bots in large-scale networks. They provided emulated infected IoT devices by Mirai in their testbed. The authors of [6] examined Mirai malware characteristics. They explored the network connections by using testbed measurements and simulations to find the correlation between bot detection delays and sampling frequencies of device packets. Tanaka et al. (2017) have modelled two IoT malware, Hajime and Mirai, that infect IoT devices in their research [7]. They also demonstrated the impact of topology on the rate of infection by Mirai by using two different network topologies. Chang et al. (2017) [8] developed an IoT sandbox to analyze malware behaviour. The sandbox supports nine different CPU architectures and includes several modules, such as an IoT Sandbox Controller, a sniffer module, an IDS module, an IoT emulator based on Qemu, and a Samba server. The IoT emulator runs the malware using the Strace command to trace system calls and record the malware's behaviour by monitoring which files the malware modifies, reads, or writes. Sivanathan et al. (2016) proposed a method to detect threats in smart home networks by monitoring network traffic at flow-level granularity. In [9], they recommended using lightweight and protocol agnostic features to reduce the cost of investigating packets at a deep level and designed the algorithm to be low memory implementation to optimize memory usage. Doshi et al. (2018) in [10] aimed to detect DoS attacks in smart home LAN by machine learning algorithms on IoT's network traffic. They collected traffic and grouped packets by device and time, sorted them based on source IP addresses, and divided them into non-overlapping time windows. They extracted both stateless features like packet size and protocol and stateful features like bandwidth and the number of unique destination IP addresses within a 10-second window. In [11], Ozawa et al. (2020) developed a darknet analysis method using association rule learning. They used TCP SYN packets collected from July 1, 2016, to July 31, 2018, with the NICT/16 darknet sensor to create transaction sets with all TCP/IP header data. Scanning all hosts showed a known feature of Mirai malware, which is the equality of the sequence number and destination IP. In [12], the authors investigated the potential of neural networks to detect and classify malware using an IoT network dataset comprising 461,043 records, of which 300,000 are benign and 161,043 are malicious with a malware detection accuracy of 94.17% and a classification accuracy of 97.08%.

Honeypot-Based Approaches. Honeypot approaches are often used to classify IoT malware families by setting up a simulated system that appears vulnerable to attracting potential attackers. In this method, researchers extract features that primarily focus on network-based characteristics and patterns exhibited by IoT malware. For example, in a study by Wang et al. (2020) [13], the researchers deployed multiple honeypots to collect IoT malware samples and analyzed the network traffic to classify the malware. They identified four main IoT malware families: Mirai, Gafgyt, Tsunami, and Bashlite, based on their unique behaviour in the honeypots. Similarly, Luo *et al.* (2017) proposed a high-interaction honeypot approach called IoTCandyJar to detect and capture IoT malware and its activities in [14]. They used a Raspberry Pi device to emulate a vulnerable IoT device, and the honeypot software was installed on it, which could interact with the attacker's commands. The high-interaction honeypot approach can provide a more realistic environment for attackers to engage with. The captured data can be analyzed to understand attack techniques and develop countermeasures. However, there are limitations including the various types of IoT devices and the lack of emulators for IoT devices. Another study [15] utilized the "Cowrie SSH/Telnet Honeypot" [16], an open-source honeypot, to capture specific information about malicious traffic behaviour in IoT devices and detect devices infected with the Mirai botnet. In a different study [17], the authors introduced a malware detection system based on images, which utilizes a software-defined networking (SDN) honeypot and Convolutional Neural Network (CNN). The authors in [17] converted binary samples into gray-scale images and extracts string-based features using deep CNN. Additionally, they utilized a two-level auto-encoder to reduce the dimensions of extracted features.

Statistical-Based and String-Based Approaches. These approaches leverage techniques such as n-grams of opcodes features, API calls, gray-scale image features, headers features, and byte sequences. Alhanahnah *et al.* (2018) in [18] developed a system to cluster IoT malware families and differentiate between malicious and benign samples using statistical and string features. The study was conducted on two datasets obtained from the IoTPOT, with 1150 and 4000 samples respectively, each labelled with a time and an MD5 name. They utilized Jaccard similarity on statistical features and the reverse of the Euclidean distance on string features to determine the inter-cluster similarity score. Clusters with an overall similarity score higher than a certain threshold could be merged. The proposed system consists of an offline section to generate IoT malware signatures and an online section for classification. Su *et al.* used CNN technique in [19] for classifying Distributed Denial-of-Service (DDoS) malware in IoT, where the samples are converted into images and features are extracted. The one-channel gray-scale image is used to represent the binary, and the approach achieves 94% accuracy for classifying malicious and benign IoT samples. The IoTPOT dataset is used, consisting of 500 malware samples, and the classification can group malware samples into two families (Gafgyt and Mirai) with an 81.8% accuracy rate. They suggested adding static features such as opcode sequences and API calls to enhance the results. Following that, in [20], a dataset of 9342 IoT malware samples was collected for further analysis. The authors converted the malware samples into gray-scale images and extracted features for performing malware family classification. In another study, [21] measured the similarity between IoT malware samples by using sequences of opcodes for each function as a feature. They analyzed 8,713 IoT malware samples from the IoTPOT [22] and found that only 1.76% of the samples were packed, indicating that the majority of IoT malware samples are not packed. Indeed, static analysis can be sufficient and efficient when it comes to examining IoT malware [21]. Azmoodeh *et al.* (2018) [23] collected a dataset consisting of 1078 benign samples and 128 IoT malware samples for their research. Their approach is based on deep learning and uses n-grams of opcodes as features to detect IoT malware. Their future research goal is to apply their method to a real-world IoT environment with diverse data. The proposed technique in [24] by Pitolli *et al.* is centred around an online clustering algorithm known as BIRCH for malware classification. The authors gathered 5,351 Windows malware samples from VirusTotal [3] and utilized an unlabeled malware dataset to create analysis reports using the Cuckoo Sandbox. The analysis reports consist of statistical features such as header fields and strings, along with dynamic features like file system access and system calls. The paper [25] proposed a multi-dimensional classification approach that utilizes Deep Learning (DL) architectures to classify IoT malware samples based on features extracted from string and image-based representations of executable binaries over 70,000 IoT malware samples. In [26], Chaganti *et al.* (2022) proposed a Deep Learning (DL) model called Bidirectional-Gated Recurrent Unit-CNN to classify IoT malware families using byte sequences from the Executable and Linkable Format (ELF) binary files as input features. The paper [27] presented a string-based technique to distinguish between malware families across diverse architectures, utilizing an intermediate representation (IR) of assembly code. In this approach, Rahat *et al.* (2024) categorized binary images according to the similarity of their functions and then subjected to analysis using call graphs.

Sensor-Based Approaches. Sensor-based features in IoT malware detection refer to the utilization of data from various sensors embedded in IoT devices to identify malicious activities. These features capture the behaviour including location data, voltage changes, and proximity sensors. Sikder *et al.* (2018) examined the potential risks posed by sensor-based threats to IoT devices. These threats involve the transmission of malicious code or the initiation of commands aimed at activating malicious behaviour, specifically targeting IoT sensors. A notable example discussed is the Cyber-Physical Voice Privacy Theft (CPVT) Trojan horse, which can compromise microphones by exploiting voice assistant applications like Apple's Siri and Google Voice search [28]. Another method of sending malicious commands is by controlling the voltage of a light source, which can trigger IoT malware in some devices to get activated or change the magnetic field. Hasan *et al.* (2013) demonstrated in [29] that changing the light intensity of the TV screen or laptop monitor can trigger a message to compromise an IoT device. Their results show that audio sensors can transfer an embedded message in an audio song to compromise a smartphone. In [26], Chaganti *et al.* (2022) proposed a Deep Learning (DL) model called Bidirectional-Gated Recurrent Unit-CNN to classify IoT malware families using byte sequences from the Executable and Linkable Format (ELF) binary files as input features.

Energy-Based and Runtime-Based Approaches. The focus of machine learning approaches in the domain of IoT malware detection is mainly on extracting features from opcodes [30] and patterns of energy consumption [23]. Santos *et al.* (2010) presented a malware family classification approach based on the frequency of opcodes. Runwal (2012) presents a similarity graph for detecting metamorphic malware based on the application's opcodes. Azmoodeh *et al.* (2018) propose a machine learning-based technique that monitors the energy usage patterns of all existing processes to distinguish between ransomware and benign software in Android devices in IoT networks [31]. Additionally, Pektas *et al.* (2017) presented a malware classification method that monitors behaviour-based features during execution, including file system, network, registry activities, and API-call sequences. Additionally, HaddadPajouh and colleagues [32] created a dataset containing 280 IoT malware and 271 benign samples proposing a IoT malware classification system based on deep Recurrent Neural Networks (RNN) with opcodes sequences and patterns of energy consumption as features.

2.2   Graph-Based Related Work

Graph-based approaches offer advantages in IoT malware analysis by capturing the interconnections and dependencies among system components. Extracting graph-based features from the graphs of the binaries can provide valuable insights, including metrics such as the number of nodes and edges, average shortest path, betweenness, closeness, and density.

IoT Malware Graph-Based Analysis Approaches. In [33], the authors conducted an analysis of Android and IoT malware samples using a graph-based method to identify similarities and differences. They utilized the IoTPOT dataset [34], which consists of 2874 IoT malware and 201 Android malware. The authors extracted Control Flow Graphs (CFGs) for both groups of malware and analyze them based on graph-based features, such as the number of nodes and edges, average shortest path, betweenness, closeness, and density. They propose using machine learning techniques with graph-based features from CFGs to classify malware samples in future work. Alasmary *et al.* (2018) presented that Android malware exhibits a higher number of nodes compared to IoT malware, as well as other distinguishing features that can be used for classification purposes. In another study, [35], Alasmary *et al.* (2019) employed the CyberIOC dataset [36], which contains 2891 Android malware and 2962 IoT malware. The authors extracted graph-based features from the generated CFGs. Alasmary *et al.* (2019) identified that Android malware samples have higher density, closeness, betweenness, and the number of nodes than IoT malware samples. However, IoT malware samples exhibit a higher number of edges and complexity than Android malware. Additionally, in [37], the authors used the IoTPOT dataset [34] which includes

2347 IoT malware samples, 261 benign IoT software, and 2891 Android malware samples. They applied various machine learning techniques, such as Logistic Regression (LR), Support Vector Machines (SVM), Random Forest (RF), and CNN, on the dataset to classify IoT malware and benign software. In [38], Nguyen *et al.* (2019) utilized Printable String Information (PSI) features. PSIs refer to a type of data representation that is primarily composed of printable characters. Authors focused on specific and small parts of FCGs rather than generating features from the complete graphs. So, the analysis is performed on smaller PSI graphs instead of the larger CFGs. The authors use this approach to analyze 7199 IoT botnets and 4001 benign software from IoTPOT [22]. Furthermore, in [39], Nguyen *et al.* (2020) propose an IoT botnet detection system that supports both ARM and MIPS architectures. They apply five machine learning algorithms, including SVM, RF, Decision Tree (DT), and k-Nearest Neighbours (kNN), on approximately 10k samples, consisting of 6165 IoT botnet samples and 3845 benign IoT samples. Recent studies have demonstrated the effectiveness of using graph-based techniques in IoT malware analysis. Control flow graphs (CFGs) have been utilized to extract graph-based features, such as the number of nodes, edges, average shortest path, betweenness, closeness, and density, for malware samples. Moreover, PSI features extracted from PSI-graphs have been employed in the classification of IoT botnet samples and benign software using machine learning algorithms.

IoT Malware Graph-Based Detection Approaches. In [40], graph-based access control is created, which can be run as a module on IoT nodes or in the network. Pahl *et al.* (2018) used a group of graph-based features like node counts, edge counts, density, degree centrality, betweenness centrality, closeness, diameter, and distribution of the shortest path. Additionally, in [41], authors used CNN classifier to detect IoT botnet based on the features from the PSI-graph. Abusnaina *et al.* (2019) work on 2281 IoT malware samples from the CyberIOC dataset. [36]. The PSI graph is simple compared to CFGs generated based on the printable string information in the malicious software's binary code. So, instead of analyzing the whole graph, Abusnaina *et al.* (2019) worked on the specific parts of the graphs that include useful information. Likewise, Nguyen *et al.* (2018) [42] proposed an approach based on PSI-graphs to collect information for static analysis. This proposed system used a graph convolution neural network classifier for the detection of IoT malware. Nguyen *et al.* (2018) used 4002 IoT malware samples from the IoTPOT dataset [22] in this research. Their system works based on generating PSI-graph to consider the linkages between PSI. The authors in [43] used the opcodes sequence to propose a detection system for IoT malware. Darabian *et al.* (2020) applied some ML techniques including k-Nearest Neighbors (KNN), SVM, random forest, decision tree, and AdaBoost on a dataset (247 IoT malware and 269 Benign samples) from [32]. Maximal Frequent Patterns (MFP) of opcodes can distinguish between IoT malware and benign samples effectively. So, Darabian *et al.* (2020) used the most frequent opcode sequences that have been detected by sequential pattern mining techniques to classify the IoT malware, benign IoT software, and polymorphic malware. [44] combined ML and deep learning to generate novel features based on PSI-rooted and sub-graph features for cross-architecture IoT botnet malware detection in a completely static way. We found an opportunity in the literature to use graph-based models for grouping IoT malware. This approach categorizes malware based on graph similarity and represents the structural interconnections within each family using family graphs. It highlights the functional attribute of binaries without execution and doesn't rely on feature extraction for machine learning algorithms. Instead, it directly utilizes graph-based models.

3   Proposed Framework

Previous studies on IoT malware analysis has mainly focused on extracting different types of features such as network activities, opcodes, and even graphs, which are then utilized with machine learning or neural network methods. These studies have primarily aimed to distinguish IoT malicious software either from benign binaries or to differentiate it from Android and Linux-based binaries. Limited research has specifically introduced methods focusing solely on IoT malware classification. For example, Su *et al.* (2018) [19] utilized CNN to classify DDoS malware in IoT by converting samples into images and extracting features. Similarly in [45], Wu u *et al.* (2023) employed FCGs and extracted opcode features to apply machine learning for classification. Although in a recent study, [27], the authors leveraged using call graphs to distinguish between malware families, the initial step involved categorizing binary images based on the similarity of their functions. In fact, this is also a string-based technique to classify malware families. Nevertheless, an IoT malware family classification relies on the similarity of the family structure, which pertains to the similarity of functions at the assembly level and the structural similarity of the family, which illustrates the connections among those functions across different CPU architectures is currently lacking.

In Function Call Graphs (FCGs), each node corresponds to a function, and edges represent calls to other functions. Consequently, FCGs provide valuable insights by reflecting the code structure and relationships between functions in the code, enabling a deeper understanding of malware operations. FCGs can be utilized as an efficient method for analysis of a large number of malware binaries since graphs can be automatically generated and can overcome code obfuscation techniques commonly used in the malware structures. Integrating FCGs with fuzzy hashing techniques further enhances malware detection. Fuzzy hashing identifies similarities between codes, even when they are obfuscated or modified. It generates unique hash values based on the assembly codes that exhibit a significant level of shared code use in comparisons with other samples. Fuzzy hashing is faster and more efficient than traditional signature-based methods since it only requires comparing hash values rather than analyzing the entire code. This approach is particularly effective in detecting unknown variants of malware and zero-day malware empowered with unpatched vulnerabilities which can spread widely without proper defense. Various studies demonstrate the effectiveness of fuzzy hashing in identifying similarities and grouping malware samples. For example, in [46], fuzzy hashing was employed as a customized distance function for clustering PC malware samples. Another study [47] utilized fuzzy hashing to create the hash graph of APIs using the tool *ssdeep* for classifying Android malware families. Figure 1 outlines the general proposed framework. The proposed framework consists of three main phases, as follows:

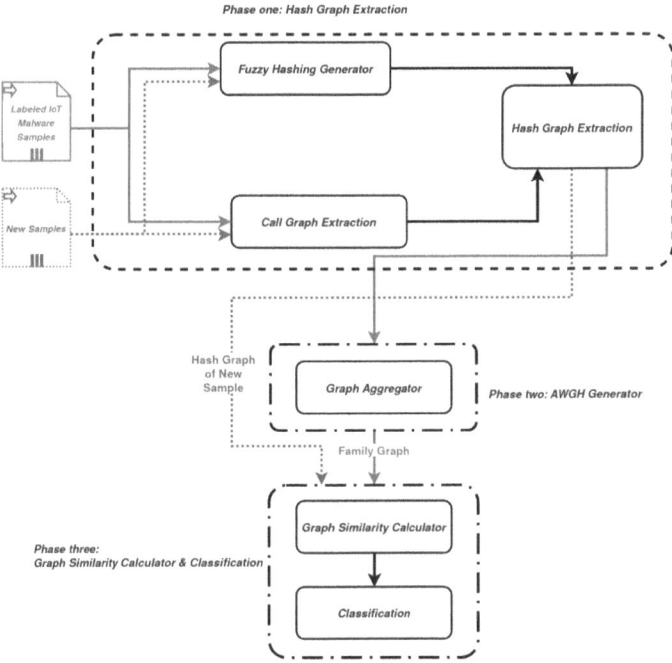

Fig. 1. Proposed System Overview

– Phase One (Hash Graph Extraction): In this phase, labeled IoT malware samples are employed as inputs to generate FCGs and fuzzy hashes of all the functions. Subsequently, the hash graph extraction component constructs a hash graph for each sample. This hash graph bears a close resemblance to the FCG, with the distinction that each node in the graph is labeled with the fuzzy hash of the corresponding function, rather than its name. To be more precise, hash graph extraction phase consists of the following components:

  1. Fuzzy Hashing Generator which takes IoT malware samples (EFL files) as inputs and extracts all their functions. It then proceeds to calculate the fuzzy hashes for the extracted functions as the output of this component. The *ssdeep* tool is employed for generating the fuzzy hashes, which are also known as Context-Triggered Piecewise Hashes (CTPH).

2. Call Graph Extraction which is tasked with generating FCGs for all IoT malware samples. To accomplish this, we utilize IDA Pro and develop Python code to automate the process of generating FCGs. **FCG of a sample** is defined as follows:

A FCG is a directed graph $G_S = (V_S, E_S)$, where $V_S = V_S(G)$ represents subroutines (functions) of a sample, and $E_S = E_S(G)$, where $E_S(G) \subseteq V_S(G) \times V_S(G)$, expresses the function calls.

3. Hash Graph Extraction utilizes the outputs of the previous steps, which are the functions' fuzzy hashes and the FCGs to generating the hash graph, which represents the relationships between functions similar to the FCGs. The hash graph consists of nodes that contain the fuzzy hashes of functions' code and edges that represent the exact call graph structure of functions within a sample. In essence, the output of this phase is the hash graphs of the inputs, where each node represents a fuzzy hash of a function and the edges reflect the function call relationships. **Hash Graph of a sample** can be defined as follows[1]:

$$G_H = (V_H, E_H),$$
$$V_H = \{(v, FZH^1(v)) | v \in V_S\},$$
$$E_H \subseteq \{(x, y) | (x, y) \in V_H \times V_H \text{ and } x \neq y\}.$$

– Phase Two (Aggregated Weighted Graph of Hashes (AWGH) Generator): In this phase, the AWGH will be generated for each IoT malware family separately based on the hash graphs of all samples in a family. AWGH or family graph is a weighted graph that is built by merging all hash graphs of samples in an IoT malware family. The Hash graph of a sample is like a FCG, in which each node keeps the function's name and the fuzzy hash of that function, unlike the typical FCGs where each node is just the function's name. An AWGH is made by merging all hash graphs of the samples in an IoT malware family and representing that malware family's structure. In AWGH, each node is a set of similar subroutines that have been merged as a super-subroutine. In other words, after generating all hash graphs for each malware's family, those hash graphs of a family will be aggregated in a weighted graph as an AWGH, which is a graph of that family. **Aggregated Weighted Graph of Hashes (AWGH) of a family** can be defined as follows:

$$G_F = (V_F, E_F),$$
$$V_F = \text{Set of SuperSubroutines},$$
$$E_F \subseteq \{(x, y) | (x, y) \in V_F \times V_F \text{ and } x \neq y\}.$$

In this step, we utilize Python and IDA Pro to implement our automated system for generating comprehensive graphs of IoT malware families. The process begins with an empty family graph, which is gradually expanded by adding the hash graphs of each sample. To incorporate a new sample into the family graph, we compare the nodes of the sample's hash graph with the existing nodes in the family graph. If a similar node is found, we merge the

---

[1] Fuzzy hash.

corresponding nodes from the sample and family graphs. If no similarity is found, the new nodes are added to the family graph. Furthermore, we update and add edges in the family graph based on the merged nodes. This ensures that the relationships between functions in the malware family are accurately represented. Through this iterative process, we incorporate all samples into the family graph, resulting in a complete AWGH that describes the structure of a specific malware family. To facilitate the aggregation of graphs and the comparison of similarities, we employ Python code that extracts function names, bodies, and other details accessible through IDA Pro. This code can be utilized as an IDA Pro plug-in for related developments or future research.

- Phase Three (Graph Similarity Calculator & Classification): The graph similarity calculator computes the similarity score between the hash graph of an incoming IoT malware sample and all AWGHs from different families. This similarity score will classify the incoming IoT malware samples into an appropriate IoT malware family. **Family Classification of a sample** is defined as follows:

For each F in Families,
$$\text{matched}_F(v) := \{v' | v' \in V_F \land Sim(v', v) > Threshold \land$$
$$\forall x \in V_F : Sim(v', v) > Sim(x, v)\}$$
$$V_{Matched(F)} = \{v | \text{matched}_F(v) \neq \varnothing\}$$
$$\text{Assigned Family} = \underset{F \in Families}{\text{argmax}} \frac{|V_{Matched(F)}|}{|V_S|}$$

In our proposed framework, we have established certain criteria for merging subroutines based on their similarity scores. Subroutines with identical names and a similarity score of 50% or higher are merged as a super-subroutine. For subroutines with different names, a minimum similarity score of 70% is required for merging. These thresholds were determined through experimentation and testing of various values.

4 Experiments

In this research, the IoT malware dataset was created by collecting all the malicious binaries from VirusTotal [3]. VirusTotal collects scan results from 75 different antivirus or antimalware systems, such as NOD32, Avast, McAfee, Kaspersky, and others to label the samples accordingly. It is important to note that there may be some disagreement in the labels assigned to the samples by VirusTotal's antivirus or antimalware resources. In such cases, the most frequent label is used for the sample. Table 1 displays the distribution of our samples based on the supporting CPU architectures.

Our proposed framework is evaluated for its effectiveness by conducting experiments on the dataset. A comparative analysis of different types of IoT

Table 1. Distribution of our malware samples based on the CPU architecture

Architecture	Total	Mirai	Gafgyt	Hajime	Tsunami	MrBlack	Dofloo	Aidra
ARM	464	234	136	4	6	31	53	0
MIPS R3000	322	148	148	3	20	2	1	0
i386	214	67	97	0	11	16	23	0
PowerPC	126	67	56	0	3	0	0	0
AMD x86-64	84	10	61	0	7	2	1	3

malware is provided based on the CPU architectures. Two types of experiments are conducted on the dataset. In the first experiment, only samples from the malware families Mirai and Gafgyt are used for each architecture. Then, 10-fold cross-validation is performed to test the proposed method's functionality between these two popular IoT malware families. In the second experiment, other families like Hajime, MrBlack, etc. are also used for testing purposes. Here, a minimum threshold of 70% for similarity is specified, and a test sample is considered a family member if their similarity is more than the threshold. However, the results of the first experiment are much better than the second one for some reasons. Firstly, the inaccuracy of VirusTotal's labels makes some samples labelled as "others" which might actually belong to families like Mirai or Gafgyt. Secondly, some malware families have similar structures to each other, such as the Hajime and Gafgyt malware families. Moreover, setting the threshold may cause the system to miss some samples with lower similarities. Table 2 below illustrates the evaluation metrics and the effectiveness of our proposed framework.

Table 2. Results of both experiments for different CPU architecture

Arch.	Expe.	Mirai			Gafgyt		
		Pre.	Rec.	F-1	Pre.	Rec.	F-1
MIPS	First	97.60%	99.18%	98.38%	99.23%	97.74%	98.48%
	Second	76.92%	81.30%	79.05%	71.75%	95.48%	81.93%
ARM	First	98.12%	100%	99.058%	100%	96.52%	98.20%
	Second	82.98%	77.03%	79.90%	91.59%	94.78%	93.16%
i386	First	97.5%	100%	98.73%	100%	98.79%	99.39%
	Second	100%	100%	100%	62.59%	98.79%	76.63%
PowerPC	First	94.73%	100%	97.29%	100%	93.87%	96.84%
	Second	94.54%	96.29%	95.41%	83.01%	89.79%	86.27%
x86-64	First	N/A	N/A	N/A	83.87%	98.11%	90.43%
	Second	N/A	N/A	N/A	N/A	N/A	N/A

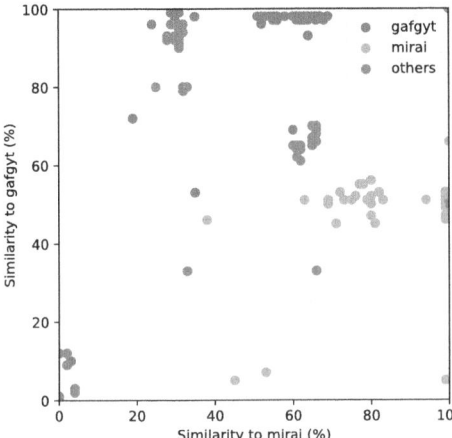

Fig. 2. Classification on MIPS samples

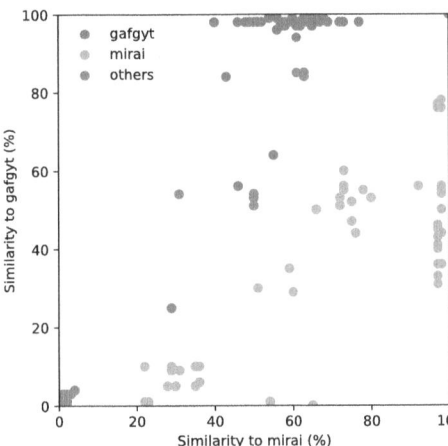

Fig. 3. Classification on ARM samples

Although there were no similar methods available for comparison, we discussed a related graph-based study in the literature review section that extracted features from FCGs. In that research, [45], with a dataset of 108,616 malware samples across seven CPU architectures, the evaluated classifiers achieved an accuracy of 98.88% rates for malware family classification with 5-fold stratified cross-validation. In contrast, our approach involved creating family graphs and comparing each FCG with the family graphs to determine the respective families. Our dataset comprised 1,212 IoT malware binaries with five distinct CPU architectures and we used 10-fold cross-validation. Mirai and Gafgyt are two of the most well-known and important families of IoT malware. Our proposed method can assist in identifying the malware family category, particularly for

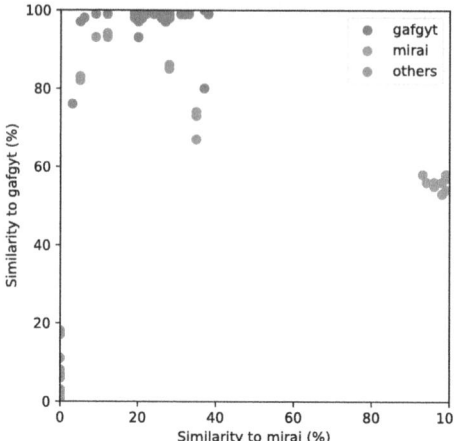

Fig. 4. Classification on i386 samples

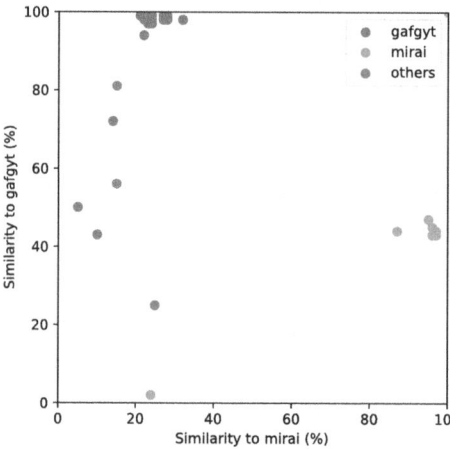

Fig. 5. Classification on PowerPC samples

Mirai and Gafgyt families that have caused some of the most significant and damaging IoT-based attacks in recent years. To assess the effectiveness of our proposed framework, we utilized precision, recall, and F1 score as evaluation metrics. While precision measures the classifier's ability to accurately identify positive instances, recall indicates how well it can locate all positive instances. F1 score, on the other hand, is a useful metric when there is an imbalanced class distribution or when both precision and recall are important. These metrics are more informative than accuracy alone that have been reported in [45].

In the AMD (x86–64) architecture group, there are only enough samples from one family (Gafgyt) to use for training the system. Therefore, we utilize samples from other families (such as Mirai, Hajime, and MrBlack) solely for testing purposes and carry out the experiment using 10-fold cross-validation. Additionally, we display the similarity of each test sample to each of the trained families for all CPU architecture groups of samples. Since there are only two families in this architecture group (Mirai and Gafgyt), we exhibit it as a two-dimensional (2D) plot, where the similarity score with the Mirai family is represented along the *x-axis* and the similarity score with the Gafgyt family is shown along the *y-axis*. Figure 2 illustrates that many of the Mirai samples (depicted as orange dots) are situated very close to the right side of the diagram for the MIPS category. On the other hand, numerous Gafgyt samples are located at the top of the diagram, indicating a high similarity score with the Gafgyt family.

Similarly, Fig. 3 demonstrates the same approach for the ARM category samples. Additionally, i386 samples similarity scores with Mirai and Gafgyt families are shown in Fig. 4 and Fig. 5 shows the similarity of the samples to the Mirai or Gafgyt families in PowerPC sample group.

5   Conclusion and Future Work

In conclusion, our research focused on addressing the lack of studies on IoT malware families and proposing an automated framework for classifying malware families. Previous studies primarily concentrated on detecting malicious software and differentiating between Android or IoT samples, rather than identifying distinct malware families based on their structure. To bridge this gap, we developed a novel framework that combines fuzzy hashing and FCGs to effectively identify IoT malware families. By generating FCGs and employing fuzzy hashing, we constructed family graphs representing the structure of each IoT malware family. The Aggregated Weighted Graph of Hashes (AWGH) was introduced to represent the structure of each family, enabling comparison with individual IoT malware graphs to find the best match.

The evaluation of our proposed framework involved conducting 10-fold cross-validation on a dataset and analyzing various types of IoT malware with different CPU architectures. The results demonstrated the effectiveness of our classification system in distinguishing between IoT malware families.

As part of our future work, we propose three avenues for further investigation and improvement in the field of IoT malware detection and classification. Firstly, we suggest combining graph-based features that describe individual aspects of binaries with our family graph representation. Secondly, we recommend training a comprehensive classification system by conducting experiments with a more diverse set of IoT malware samples encompassing various CPU architectures.

Thirdly, a limitation of our work is its sensitivity to parameter settings. In our study, we established similarity thresholds by experimenting with various values. However, more rigorous parameter tuning is needed to identify the optimal values for these thresholds. Addressing this issue will be an important focus for future research to enhance the precision and effectiveness of our framework.

References

1. SA, H.-R.: Ida pro. https://www.hex-rays.com. Accessed Nov 2020
2. ssdeep project. https://github.com/ssdeep-project/ssdeep. Accessed Nov 2020
3. Virustotal-free online virus, malware and URL scanner. https://www.virustotal.com. Accessed Nov 2020
4. Gopal, T. S., Meerolla, M., Jyostna, G., Eswari, P.R.L., Magesh, E.: Mitigating mirai malware spreading in IoT environment. In: 2018 International Conference on Advances in Computing, Communications and Informatics (ICACCI), pp. 2226–2230. IEEE (2018)
5. Kambourakis, G., Kolias, C., Stavrou, A.: The mirai botnet and the IoT zombie armies. In: MILCOM 2017-2017 IEEE Military Communications Conference (MILCOM), pp. 267–272. IEEE (2017)
6. Kumar, A., Lim, T.J.: Early detection of Mirai-like IoT bots in large-scale networks through sub-sampled packet traffic analysis. In: Arai, K., Bhatia, R. (eds.) FICC 2019. LNNS, vol. 70, pp. 847–867. Springer, Cham (2020). https://doi.org/10.1007/978-3-030-12385-7_58
7. Tanaka, H., Yamaguchi, S.: On modeling and simulation of the behavior of IoT malwares Mirai and Hajime. In: 2017 IEEE International Symposium on Consumer Electronics (ISCE), pp. 56–60. IEEE (2017)
8. Chang, K.-C., Tso, R., Tsai, M.-C.: IoT sandbox: to analysis IoT malware Zollard. In: Proceedings of the Second International Conference on Internet of things, Data and Cloud Computing, p. 4. ACM (2017)
9. Sivanathan, A., Sherratt, D., Gharakheili, H.H., Sivaraman, V., Vishwanath, A.: Low-cost flow-based security solutions for smart-home IoT devices. In: 2016 IEEE International Conference on Advanced Networks and Telecommunications Systems (ANTS), pp. 1–6. IEEE (2016)
10. Doshi, R., Apthorpe, N., Feamster, N.: Machine learning DDOS detection for consumer internet of things devices. In: 2018 IEEE Security and Privacy Workshops (SPW), pp. 29–35. IEEE (2018)
11. Ozawa, S., Ban, T., Hashimoto, N., Nakazato, J., Shimamura, J.: A study of IoT malware activities using association rule learning for darknet sensor data. Int. J. Inf. Secur. **19**(1), 83–92 (2020)
12. Jamal, A., Hayat, M.F., Nasir, M.: Malware detection and classification in IoT network using ANN. Mehran Univ. Res. J. Eng. Technol. **41**(1), 80–91 (2022)
13. Wang, B., Dou, Y., Sang, Y., Zhang, Y., Huang, J.: IoTCMAL: towards a hybrid IoT honeypot for capturing and analyzing malware. In: ICC 2020 - 2020 IEEE International Conference on Communications (ICC), pp. 1–7 (2020)
14. Luo, T., Xu, Z., Jin, X., Jia, Y., Ouyang, X.: IoTcandyJar: towards an intelligent-interaction honeypot for IoT devices. Black Hat (2017)
15. Feng, X., Li, Q., Wang, H., Sun, L.: Acquisitional rule-based engine for discovering internet-of-things devices. In: 27th {USENIX} Security Symposium ({USENIX} Security 18), pp. 327–341 (2018)
16. Oosterhof, M.: Cowrie SSH/Telnet honeypot (2016)
17. Kumar, S., Kumar, A.: Image-based malware detection based on convolution neural network with autoencoder in industrial internet of things using software defined networking honeypot. Eng. Appl. Artif. Intell. **133**, 108374 (2024)
18. Alhanahnah, M., Lin, Q., Yan, Q., Zhang, N., Chen, Z.: Efficient signature generation for classifying cross-architecture IoT malware. In: 2018 IEEE Conference on Communications and Network Security (CNS), pp. 1–9. IEEE (2018)

19. Su, J., Vasconcellos, V.D., Prasad, S., Daniele, S., Feng, Y., Sakurai, K.: Lightweight classification of IoT malware based on image recognition. In: 2018 IEEE 42nd Annual Computer Software and Applications Conference (COMPSAC), vol. 2, pp. 664–669. IEEE (2018)
20. Naeem, H., Guo, B., Naeem, M.R.: A light-weight malware static visual analysis for IoT infrastructure. In: 2018 International Conference on Artificial Intelligence and Big Data (ICAIBD), pp. 240–244. IEEE (2018)
21. Isawa, R., Ban, T., Tie, Y., Yoshioka, K., Inoue, D.: Evaluating disassembly-code based similarity between IoT malware samples. In: 2018 13th Asia Joint Conference on Information Security (AsiaJCIS), pp. 89–94. IEEE (2018)
22. Pa, Y.M.P., Suzuki, S., Yoshioka, K., Matsumoto, T., Kasama, T., Rossow, C.: IoTpot: analysing the rise of IoT compromises. In: 9th {USENIX} Workshop on Offensive Technologies ({WOOT} 15) (2015)
23. Azmoodeh, A., Dehghantanha, A., Choo, K.-K.R.: Robust malware detection for internet of (battlefield) things devices using deep eigenspace learning. IEEE Trans. Sustain. Comput. (2018)
24. Pitolli, G., Laurenza, G., Aniello, L., Querzoni, L., Baldoni, R.: Malfamaware: automatic family identification and malware classification through online clustering. Int. J. Inf. Secur. 1–16 (2020)
25. Dib, M., Torabi, S., Bou-Harb, E., Assi, C.: A multi-dimensional deep learning framework for IoT malware classification and family attribution. IEEE Trans. Netw. Serv. Manag. **18**(2), 1165–1177 (2021)
26. Chaganti, R., Ravi, V., Pham, T.D.: Deep learning based cross architecture internet of things malware detection and classification. Comput. Secur. **120**, 102779 (2022)
27. Rahat, M.A., Banerjee, V., Bloom, G., Zhuang, Y.: Cimalir: cross-platform IoT malware clustering using intermediate representation. In: 2024 IEEE 14th Annual Computing and Communication Workshop and Conference (CCWC), pp. 0460–0466 (2024)
28. Sikder, A.K., Petracca, G., Aksu, H., Jaeger, T., Uluagac, A.S.: A survey on sensor-based threats to internet-of-things (IoT) devices and applications. arXiv preprint arXiv:1802.02041 (2018)
29. Hasan, R., Saxena, N., Haleviz, T., Zawoad, S., Rinehart, D.: Sensing-enabled channels for hard-to-detect command and control of mobile devices. In: Proceedings of the 8th ACM SIGSAC Symposium on Information, Computer and Communications Security, pp. 469–480. ACM (2013)
30. Azmoodeh, A., Dehghantanha, A., Conti, M., Choo, K.-K.R.: Detecting crypto-ransomware in IoT networks based on energy consumption footprint. J. Ambient Intell. Human. Comput. 1–12 (2017)
31. Caviglione, L., Gaggero, M., Lalande, J.-F., Mazurczyk, W., Urbański, M.: Seeing the unseen: revealing mobile malware hidden communications via energy consumption and artificial intelligence. IEEE Trans. Inf. Forensics Secur. **11**(4), 799–810 (2015)
32. HaddadPajouh, H., Dehghantanha, A., Khayami, R., Choo, K.-K.R.: A deep recurrent neural network based approach for internet of things malware threat hunting. Futur. Gener. Comput. Syst. **85**, 88–96 (2018)
33. Alasmary, H., Anwar, A., Park, J., Choi, J., Nyang, D., Mohaisen, A.: Graph-based comparison of IoT and android malware. In: Chen, X., Sen, A., Li, W.W., Thai, M.T. (eds.) CSoNet 2018. LNCS, vol. 11280, pp. 259–272. Springer, Cham (2018). https://doi.org/10.1007/978-3-030-04648-4_22

34. Pa, Y.M.P., Suzuki, S., Yoshioka, K., Matsumoto, T., Kasama, T., Rossow, C.: IoTpot: analysing the rise of IoT compromises. In: 9th USENIX Workshop on Offensive Technologies (WOOT 15), (Washington, D.C.), USENIX Association (2015)

35. Alasmary, H., et al.: Analyzing and detecting emerging internet of things malware: a graph-based approach. IEEE Internet Things J. **6**(5), 8977–8988 (2019)

36. Public cyberiocs repository. https://freeiocs.cyberiocs.pro/. Accessed Nov 2020

37. Alasmary, H., et al.: Poster: analyzing, comparing, and detecting emerging malware: a graph-based approach (2019)

38. Nguyen, H.-T., Ngo, Q.-D., Le, V.-H.: A novel graph-based approach for IoT botnet detection. Int. J. Inf. Secur. 1–11 (2019)

39. Nguyen, H.-T., Ngo, Q.-D., Nguyen, D.-H., Le, V.-H.: Psi-rooted subgraph: A novel feature for IoT botnet detection using classifier algorithms. ICT Express (2020)

40. Pahl, M.-O., Aubet, F.-X., Liebald, S.: Graph-based IoT microservice security. NOMS 2018-2018 IEEE/IFIP Network Operations and Management Symposium, pp. 1–3. IEEE (2018)

41. Abusnaina, A, et al.: Breaking graph-based IoT malware detection systems using adversarial examples: poster. In: Proceedings of the 12th Conference on Security and Privacy in Wireless and Mobile Networks, pp. 290–291 (2019)

42. Nguyen, H.-T., Ngo, Q.-D., Le, V.-H.: IoT botnet detection approach based on psi graph and DGCNN classifier. In: 2018 IEEE International Conference on Information Communication and Signal Processing (ICICSP), pp. 118–122. IEEE (2018)

43. Darabian, H., Dehghantanha, A., Hashemi, S., Homayoun, S., Choo, K.-K.R.: An opcode-based technique for polymorphic internet of things malware detection. Concurr. Comput. Pract. Exp. **32**(6), e5173 (2020)

44. Nguyen, H.-T., Nguyen, D.-H., Ngo, Q.-D., Tran, V.-H., Le, V.-H.: Towards a rooted subgraph classifier for IoT botnet detection. In: Proceedings of the 2019 7th International Conference on Computer and Communications Management, pp. 247–251 (2019)

45. Wu, C.-Y., Ban, T., Cheng, S.-M., Takahashi, T., Inoue, D.: IoT malware classification based on reinterpreted function-call graphs. Comput. Secur. **125**, 103060 (2023)

46. Li, Y., Sundaramurthy, S.C., Bardas, A.G., Ou, X., Caragea, D., Hu, X., Jang, J.: Experimental study of fuzzy hashing in malware clustering analysis. In: 8th Workshop on Cyber Security Experimentation and Test ({CSET} 15) (2015)

47. Mirzaei, O., Suarez-Tangil, G., de Fuentes, J.M., Tapiador, J., Stringhini, G.: Andrensemble: Leveraging API ensembles to characterize android malware families. In: Proceedings of the 2019 ACM Asia Conference on Computer and Communications Security, pp. 307–314 (2019)

Error Resiliency and Adversarial Robustness in Convolutional Neural Networks: An Empirical Analysis

Mario Barbareschi[1] , Salvatore Barone[1] , Valentina Casola[1] ,
and Salvatore Della Torca[1,2]([✉])

[1] University of Naples Federico II, 80125 Naples, Italy
{mario.barbareschi,salvatore.barone,casolav,
salvatore.dellatorca}@unina.it
[2] University of Bergamo, 24044 Dalmine, Italy

Abstract. The increasing pervasiveness of Artificial Intelligence (AI), and Convolutional Neural Networks (CNNs) in edge-computing and Internet of Things applications pose several challenges, including the hunger for computational and power resources of predictive models, and their robustness w.r.t. security threats, e.g., adversarial attacks. As for the former, the approximate computing emerged as one of the most promising solutions to lower the computational effort of AI, since the output of approximate application is usually barely distinguishable from the exact one. Nevertheless, alterations to predictive models through approximation may actually jeopardize inner characteristics of CNNs, such as their adversarial robustness, that is their ability to discern legitimate inputs from systematically crafted malicious ones.

In this paper, we investigate the vulnerability of the approximate CNNs to adversarial attacks. Specifically, we target approximate CNNs while resorting to different adversarial attacks in an aversion scenario, and we empirically prove approximation may actually compromise adversarial robustness.

Keywords: Convolutional Neural Networks · Approximate Computing · Adversarial Attacks

1 Introduction

Deep learning, and Convolutional Neural Networks (CNNs) in particular, are one of the most widely used predictive models in Artificial Intelligence (AI), since the major breakthroughs they achieved in several challenges, including image-classification, object- and speech-recognition [31]. Consequently, they have gone from being primarily employed for research purposes to being deployed in a large variety of applications, including edge-computing and Internet of Things (IoT), since the need to process large volumes of information in a timely and

---

All the authors have contributed equally to this research.

© IFIP International Federation for Information Processing 2025
Published by Springer Nature Switzerland AG 2025
G. Rey et al. (Eds.): IFIPIoT 2024, IFIP AICT 737, pp. 149–160, 2025.
https://doi.org/10.1007/978-3-031-81900-1_9

reliable manner. CNNs performance, however, has come with enormous power and computational need, which is actually hindering any wider adoption.

As demonstrated in the scientific literature, machine-learning, and CNNs in particular, are the ideal field of application for the Approximate Computing (AxC) design paradigm [15,37], that trades the quality of results for performance gains [13]. Indeed, the generalization property induced by noisy and redundant training data as well as training algorithms, make CNNs fairly error resilient, which is exploited by AxC to lower CNNs computational demand [7].

Although approximation methodologies aim to introduce the least alterations to CNNs, learned parameters may be heavily modified [25,35]; hence, inner properties may be affected. For instance, Deep Neural Networks (DNNs) are well known to be vulnerable to adversarial attacks, that are inputs systematically crafted to force a misclassification; thus, it is undoubtedly legitimate to wonder whether any correlation between error induced by approximation and adversarial robustness may actually exist.

In terms of security, a number of approaches have been developed to generate more precise and robust adversarial attacks [5,20,22,38], both in white-box and black-box scenarios. Nevertheless, despite the relevance of these issues, resource requirements and adversarial attacks are rarely considered together, and the scientific literature often gives conflicting results. Guesmi et al. [17] refer to the AxC design paradigm as a defense strategy against adversarial attacks. In contrast, Siddique et al. [32] empirically demonstrated that it is still possible to transfer adversarial attacks from the original neural network to its approximate counterpart. This implies that an adversarial sample crafted to fool the original DNN also fools the approximate one. In their study, Askarizadeh et al. [6] examine the susceptibility of the Approximated Neural Network (AxNN) model to adversarial attacks. However, their analysis is limited to gradient-based adversarial algorithms. Finally, the aforementioned approaches approximate the DNNs by deploying a single approximate component throughout the network, a strategy that has been demonstrated to result in suboptimal performance. Indeed, contemporary methodologies aimed in designing AxNNs typically employ a combination of approximate multipliers [25,35].

This paper examines the vulnerability of the AxNNs to adversarial attacks. Specifically, (i) we first identify a suitable combination of approximate multipliers that strikes an optimal balance between resource requirements and the accuracy lost due to the approximation. (ii) Consequently, we design the AxNN by replacing the multipliers selected in the previous stage in both the convolutional and dense layers of the original CNN. (iii) Finally, we target the AxNN with both white-box and black-box adversarial attacks in an evasion scenario, wherein the test dataset is considered solely.

The experimental results indicate that while the AxNNs are particularly robust against white-box gradient-based adversarial attacks, they exhibit the same vulnerability to both black-box attacks and white-box attacks, such as the DeepFool (DP) and Carlini-Wagner (CW), as the original CNNs.

The remainder of this paper is organized as follows: Sect. 2 provides the reader with a technical background pertaining to the AxC design paradigm, and adversarial attacks. Section 3 discusses how we conduct our analysis, while Sect. 4 reports the results of our analysis. Finally, Sect. 5 draws the conclusion and discusses future works.

2   Technical Background

This Section provides details concerning the AxC design paradigm, and adversarial attacks, in order to fully understand our work.

2.1   Approximate Neural Networks

The AxC design-paradigm allows leveraging sources of error resiliency in applications by systematically trading off the quality of output results for performance gains or resource savings [13,37]. Indeed, approximate and exact results are hardly distinguishable for a vast plethora of applications [11], including audio, image, and video processing [3,8], logic circuits [10,11,30], safety-critical applications [16,36], and, of course, machine learning and artificial intelligence applications [2,7,9].

Specifically for DNNs, a significant amount of research focused on reducing the computational effort of training and inference, both in terms of time and hardware resource requirements. Regarding the latter, multipliers in convolutions and fully connected layers are recognized as the most demanding component in terms of overhead [4,29]. In [25], for instance, approximate multipliers are exploited in convolutional layers to decrease the energy consumption, and the error entailed by approximation is simultaneously minimized through Multi-Objective Optimization (MOO). Besides, weight-tuning procedure and bias terms are commonly exploited to compensate for the systematic error being introduced [25,35]. These, anyway, affect the learned parameters, which means the robustness of the network against additional sources of error, such as glitch or adversarial attacks, may be weakened.

2.2   Adversarial Attacks

CNNs models are susceptible to adversarial attacks, which entail the addition of imperceptible perturbations to the original input images. The objective of such attacks is to induce the CNN to misclassify the perturbed image with a high degree of confidence [34]. The generation of adversarial samples is typically accomplished through the application of Equation (1):

$$x_{adv} = x + \delta_x \tag{1}$$

The additive perturbation δ_x may lead to a different classification, between x and x_{adv}, if its norm L_∞ is greater than a threshold ϵ, that defines the precision of an input feature.

Depending on the level of knowledge an attacker has about the model being attacked, they may be classified as white or black box attacks. In white-box attacks, the attacker has full knowledge of and access to the model. This includes the model architecture, the parameters, training data, and the specific type of learning algorithm used. Thus, the perturbation needed to fool the model can be precisely calculated [23]. In black-box attacks, the attacker only has access to the model's input and output. Despite this lack of information, black-box attacks can still be effective by leveraging techniques such as transferability, which exploits the fact that adversarial examples created for one model typically mislead other models [28]. Black-box attacks reflect a more common scenario where an external attacker has limited knowledge about the model.

3   Methodology

As anticipated in Sect. 1, we leverage the AxC design paradigm to approximate CNNs in order to generate AxNNs and analyze their behavior w.r.t. adversarial attacks. Thus, we (i) first build and train CNNs; then, (ii) we select a suitable approximate configuration in order to approximate CNNs, and, finally, (iii) we target AxNN with both black-box and white-box adversarial attacks in an evasion scenario, i.e., we craft adversarial examples on samples from the test-set. In the next subsection, we will detail how we conduct our analysis.

3.1   Neural Network Approximation

As previously indicated in Sect. 1, we approximate CNNs by replacing the original multipliers within the convolutional and dense layers with approximate ones in order to reduce power consumption, as evidenced in [25,35]. However, the design of AxNNs is not a trivial task, since both resource-requirements – power-consumption, area occupied on the silicon, inference-time – and the accuracy lost due to the approximate multipliers have to be kept low.

Hence, we resort to MOO-based Design-Space Exploration (DSE) in order to address the design of AxNNs, that is, a Multi-Objective Optimization Problem (MOP) with a set of fitness-function to optimize and a set of constraints. Note that this is a complex MOP, with multiple feasible solutions that separately optimize different fitness-function. Therefore, we search for the *non-dominated* solutions – Pareto-optimal solutions –, that is, feasible solutions that cannot be further optimized without degrading other objectives or violating constraints. Specifically, we resort to the Non-dominated Sorting Genetic Algorithm-II (NSGA-II) heuristic to solve the MOO, in order to save computational-time.

In our case, a Pareto-solution is a specific approximate configuration for the CNN, that selects the appropriate approximate multipliers for each convolutional and dense layer. Figure 1 depicts our approach to generate AxC configurations, in order to generate AxNNs.

In order to generate approximate configurations, our approach requires both the CNN to be approximated and the approximate multipliers to be substituted

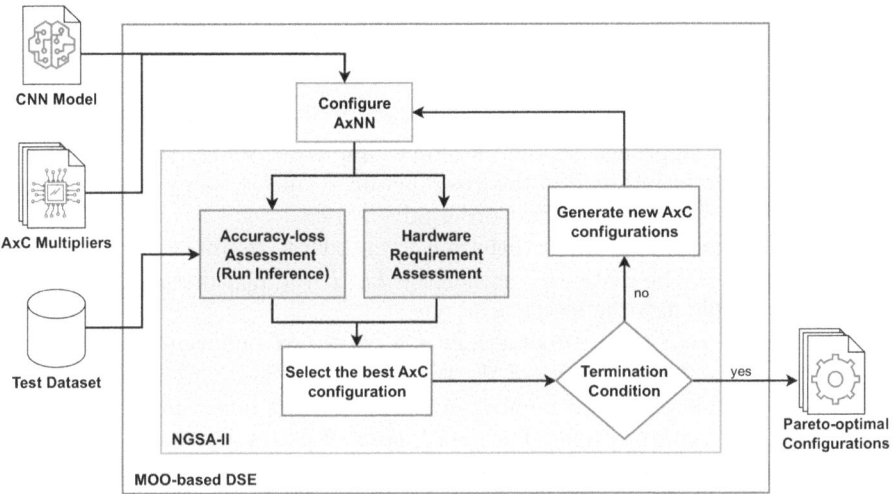

Fig. 1. Our Approximation approach

within the convolutional and dense layers. Furthermore, the test dataset must be run through an inference process in order to assess the accuracy lost due to the approximation. Specially, we need to specify 1. the architecture of the CNN, including the layers and parameters such as stride and padding, and 2. the learned weights and biases, for each of the convolutional and dense layers.

Solving the MOO-based DSE requires minimizing the hardware-requirement and error (accuracy-loss) fitness-functions. Thus, the NSGA-II selects the best approximate configurations that provide a trade-off between the above-mentioned function. Finally, we exploited the running performance metric and termination criterion from [12].

3.2 Adversarial Sample Generation

Once we generate AxNNs, we target them with both white-box and black-box adversarial attack in an evasion scenario. We selected the following adversarial-sample generation algorithm from the State-of-the-ART (SotA).

1) Basic Iterative Method (BIM) [19]: it is the iterative version of the Fast Gradient Sign Method (FGSM). Thus. it iteratively adds to an input sample x, whose true class is denoted as t, the perturbation $\delta_x = \epsilon \cdot sign(\nabla_x \mathcal{L}(f(x), t))$, where $\nabla_x \mathcal{L}(f(x), t)$ is the gradient of the loss function. The resulting element is clipped in the range $[x - \epsilon, x + \epsilon]$ each iteration.

2) DP [23]: it is optimized for the L_2 distance metric and designed by assuming the linearity of the Deep Learning (DL) model, with a decision boundary separating each class. The perturbation δ_x is computed iteratively as an orthogonal projection vector that project the sample x onto the closest decision boundary, each iteration.

3) Projected Gradient Descent (PGD) [21]: it is an iterative attack based on BIM. PGD initialize the attack at a random point of the L_ρ ball around the input sample x, and, iteratively, projects the adversarial sample back onto the L_ρ ball. Furthermore, it has been proved that PGD is a *universal* adversary among first-order approaches –they leverage first order information about the networks, such us the gradient of the loss function –, that is, being robust against it yields robustness against all first-order adversaries.

4) CW [14]: computes the perturbation δ_x in order to minimize $\mathcal{D}(x, x+\delta_x) = \mathcal{D}(x, x_{adv})$, that is, the distance – either the L_0, L_2 or L_{inf} distance – between the original sample and the adversarial one.

5) One-Pixel (OP) [33]: this method is a black-box one, requiring only the probability labels of the outputs of the target neural network. The main idea is to modify the value of a fixed number of pixels of input image in order to craft a successful adversarial sample. The coordinates of pixels are searched through the Differential Evolution (DE) genetic algorithm.

We generated adversarial samples against both the original CNN and its approximate version AxNN, whose configuration was selected while solving the MOO-based DSE. Finally, we analyze the success-rate of each adversarial sample generation-algorithm, highlighting the differences between both the original and approximate DNNs.

4   Experimental Results

In this Section, we present the results obtained through an experimental evaluation conducted on three different CNNs and their respective approximate versions. Specifically, we designed, trained and approximate each network. Subsequently, we target each CNN and AxNN with adversarial algorithms, as specified in Sect. 3. Note that, given a convolutional neural model CNN_1 and its approximate version $AxNN_1$, we generate adversarial samples while considering only the original samples from the test dataset that were correctly classified by both CNN_1 and $AxNN_1$. Finally, we evaluate the success rate of adversarial samples against all the CNNs and AxNNs.

We conduct the experiments on a machine equipped with an AMD Ryzen Threadripper PRO 5945 WX and a NVIDIA RTX A5000.

Our experiments take into account the custom CNN MinNet, whose details are reported in Table 1, and two ResNet networks, that is, Resnet8 and ResNet24, designed and trained with the TensorFlow Python library [1].

All these networks were trained on the CIFAR-10 [18] dataset, consisting of 60000 32×32 RGB images – 50k images for training, and 10k for testing –, using cross-entropy as loss-function, and Adam as optimizer. Finally, the training lasted 200 epochs, with a batch size of 64.

Each network was approximated by replacing the original floating-point 32 multipliers within convolutional and dense layers with the 8-bit integer one from the EvoApprox8b library [24], hose details are reported in Table 2. Note that each network was Quantized-aware trained [27] by resorting to TensorFlow-Lite,

Table 1. Architectural details of the MinNet CNN

Layer	Input Shape	Output Shape	# of Parameters
Conv2D	$1 \times 32 \times 32 \times 32$	$1 \times 30 \times 30 \times 32$	896
MaxPooling2D	$1 \times 30 \times 30 \times 32$	$1 \times 15 \times 15 \times 32$	0
Conv2D	$1 \times 15 \times 15 \times 32$	$1 \times 13 \times 13 \times 64$	18496
MaxPooling2D	$1 \times 13 \times 13 \times 64$	$1 \times 6 \times 6 \times 64$	0
Flatten	$1 \times 6 \times 6 \times 64$	1×2304	0
Dense	1×2304	1×64	147520
Dense	1×64	1×10	650

in order to quantize weights into from floating-point 32 bit to 8-bit integer, since we approximate by using 8-bit integer multipliers.

Table 2. Error characterization and hardware requirements for approximate circuits taken from the EvoApproxLib-Lite library, as reported in [26].

Circuit	MAE (%)	AWCE (%)	MRE (%)	Power (mW)	Area (μm^2)
1KV6	0.00	0.00	0.00	0.425	729.8
1KV8	0.0018	0.0076	0.28	0.422	711.0
1KV9	0.0064	0.026	0.90	0.410	685.2
1KVA	0.019	0.075	2.53	0.391	641.1
1KVM	0.049	0.20	2.40	0.369	652.8
1KVP	0.051	0.21	2.73	0.363	635.0
1KVQ	0.056	0.25	3.64	0.351	599.8
1KX5	0.15	0.69	8.93	0.289	543.0
1KXF	0.34	1.37	15.72	0.237	482.4
1L2J	0.081	0.39	4.41	0.301	558.9
1L2L	0.23	1.16	12.26	0.200	411.6
1L2N	0.52	2.66	27.44	0.126	284.9
1L12	3.08	12.30	135.77	0.052	172.2

Table 3 report details regarding the accuracy, and the hardware-requirements, of MinNet, ResNet8, and ResNet24. We estimated the power-consumption and the area occupied on the silicon as done in [25]. From this point forward, we will refer to the floating-point networks MinNet, ResNet8, and ResNet24 networks as FpM, $FpR8$, and $FpR24$, respectively. Consequently, $AxCM$, $AxCR8$, and $AxCR24$ will refer to the approximate versions of MinNet, ResNet8, and ResNet24, respectively.

With regard to the generation of adversarial samples, as previously stated at the outset of this Section, we have solely considered the images from the test

Table 3. Accuracy, and estimated resource requirements for MinNet, ResNet8 and ResNet24 implementations.

Model	Accuracy (%)	Power (mW)	Area (μm^2)
FpM	80.08	125.27	4860.35
$AxCM$	75.02	14.73	1990.2
$FpR8$	86.36	1390.12	13365.97
$AxCR8$	83.76	202.30	6451.9
$FpR24$	84.39	2487.87	25516.85
$AxCR24$	87.59	544.96	12575.09

Table 4. Success rate of OP, BIM, DP, PGD, and CW against the floating-point, and approximate versions of MinNet, ResNet8, and ResNet24.

Model	OP	BIM	DP	PGD	CW
FpM	75.73	100	75.84	100	34.80
$AxCM$	75.92	31.40	65.72	33.46	24.15
$FpR8$	66.16	99.83	71.26	99.83	17.08
$AxCR8$	27.79	15.88	61.71	13.90	7.29
$FpR24$	58.04	99.41	69.62	99.41	14.37
$AxCR24$	42.60	12.95	61.68	12.09	7.06

set that are correctly classified by both the original CNN and its approximate counterpart. This means that adversarial sample were generated basing on (i) 7183 images in case of FpM and $AxCM$, (ii) 7650 images while targeting $FpR8$ and $AxCR8$, and (iii) 7757 images in case of $FpR24$ and $AxCR24$.

With regard to the generation settings, the OP algorithm was set to modify 20 pixels of the original images within 51 iterations (generations of the DE algorithm). Furthermore, the maximum perturbation and the maximum number of iterations were set to 20 and 50, respectively, with respect to the BIM, PGD, DP, and CW algorithms, with a perturbation step of 1. It should be noted that, due to the 8-bit representation of RGB images of CIFAR-10, the perturbation step of iterative algorithms must be an integer and at least 1. Table 4 depicts the success rate of each algorithm against floating-point CNNs and AxNNs, i.e., the percentage of successful adversarial images that were generated.

As Table 4 illustrates, the approximate versions of all the CNN are susceptible to adversarial attacks. In particular, MinNet is the most susceptible network, in both its floating-point and approximate versions. The less-effective attacks against both the floating-point and approximate versions of all the CNNs are represented by CW. In contrast, the most successful adversarial attack against the AxNNs is represented by DP. This attack has a success rate greater than 61%. The behavior of OP is analogous to that of DP, except for the $AxCR8$ case, where the success rate is less than 28%. Finally, the success rates diverge significantly in the case of the BIM and PGD attacks. While their success rates are consistently above 99% in the case of floating-point CNNs, they are below 35% when targeting $AxCM$ and below 16% when targeting approximate ResNet networks.

Consequently, the AxNNs are resilient to gradient-based adversarial attacks. This resilience is attributed to the fact that quantization and then approximation desegregate the gradient of the loss functions, rendering gradient-based adversarial attacks less effective against such networks. With regard to other types of adversarial attack, the AxNNs are similarly robust to those attacks as their floating-point counterparts.

5   Conclusions

The objective of this paper was to examine the vulnerability of Convolution Neural Networks (CNNs) approximated by leveraging the Approximate Computing (AxC) design paradigm. Specifically, we first identified a combination of approximate multipliers that optimally balances the resource requirements and the accuracy loss due to approximation. Subsequently, we proceeded to design the Approximate Neural Network (AxNN) by replacing the selected multipliers in both the convolutional and dense layers of the original CNN model. Finally, the AxNN was subjected to both white-box and black-box adversarial attacks in an evasion scenario, with the test dataset exclusively considered.

The experimental results indicate that AxNNs exhibit significant robustness against gradient-based white-box adversarial attacks. However, they share the same vulnerability to black-box attacks and other white-box attacks, such as DeepFool (DP), Carlini & Wagner (CW), and One Pixel (OP) as the original CNNs.

These findings indicate that, despite the substantial benefits of approximation in terms of computational and energy efficiency, robustness to adversarial attacks remains a critical challenge. Consequently, future research should concentrate on the investigation of approximation techniques that not only reduce resource consumption but also enhance the robustness of AI models against a wide range of adversarial attacks.

References

1. Abadi, M., et al.: TensorFlow: a system for large-scale machine learning. Technical report, The Google Brain Team (2015). https://www.tensorflow.org/
2. Ahmadilivani, M.H., et al.: Special session: approximation and fault resiliency of DNN accelerators. In: 2023 IEEE 41st VLSI Test Symposium (VTS), pp. 1–10 (2023). https://doi.org/10.1109/VTS56346.2023.10140043. iSSN: 2375-1053
3. Almurib, H.A., Kumar, T.N., Lombardi, F.: Approximate DCT image compression using inexact computing. IEEE Trans. Comput. **67**(2), 149–159 (2018). https://doi.org/10.1109/TC.2017.2731770

4. Ansari, M.S., Mrazek, V., Cockburn, B.F., Sekanina, L., Vasicek, Z., Han, J.: Improving the accuracy and hardware efficiency of neural networks using approximate multipliers. IEEE Trans. Very Large Scale Integr. (VLSI) Syst. **28**(2), 317–328 (2020). https://doi.org/10.1109/TVLSI.2019.2940943

5. Arjomandi, H.M., Khalooei, M., Amirmazlaghani, M.: Low-epsilon adversarial attack against a neural network online image stream classifier. Appl. Soft Comput. 110760 (2023). https://doi.org/10.1016/j.asoc.2023.110760. https://www.sciencedirect.com/science/article/pii/S1568494623007780

6. Askarizadeh, M.J., Farahmand, E., Castro-Godinez, J., Mahani, A., Cabrera-Quiros, L., Salazar-Garcia, C.: Exploring DNN Robustness Against Adversarial Attacks Using Approximate Multipliers (2024). http://arxiv.org/abs/2404.11665. arXiv:2404.11665

7. Barbareschi, M., Barone, S.: Investigating the resilience source of classification systems for approximate computing techniques. IEEE Trans. Emerg. Top. Comput. **01**, 1–12 (2024). https://doi.org/10.1109/TETC.2024.3403757. https://www.computer.org/csdl/journal/ec/5555/01/10542568/1XmMGLjxlRe

8. Barbareschi, M., Barone, S., Bosio, A., Han, J., Traiola, M.: A genetic-algorithm-based approach to the design of DCT hardware accelerators. ACM J. Emerg. Technol. Comput. Syst. **18**(3), 1–25 (2022). https://doi.org/10.1145/3501772. https://dl.acm.org/doi/10.1145/3501772

9. Barbareschi, M., Barone, S., Mazzocca, N.: Advancing synthesis of decision tree-based multiple classifier systems: an approximate computing case study. Knowl. Inf. Syst. 1–20 (2021). https://doi.org/10.1007/s10115-021-01565-5. https://link.springer.com/article/10.1007/s10115-021-01565-5

10. Barbareschi, M., Barone, S., Mazzocca, N., Moriconi, A.: A catalog-based AIG-rewriting approach to the design of approximate components. IEEE Trans. Emerg. Top. Comput. (2022). https://doi.org/10.1109/TETC.2022.3170502

11. Barone, S., Traiola, M., Barbareschi, M., Bosio, A.: Multi-objective application-driven approximate design method. IEEE Access **9**, 86975–86993 (2021). https://doi.org/10.1109/ACCESS.2021.3087858

12. Blank, J., Deb, K.: A running performance metric and termination criterion for evaluating evolutionary multi- and many-objective optimization algorithms. In: 2020 IEEE Congress on Evolutionary Computation (CEC), Glasgow, United Kingdom, pp. 1–8. IEEE (2020). https://doi.org/10.1109/CEC48606.2020.9185546. https://ieeexplore.ieee.org/document/9185546/

13. Bosio, A., Ménard, D., Sentieys, O. (eds.): Approximate Computing Techniques: From Component- to Application-Level. Springer, Cham (2022). https://doi.org/10.1007/978-3-030-94705-7. https://link.springer.com/10.1007/978-3-030-94705-7

14. Carlini, N., Wagner, D.: Towards evaluating the robustness of neural networks. In: 2017 IEEE Symposium on Security and Privacy (SP), pp. 39–57 (2017). https://doi.org/10.1109/SP.2017.49. https://ieeexplore.ieee.org/document/7958570. iSSN: 2375-1207

15. Chippa, V.K., Mohapatra, D., Roy, K., Chakradhar, S.T., Raghunathan, A.: Scalable effort hardware design. IEEE Trans. Very Large Scale Integr. (VLSI) Syst. **22**(9), 2004–2016 (2014). https://doi.org/10.1109/TVLSI.2013.2276759

16. Deveautour, B., Traiola, M., Virazel, A., Girard, P.: QAMR: an approximation-based fully reliable TMR alternative for area overhead reduction. In: 2020 IEEE European Test Symposium (ETS), pp. 1–6 (2020). https://doi.org/10.1109/ETS48528.2020.9131574. iSSN: 1558-1780

17. Guesmi, A., et al.: Defensive approximation: securing CNNs using approximate computing. In: Proceedings of the 26th ACM International Conference on Architectural Support for Programming Languages and Operating Systems, Virtual USA, pp. 990–1003. ACM (2021). https://doi.org/10.1145/3445814.3446747. https://dl.acm.org/doi/10.1145/3445814.3446747

18. Krizhevsky, A., Nair, V., Hinton, G.: CIFAR-10 (Canadian institute for advanced research) (2010). https://www.cs.toronto.edu/~kriz/cifar.html

19. Kurakin, A., Goodfellow, I., Bengio, S.: Adversarial examples in the physical world (2017). http://arxiv.org/abs/1607.02533. arXiv:1607.02533

20. Li, J., Hu, Y., Xia, F.: A variable adversarial attack method based on filtering. Comput. Secur. **134**, 103431 (2023). https://doi.org/10.1016/j.cose.2023.103431. https://www.sciencedirect.com/science/article/pii/S0167404823003413

21. Madry, A., Makelov, A., Schmidt, L., Tsipras, D., Vladu, A.: Towards Deep Learning Models Resistant to Adversarial Attacks (2019). https://doi.org/10.48550/arXiv.1706.06083. http://arxiv.org/abs/1706.06083. arXiv:1706.06083

22. Manikantta Reddy, K., Vasantha, M.H., Nithin Kumar, Y.B., Keshava Gopal, C., Dwivedi, D.: Quantization aware approximate multiplier and hardware accelerator for edge computing of deep learning applications. Integration **81**, 268–279 (2021). https://doi.org/10.1016/j.vlsi.2021.08.001. https://www.sciencedirect.com/science/article/pii/S0167926021000869

23. Moosavi-Dezfooli, S.M., Fawzi, A., Frossard, P.: DeepFool: a simple and accurate method to fool deep neural networks. In: 2016 IEEE Conference on Computer Vision and Pattern Recognition (CVPR), Las Vegas, NV, USA, pp. 2574–2582. IEEE (2016). https://doi.org/10.1109/CVPR.2016.282. http://ieeexplore.ieee.org/document/7780651/

24. Mrazek, V., Hrbacek, R., Vasicek, Z., Sekanina, L.: EvoApprox8b: library of approximate adders and multipliers for circuit design and benchmarking of approximation methods. In: Design, Automation Test in Europe Conference Exhibition (DATE), pp. 258–261 (2017). https://doi.org/10.23919/DATE.2017.7926993. iSSN: 1558-1101

25. Mrazek, V., Vasicek, Z., Sekanina, L., Hanif, M.A., Shafique, M.: ALWANN: automatic layer-wise approximation of deep neural network accelerators without retraining. In: 2019 IEEE/ACM International Conference on Computer-Aided Design (ICCAD), pp. 1–8 (2019). https://doi.org/10.1109/ICCAD45719.2019.8942068. http://arxiv.org/abs/1907.07229. arXiv: 1907.07229

26. Mrazek, V., Vasicek, Z., Sekanina, L., Jiang, H., Han, J.: Scalable construction of approximate multipliers with formally guaranteed worst case error. IEEE Trans. Very Large Scale Integr. (VLSI) Syst. **26**(11), 2572–2576 (2018). https://doi.org/10.1109/TVLSI.2018.2856362

27. Nagel, M., Fournarakis, M., Bondarenko, Y., Blankevoort, T.: Overcoming oscillations in quantization-aware training. In: Proceedings of the 39th International Conference on Machine Learning, pp. 16318–16330. PMLR (2022). https://proceedings.mlr.press/v162/nagel22a.html. iSSN: 2640-3498

28. Nowroozi, E., Mekdad, Y., Berenjestanaki, M.H., Conti, M., Fergougui, A.E.: Demystifying the transferability of adversarial attacks in computer networks. IEEE Trans. Netw. Serv. Manage. **19**(3), 3387–3400 (2022). https://doi.org/10.1109/TNSM.2022.3164354. https://ieeexplore.ieee.org/document/9747933/

29. Sarwar, S.S., Venkataramani, S., Ankit, A., Raghunathan, A., Roy, K.: Energy-efficient neural computing with approximate multipliers. ACM J. Emerg. Technol. Comput. Syst. **14**(2), 1–23 (2018). https://doi.org/10.1145/3097264. https://dl.acm.org/doi/10.1145/3097264

30. Scarabottolo, I., Ansaloni, G., Constantinides, G.A., Pozzi, L., Reda, S.: Approximate logic synthesis: a survey. Proc. IEEE **108**(12), 2195–2213 (2020). https://doi.org/10.1109/JPROC.2020.3014430

31. Schmidhuber, J.: Deep learning in neural networks: an overview. Neural Netw. **61**, 85–117 (2015). https://doi.org/10.1016/j.neunet.2014.09.003. https://linkinghub.elsevier.com/retrieve/pii/S0893608014002135

32. Siddique, A., Hoque, K.A.: Is approximation universally defensive against adversarial attacks in deep neural networks? In: 2022 Design, Automation & Test in Europe Conference & Exhibition (DATE), pp. 364–369 (2022). https://doi.org/10.23919/DATE54114.2022.9774563. iSSN: 1558-1101

33. Su, J., Vargas, D.V., Sakurai, K.: One pixel attack for fooling deep neural networks. IEEE Trans. Evol. Comput. **23**(5), 828–841 (2019). https://doi.org/10.1109/TEVC.2019.2890858

34. Szegedy, C., et al.: Intriguing properties of neural networks (2014). http://arxiv.org/abs/1312.6199. arXiv:1312.6199

35. Tasoulas, Z.G., Zervakis, G., Anagnostopoulos, I., Amrouch, H., Henkel, J.: Weight-oriented approximation for energy-efficient neural network inference accelerators. IEEE Trans. Circ. Syst. I Regul. Pap. **67**(12), 4670–4683 (2020). https://doi.org/10.1109/TCSI.2020.3019460

36. Traiola, M., Echavarria, J., Bosio, A., Teich, J., O'Connor, I.: Design space exploration of approximation-based quadruple modular redundancy circuits. In: 2021 IEEE/ACM International Conference On Computer Aided Design (ICCAD), pp. 1–9 (2021). https://doi.org/10.1109/ICCAD51958.2021.9643561. iSSN: 1558-2434

37. Xu, Q., Mytkowicz, T., Kim, N.S.: Approximate computing: a survey. IEEE Des. Test **33**(1), 8–22 (2016). https://doi.org/10.1109/MDAT.2015.2505723

38. Yang, X., Lin, J., Zhang, H., Yang, X., Zhao, P.: Improving the transferability of adversarial examples via direction tuning. Inf. Sci. **647**, 119491 (2023). https://doi.org/10.1016/j.ins.2023.119491. https://www.sciencedirect.com/science/article/pii/S0020025523010769

Cyber Security/Privacy/Trust for IoT and CPS

A Blockchain and IPFS-Enhanced Model for Attack Detection and Resource Efficiency

Raouf Jmal[1]([⊠])(iD), Mariam Masmoudi[2,3](iD), Ikram Amous[1](iD),
and Florence Sèdes[3](iD)

[1] MIRACL, Enet'Com, Sfax University, Sfax, Tunisia
`raouf.jmal14@gmail.com, ikram.amous@enetcom.usf.tn`
[2] MIRACL, FSEGS, Sfax University, Sfax, Tunisia
[3] IRIT, Paul Sabatier University, Toulouse, France
`Florence.Sedes@irit.fr`

Abstract. The Social Internet of Things (SIoT) facilitates seamless interactions between IoT devices, providing users with quick and convenient services. However, this domain is vulnerable to manipulation by malicious nodes that issue false recommendations and services to inflate their reputation, leading to trust-related attacks. Developing trust models to detect these attacks in each interaction is challenging due to the complexity of the patterns and features required for accurate prediction. Furthermore, trust metrics are not consistently updated for each node, resulting in inefficiencies and unnecessary resource consumption. To address these challenges, we propose a system that analyzes the context of the current interaction and incorporates temporal factors to monitor node behavior. Our approach employs a decentralized system based on blockchain and IPFS storage, reducing costs and making the process of trust evaluation more efficient and practical for real-time scenarios. This method enhances the detection of trust-related attacks while optimizing resource allocation and execution time.

Keywords: SIoT · Trust · Real-Time attack detection · Blockchain · IPFS

1 Introduction

The social internet of things represents an advanced paradigm within the IoT framework, where devices are not only interconnected but also capable of autonomously establishing social relationships, akin to human social interactions. In this context, SIoT extends the traditional IoT by enabling devices to discover and interact with each other based on their social relationships, thereby enhancing overall functionality and user experience [6,30]. The primary goal of SIoT is to create a socially aware network of smart objects that can cooperate, share resources, and provide services efficiently and effectively [7]. This

© IFIP International Federation for Information Processing 2025
Published by Springer Nature Switzerland AG 2025
G. Rey et al. (Eds.): IFIPIoT 2024, IFIP AICT 737, pp. 163–174, 2025.
https://doi.org/10.1007/978-3-031-81900-1_10

novel approach introduces unique opportunities and challenges, particularly in the realms of security and trust management.

A significant challenge in SIoT is ensuring secure interactions based on trust assessment [4] among the involved parties. These interactions may involve exchanging various digital content forms, such as songs, videos, images, and texts. In each interaction, the trustworthiness of the parties involved remains uncertain, highlighting the importance of effective trust evaluation. To address this, several trust management models have been proposed in the literature for assessing trust [1,2,28].

According to state-of-the-art research [26,34,35,40], trust management typically involves four fundamental phases: trust composition, trust aggregation, trust propagation, and trust update. Trust composition involves selecting features to evaluate trustworthiness in interactions, including information about each user's behavior and the quality of services provided to other nodes. The aggregation phase, which has garnered significant attention, involves using machine learning, deep learning, and Bayesian techniques to classify transactions and identify malicious nodes. Machine learning techniques, in particular, have significantly advanced trust aggregation, outperforming traditional static methods in detecting trust-related attacks [3,24,27]. Trust propagation involves broadcasting trust scores and information among nodes, while the trust update phase ensures dynamic updates to trust information, either after each transaction or at arbitrary intervals.

An effective solution for trust management systems is the use of decentralized systems like blockchain. The integration of blockchain technology into trust management systems benefits from its distributed architecture [8,19,23,29]. Blockchain offers valuable properties such as immutability, ensuring that transactions remain unalterable post-validation and are securely encrypted [42]. This decentralized approach enhances trust management by improving data sharing reliability and detecting trust-related attacks [5,38].

Employing a consensus protocol in trust management systems typically involves reliance on third parties for trust aggregation, which can be both time-consuming and resource-intensive. Smart contracts present a promising alternative by leveraging blockchain's distributed architecture to mitigate the complexity and issues associated with consensus protocols. These contracts execute automatically, ensuring validity by adhering to predefined constraints without manual intervention [13]. Their integration into trust management systems can reduce the overhead associated with consensus protocols. This paper explores the deployment of smart contracts for detecting abnormal behavior and managing sensitive data storage.

Although prior studies have applied machine learning and deep learning algorithms to identify trust-related attacks from malicious nodes [10,17,25,33], their practical implementation requires extensive data preprocessing. Addressing issues related to feature extraction and suspicious behaviors can be more effectively managed by monitoring and analyzing node states, which helps detect behavioral changes rather than applying a trust-related attack model directly to each interaction [43].

The objective of this paper is to develop a behavior monitoring model that utilizes contextual information applicable to real-world scenarios such as vehicular communication. By considering factors like location, time, and type of action, this model aims to improve the detection of malicious vehicles.

Furthermore, while storing transactions on the blockchain enhances security due to its immutability, the cost of preserving sensitive data can be high. The InterPlanetary File System (IPFS) [16], a decentralized and peer-to-peer protocol for file storage and retrieval, offers an alternative. Governed by smart contracts [14], IPFS operates through a distributed network of nodes, providing secure and cost-effective storage compared to traditional blockchain solutions.

The remainder of this paper is organized as follows: Sect. 2 reviews related work, providing context and background. Section 3 details the proposed system, with a focus on tracking nodes' behaviors and using IPFS for trust metrics storage. Section 4 presents the results of the proposed model. Finally, Sect. 5 concludes the paper and suggests areas for future research.

2   Related Works

Trust management utilizing blockchain and machine learning techniques has made significant advancements in recent years. In [23], authors highlighted the use of blockchain to enhance trust management by providing transparent and tamper-proof records of transactions, significantly reducing the risk of trust-related attacks.

Similarly, in [36], researchers proposed a blockchain-based trust management framework for IoT networks, emphasizing the use of smart contracts to automate trust evaluations and updates. However, blockchain-based consensus protocols often relied on third parties for trust aggregation and authentication verification, which could be time-consuming and resource-intensive, posing a significant limitation.

The study in [39] demonstrated the use of deep learning models to predict trust scores in IoT environments, showing improved accuracy over traditional methods.

In [44], authors employed reinforcement learning to dynamically adjust trust scores based on nodes' behavior over time, enhancing the adaptability of trust management systems. Despite these advancements, the complexity and high-dimensionality of features used to detect trust-related attacks remained a significant challenge. These features required extensive preprocessing and computational resources, limiting the real-time applicability of such models.

The authors in [11] focused on utilizing anomaly detection techniques to identify malicious nodes in a network. Their approach combined supervised learning with behavioral analysis to detect deviations from expected patterns, achieving high detection rates.

In [22], the study explored the use of adversarial machine learning to anticipate and mitigate attacks on trust management systems, enhancing system robustness. However, the reliance on extensive datasets and the complexity of feature engineering presented ongoing challenges in accurately detecting trust-related attacks.

In [18], authors integrated behavior analysis with ML algorithms to continuously assess node trustworthiness in real-time, improving response times to potential threats. The approach in [15] used deep learning to model and predict node behavior in complex environments, providing a proactive approach to trust management. Yet, the high computational cost and the need for large-scale data remained significant barriers to the widespread adoption of these techniques.

In [32], researchers discussed the integration of the InterPlanetary File System with blockchain to store trust-related data securely and cost-effectively.

Indeed, in [31] authors proposed a hybrid approach combining blockchain and IPFS for secure data storage, emphasizing the role of smart contracts in managing access controls and data integrity. While IPFS offered a decentralized and efficient alternative for data storage, the costs associated with preserving sensitive data on the blockchain remained high. Additionally, the complexity of managing extensive trust-related information from diverse nodes required robust database systems capable of handling high-data relationships effectively.

The study in [21] devised a hybrid reputation-based system that integrates both direct and indirect trust metrics to evaluate node trustworthiness in IoT networks. Their model incorporated user feedback and historical transaction data to compute reputation scores, aiming to mitigate the impact of malicious nodes. However, the system faced challenges related to the aggregation and storage of large volumes of reputation data, necessitating robust database solutions and efficient algorithms to ensure scalability and real-time performance.

Furthermore, in [37], authors developed a recommendation-based trust management system that utilized collaborative filtering techniques to predict trustworthiness of nodes based on similar past interactions. Their approach improved the accuracy of trust assessments by leveraging the collective experiences of multiple nodes. Despite its effectiveness, the system's reliance on extensive data storage and processing capabilities presented significant limitations, particularly in resource-constrained environments such as IoT networks.

From these studies, various techniques have been proposed to detect such attacks, including anomaly detection, reputation-based systems, and behavior analysis. Despite significant advancements, challenges such as the limitations of blockchain-based consensus protocols, the complexity of feature extraction for detecting trust-related attacks, and the high costs of storing sensitive data on the blockchain continue to pose obstacles to the development of effective trust management solutions.

This study aims to demonstrate a method for tracking nodes' behaviors in the social internet of things through the analysis of their interactions and temporal dependencies. This method focuses on detecting state changes from normal to abnormal, indicating potential trust-related attacks. It addresses scalability and reliability concerns by avoiding computationally intensive consensus protocols and instead adopts a lightweight approach that analyzes interactions and temporal dependencies to identify abnormal behavior. By employing this approach, the detection of trust-related attacks can become more efficient and effective, ensuring the security and privacy of users in social internet of things networks.

3   Behavior Monitoring Model for Trust Management System

Our approach is designed to maintain trust in social internet of things environments by dynamically classifying nodes in real-time during their interactions, thereby ensuring robust temporal trust management. Traditional methods often relied on complex feature extraction to detect trust-related attacks, which can be both resource-intensive and costly. In contrast, our model leverages the efficiency of recurrent neural networks to monitor and classify node behavior more effectively. We developed a Long Short-Term Memory (LSTM) model, referred to as "SeqLSTM," to classify the states of nodes based on long-term dependencies. This approach is particularly effective in identifying and eliminating nodes that exhibit abnormal behavior, thereby preserving the trustworthiness of the SIoT network.

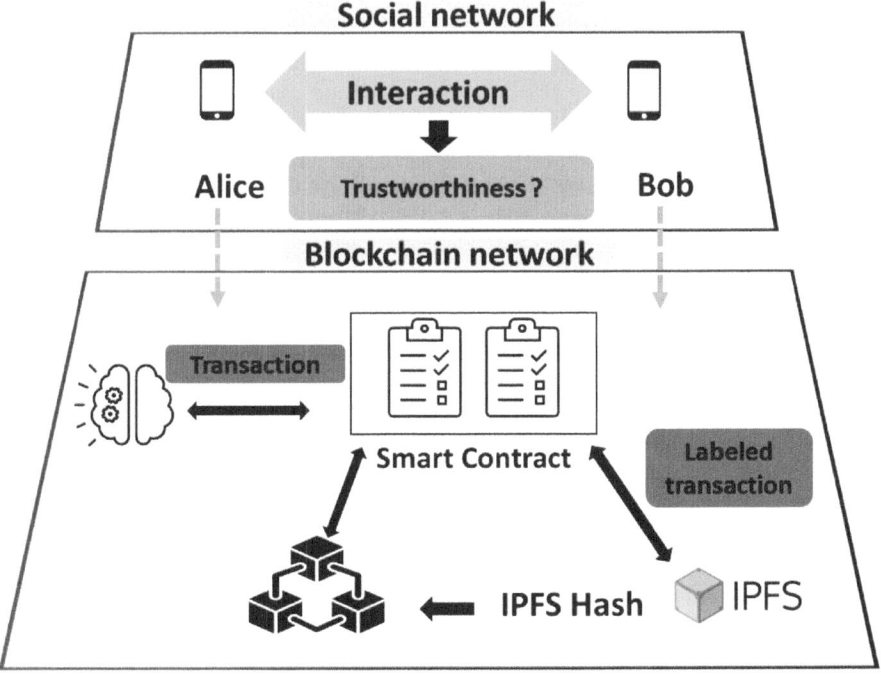

Fig. 1. Blockchain-based smart contract for behavior assessment in SIoT.

As illustrated in Fig. 1, node interactions within the SIoT environment are fundamentally dependent on trust evaluation. Effective trust assessment is achieved through continuous monitoring of node behaviors. Our approach begins with the cost-effective storage of node features and behavioral patterns in IPFS, while only the corresponding IPFS hash is stored on the blockchain, linked to each node's ID. Data access and control are governed by smart contracts, which interface with the classification model to predict whether a node's behavior is normal or abnormal based on the features collected for each new transaction. This decentralized system facilitates real-time monitoring of node behaviors, drawing on historical interactions and patterns to inform predictions and sustain trust across the network.

Algorithm 1: Smart contract for trust management

1: function manageTrust(address nodeId, string memory ipfsHash, bytes32 features) public {
2: // Check if the IPFS hash is valid
3: require(bytes(ipfsHash).length != 0, "Invalid IPFS hash");
4: // Verify if the node is already registered
5: if (nodes[nodeId].id == address(0)) {
6: // Node is not registered, initiate registration process
7: revert("Node not registered. Please register the node first.");
8: }
9: // Node is registered, proceed to retrieve features from IPFS
10: bytes32 retrievedFeatures = // Logic to retrieve features from IPFS
11: require(verifyFeatures(retrievedFeatures), "Features do not match predefined schema");
12: // Predict node behavior using SeqLSTM model
13: bool isTrustworthy = // Call SeqLSTM model with retrieved features
14: if (isTrustworthy) {
15: // Node is deemed trustworthy, continue interactions
16: nodes[nodeId].ipfsHash = ipfsHash; // Update node's IPFS hash
17: } else {
18: // Node is flagged for abnormal behavior, reject interactions
19: revert("Node behavior is abnormal. Interaction rejected.");
20: }
21: }

Algorithm 1 outlines the steps taken by the smart contract to manage trust within a SIoT environment. The algorithm initiates by validating the provided IPFS hash, ensuring it is both valid and non-empty. Subsequently, it verifies whether the node is registered within the system. If the node is not registered, the contract rejects the request and prompts the user to complete the registration process. For registered nodes, the contract retrieves the features associated with the IPFS hash from IPFS, ensuring that these features conform to a predefined schema to maintain data consistency. This step is critical as it guarantees that the features used for prediction are properly structured and compatible with the model's requirements. Once the features are validated, they are fed into the SeqLSTM model for behavior prediction. If the model determines that the node's behavior is trustworthy, the smart contract updates the node's IPFS hash with the new data and permits the node to continue interacting with other nodes. Conversely, if the behavior is flagged as abnormal, the contract denies further interactions from the node and flags it for potential exclusion from the network.

This streamlined process enables effective real-time trust management in SIoT environments, utilizing blockchain for secure data storage and SeqLSTM for precise behavior prediction, all while ensuring the integrity and reliability of node interactions.

4   Experimental Evaluation

We delineated machine learning and deep learning models designed to detect the user's state, distinguishing between normal and abnormal behaviors. In real-world scenarios such as those encountered in the SIoT context, these models rely heavily on temporal and contextual patterns. Factors such as the frequency, type, and size of frames (interactions), session timestamps, energy consumption, and other contextual cues play pivotal roles in informing these models. By incorporating such multifaceted features, our approach strives to enhance the accuracy and robustness of anomaly detection within SIoT environments.

4.1   Experimental Setup

This section provides an overview of the dataset utilized in the experimentation and delineates the evaluation metrics employed to assess the efficacy of the models and their variants. Given the absence of authentic dataset pertaining to user or node interactions within behavior state features in the SIoT domain, alternative dataset was explored.

In order to forecast state changes, [20], authors meticulously curated a Massive Open Online Course (MOOC) dataset. This dataset is tailored to forecast whether an interaction would precipitate a behavioral alteration in users. It documents the activities undertaken by students within a MOOC, such as watching videos or submitting answers. It involves 7,047 users engaging with 98 items, resulting in over 411,749 interactions. Among these interactions, there are 4,066 drop-out events, accounting for 0.98% of the dataset. The dataset is dichotomized into two classes: class '0' denotes normal behavior, where users neither face bans nor drop out, and class '1' signifies abnormal behavior, indicative of users encountering bans or dropping out. Additionally, we evaluate the models using the area under the curve (AUC) metric, which is standard for tasks with highly imbalanced labels, to ensure a comprehensive assessment of their performance.

4.2   Models Evaluation

The SeqLSTM model proposed in this study integrates temporal factors to enhance the predictive capabilities of traditional LSTM architectures. By including the timestamp feature, the model effectively captures temporal dependencies

Table 1. Parameters for XGBoost, AdaBoost, and SeqLSTM models

SeqLSTM	Parameter	Grid search values	Best values
	Hidden layers number		2
	Units per layer	50, 100, 150	50
	Learning rate	0.0001, 0.0001, 0.001	0.001
	Optimizer	Adam, rmsprop	Adam
	Folds for cross-validation		5
	Batch size		32
	Epochs		25
Xgboost	Estimators number	150, 200, 250, 300, 400	300
	Max depth	4, 5, 6, 7	6
	Subsample	0.7, 0.8, 0.9, 1.0	0.8
	Learning rating	0.00001, 0.0001, 0.001	0.001
	Folds for cross-validation		5
AdaBoost	Estimators number	7,10, 15, 20, 30	10
	Learning rate	0.00001, 0.0001, 0.001	0.0001
	Folds for cross-validation		5

alongside spatial relationships in the data, thereby improving its performance in time-series analysis tasks. Unlike conventional LSTM models, which primarily focus on feature values across different time steps, this enhanced model leverages temporal context to gain deeper insights into sequential patterns. The effectiveness of the model is rigorously evaluated through k-fold cross-validation, which ensures robustness and guards against overfitting by assessing its performance across various data subsets. The selection of the model with the highest AUC score during cross-validation demonstrates its superior discriminatory power. Subsequent evaluation on an independent test set further validates the model's ability to generalize to unseen data.

For a comprehensive evaluation of behavior monitoring through state change prediction, we employed machine learning models. We chose XGBoost and AdaBoost classifiers for their robust performance in handling complex datasets and their ability to capture nonlinear relationships and interactions among features. Similarly, for our SeqLSTM model, we utilized grid search and cross-validation techniques to fine-tune hyperparameters, ensuring optimal performance.

Table 1 provides an overview of the hyperparameters explored during the grid search process for the three models: XGBoost, AdaBoost, and SeqLSTM. It outlines the range of values investigated for each parameter and identifies the best values that contributed to the selection of the optimal model configuration.

4.3   Experimental Results

Table 2 summarizes the AUC scores achieved by different models based on the MOOC dataset, including traditional methods and our proposed SeqLSTM model.

Table 2. AUC scores of various models on the MOOC dataset

Method	Area Under the Curve
LSTM [45]	0.686
Time-LSTM [45]	0.711
RRN [41]	0.558
LatentCross [9]	0.686
DeepCoevolve [12]	0.671
JODIE [20]	0.756
SeqLSTM	0.924
XGBoost	0.720
AdaBoost	0.648

In comparing the AUC scores, it is evident that the SeqLSTM model achieved a superior result, with an AUC of 0.924, significantly outperforming both XGBoost and AdaBoost. While XGBoost obtained a respectable AUC score of 0.720 and AdaBoost achieved 0.648, these scores were still lower compared to SeqLSTM. Our model also outperformed all other models listed in the table, with the second-best model, JODIE, achieving an AUC of 0.756. This indicates that SeqLSTM surpassed JODIE by approximately 0.16 in AUC, highlighting its enhanced capability to capture temporal dependencies and sequential patterns, leading to a more accurate and reliable prediction of node behaviors in the SIoT environment.

The results demonstrate that while XGBoost and AdaBoost performed well, their capabilities were surpassed by the SeqLSTM model. The inclusion of temporal factors in SeqLSTM allowed for better understanding and prediction of behavior patterns, providing a significant improvement over other models. This underscores the importance of leveraging advanced neural network architectures like SeqLSTM for tasks involving temporal and sequential data, proving its superior effectiveness in maintaining trust in SIoT networks.

5   Conclusion

Our decentralized system, based on the SeqLSTM model, effectively classifies nodes as either normal or abnormal by leveraging temporal factors and contextual patterns using long-term dependencies to monitor node states. This approach achieved superior results in terms of AUC compared to other models.

Additionally, the behavior monitoring model offers improvements in execution time and resource allocation, as it relies on features directly related to the current interaction, rather than using a trust model dependent on complex features to predict attacks. Furthermore, we incorporated IPFS storage for behavior data and trust metrics, governed through smart contracts, which reduces storage costs by storing only the IPFS hash on the blockchain.

In future work, we aim to develop a full Web3 application for trust management. Additionally, we plan to build a specific dataset for real-world scenarios in the SIoT domain to enable further experimentation and testing. This will enhance the applicability and robustness of our trust management system in practical environments.

References

1. Abdelghani, W., Zayani, C.A., Amous, I., Sèdes, F.: Trust management in social internet of things: a survey. In: Dwivedi, Y.K., et al. (eds.) I3E 2016. LNCS, vol. 9844, pp. 430–441. Springer, Cham (2016). https://doi.org/10.1007/978-3-319-45234-0_39
2. Alam, S., Zardari, S., Noor, S., Ahmed, S., Mouratidis, H.: Trust management in social internet of things (SIOT): a survey. IEEE Access **10**, 108924–108954 (2022)
3. Alghofaili, Y., Rassam, M.A.: A dynamic trust-related attack detection model for IoT devices and services based on the deep long short-term memory technique. Sensors **23**(8), 3814 (2023)
4. Amin, F., Ahmad, A., Sang Choi, G.: Towards trust and friendliness approaches in the social internet of things. Appl. Sci. **9**(1), 166 (2019)
5. Arshad, Q.U.A., Khan, W.Z., Azam, F., Khan, M.K., Yu, H., Zikria, Y.B.: Blockchain-based decentralized trust management in IoT: systems, requirements and challenges. Complex Intell. Syst. **9**(6), 6155–6176 (2023)
6. Atzori, L., Iera, A., Morabito, G.: SIOT: giving a social structure to the internet of things. IEEE Commun. Lett. **15**(11), 1193–1195 (2011)
7. Atzori, L., Iera, A., Morabito, G.: From "smart objects" to "social objects": the next evolutionary step of the internet of things. IEEE Commun. Mag. **52**(1), 97–105 (2014)
8. Awan, S., Javaid, N., Ullah, S., Khan, A.U., Qamar, A.M., Choi, J.G.: Blockchain based secure routing and trust management in wireless sensor networks. Sensors **22**(2), 411 (2022)
9. Beutel, A., et al.: Latent cross: making use of context in recurrent recommender systems. In: Proceedings of the Eleventh ACM International Conference on Web Search and Data Mining (WSDM) (2018)
10. Bhandari, A., Cherukuri, A.K., Kamalov, F.: Machine learning and blockchain integration for security applications. In: Big Data Analytics and Intelligent Systems for Cyber Threat Intelligence, pp. 129–173. River Publishers (2023)
11. Chen, Y., Liu, J., Zhang, H.: Anomaly detection for trust management in IoT networks. Sensors **21**(5), 1720 (2021)
12. Dai, H., Wang, Y., Trivedi, R., Song, L.: Deep coevolutionary network: embedding user and item features for recommendation. arXiv preprint arXiv:1609.03675 (2016)

13. Dhelim, S., Aung, N., Kechadi, M.T., Ning, H., Chen, L., Lakas, A.: Trust2vec: large-scale IoT trust management system based on signed network embeddings. IEEE Internet Things J. **10**(1), 553–562 (2022)
14. Dwivedi, S.K., Amin, R., Vollala, S.: Smart contract and IPFS-based trustworthy secure data storage and device authentication scheme in fog computing environment. Peer-to-Peer Netw. Appl. **16**(1), 1–21 (2023)
15. Gupta, P., Singh, R., Kumar, S.: Deep learning for predictive behavior modeling in trust management. Pattern Recogn. Lett. **158**, 44–52 (2023)
16. Jain, S.M.: A Brief Introduction to Web3: Decentralized Web Fundamentals for App Development. Springer, Cham (2023). https://doi.org/10.1007/978-1-4842-8975-4
17. Jmal, R., Masmoudi, M., Amous, I., Zayani, C.A., Sèdes, F.: Apache spark based deep learning for social transaction analysis. In: WEBIST, pp. 365–372 (2023)
18. Kim, J., Lee, H., Kim, K.: Real-time behavior analysis for trust management in IoT. Futur. Gener. Comput. Syst. **114**, 224–233 (2021)
19. Kudva, S., Badsha, S., Sengupta, S., La, H., Khalil, I., Atiquzzaman, M.: A scalable blockchain based trust management in Vanet routing protocol. J. Parallel Distrib. Comput. **152**, 144–156 (2021)
20. Kumar, S., Zhang, X., Leskovec, J.: Predicting dynamic embedding trajectory in temporal interaction networks. In: Proceedings of the 25th ACM SIGKDD International Conference on Knowledge Discovery and Data Mining, pp. 1269–1278 (2019)
21. Liu, P., Zhang, Y., Shi, W.: Hybrid reputation-based trust management system for IoT networks. IEEE Trans. Industr. Inf. **17**(2), 1494–1503 (2021)
22. Liu, S., Huang, Q., Wang, Z.: Adversarial machine learning for trust management systems. IEEE Access **10**, 45345–45355 (2022)
23. Liu, Y., Wang, J., Yan, Z., Wan, Z., Jäntti, R.: A survey on blockchain-based trust management for internet of things. IEEE Internet Things J. **10**(7), 5898–5922 (2023)
24. Marche, C., Nitti, M.: Trust-related attacks and their detection: a trust management model for the social IoT. IEEE Trans. Netw. Serv. Manag. **18**(3), 3297–3308 (2020)
25. Masmoudi, M., Abdelghani, W., Amous, I., Sèdes, F.: Deep learning for trust-related attacks detection in social internet of things. In: Chao, K.-M., Jiang, L., Hussain, O.K., Ma, S.-P., Fei, X. (eds.) ICEBE 2019. LNDECT, vol. 41, pp. 389–404. Springer, Cham (2020). https://doi.org/10.1007/978-3-030-34986-8_28
26. Masmoudi, M., Amous, I., Zayani, C.A., Sèdes, F.: Real-time mitigation of trust-related attacks in social IoT. In: Mosbah, M., Kechadi, T., Bellatreche, L., Gargouri, F. (eds.) MEDI 2023. LNCS, vol. 14396, pp. 303–318. Springer, Cham (2023). https://doi.org/10.1007/978-3-031-49333-1_22
27. Masmoudi, M., Amous, I., Zayani, C.A., Sèdes, F.: Real-time prevention of trust-related attacks in social IoT using blockchain and apache spark. Comput. Commun. **225**, 65–82 (2024)
28. Masmoudi, M., Amous, I., Zayani, C.A., Sèdes, F.: Trust attack prevention based on spark-blockchain in social IoT: a survey. Int. J. Inf. Secur. 1–20 (2024)
29. Masmoudi, M., Zayani, C.A., Amous, I., Sèdes, F.: A new blockchain-based trust management model. Procedia Comput. Sci. **192**, 1081–1091 (2021)
30. Nitti, M., Atzori, L., Cvijikj, I.P.: Network navigability in the social internet of things. In: 2014 IEEE World Forum on Internet of Things (WF-IoT), pp. 405–410. IEEE (2014)

31. Patel, M., Thakkar, P., Parikh, M.: Hybrid blockchain-IPFS architecture for secure data storage. Inf. Syst. **110**, 101987 (2023)
32. Roy, S., Das, A., Chatterjee, P.: Secure data storage using IPFS and blockchain. J. Parallel Distrib. Comput. **153**, 180–190 (2022)
33. Sagar, S., Mahmood, A., Sheng, M., Zaib, M., Zhang, W.: Towards a machine learning-driven trust evaluation model for social internet of things: a time-aware approach. In: MobiQuitous 2020-17th EAI International Conference on Mobile and Ubiquitous Systems: Computing, Networking and Services, pp. 283–290 (2020)
34. Saied, Y.B., Olivereau, A., Zeghlache, D., Laurent, M.: Trust management system design for the internet of things: a context-aware and multi-service approach. Comput. Secur. **39**, 351–365 (2013)
35. Sharma, A., Pilli, E.S., Mazumdar, A.P., Gera, P.: Towards trustworthy internet of things: a survey on trust management applications and schemes. Comput. Commun. **160**, 475–493 (2020)
36. Singh, S., Raj, A., Choudhury, T.: Blockchain-based trust management framework for IoT networks. J. Netw. Comput. Appl. **202**, 103432 (2023)
37. Sun, X., Li, J., Wang, Q.: Recommendation-based trust management system using collaborative filtering for IoT. IEEE Access **10**, 20432–20445 (2022)
38. Tariq, N., Asim, M., Khan, F.A., Baker, T., Khalid, U., Derhab, A.: A blockchain-based multi-mobile code-driven trust mechanism for detecting internal attacks in internet of things. Sensors **21**(1), 23 (2020)
39. Wang, T., Zhang, Y., Sun, W.: Deep learning-based trust evaluation for IoT environments. IEEE Internet Things J. **8**(4), 2216–2225 (2021)
40. Wei, L., Yang, Y., Wu, J., Long, C., Li, B.: Trust management for internet of things: a comprehensive study. IEEE Internet Things J. **9**(10), 7664–7679 (2022)
41. Wu, C.Y., Ahmed, A., Beutel, A., Smola, A.J., Jing, H.: Recurrent recommender networks. In: Proceedings of the Tenth ACM International Conference on Web Search and Data Mining (WSDM) (2017)
42. Yaga, D., Mell, P., Roby, N., Scarfone, K.: Blockchain technology overview. arXiv preprint arXiv:1906.11078 (2019)
43. Zaki, W., Abdullah, R.S., Yassin, W., Selamat, S.R., Rosli, M.S., Yahya, S.: Constructing IoT botnet detection model based on degree centrality and path analysis. J. Adv. Inf. Technol. **15**(3) (2024)
44. Zhang, H., Wu, Q., Shen, X.: Reinforcement learning for dynamic trust management in IoT systems. IEEE Trans. Industr. Inf. **18**(3), 1654–1663 (2022)
45. Zhu, Y., et al.: What to do next: modeling user behaviors by time-LSTM. In: Proceedings of the 26th International Joint Conference on Artificial Intelligence (IJCAI) (2017)

Hardware Trojan Key-Corruption Detection with Automated Neural Architecture Search

Franco Mezzarapa⬤, Jenna Goodrich⬤, Andey Robins⬤,
and Mike Borowczak(✉)⬤

University of Central Florida, Orlando, FL, USA
`mike.borowczak@ucf.edu`

Abstract. This work presents a model hardware trojan which intermittently is capable of corrupting an encryption operation occurring on a device. It asks whether this trojan can be detected via power-based, side-channel attacks only instrumenting the encryption itself, not the control flow of the trojan itself. By applying Automated Machine Learning techniques to search neural architecture, a classification of corrupted encryption operations is able to completely identify whether the operation corresponded with a corrupted operation or not. Through a number of experiments, we demonstrate this fact holds regardless of variable or constant plaintext, rotating encryption keys, or even with different corrupted keys.

Keywords: Side Channels · Hardware Trojan · Power Analysis · Deep Neural Network

1 Introduction

Information leakage has become a power approach for data exfiltration in modern systems. The advent of the field of side-channel attacks, having built upon abstractions and representations of specific hardware models over the last few decades, has enabled an entirely new class of exploits that require hardware designers to consider the data embedded in the power consumed by a device over the time it is operating. This change in the conceptualization of secure design, and the offensive explorations of devices this threat model enables.

At the same time as information extraction from power usage has begun to demonstrate the potential for key recovery [13], control flow recovery [18], and even classes of machine learning (ML) hyper-parameters [21], an increasingly relevant threat has emerged throughout the semiconductor manufacturing supply chain: hardware trojans (HT). A HT is additional hardware logic which modifies the intended behavior of a circuit.

As hardware components continue to be critical to modern technological advanced and society (e.g., scientific computing, healthcare, generative AI) the insertion of a service denying component into the hardware has the potential to be catastrophic. Developing measures for automated detection of HTs is critical.

© IFIP International Federation for Information Processing 2025
Published by Springer Nature Switzerland AG 2025
G. Rey et al. (Eds.): IFIPIoT 2024, IFIP AICT 737, pp. 175–185, 2025.
https://doi.org/10.1007/978-3-031-81900-1_11

1.1   Threat Model

This work is predicated on a specific and particular threat model. Under this threat model, we have a known 'good' device which we can confirm does not have a HT. This device can therefore be used to develop a characterization model of the specific task being performed by the device. For the purposed of this discussion, the task performed by the device is a lightweight, XOR-based, encryption of data using a stored embedded key. Other 'unknown' devices performing the same task may or may not contain a trojan, which performs ephemeral modifications to the internal embedded key outside of the realm of direct observability (e.g., perfectly obfuscated hardware).

When active, the trojan supplies a 'bad' key to the encryption operation. This is a valid key in that it is within the key space which the 'good' keys sample from, but it is considered 'bad' as it is not the key provided by the device operator. This thus corrupts the encryption operation so that a decryption operation performed with the key provided by the user to encrypt the data fails to correctly decrypt the data.

As a result of this behavior, even though the trojan may only be active a small portion of the time, all encryption operations performed on the potentially 'bad' device must be validated. This could require the encrypted data be immediately decrypted and validated on the bad device, raising questions about the trustworthiness of that assertion on a device which may be corrupted, or the encryption must be validated on a secondary device, vastly increasing the computational load of a simple encryption and distributing work across multiple devices.

This work addresses this threat by constructing an ML model which detects whether a specific operation on the potentially 'bad' board had the modeled trojan active or not. The exact mechanics of the trojan are left abstract by instrumenting our power trace capture to assume that all of the work to fetch and prepare keys and message data occurs outside the trace capture. Only the actual encryption is measured and then whether the trojan has corrupted the key or not is labeled by the ML model as a classification target.

This work is organized as follows. Section 2 explores foundations of HTs, power-based side-channel attacks, and applications of automated ML in those fields. Section 3 discusses experimental setup and design as well as the modeling techniques used to create the device trojan evaluated in this work. Section 4 and Sect. 5 present the findings of this work and discuss the context and implications of them within the wider field. Finally, we conclude in Sect. 6 with a discussion of future works, extensions, and the limitations bounding the claims laid out in this work.

2   Related Works

2.1   Overview of Side Channel Attacks

A side channel attack (SCA) is a class of attacks through which sensitive information can be obtained by exploiting information leakage whether it be physical or otherwise [10]. Much of the realm of SCA research involves a back and forth between developing new attacks which leverage the latest tools and algorithms to defeat existing countermeasures, and developing new countermeasures to combat those attacks. One SCA-resistant countermeasure proposed performs Hamming distance (HD) redistribution to make the HD probabilities unable to be distinguished from correct and incorrect keys [19]. Another countermeasure equalizes the electromagnetic profile of a chip by adjusting the power grid impedance to protect against electromagnetic analysis [20]. An example of developing an attack to circumvent a countermeasure can be found in Cagli et al. where a convolutional neural network was used against jitter-based countermeasures [3]. This work falls directly under neither umbrella of attacks or countermeasures, instead acting as an attack discovery tool.

There are many other works in the last decade which explore the different types of SCAs, several of which are highlighted in the survey performed by Hettwer et al. [7]. Some of the most common SCAs include timing attacks, power analysis attacks, and electromagnetic analysis attacks, though there are several others which exploit areas such as audio and optics [6,10,14]. Some attacks, including power analysis attacks, can be further categorized. Simple Power Analysis (SPA) is the most base form of power based SCAs in that SPA involves directly interpreting power traces. Differential Power Analysis (DPA) is a similar but stronger because it can differentiate between power traces and reveal data leakage that may provide a correct key being guessed [15]. Both analyze power traces and are considered passive attacks because they are observational at their core, unlike some of their active SCA counterparts such as fault injection attacks which interfere with a program by inducing errors into computation [18].

2.2 Information Recovery from Power Based Side Channel Attacks

It has been shown that DPA excels at recovering keys and other information. In Carper at al., power based attacks on an embedded state machine revealed a maximum 81% of state transitions, and up to 100% in cases where dimensionality was reduced [4] which validated information-theory-based side channel risks in Finite State Machines proposed by Borowczak and Vemuri a decade earlier [2]. DPA is a particularly powerful SCA because it leverages the statistical power of a large number of power traces to overcome the low signal-to-noise ratios seen in most devices when trying to identify a single interesting operation amongst thousands of extraneous operations. Due to the success of these attacks, it is essential to address vulnerabilities, and though work has been done to protect against DPAs, little has been done using side channels to identify an attacker that has infiltrated a design. Herein lies the motivation for this work's ML model and power analysis based detection of HTs within a system.

2.3 Applications of Machine Learning

ML has been utilized in both an adversarial and a defensive manner within the SCA space. A multitude of ML models can be, and have been, applied to SCAs including support vector machines, decision trees, random forests, k-nearest neighbors [4], neural networks (NN) [3] and deep neural networks, otherwise known as deep learning [11]. Other documented uses of ML include: support vector machines in recovery of intermediate cipher states and mask recovery, random forests in direct key recovery via attacking individual key bits, and neural networks for leakage modeling [7].

In particular, deep neural networks (DNNs) form one interesting avenue for HT detection. In a survey of ML models for trojan detection, NNs using on-chip data such as power consumption performed better than their counterparts which used design netlist data and runtime traffic data [12]. The particular study which used NNs and on-chip data sought to embed detection within a device to detect trojans that were dormant during the validation phase [9]. This work has no restrictions on what time in the process the capture and evaluation of power traces is performed. Additionally, Jin et al. used spice-level Monte-Carlo simulation to generate instances of the trojan-free chips, and only collected current measurements when a pre-selected 64-bit block was transmitted [9], unlike this work which does not depend on simulation.

This study uses the automated ML system AutoKeras [8], an automated ML (AutoML) framework, to automatically select and tune a ML model capable of distinguishing between normal device operation and HT-enabled device operation. Utilizing AutoKeras avoids potential biases introduced by human selection of the deep neural network architecture by instead exploring the space of valid models. Multiple researchers have posited that there is no guarantee that an algorithm selected for a task is the optimal one, sometimes referred to as the 'no free lunch' theorem [7,17]. Use of automated ML mitigates this risk by comparing multiple models and parameter selection in order to identify the best candidate model [8]. For an in-depth discussion of the ML methods used see Sect. 3.2.

3   Methods

3.1   Hardware Trojan Model

If the presence of a HT can be detected based on the power consumption characteristics of a device, an experiment can be architected to capture power traces from an embedded system at specific points during programmatic execution. The malicious system being tested in this experiment is a denial-of-service trojan that modifies the base address of the key given to the system (expected key) with its malicious key (trojan key) to prevent decryption. Data captured is then used to train an ML model to determine if power traces can accurately assess the presence of a HT on the device.

Power and Communications captured were performed using an automated Python script referred to as the "host" and the Chipwhisperer Nano embedded systems board. The Chipwhisperer consists of two main components a capture component and a target component (STM32F030); while both components are built into the Chipwhisperer, they are separately mentioned throughout this work. Figure 1 illustrates the architectural layout of the experiment detailed in this work.

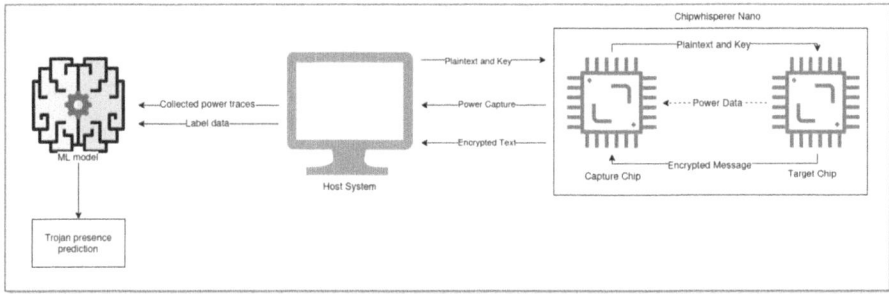

Fig. 1. The architecture detailed in this figure demonstrates the flow of information between the Chipwhisperer Nano's onboard components, the host system, and the ML model.

Hardware Platform: STMicroelectronics' ARM Cortex-M0 based STM32-F030 MCU was used as the experiment target since a hardware re-configurable system, such as an FPGA, would exhibit different trace characteristics than a fabricated processor addressed by the threat model. The Chipwhisperer [16] is a family of devices from NewAE Technologies' line of side-channel analysis-ready embedded systems boards which package a target device and power trace capture equipment onto a single or interoperable device. The device also exposes an API that makes use of an on-board capture chip to provide a serial communication protocol (referred to as 'simpleserial') alongside an interface to measure differential voltage through a shunt resistor facilitating power capture data and communications sent between the target system and host.

Target Implementation: The target board contains a firmware implementation of an XOR encryption scheme that utilizes messages and keys generated by the host system; information on key generation is further detailed in Sect. 4. Following key generation, the keys are transmitted serially and stored with a data structure which will be used to perform the encryption. Under normal operation the encryption process uses the key and message provided by the host. However, when the trojan is active, calling the encryption function will invoke a malicious key that is used to encrypt, causing data corruption which manifests as a denial of service.

In order to simplify post-processing, the firmware implementation within the target also contains trigger signals which the hardware platform uses to capture power consumption. The triggers are placed within the code such that the power consumption is only captured during encryption; the control flow, including data and key loading and activation of the trojan, is not captured within the trace. When the trojan is inactive and the trigger signal is driven high, the encryption structure containing all non-malicious data is accessed to perform the encryption. Once the encryption is complete, the trigger is driven low, concluding the trace; the result is sent back to the host machine. When the trojan is active, a malicious data structure is assigned a predetermined key of the same length replacing the expected key. Throughout the data capture process, visualized in Fig. 2 and Fig. 3, the encryption is repeated for each power trace until the necessary data is collected. Figure 4 illustrates the relative positioning of the relevant data mutation operations as well as the oscilloscope triggers and encryption operation.

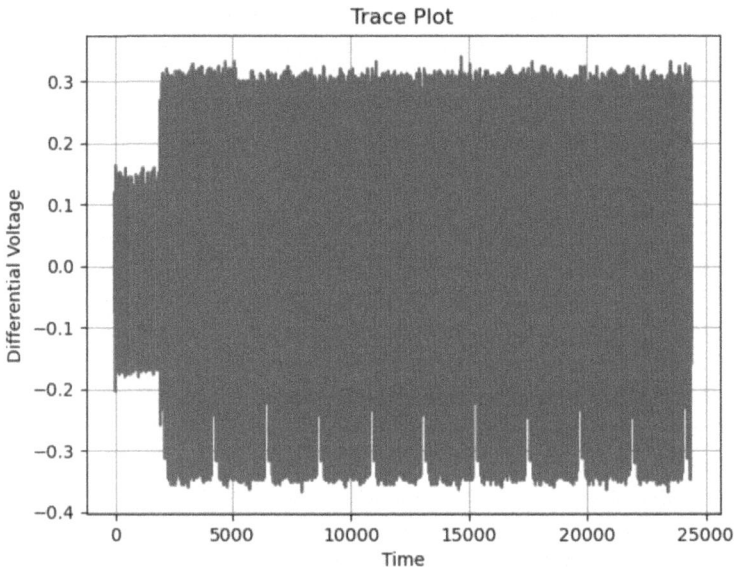

Fig. 2. Power trace without an active hardware trojan.

3.2   Machine Learning Methods

The HT detector was developed using existing ML/Deep Learning tools and pipelines running on a performance-enhanced desktop. Specifically, AutoML was used to develop DNN models while calculation acceleration was handled using Tensorflow [1] running on an Nvidia 4090 GPU on a system running Arch Linux with kernel version 6.9.2 and with 32 GB of available RAM. The automated neural architecture search (NAS) approach made use of the AutoML package AutoKeras [8] which is itself built upon the Keras deep learning library [5]. Following the data capture process previously detailed, this technology stack was utilized for the machine learning pipeline.

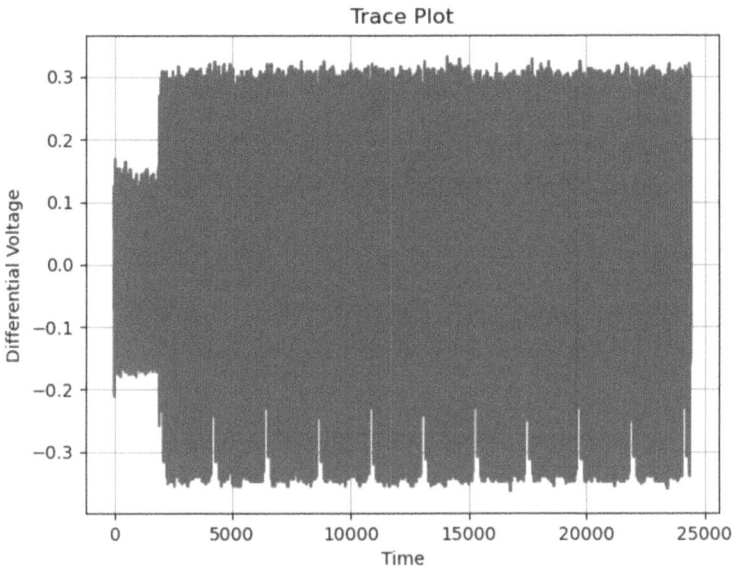

Fig. 3. Power trace of an active hardware trojan.

Each experiment begins with collecting 'trojan' and 'non-trojan' powertraces by randomly selecting a message from the entire message space ($B^{64} = 2^{64}$) and encrypting it with either the 'trojan' or 'non-trojan' logic. Over all experiments, the most 'trojan' and 'non-trojan' samples collected was 100K for each. Though there is a non-zero likelihood of message-collision the likelihood of significant overlap is incredibly unlikely as each collection of 100K messages/traces represents less than 0.15% of the message space.

```
if TROJAN then
    key = trojan_key
end if
trigger-high()                                    ▷ Begin Trace Capture
for n = 0, ..., Message-size do
    ciphertext[n] = message[n] ⊕ key[n  mod  Key_Size]
end for
trigger-low()                                     ▷ Stop Trace Capture
if TROJAN then
    key = expected_key
end if
```

Fig. 4. Trigger locations in relation to encryption and key provision code. 'TROJAN' is a signal value which could be derived from a control line in a physical trojan but is simulated as a variable in the model detailed herein.

Once collected, the dataset, consisting of an equal number of labeled 'trojan' and 'non-trojan' powertraces was randomly shuffled. The dataset was then split 80/20 into a training and testing dataset. The testing data set was never shown to the AutoKeras tool. The training dataset was then used in the AutoKeras pipeline which further split the data into a training and validation dataset again with a 80/20 split uniformly sampling from traces with a trojan and without one ensuring that no traces are present in both the training and validation data sets. AutoKeras was then configured to explored 50 unique deep learning network architectures for 25 training epochs before selecting the best-performing model. The best model was automatically selected by AutoKeras according to accuracy and training loss. Finally, the reserved testing dataset was used to further confirm the accuracy of the model.

Following this phase of exploring the neural architecture space, the model that performed the best was trained for a full 100 training epochs before the final model performance was evaluated. All of the performance metrics presented in this work are the metrics of this fully trained model unless otherwise specified.

4   Results

The experimental configurations used for experimentation underwent various revisions tested using the same ML configuration and a 4:1 split of the data. All of the data present in the training set, the larger of the two sets was only used for training while all of the data in the validation set, the smaller of the two, was only used for determining validation performance. The configurations will be detailed in order of increasing sophistication and expected difficulty for trace recovery.

The initial trial was configured to use a predetermined expected key and message of lengths 4 and 64 bytes respectively. The trojan configuration used a 1-byte trojan key to replace the expected key. The ML model reported that the validation accuracy was 100% with a validation loss of 0.00.

The secondary trial configuration included the implementation of random expected keys and messages with the same predetermined lengths to help mitigate any static key detection bias from the power traces captured. The trojan configuration remained the same for this trial. The ML model reported that the validation accuracy was 100% with a validation loss of 0.00.

The final trial configuration consisted of a change to the trojan where the trojan key had the same length as the expected key. Two trojan keys were tested during this phase to mitigate further biased detection of a malicious key, where one key had a hamming weight of 4 and another of 16. The ML model reported that the validation accuracy was 100% with a validation loss of 0.00.

The models selected during the NAS had similar architecture across all variations of the experiments. The specific architecture for the experiment conducted with randomly sampled messages, randomly sampled keys, and an expected hamming weight trojan key is detailed in Table 1. In this table, the output count is the number of outputs from a layer and the 'Params' value is the number of tunable model parameters present in that layer of the neural network. The model had a final, trained size of 47.72MB, which represents an 1000x reduction in the size when compared to the raw dataset of traces which is 39 GB in size, uncompressed.

Table 1. The deep learning model layered architecture including descriptions of size and parameter counts. Layer types are derived from the Autokeras reporting of the trained model.

Layer Type	Output Count	Params
Input Layer	24400	0
Cast to Float32	24400	0
Dense	512	12,493,312
ReLU	512	0
Dropout	512	0
Dense	32	16,416
ReLU	32	0
Dropout	32	0
Dropout	32	0
Dense	1	32
Activation	1	0

5 Discussion

Contrasted to related works in HT detection which were simulated [9] or depended on combinations of on-chip data, netlist data, and runtime traffic data [12] the results of this work show that it is possible to detect a simulated hardware trojan when observing the power consumption utilized for the encryption function depending on if the expected or malicious key is used. Originally it was hypothesized that it would be possible to detect a simulated HT, however, the accuracy at which the ML model performed this task exceeded the target accuracy of 95% achieving an accuracy of 100%; attempts to increase the sophistication of the attack by randomizing messages; randomizing expected keys; and padding the length of the trojan key to that of the expected key, all yielded the same accuracy by the ML model. Further investigation is required to asses how the ML model accomplished this level of accuracy.

It is recognized that this is a firmware implementation for a static chip to emulate a HT and power capture data may present itself differently in a production environment. To further expand upon this work, chip fabrication may be an option to get a more comparable result to an environment where the trojan is built into the package of a chip. Further works may expand on power exploitation as a method to retrieve workflow from fabricated chips and as an avenue for enabling a HT on fabricated devices.

6   Conclusion

This work presents an approach for developing a side channel-based trojan-detecting model with AutoML. Whether the encryption keys were rotated, the messages were randomized, or another corrupt key was utilized by the trojan, this approach led to complete recovery and identification of the traces as either being created by the device with the trojan or without it.

Future work plans to explore the volume of each type of data necessary to develop these models. Currently, the threat model we are working under requires extensive characterization work. A model which requires fewer correct or 'bad' traces would be valuable as it simplifies the construction of these models outside of the idealized environment created within the research lab. Furthermore, we plan to explore the potential for these models to be integrated into larger, stream-based detection systems to drive them from an offline detection model to an online model.

Acknowledgments. This study was funded in part by the ORCGS Fellowship at the University of Central Florida.

Disclosure of Interests. The authors have no competing interests to declare that are relevant to the content of this article.

References

1. Abadi, M., et al.: TensorFlow: large-scale machine learning on heterogeneous systems (2015). https://www.tensorflow.org/. Software available from tensorflow.org
2. Borowczak, M., Vemuri, R.: S* fsm: a paradigm shift for attack resistant FSM designs and encodings. In: 2012 ASE/IEEE International Conference on BioMedical Computing (BioMedCom), pp. 96–100. IEEE (2012)
3. Cagli, E., Dumas, C., Prouff, E.: Convolutional neural networks with data augmentation against jitter-based countermeasures. In: Fischer, W., Homma, N. (eds.) CHES 2017. LNCS, vol. 10529, pp. 45–68. Springer, Cham (2017). https://doi.org/10.1007/978-3-319-66787-4_3
4. Carper, C., Robins, A., Borowczak, M.: Transition recovery attack on embedded state machines using power analysis. In: 2022 IEEE 40th International Conference on Computer Design (ICCD), pp. 572–576. IEEE (2022)
5. Chollet, F., et al.: Keras (2015). https://github.com/fchollet/keras
6. Devi, M., Majumder, A.: Side-channel attack in internet of things: a survey. In: Mandal, J.K., Mukhopadhyay, S., Roy, A. (eds.) Applications of Internet of Things. LNNS, vol. 137, pp. 213–222. Springer, Singapore (2021). https://doi.org/10.1007/978-981-15-6198-6_20
7. Hettwer, B., Gehrer, S., Güneysu, T.: Applications of machine learning techniques in side-channel attacks: a survey. J. Cryptogr. Eng. **10**(2), 135–162 (2020)
8. Jin, H., Chollet, F., Song, Q., Hu, X.: Autokeras: an autoML library for deep learning. J. Mach. Learn. Res. **24**(6), 1–6 (2023). http://jmlr.org/papers/v24/20-1355.html

9. Jin, Y., Maliuk, D., Makris, Y.: Post-deployment trust evaluation in wireless cryptographic ics. In: Proceedings of the Conference on Design, Automation and Test in Europe. DATE '12, pp. 965–970. EDA Consortium, San Jose, CA, USA (2012)

10. Joy Persial, G., Prabhu, M., Shanmugalakshmi, R.: Side channel attack-survey. Int. J. Adv. Sci. Res. Rev **1**(4), 54–57 (2011)

11. Kubota, T., Yoshida, K., Shiozaki, M., Fujino, T.: Deep learning side-channel attack against hardware implementations of AES. Microprocess. Microsyst. **87**, 103383 (2021). https://doi.org/10.1016/j.micpro.2020.103383

12. Kundu, S., Meng, X., Basu, K.: Application of machine learning in hardware trojan detection. In: 2021 22nd International Symposium on Quality Electronic Design (ISQED), pp. 414–419 (2021). https://doi.org/10.1109/ISQED51717.2021.9424362

13. Lathrop, L.: Differential power analysis attacks on different implementations of AES with the Chipwhisperer Nano. Cryptology ePrint Archive (2020)

14. Méndez Real, M., Salvador, R.: Physical side-channel attacks on embedded neural networks: a survey. Appl. Sci. **11**(15), 6790 (2021)

15. Owen Lo, W.J.B., Carson, D.: Power analysis attacks on the aes-128 s-box using differential power analysis (DPA) and correlation power analysis (CPA). J. Cyber Secur. Technol. **1**(2), 88–107 (2017).https://doi.org/10.1080/23742917.2016.1231523

16. O'Flynn, C., Chen, Z.D.: ChipWhisperer: an open-source platform for hardware embedded security research. In: Prouff, E. (ed.) COSADE 2014. LNCS, vol. 8622, pp. 243–260. Springer, Cham (2014). https://doi.org/10.1007/978-3-319-10175-0_17

17. Picek, S., Heuser, A., Guilley, S.: Template attack versus Bayes classifier. J. Cryptogr. Eng. **7**(4), 343–351 (2017)

18. Robins, A., Olguin, S., Brown, J., Carper, C., Borowczak, M.: Power-based side-channel attacks on program control flow with machine learning models. J. Cybersecur. Privacy **3**(3), 351–363 (2023)

19. Shan, W., Zhang, S., Xu, J., Lu, M., Shi, L., Yang, J.: Machine learning assisted side-channel-attack countermeasure and its application on a 28-nm AES circuit. IEEE J. Solid-State Circuits **55**(3), 794–804 (2019)

20. Wang, C., Cai, Y., Wang, H., Zhou, Q.: Electromagnetic equalizer: an active countermeasure against EM side-channel attack. In: 2018 IEEE/ACM International Conference on Computer-Aided Design (ICCAD), pp. 1–8 (2018).https://doi.org/10.1145/3240765.3240804

21. Wolf, S., Hu, H., Cooley, R., Borowczak, M.: Stealing machine learning parameters via side channel power attacks. In: 2021 IEEE Computer Society Annual Symposium on VLSI (ISVLSI), pp. 242–247. IEEE (2021)

IoT or CPS Applications and Use Cases

Actuation Conflict Management in Internet of Things Systems DevOps: A Discrete Event Modeling and Simulation Approach

Laurent Capocchi[1]($\boxtimes$), Jean-Francois Santucci[1]🆔, Jean-Yves Tigli[2]🆔,
Thibault Gomnin[2], Stephane Lavirotte[2]🆔, and Gerald Rocher[2]🆔

[1] SPE UMR CNRS 6134, Univ. of Corsica, Campus Mariani, 20250 Corte, France
`{capocchi,santucci}@univ-corse.fr`
[2] I3S UMR CNRS 7271, Campus SophiaTech, 06903 Sophia Antipolis, France
`{jean-yves.tigli,thibault.gomnin,stephane.lavirotte,`
`gerald.rocher}@unice.fr`

Abstract. In IoT DevOps, simulating actuation conflict management is crucial for enhancing conflict detection and resolution in concurrent IoT applications. This paper introduces a new discrete event modeling and simulation approach for IoT systems during the design phase. Its objectives are to identify potential conflicts arising from competing smart applications accessing shared actuators or physical properties and to validate actuation conflict management specifications aimed at resolving conflicts among concurrent access attempts to IoT devices. The formalism of discrete event system specification is employed to model IoT systems formally, incorporating an actuation conflict management simulation model. This aids designers in the resolution of actuation conflicts.

Keywords: Actuation Conflicts · Discrete-Event · Internet of Things · Modeling · Discrete-Event Simulation

1 Introduction

Detecting and managing actuation conflicts in IoT systems is crucial to ensure the smooth operation, reliability and security of these systems. Work in this area aims to develop methods, tools and techniques to identify, prevent and resolve conflicts between actuators, taking into account the specific needs of IoT applications.

In the field of IoT conflict management, validation plays an important role in verifying conflicts by considering events and possible actions on actuators [1] managed by concurrent smart applications. However, new challenges appear when smart applications become available to control shared IoT devices that involve actuators that process commands into physical effects. One of these challenges is managing *actuation conflicts* that can arise when various applications

© IFIP International Federation for Information Processing 2025
Published by Springer Nature Switzerland AG 2025
G. Rey et al. (Eds.): IFIPIoT 2024, IFIP AICT 737, pp. 189–206, 2025.
https://doi.org/10.1007/978-3-031-81900-1_12

compete to access shared actuators (*direct conflicts*) or shared physical properties (*indirect conflicts*). Consider, for example, a smart home scenario in which a first application that controls lights and blinds to reduce energy consumption competes with a second application that contributes to user well-being by controlling the same lights and blinds and all other actuators relevant to this end. At any given time, either of the applications may trigger the *antagonistic commands* on these shared actuators, causing a direct conflict to develop. Based on the previous scenario, you can also consider concurrent applications for controlling home temperature by heating, cooling, blinding, etc. at the same time. In such a context, an indirect conflict may occur when both applications trigger heating and cooling commands, i.e., *to different actuators competing for the same physical property*, temperature in this case.

These actuation conflicts must be considered by designers and not delegated to end users. The goal is to provide actuation conflict management (ACM) mechanisms that identify and address direct and indirect actuation conflicts early in the design phase. According to ACM specifications, validation is crucial for verifying ACM properties, especially considering IoT-based application events and potential actuator actions in simulated environments. This validation is essential to ensure ACM specifications hold true in real-world scenarios, particularly in cases of direct and indirect conflicts (ACM, [9]).

In software development, testing is paramount, especially in the DevOps cycle. However, in IoT-oriented development, creating a production-like environment for testing can be challenging. Accessing devices, sensors, and actuators in their intended deployment environments is often difficult due to various constraints. Physical networks are typically dedicated to production software, making testing on them cumbersome and potentially disruptive to operations. Software simulators offer a solution by providing developers with a testing environment to begin application testing. While simulators alleviate some challenges, they fall short when applications rely on external networks of sensors and actuators. In such cases, IoT testbeds become crucial. Testbeds, like IoT-Lab and SmartSantander, offer real-world environments for application testing, though they may have predefined configurations and shared access, posing challenges for performance measurement.

Discrete Event Modeling and Simulation (M&S) can validate ACMs early in the design stage using the DEVS formalism. DEVS models allow for modular and hierarchical modeling, enabling simulation-based validation of ACM components in a simulated physical environment. Additionally, custom ACM formal verifications can be complemented with tests on concrete ACMs to ensure validated properties are preserved.

2   Contribution

The proposed article follows [3] and its main contribution appears at the last two levels of the following custom ACM design process (Fig. 1):

– At a first level, *Logical ACM Design* allows custom ACMs *logical properties* (e.g. completeness, safety, liveness, etc.) to be formally verified by using state-of-the-art methodologies (Model Checking [4,5]). In this paper, custom ACMs are thus defined through Finite State Machines (FSM) and are given by the designer.

– At a second level, *Model Validation* allows custom ACMs *conflict resolution effects on the environment* to be validated using DEVS (Discrete EVent system Specification) [12] simulation. The ACM DEVS model is obviously obtained from the ACM FSM including temporal properties (e.g. delayed events, state duration, etc.).

– At the third level, *Model Deployment* allows custom DEVS ACMs *temporal properties* to be formally verified through different *asynchronous execution machine strategies* associated with the ACM FSM. DEVS formalism is used to simulate the different implementation strategies. This level is not discussed in this paper and will be included in future work.

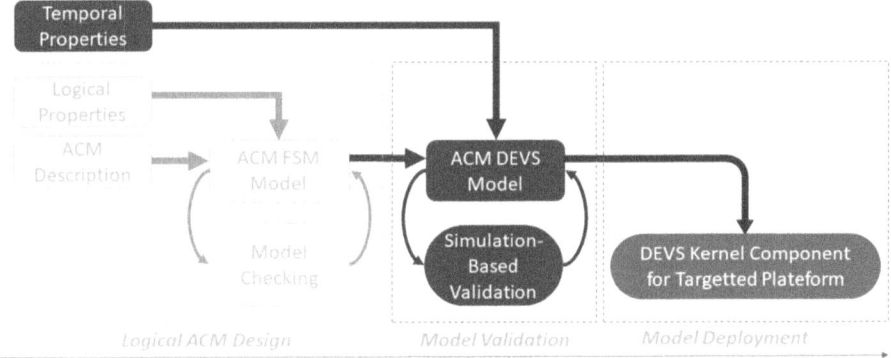

Fig. 1. Custom ACM design process. The *Model Validation* and *Model Deployment* levels which include DEVS formalism represent the contribution of the proposed approach.

The proposed approach is based on the assumption of perfect knowledge of ACM rules defined as an automaton by the designer facing two kinds of issue. He has indeed to wait for the deployment phase in order to: (i) appreciate the effect of the conflict resolution (via the ACM rules) on the physical environment and (ii) take into account temporal aspects involved in the execution machine associated with ACM FSM (for instance, the trigger condition on the input events of the FSM).

In this article, a new discrete event M&S approach is introduced during the design phase of IoT systems to validate the ACM specifications, allowing one to answer the two previous issues.

The main contributions of the proposed M&S approach deal with the previous first issue and are as follows:

– Formally represent IoT systems as a DEVS system of systems to characterize event flow and component interactions.

- Automatically generating the list of potential conflicts from a DEVS formal description of the application flows: (i) physical effects on the environment for the indirect conflicts, and (ii) coupling for the direct conflicts.
- Modeling ACM rules as a DEVS generic component in a simulated environment composed of an assembly of actuators and sensor DEVS components.
- Simulating the conflict resolution based on a pseudo-random application flows events until all the conflict belonging to the previous list of potential conflicts have been considered.
- Measuring the quality of the ACM rules by introducing a component that analyzes the physical effects of the application flows from the sensors outputs.
- Investigating the effectiveness of the proposed approach using a smart home case study that involved IoT devices controlled by concurrent application flows that command actuators.

3   Background

3.1   ACM Assisted Design Principles

The DevOps approach facilitates continuous and swift software deployment. Designers are provided with pre-configured, off-the-shelf ACMs for local conflict resolution. A formal verification flow is recommended for designing reusable custom ACMs. Edge platforms are diverse, resource-constrained, and often operate with asynchronous events (van Steen, [10]).

The ACM component model can be represented as two entities: a Synchronizer that receives events from application flows and makes the Logical Behavior evolve from the inputs it transmits (Fig. 2).

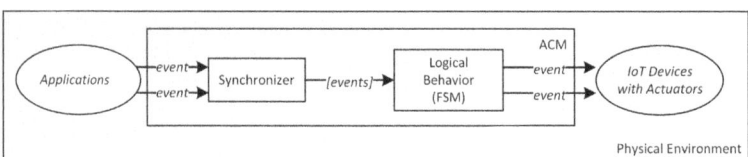

Fig. 2. The ACM component model with its Synchronizer and Logical Behavior models embedded in a Physical Environment including Application flows and IoT Devices (Actuators).

Designers typically employ a Logical Behavior component, represented as a Finite State Machine (FSM), to outline conflict resolution rules through state transitions and output functions. An execution engine is necessary to trigger these functions upon receiving inputs and generating outputs.

While a classic model-checking approach can validate the logic of the FSM-based Logical Behavior, it may not cover synchronization temporal aspects.

The Synchronization policy significantly influences the properties of the Logical Behavior component. The Synchronizer component aims to preprocess input events (actions from IoT-based application flows) by synchronizing and serializing them based on a strategy defined during the design phase. This strategy could involve waiting for all input events before triggering output, sending input events as soon as possible, or adhering to specific time intervals.

Designers rely on estimating application dynamics to define strategies, but finding the best strategy without testing during deployment is challenging. Validating strategies through discrete event M&S before deployment enables designers to choose strategies ensuring synchronization between applications and conflict resolution. In the DevOps for IoT context, deploying to a real target for bench testing is often impossible. Discrete event simulation integrates the IoT physical environment into conflict management, allowing anticipation of conflict detection and resolution in complex scenarios before deployment.

3.2 Discrete Event System Specification

The discrete event system specification (DEVS) formalism, introduced by Zeigler in the 1970s [12], introduced a hierarchical and modular approach to the design of a discrete event system. DEVS formalizes what a model is, what should contain and what should not include (Experimentation and Simulation Control Parameters are not contained in the model). All systems that accept events as input in time and generate events as output over time are equivalent to DEVS. Using DEVS, large-system model can be separated into small-model components with connections between them. DEVS formalism defines two types of models: (i) atomic models, which represent basic models providing subsystem dynamics specifications through function transitions, and (ii) coupled models, which describe how several component models (which may be atomic or coupled models) are combined to form new models. The atomic DEVS model can be thought of as an automaton (like the Mealy finite state machine) with a set of states and transition functions for state change when an event takes place or not. When no event occurs, the state of the atomic model can be modified using an internal transition function (δ_{int}). When external events occur, an atomic model can intercept them and change their state by applying an external transition function (δ_{ext}). The lifetime of a state is determined by the t_a time advance function. Each state change can generate an output message through the output function λ. In classic DEVS with port formalism, an atomic model AM is defined as follows:

$$AM =< X, Y, S, \delta_{int}, \delta_{ext}, \lambda, t_a >$$

where:

- $X : \{(p, v) \mid (p \in InputPorts, v \in X_p)\}$ is the set of input ports and values
- $Y : \{(p, v) \mid (p \in OutputPorts, v \in Y_p)\}$ is the set of output ports and values
- S: is the set of sequential states
- $\delta_{int} : S \rightarrow S$ is the internal transition function that will move the next state after the time returned t_a

- $\delta_{ext} : Q \times X \rightarrow S$ is the external transition function that will schedule the changes of the states in reaction to an external input event
- $Q = \{(s,e) \mid s \in S, 0 < e < t_a(s)\}$ is the set of total states where e is the elapsed time since the last transition and s the partial set of states for the duration of $t_a(s)$ if no external event occur
- $\lambda : S \rightarrow Y$ is the output function that will generate external events before the δ_{int} takes places
- $t_a : S \rightarrow \mathbb{R}^+_{0,\infty}$ is the time advance function, which will give the life time of the current state.

The dynamic interpretation is as follows: the state set $Q = \{(s,e) \mid s \in S^h, 0 < e < t_a(s)\}$ includes s, the partial state, and e, the elapsed time since the last transition. The internal transition δ_{int} moves the model from s to $s' = \delta_{int}(s)$ if no external event occurs before $t_i + t_a(s)$. For an external event, δ_{ext} updates the state to s', resetting e to 0. The output function λ is executed before an internal transition, placing the model in a transient state. States with infinite lifetime are passive (*steady state*), while others are active (*transient*). Passive states change only with an input event.

Connections between various atomic models can be made with a coupled model (CM). Coupled models tell us how to create a new model when multiple component models are joined together. This type of model can be used as a component of a larger coupled model and allows complex models to be constructed hierarchically. The DEVS coupled model CM has the following structure:

$$CM = < X, Y, D, \{M_d \in D\}, EIC, EOC, IC >$$

where:

- X is the set of input ports for the reception of external events.
- Y is the set of output ports for the emission of external events.
- D is the set of components (coupled or basic models).
- M_d is the DEVS model for each $d \in D$.
- EIC is the set of input links that connects the input of the coupled model to one or more of the inputs of the components that it contains.
- EOC is the set of output links that connect the output of one or more of the contained components to the output of the coupled model.
- IC is the set of internal links that connect the output ports of the components to the input ports of the components in coupled models.

In a coupled model, an output port from a model $M_d \in D$ can be connected to the input of another $M_d \in D$ but cannot be connected directly to itself. The coupled model shows how to couple (bind) multiple model components to form a new model in a coupled model. The latter model itself can be used to be a component of an integral model, resulting in a hierarchical structure.

In the context of the DEVS formalism, a simulator is associated with it to perform the instructions of the combined model to actually generate its behavior. DEVS simulation system is derived from abstract simulator concepts associated with hierarchical and modular DEVS formalisms.

As part of designing custom ACMs, the DEVS formalism has the following main advantages:

1. Provides a common representation of the various existing discrete event modeling formalisms (including Petri Nets, FSM, and different state machines) [13]. Therefore, designers do not have to be limited to a specific modeling framework when designing custom ACMs.
2. It allows one to build a library of reusable DEVS-based ACMs (a.k.a., DEVS kernels) targeting different implementation strategies (i.e., hardware platforms).
3. Allows the encapsulation of discrete synchronous event models in asynchronous environments [10]. This is absolutely crucial when considering the fact that software components are likely to be installed on various *resource-constrained* hardware platforms at the edge of infrastructure.
4. As mentioned in [11], according to the DEVS design pattern-based approach, "DEVS may be the best candidate to implement conflict resolution in today's complex systems of system design problems".

4   DEVS-Based Validation of Conflict Detection and Resolution in IoT Systems

This section provides a formal description of the proposed approach, including direct and indirect conflict definitions and DEVS modeling of IoT systems in the context of action conflict management. A practical example is provided to illustrate the validation process.

4.1   Overview

A DEVS general ACM test model comprises various types of atomic models, as shown in Fig. 2. An ACM component relies on a logical behavior description executed within an execution engine, equipped with a synchronizer to manage its logical behavior model based on asynchronous events. Consequently, the DEVS formalism represents an ACM component with a coupled model consisting of two atomic models, as detailed in Sect. 3.1.

To compare different ACM components, a pseudo-random test pattern is defined to automatically generate test sequences, aiming for efficiency. These sequences involve events sent to actuator devices by applications in the IoT system under test. The test sequence length is determined based on the percentage of conflicts detected by the current test pattern, derived from potential conflicts arising from application flows. Once a satisfactory conflict detection rate is achieved, the pseudo-test pattern generation ceases, and a simulation process calculates the conflicts detected by the sequence.

Subsequent sections discuss IoT conflict definitions and formal DEVS descriptions of ACM component test models, employing the following notation: N denotes the number of application flows, where an application flow app_k^d emits $k \in K^{app}$ events to device $d \in D$. D represents the set of M IoT devices, while $N^d \in N$ signifies the number of applications controlling the same device d.

4.2 Direct and Indirect Conflicts Definition

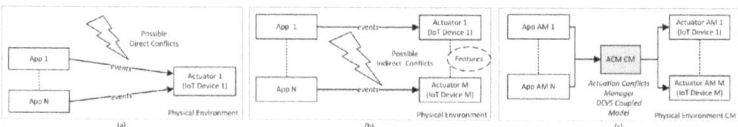

Fig. 3. Two types of conflicts in IoT systems: (**a**) Direct conflicts between N application flows and an IoT device (actuator) that is affected by one of its characteristics (**b**) Indirect conflicts between N application flows and M IoT devices that affect characteristics related to the physical environment (noise, for example) (**c**) ACM DEVS Coupled Model has been introduced to detect and validate by simulation the possible resolution of both direct and indirect conflicts.

Conflicts in IoT systems arise when their safety properties (feature of the actuators or environment) are violated, for example, when multiple application flows attempt to control the same IoT device (actuator) and affect one feature of the same IoT device. Some conflicts can be classified as direct as in the previous case (Fig. 3(a)) and indirect when, for example, application flows affect a property of IoT devices included in the physical environment contradictorily (Fig. 3(b)). The proposed simulation-based approach aims to intercept all events between application flows (actions) and IoT devices (actuators) to detect potentially direct and indirect conflicts and validate specific strategies applied by a specific component called Actuation Conflict Management (ACM) (Fig. 3(c)), which can then try to resolve conflicts.

Actuation conflicts can occur when applications have shared concurrent access to an actuator and when actuators produce contradictory actions within a common physical and local environment.

A direct conflict between N applications ($N \geq 2$) that send opposite N events e on a device d during a period of time Δ_t ($\Delta_t \in \mathbb{R}_{0,\infty}^+$) can be specified as follows:

$$('direct', [app_i/(e_i, t_i), app_j/(e_j, t_j)], d) | i \neq j, e_i \neq e_j,$$
$$|t_j - t_i| \leq \Delta_t, i \in [0, N], j \in [0, N].$$

Direct conflicts can typically also be considered when $\Delta_t = 0$ (events at the same time) on an IoT device that receives events from apps simultaneously.

An indirect conflict related to a device d in a state s that affects a feature f (property) and N apps that send an event e to other devices that affect the same feature in a not desired way. It can be specified as follows:

$$('indirect', [app, (e, t)], (d, s), f).$$

Direct and indirect conflicts can occur simultaneously and affect the same devices. In such a case, the resolution should apply specific rules to solve both concurrent conflicts.

Let us consider the hypothesis in which one application commands only one device, the number K^{app} of events sent by an app is equal to the number of events K^d received by the associated device d. The number of possible direct conflicts Nb^{dc} is determined as follows:

$$Nb^{dc} = \sum_{d \in D} K^d \sum_{i \in [1, N^d]} (N^d - i). \tag{1}$$

Regarding the number of possible indirect conflicts, consider the characteristic property as: $features = \{f : [\{(d, s)\}, \{(app, e)\}] \mid d \in D, s \in S_d \text{ and } e \in K^{app}\}$ is a dictionary with environmental characteristics f as keys and associated set of tuples containing the IoT device d in the current state s that can affect the characteristic f (noted A^f) and as values the tuple of app app that generate events e that produce an effect on a device that affects the characteristic f. The number of possible indirect conflicts Nb^{idc} can be obtained using the following formula:

$$Nb^{idc} = \sum_{f \in features} \sum_{app \in f} \mid A^f - (d^{app}, s) \mid, \tag{2}$$

where d^{app} is the device controlled by app and $\forall s \in S_{d^{app}}$.

4.3   DEVS Modeling

The DEVS Synchronizer model (Fig. 2) generates the Logical Behavior input according to the asynchronous input events of the application flows. The DEVS Synchronizer entity is modeled by the following DEVS atomic model:

$$Synchronizer = < X, Y, S, \delta_{int}, \delta_{ext}, \lambda, t_a >$$

where:

- $X : \{(p, v) \mid p \in [In_0, \ldots, In_N], v = (d, e) \mid d \in D, e \in E\}$ is the set of N input ports that can receive K events e from N application flows to control M IoT devices identified by their id d.
- $Y : (Out, [v]) \mid v = (d, e)$ is the set of unique output ports Out and the list of events sent $[v]$ depending on the selected trigger strategies
- $sigma \in \mathbb{R}^+_{0,\infty}$ is the variable introduced to manage the time advance function
- $state \in \{'IDLE', 'SEND'\}$ is the state space
- $buffer : \{p : [v]\}$ is a dictionary object with input ports p as keys and FIFO lists of received input events v (with a specific limit size) as values
- $condition$ is a string corresponding to the trigger condition defined at design phase
- $S : state \times sigma \times buffer$ is the set of sequential states
- $\delta_{int}(S \to S) :$ if $state ==' SEND'$ then $state \leftarrow ('IDLE', \infty, buffer)$

- $\delta_{ext}(Q \times X \to S)$:
  1.   loop p in X:
  2.   device,event $\leftarrow$ peek(p)
  3.   buffer[p] $\leftarrow$ [(device,event)]
  4.   S $\leftarrow$ ('SEND', 0, buffer) if *condition* otherwise (state, ∞, *buffer*)
- $\lambda(S \to Y)$:
  5.   output $\leftarrow$ filter(buffer)
  6.   send(Out,output) if state=='SEND'
  7.   buffer $\leftarrow$ []
- $t_a(S \to \mathbb{R}_{0,\infty}^+) \leftarrow sigma$

According to a selected triggering strategy, the *filter* function (line 5 in the previous DEVS specifications) is used to translate the buffer into an output message that includes input events to be sent to the Logical Behavior model. Different synchronizers correspond to different strategies and, therefore, different specifications for the parameter *condition* (line 4). For example, the first one can be based on a strategy called ASAP (as soon as possible). It triggers an execution cycle of the Logical Behavior as soon as an input event is received. The second can be based on conditional input and delayed triggering. This triggers a Logical Behavior execution cycle with the value of the received event if a delay has elapsed without any other events occurring before. If another event occurs in the meantime, the execution cycle is triggered with another value as input to the Logical Behavior.

A logical behavior entity is modeled as a DEVS atomic model with one input port and N output ports as:

$$Logical\_Behavior =< X, Y, S, \delta_{int}, \delta_{ext}, \lambda, t_a >$$

where:

- $X : (In, [v])$ *with* $v = (d, e), d \in D, e \in E$ is the unique input port In with the list of tuples (d, e) received from the Synchronizer model
- $Y : \{(p, v) \mid p \in [Out_0, Out_1] \cup [Out_2, \ldots, Out_M + 2], v \in D \cup E\}$ is the set of $M + 2$ output ports p corresponding to the first two output ports that give the direct and indirect conflict detection rate during simulation and the M output ports associated with the list of events resolved by the rules when a conflict occurred on M possible IoT devices.
- $sigma \in \mathbb{R}_{0,\infty}^+$ is the variable introduced to manage the t_a
- $state \in \{'IDLE', 'SEND'\}$ is the state space
- $inputs : \{app : [v]\}$ is a dictionary with the ID of the app (app) as keys and the following tuple as values: $v = (d, e, t) \mid d \in D, e \in E, t \in \mathbb{R}_{0,\infty}^+$ representing the event e sent at time t by the app to the device d
- $outputs : \{app : e\}, e \in K^{app}$ is a dictionary object with the ID of the app (app) as keys and no conflicting (or resolved) event to send on the IoT devices as values

- $current\_states : \{app : s\} \mid s \in S_d$ is the dictionary object with the ID of the app (app) as keys and the associated last received input events that correspond to the current state s of the IoT device d controlled by the app. S_d is the set of states of the IoT device d.
- $features$: is defined in Sect. 4.2. This list is defined by the designer who has knowledge of the states and events that will influence the features
- $conflicts$: is the list of direct or indirect conflicts between possible N applications (see Sect. 4.2). This attribute is initialized during the instantiation of the model using a method called $getConflictsList$ that accepts three input parameters: $inputs, features$, and $current\_states, \Delta_t$
- $\Delta_t \in \mathbb{R}_{0,\infty}^+$ is the period considered for the direct conflict
- fsm: is the finite state machine used to resolve conflicts
- $S : state \times sigma \times features \times current\_states$ is the set of sequential states
- $\delta_{int}(S \to S) : state \leftarrow ('IDLE', \infty, features, current\_states)$
- $\delta_{ext}(Q \times X \to S) :$
  1.   outputs $\leftarrow$ peek(In)
  2.   if $conflicts$ is not empty then:
  3.   c $\leftarrow getDirectConflict(outputs, \Delta_t) +$
         $getInDirectConflict(outputs, features, current\_states)$
  4.   if c is not empty then
  5.   outputs $\leftarrow ResolveConflict(c, fsm)$
  6.   del $conflicts[c]$
  7.   state $\leftarrow$ ('SEND', 0, features, $current\_states$)
  8.   else:
  9.   state $\leftarrow$ ('IDLE', ∞, features, $current\_states$)
- $\lambda(S \to Y) :$
  10.   send(0,$getDirectConflictRate()$)
  11.   send(1,$getInDirectConflictRate()$)
  12.   loop p in Y[2:]:
  13.   send(p,outputs[p])
- $t_a(S \to \mathbb{R}_{0,\infty}^+) \leftarrow sigma$

The $getDirectConflict$ (resp. $getInDirectConflict$) function returns the list of direct (resp. indirect) conflicts that can appear after having peeked the input events and stored them in the $outputs$ variable (line 1 of the δ_{ext} function of the DEVS model of Logical Behavior).

The algorithm $getConflictList$ is obtained by adding the results of the functions $getDirectConflict$ and $getInDirectConflict$. It is performed during the initialization phase of the Logical Behavior model and is executed while the length of the resulting list is not equal to the total number of conflicts obtained by adding Eqs. 1 and 2.

The $ResolveConflict$ function allows to resolve conflicts by applying rules implemented in the design phase using textual rules or FSMs. This function updates the variable $current\_state$.

The ACM model includes a Synchronizer and a Logical Behavior models and is modeled by a DEVS coupled model as:

$$ACM =< X, Y, D, \{M_d \in D\}, EIC, EOC, IC >$$

where:

- $X \leftarrow \{(p, v) \mid (p \in [In_0, \ldots, In_N], v \in [Event_0, \ldots, Event_M]\}$ is the set of input ports and the values of N.
- $Y \leftarrow \{(p, v) \mid (p \in [Out_0, \ldots, Out_N], v \in [Event_0, \ldots, Event_M]\}$ is the set of N output ports and the list of events resolved by the rules when a conflict occurred.
- $D \leftarrow \{Synchronizer, Logical\_Behavior\}$
- $\{M_d\}: \{M_{Synchronizer}, M_{Logical\_Behavior}\}$
- $EIC \leftarrow \{(In_0^{ACM}, In_0^{Synchronizer}), \ldots, (In_N^{ACM}, In_N^{Synchronizer})\}$
- $EOC \leftarrow \{(Out_0^{ACM}, Out_0^{Logical\_Behavior}), \ldots, (Out_N^{ACM}, Out_N^{Logical\_Behavior})\}$
- $IC \leftarrow \{(Out^{Synchronizer}, In^{Logical\_Behavior})\}$

4.4   Illustration on a Case Study

This section presents the modeling of a custom ACM within a smart home scenario using DEVSimPy [2]. Conflict detection in IoT-based smart homes is a growing research topic [7,8]. The scenario involves managing 216 applicative flows that control 37 actuators, including 13 types such as Window, Air Conditioner, and Light. Each actuator can be controlled by multiple applications, leading to potential access conflicts. For instance, both application 14 and application 134 can control the TV, generating conflicts like turning it on or off. DEVSimPy utilizes wxPython General User Interface for modeling systems based on the DEVS formalism, allowing the interconnection of atomic and coupled DEVS models from libraries. The custom ACM component is essential for detecting and resolving conflicts, such as direct conflicts in TV commands and indirect conflicts like "ambient noise level" caused by controlling both the Speaker and TV, both being sources of noise.

DEVSimPy Modeling: Figure 4 shows all DEVSimPy models defined to validate the proposed approach that focuses on ACM model validation (Fig. 1).

The applicative flows are modeled by the *AppGen* atomic model that randomly generate output events corresponding to actions sent by the apps. They can be configured using two parameters: (i) the list l of events that will be sent randomly (ON or OFF); (ii) the pair (min, max) of the minimum and maximum time values of the set used to define the occurrence time of the randomly generated event.

How is the ACM DEVS Coupled Model Configured? The coupled model *ACM* comprises the *Synchronizer* and *LogicalBehavior* models, tracked by atomic models *MessageCollector*1 and *MessageCollector*2. In Fig. 4, the first two output ports of *MessageCollector*2 observe direct and indirect conflict

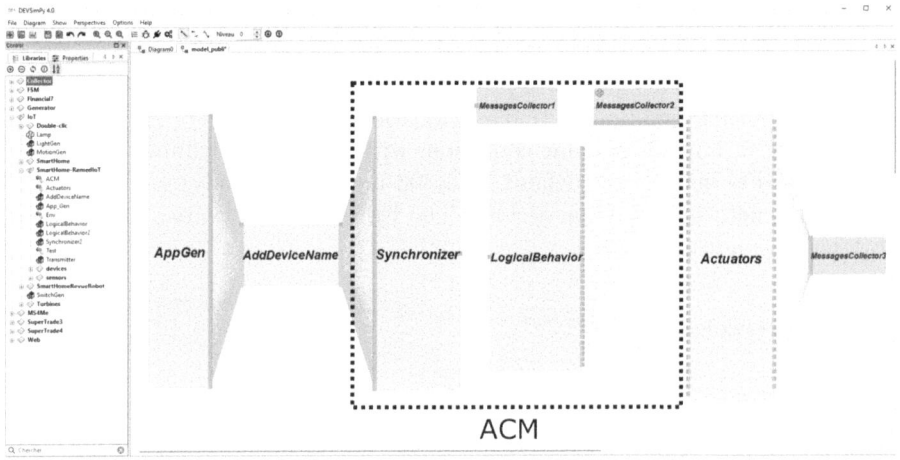

Fig. 4. DEVSimPy modeling of the Smart Home scenario with the ACM model connected the application flows and the Actuators coupled model. The Synchronizer and LogicalBehavior models belong to the ACM coupled model.

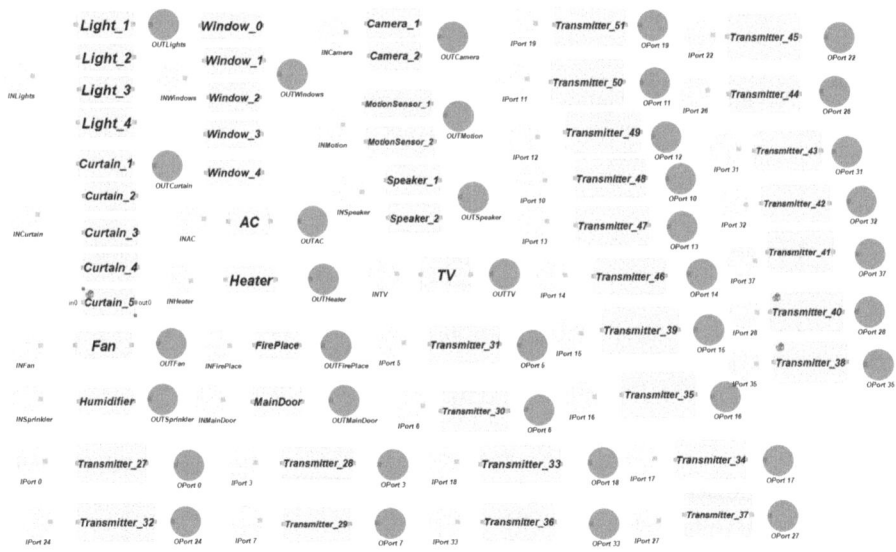

Fig. 5. Composition of the Actuators coupled model with the 37 atomic models corresponding to the actuators involved in the case study. The circles correspond to the input/output ports represented in green/red in the figure. (Color figure online)

detection rates during simulation. In the smart home use case, a complex policy requiring all inputs before sending output is adopted. This policy, defined in *Synchronizer*'s *filter* function, utilizes logical AND operators. For example,

"Input(1,0) != null OR Input(2,0) != null OR Input(3,0) != null" ensures ASAP behavior. Here, $Input(i)$ denotes events from different application flows, renamed according to their occurrence rank j. The trigger condition can also depend on a time period (clk), overriding textual specifications. The $Synchronizer$ model, as shown in Fig. 6, implements this condition, with properties defining the trigger condition, FIFO queue size (default 100, 300 in the case study), and time step for output generation based on a clock. The FIFO queue serializes input events per Trigger Condition rules.

Attribut	Valeur	Information
label	Synchronizer	Nom
label_pos	center	Position du nom
pen	['#add8e6', 1, 100]	Couleur et taille du pinceau
fill	['#add8e6']	Couleur de fond
font	[12, 74, 93, 700, 'Arial']	Police
image_path		Image de fond
input	216	Port d'entrée
output	1	Port de sortie
clk	0,000000	output frequency
eca_trigger_condition	Input(1,0) != null && Input(2,0)	the eca condition rule to
queue_size	300	size of the event queue of
python_path	Synchronizer2.py	Chemin du fichier python

Fig. 6. DEVSimPy Synchronizer model properties obtained by a double click. The *eca_trigger_condition* can be defined as a string. The *queue_size* defines the size of the input events FIFO buffer.

The specification of the *LogicalBehavior* DEVS model is defined by the designer:

- $X = \{In\}$, $Y = \{Out_i\}$ with $i \in [0, 36]$
- $inputs = \{$ "i" : ({"*device*" : "j", "*event*" : "ON", "*time*" : 0.0}, {"*device*" : "j", "*event*" : "OFF", "*time*" : 0.0}, ... "N" : ({"*device*" : "M", "*event*" : "ON", "*time*" : 0.0}, {"*device*" : "M", "*event*" : "OFF", "*time*" : 0.0})}$ for $i \in [1, N]$ and $j \in [1, M]$, N=266 and M=37 the number of app and the number of devices
- $outputs = \{0 : \emptyset, 1 : \emptyset, \ldots, 36 : \emptyset\}$
- $current\_states = \{1 : ON, 2 : OFF\}$ which is randomly initialized
- features={
  STATIONARITY:(camera,OFF; motion,OFF),
  ABSENCE:(user,OFF; camera,OFF, user_away_mode,OFF, wfh,OFF),
  COOL WITH HIGHT EXTERNAL TEMP: (ac,ON, windows,OFF, fan,ON),
  COOL WITH LOW EXTERNAL TEMP: (ac,ON, windows,ON, fan,ON),
  HOT WITH HIGHT EXTERNAL TEMP: (heater,ON, windows,ON, fireplace,ON),
  HOT WITH LOW EXTERNAL TEMP": (heater,ON, windows,OFF, fireplace,ON),

VENTILATION: (fan,ON, windows,ON, door,ON),
HUMIDITY: (fan,OFF, valve,OFF),
LUMINATION: (light,ON, lights,ON, curtain,ON),
ENERGY: (high_power,OFF, low_power,ON),
CONFORT: (curtain,OFF, lights,OFF, speaker,OFF),
SAFETY: (windows,OFF, camera,ON, door,OFF, alarm,ON,
electric_devices,OFF)}
– $\Delta_t = 0$

The state variable *inputs* contains i keys for each application flow, representing devices, events, and their respective occurrence times. For instance, app 1 activates the TV at time 0 with *"device"* : *"TV"*, *"event"* : *"ON"*, *"time"* : 0.0. The variable *features* outlines devices and applications with potential effects on the physical environment. Based on *inputs* and *features*, formulas 1 and 2 yield 3124 (direct) and 673 (indirect) conflicts. *AddDeviceName* links randomly generated events (ON/OFF from *AppGen*) to their originating applications. The *Actuators* DEVS coupled model comprises 37 device models built from 13 basic atomic models. The 12 other automata corresponding to the other actuator types have been designed in the same way.

How Are the Resolution Rules Defined? All detection and resolution processes consider previous information and the variable *fsm* corresponding to the designer's proposed FSM. The resolution rule for the case study is straightforward: the last app event is sent to a device with the first command. For instance, in a direct conflict on the light device between apps 216 (sending ON) and 85 (sending OFF), the event ON is sent to the light device (('direct', ('216/ON', '85/OFF'), 'light') → ('light', ON)). When both direct and indirect conflicts arise on the same device, indirect conflict resolution takes precedence over direct conflict resolution. While this rule is simplistic, designers can make it more complex, potentially involving users and artificial intelligence algorithms in conflict resolution. Users may be presented with a set of resolution rules by the algorithm, contributing to its learning database by making choices. This process empowers the algorithm to autonomously resolve conflicts without constantly seeking user input.

Three observer models (*MessageCollector* 1, 2, and 3 DEVS models) are presented to monitor temporal properties, outlined in Sect. 3.1. Specifically, *MessageCollector*3 represents the physical effects of 37 actuator devices, emphasizing adverse environmental impacts. *MessageCollector*2 measures the rate of conflicts detected (direct and indirect) throughout the simulation.

DEVS Simulation: The DEVSimPy simulation model shown in Fig. 4 is simulated to generate test patterns that allow us to point out all direct and indirect conflicts and validate that all conflicts are solved by the ACM model. Different types of conflict can arise on the devices, such as: window is ON and OFF at the same time, the lights are ON and OFF at the same time, etc.

The generator model *AppGen* is configured to send random actions (ON or OFF) at different simulation time-step intervals to simulate several scenarios, allowing the best possible conflict coverage rate.

The atomic model *AddDeviceName* makes a correspondence between the output port of *AppGen* and the corresponding application name.

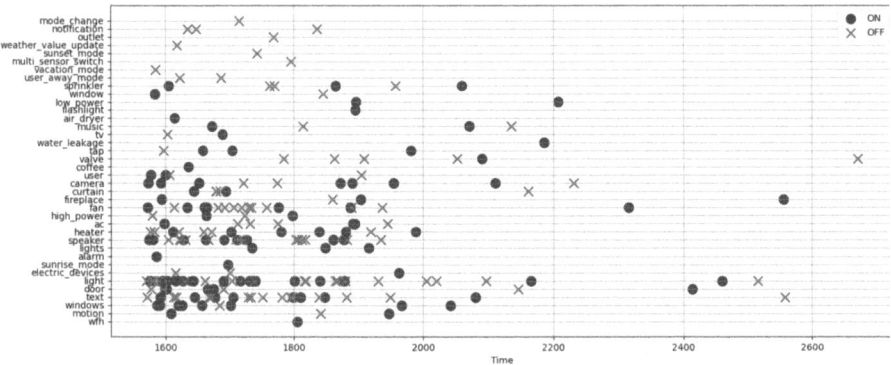

Fig. 7. Example of an output from *AddDeviceName* displaying randomly generated events (ON or OFF) from the presented applications on the ordinate axis. Events can be generated by different applications simultaneously and cause direct or indirect conflicts.

The Fig. 7 provides an example of the output of the *AddDeviceName* model, which serves as an input to the *Synchronizer* model. During the simulation, *AppGen* and *AddDeviceName* will generate multiple messages of this type, varying the event and the generation time for each application. The simulation ends when all conflicts included in the *conflicts* list are detected (when the *conflicts* list is empty, line 8 of the *LogicalBehavior* DEVS specification in Sect. 4.3).

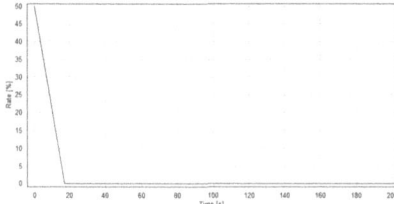
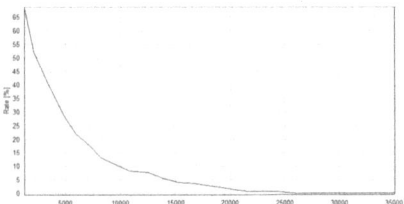

(a) Rate of undetected direct conflicts after 200 simulation steps.

(b) Rate of undetected indirect conflicts after 35000 simulation steps.

Fig. 8. Comparison of conflict detection rates.

Figure 8b that 30% of indirect conflicts are detected at the start of the simulation and the other 50% before the 2500 simulation time step. Figure 8a shows that direct conflicts are more difficult to raise, since we have to wait 30 time steps to obtain a 100% detection.

These two figures indicate that these test patterns allow us to highlight all direct and indirect conflicts after 30000 simulation time steps.

5   Conclusion and Future Work

This paper presents a novel simulation-based discrete event approach for validating actuation conflict management strategies in IoT systems. The key contribution lies in validating ACM specifications to resolve conflicts in the physical environment using pseudo-random application flow generators. This validation is achieved through DEVS simulations with and without the ACM component, demonstrated through a case study involving apartment actuators controlling comfort and communication features. A comprehensive formal verification flow is proposed for designing reusable custom ACMs. Given the heterogeneous and resource-constrained nature of edge platforms, temporal property verification in DEVS formalism is proposed to validate ACM behavior alongside logical properties. DEVS also enables building a library of reusable DEVS-based ACMs for different hardware platforms.

Future work aims to leverage this approach to expedite IoT software development by providing standard conflict management solutions for diverse hardware platforms and middleware solutions (e.g., node-red, ThingML) using an automatic implementation of DEVS simulation kernel. Additionally, exploring DEVS M&S potentialities, such as synchronization strategies, conflict resolution algorithms, realistic actuator behavior modeling, and environment modeling based on real sensor signals and continuous models, could further aid ACM component validation.

Acknowledgments. The research that led to these results has received funding from the European Commission's H2020 program under grant agreement numbers 780351 [6] (ENACT).

References

1. Al Farooq, A., Al-Shaer, E., Moyer, T., Kant, K.: IoTC2: a formal method approach for detecting conflicts in large scale IoT systems. In: 2019 IFIP/IEEE Symposium on Integrated Network and Service Management (IM), pp. 442–447 (2019)
2. Capocchi, L.: DEVSimPy. https://github.com/capocchi/DEVSimPy. Accessed 10 Oct 2019
3. Capocchi, L., Santucci, J.F., Tigli, J.Y., Gonnin, T., Lavirotte, S., Rocher, G.: A new discrete-event simulation based approach for validating actuation conflict management in IoT systems. In: 2021 Annual Modeling and Simulation Conference (ANNSIM), pp. 1–12 (2021). https://doi.org/10.23919/ANNSIM52504.2021.9552098

4. Clarke Jr, E.M., Grumberg, O., Kroening, D., Peled, D., Veith, H.: Model Checking. MIT Press (2018)
5. Fang, Z., et al.: A model checking-based security analysis framework for IoT systems. High-Confidence Comput. **1**(1), 100004 (2021). https://doi.org/10.1016/j.hcc.2021.100004
6. Ferry, N., et al.: ENACT: development, operation, and quality assurance of trustworthy smart IoT systems. In: Bruel, J.-M., Mazzara, M., Meyer, B. (eds.) DEVOPS 2018. LNCS, vol. 11350, pp. 112–127. Springer, Cham (2019). https://doi.org/10.1007/978-3-030-06019-0_9
7. Huang, B., Chaki, D., Bouguettaya, A., Lam, K.Y.: A survey on conflict detection in IoT-based smart homes. ACM Comput. Surv. **56**(5) (2023). https://doi.org/10.1145/3629517
8. Pradeep, P., Kant, K.: Conflict detection and resolution in IoT systems: a survey. IoT **3**(1), 191–218 (2022). https://doi.org/10.3390/iot3010012. https://www.mdpi.com/2624-831X/3/1/12
9. Rocher, G., et al.: An actuation conflicts management flow for smart IoT-based systems. In: 2020 7th International Conference on Internet of Things: Systems, Management and Security (IOTSMS), pp. 1–8 (2020). https://doi.org/10.1109/IOTSMS52051.2020.9340196
10. Van Der Schaft, A.J., Schumacher, J.M.: An Introduction to Hybrid Dynamical Systems, vol. 251. Springer, London (2000)
11. Zeigler, B.: DEVS-based building blocks and architectural patterns for intelligent hybrid cyberphysical system design. Information **12**(12) (2021). https://doi.org/10.3390/info12120531. https://www.mdpi.com/2078-2489/12/12/531
12. Zeigler, B.P., Muzy, A., Kofman, E.: Theory of Modeling and Simulation: Discrete Event & Iterative System Computational Foundations. Academic Press (2018)
13. Zheng, T., Wainer, G.A.: Implementing finite state machines using the CD++ toolkit. In: Proceedings of the SCS Summer Computer Simulation Conference, 2003. atomic model, 1 CD++, 1 coupled model, 1 DEVS, 1 DEVS Graph, 1 discrete-event modeling. Citeseer (2003)

Leveraging Task-Specific VAEs
for Efficient Exemplar Generation in HAR

Bonpagna Kann[1,2]([⊠]), Sandra Castellanos-Paez[1], Romain Rombourg[3],
and Philippe Lalanda[1]

[1] Univ. Grenoble Alpes, CNRS, Grenoble INP, LIG, 38000 Grenoble, France
{bonpagna.kann,sandra.castellanos,
philippe.lalanda}@univ-grenoble-alpes.fr
[2] Institute of Digital Research and Innovation, Cambodia Academy of Digital
Technology, Phnom Penh 121002, Cambodia
[3] Univ. Grenoble Alpes, CNRS, Grenoble INP, G2Elab, 38000 Grenoble, France
romain.rombourg@univ-grenoble-alpes.fr

Abstract. The emerging technologies of smartphones and wearable
devices have transformed Human Activity Recognition (HAR), offering
a rich source of sensor data for building an automated system to recognize people's daily activities. The sensor-based HAR data also enables
Machine Learning (ML) algorithms to classify various activities, indicating a new era of intelligent systems for health monitoring and diagnostics.
However, integrating ML into these systems faces the challenge of catastrophic forgetting, where models lose proficiency in previously learned
activities when introduced to new ones by users. Continual Learning
(CL) has emerged as a solution, enabling models to learn continuously
from evolving data streams while reducing forgetting of past knowledge.
Within CL methodologies, the use of generative models, such as Variational Autoencoders (VAEs), for example, has drawn significant interest for their capacity to generate synthetic data. This reduces storage
demands by creating on-demand samples. However, the application of
VAEs with a CL classifier has been limited to low-dimensional data or
fine-grained features, leaving a gap in harnessing raw, high-dimensional
sensor data for the HAR model. Our research aims to bridge this gap by
constructing VAEs with a filtering mechanism for direct training with
raw sensor data from the HAR dataset, enhancing CL models' capability
in class-incremental learning scenario. We demonstrate that VAE with
a boundary box sampling and filtering process significantly outperforms
both traditional and hybrid exemplar CL methods, offering a more balanced and diverse training set that enhances the knowledge acquisition
of the model. Our findings also emphasize the importance of sampling
strategies in the latent space of VAEs to maximize data diversity, crucial
for recognizing the variability in human activities for better representation of each activity in each CL task.

Keywords: Continual Learning · HAR · Replay Methods · VAE

© IFIP International Federation for Information Processing 2025
Published by Springer Nature Switzerland AG 2025
G. Rey et al. (Eds.): IFIPIoT 2024, IFIP AICT 737, pp. 207–225, 2025.
https://doi.org/10.1007/978-3-031-81900-1_13

1 Introduction

With the introduction of smartphones and wearable devices, a wealth of sensor data has become available, offering a more nuanced and automated approach to understanding human activities in HAR systems. These devices, carried by millions of users, continuously collect data through built-in sensors, such as accelerometers and gyroscopes, capturing the information of users' daily movements and behaviors. These data-driven HAR systems enable the development of ML algorithms to identify different activities through the patterns inherent in this sensor data. The shift towards leveraging ML models to interpret this data shows a promising insight into human activity, paving the way for intelligent systems capable of enhancing personal health tracking, and diagnosis.

However, the ever-changing nature of real-world data streams [3,30] poses a fundamental problem to classical ML approaches. More particularly, classically trained models tend to forget previously acquired knowledge when exposed to new data, a phenomenon called catastrophic forgetting. This issue is particularly relevant in HAR [35], where data streams come from sensors on smartphones or wearable devices, capturing activities of users such as walking, running, or sitting over time. As new activities are introduced, a traditional ML model might lose its ability to recognize the activities it was previously trained on. To alleviate this problem, Continual Learning (CL) is introduced, focusing on developing algorithms and methodologies that allow models to learn from changing data streams while retaining prior knowledge. In the context of CL, a *task* refers to learning how to recognize a set of activities, and a CL classifier is a model whose goal is to learn from a sequence of tasks. When a user performs more activities, additional tasks are added to the model training. CL approaches are thus applied to the model training to enable the model to adapt to new tasks sequentially without losing old knowledge. However, with the limitation in the size of training data in the context of sensor-based HAR, it is challenging to apply CL approaches in training a model from scratch. To mitigate this issue, using a pre-trained model in CL training provides a promising solution, as demonstrated in [15].

Among the strategies in CL, *replay methods* stand out for their ability to mitigate forgetting by revisiting a subset of old data when learning new tasks, thus preserving earlier knowledge. Despite their promise, storage constraints make it impractical and costly. Two approaches exist to address this issue: storing and exploiting a small subset of examples or training a generative model to generate as many examples as needed on the fly. The first approach naturally leads to heavy data imbalance while the second is more complex, and some generative models are notoriously hard to train.

Employing generative models, specifically Variational Autoencoders (VAEs), in CL can be a compelling solution. VAEs offer several key advantages in the context of CL on smart devices. They are lightweight, easy to train (contrary to GANs) and can generate samples at a low computational cost (contrary to Normalizing Flows or Score Matching methods).

By leveraging VAEs, smart systems can continuously learn and adapt to new activities without the limitations of data access size, ensuring that the storage costs are minimized. However, prior implementations have predominantly focused on low-dimensional data and engineered features. This leaves a gap in the application and effectiveness of these models when dealing with the complexity and high dimensionality characteristic of raw sensor-based HAR data.

Our work proposes an approach that uses task-specific VAEs for generating synthetic data for previous tasks from raw sensor data without the need for extensive pre-processing or feature engineering process, and trains the CL model on real data for the new classes and synthetic data for old classes. In Sect. 2, we present an overview of CL, elaborating different CL methodologies and their implementations across different fields, followed by a discussion on how VAEs contribute to support the CL model in mitigating forgetting while learning new knowledge. In Sect. 3, we describe the VAE-Based CL framework. In Sect. 4, we delve into experimental protocol details regarding CL training with both real and synthetic data samples. Experimental settings are presented in Sect. 5 and we discuss our findings in Sect. 6. Finally, we conclude our work and suggest future research directions.

2   Background and Related Work

In the domain of HAR, a number of previous works have been conducted on sensor-based HAR, emphasizing feature extraction methods and training process. Bulling et al. [4] investigated different feature extraction techniques based on statistical analysis on the features of the HAR data. Despite displaying encouraging results, the extracted features were carefully engineered and heuristic in the process, lacking a generalized or systematic approach for accurately classify human activities. To overcome this limitation, Hammerla et al. [10] examined the use of convolutional neural networks (CNNs), and recurrent neural networks (RNNs) across multiple HAR datasets [2,6,27], which comprised movement data from wearable sensors. Their findings suggested that deep learning models excel at identifying local patterns within sensor data, and the inherent translational invariance of these models contributes to their high accuracy in activity recognition. Nonetheless, new issues arise as these models were trained on predefined activities, posing difficulties in adapting to new activities that users do in their daily routine [29].

To alleviate this issue, the research in Continual Learning (CL) is gaining interest for its ability to enable models to adapt to new data while retaining previously acquired knowledge. CL displays promising applications in smart homes [8], sports training [22], and healthcare [33]. CL employs various strategies to maintain past knowledge when facing new tasks. Architecture-based methods [7,25,31] ensure minimal interference between tasks by modifying the network's structure for new information, but this leads to increased complexity and potential scalability issues. To address this, regularization strategies [1,16,20] keep the model architecture fixed, applying constraints on weight updates to protect old knowledge. However, they struggle in class-incremental scenarios where there is significant similarity between classes in each task [11,14].

Replay approaches [21,24,26] address this issue by incorporating a subset of data from previous tasks alongside current task data during training, which consists of either real or synthetically generated samples. Real data ensures direct knowledge recall but raises issues like increased memory use and potential data distribution misrepresentation. To overcome these, generative models [9,17] are used to create synthetic data, which reduces memory storage and addresses privacy concerns, all while ensuring the synthetic samples accurately reflect essential task-specific features.

The use of generative models to improve model performance in CL has been widely implemented on computer vision with remarkable outcomes [23,32]. However, in sensor-based HAR, the collected data is time-series data which is high-dimensional. As a result, it poses a big challenge in applying CL methods to train the model in CL scenarios. Ye et al. [38] applied the work of Shin et al. [32], Deep Generative Replay (DGR), to HAR datasets, using Generative Adversarial Networks (GANs) to generate samples for CL tasks. This approach can lead to significant computational costs due to the necessity of separate GANs and classifiers for each task, contradicting the CL paradigm of using a singular classifier. Moreover, they further adopted the strategy from Van and Tolias [36] of integrating a VAE directly into the primary classifier. Despite being innovative, this approach also introduces the risk of overfitting due to an increase in parameters and model complexity, particularly when limited training data is available. Additionally, they also proposed HAR-GAN, which incorporates GANs as one part of their CL framework. While showing encouraging results, their CL framework has a limitation regarding scalability issues as the network grows with each new class, making it less suitable for resource-constrained environments. In addition, the limitation also lies in the data imbalance despite their effort in including a method to deal with it.

From the benchmark results of Jha et al. [13] on different CL approaches with a variety of HAR datasets, Learning a Unified Classifier Incrementally via Rebalancing (LUCIR) [12] has demonstrated a significant contribution in tackling the issue of data imbalance using cosine normalization. Despite the effort from previous studies, most of them are conducted with low-dimensional data and fine-grained features extracted from the HAR dataset without any systematic feature extraction process. While shown effective, the limitation lies in the training of generative models, particularly when involving with the high dimensional data, including raw sensor data. Besides, not only is sensor data high-dimensional, but there is also a high variance in sensor data of each activity due to the different individual [19] or sensor quality [39]. Despite multiple applications of existing CL approaches across different domains, the study on conducting a CL strategy with the raw sensor-based HAR data is still limited.

3   VAE-Based CL Framework with Classifier and Filtering Process

In our work, we aim to reduce the complexity associated with training generative models by developing a task-specific VAE to assist the CL classifier in a class-incremental learning scenario.

This approach is designed to directly expose the model to raw sensor data from new activities in each task, leveraging the VAE to generate exemplars. This strategy facilitates knowledge retention, addresses storage constraints and naturally avoids training challenges related to data imbalance between the exemplars and training data in the new task. By focusing on training with raw sensor data, our study seeks to create a more direct and efficient method for accommodating new activities while accounting for the inherent variability and high dimensionality of sensor data in HAR.

3.1 VAE and CL Classifier Architecture

We construct a VAE with three main components: an encoder, a decoder, and a classifier as displayed in Fig. 1(a). The encoder transforms high-dimensional input data into a lower-dimensional latent space, creating a compressed representation that captures essential features of the data. From this latent space, sampled latent vectors are passed to the decoder, which reconstructs the input data. The VAE classifier, built upon the latent representation, is used for labeling reconstructed data. This classifier also imposes additional structure on the latent space, enhancing feature distinction between different classes. This dual capability makes VAEs valuable for generating meaningful and diverse samples with accurate labels. The reconstructed data can then be used as generated data to combine with the data from the new task to train the CL classifier during the CL training process.

The encoder consists of five 1D convolutional layers, each followed by batch normalization and LeakyReLU activation. Max-pooling operations with the kernel size and stride of 2 are also applied between each convolutional layer to reduce the spatial dimensions of the feature maps. In the first 3 convolutional layers, a kernel size of 3 is used and the number of kernels is arranged as 16, 32, and 64 respectively. Finally, the final 2 convolutional layers have 64 filters with a kernel size of 5. The tensor is then fed into two separate fully connected layers with 64 neurons to produce the mean and log variance of the latent distribution, denoting the parameters for the probabilistic encoding of the inputs.

The decoder begins with a fully connected layer with the size of 384. After that, another series of three transposed convolutional layers, each equipped with LeakyReLU activation. The first two layers use 16 filters with the kernel sizes of 5 and 3. The final transposed convolutional layer has 6 filters and a kernel size of 3.

Lastly, the VAE classifier is a MLP (multilayer perceptron) with a single hidden layer of 32 neurons with LeakyReLU activation. The softmax activation function is applied in the final layer to obtain a probability distribution over the class labels.

On the other hand, the CL classifier, which is responsible for learning tasks incrementally, is a Convolutional Neural Network (CNN) with four convolutional layers with 16, 32, 32, 64 filters respectively. The first two layers use a filter size of 3, and the following two layers use a filter size of 5. Each convolutional layer is equipped with a batch normalization, ReLU activation and a max-pooling

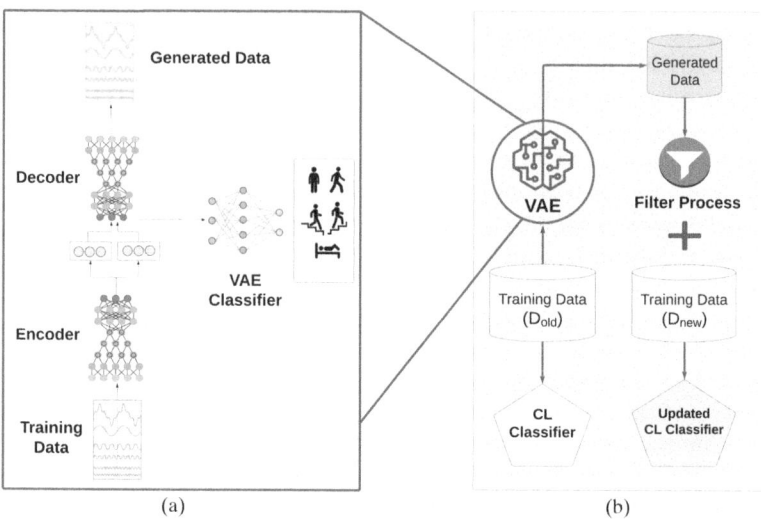

Fig. 1. (a) VAE architecture (b) Overview of VAE with filtering process framework

operation using a filter size of 2. Finally, the tensor is fed into the fully connected layer with 32 units, followed by the final output layer.

3.2 Filtering Mechanism in Generated Sample Selection

For each task in CL training, a VAE is trained individually as described in Sect. 4.3. This designed process aims to enhance the fidelity of the generated data, improving the representativeness of the generated data for each class. Through the filtering criterion that excludes samples below the prediction score threshold, this strategy can minimize the inclusion of ambiguous samples. This can improve the overall quality and reliability of the pseudo-samples, thereby optimizing the learning efficiency and predictive performance of models. This proposed framework is illustrated in Fig. 1(b).

4 Experimental Protocol

4.1 CL Training with Random Sampling from the Real Data

In this experiment, the first task consist of two classes randomly selected and input into the CL classifier for training. Each subsequent task consist of two new classes randomly selected from the remaining classes. In addition, a predetermined quantity of samples are chosen from the training data via random selection in each task. After each task is completed, the model is evaluated using a test set that includes all the classes previously encountered during the training so far.

4.2   Training with Hybrid CL Methods Using Real Data

This experiment assesses model performance when training with different CL strategies. Also, it allows us to evaluate the effectiveness of using generated samples with VAE compared to the different CL methods. The training process with hybrid CL methods is illustrated in Fig. 2.

Similarly to the previous experiment, it starts by randomly selecting two classes for the initial task. However, different methods are applied in sample selection for each CL approach such as random and herding sampling [37]. In addition, the model from the previous task is also used for different processes in each CL approach. The CL approaches selected for these experiments are Elastic Weight Consolidation with Replay (EWC Replay), Incremental Classifier and Representation Learning (iCaRL), and LUCIR.

Elastic Weight Consolidation (EWC). Proposed by Kirkpatrick et al. [18], EWC addresses catastrophic forgetting in CL by identifying and preserving the weights crucial for previously learned tasks. In this approach, the Fisher Information Matrix (FIM) is constructed to calculate the importance of each parameter for each task. When learning new tasks, a penalty is applied to the loss function for significant changes from the important parameters. In our implementation, EWC serves as a weight regularizer for the CL classifier to maintain knowledge of previous tasks, complemented by exemplars randomly selected from the training data for each task.

Incremental Classifier and Representation Learning (iCaRL). iCaRL, introduced by Rebuffi et al. [26], is a hybrid approach in CL that leverages knowledge distillation and memory replay. In each task, exemplars are selected using the herding sampling technique from each class of training data and stored in a fixed memory. In herding sampling, samples are selected based on their closeness to the class mean in the feature space to ensure a comprehensive representation of each class. During model training, the loss function of iCaRL combines Cross-Entropy (CE) loss for new class learning with Knowledge Distillation (KD) loss for the preservation of previously acquired knowledge, facilitating seamless knowledge transfer. With this combination of components, iCaRL allows for updating the model with new data without forgetting old knowledge, enabling the network to perform well in different CL scenarios.

Learning a Unified Classifier Incrementally via Rebalancing (LUCIR). LUCIR is a hybrid CL approach which is implemented in our experiment with the use of exemplars. Proposed by Hou et al. [12], this method combines the three components to deal with the data imbalance that naturally occurs when using exemplars. The first component, Cosine Normalization, is applied to the final layer to level the differences caused by the varying magnitudes of embeddings and biases as those of the new classes tend to be significantly higher than those from previous tasks. The second component, the Less-Forget Constraint, is applied to preserve the integrity of knowledge from earlier tasks. It maintains the established geometric configuration of the embeddings of old classes throughout subsequent tasks. The last component, Inter-Class Separation, applies margin ranking loss to create a distinction between old and new class samples within the training data.

With the combination of these three elements, LUCIR has been shown to be an effective CL algorithm for preserving knowledge from earlier tasks [12,13]. Hence, in this study, we are going to implement this method with real-data exemplars to compare the results with the use of VAE in the class-incremental learning scenario.

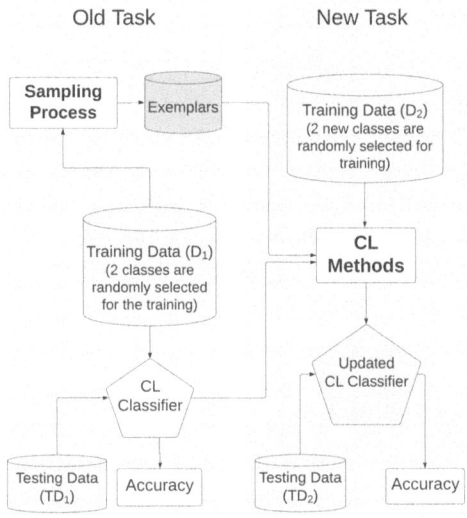

Fig. 2. Training process with CL methods using real data as exemplars

4.3 CL Training with Generated Data from VAE and the Filtering Process

For our approach, the CL classifier is initially trained with the first two randomly selected classes. In addition, the training data from the current task is also used to train a VAE specialized in generating samples from the current task. In each of the following tasks, two of the remaining unseen classes are randomly selected for training the CL classifier. The saved VAEs from each of the previous tasks are also loaded to generate data for their respective classes according to their assigned tasks of the VAEs.

In the data generation process, we use two strategies for sampling latent vectors from the latent space:

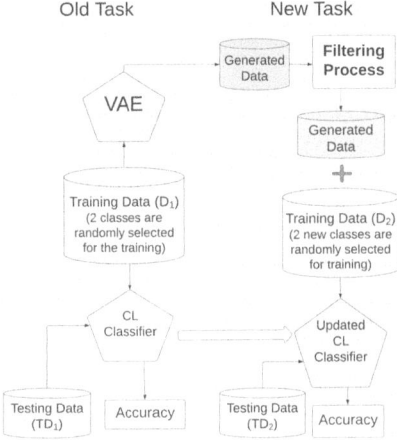

Fig. 3. Training process with VAE as a generative model.

- Adaptive Boundary Sampling: Adjusting boundaries in each latent space dimension based on data distribution percentiles, ensuring coverage of key variations learned by the VAE. However, this can lead to a lack of diversity in the data representation. Latent vectors are generated by sampling random uniform values within these adapted boundaries.
- Boundary Box Sampling: Setting fixed boundaries using the minimum and maximum values for each latent space dimension, enhancing data diversity but potentially including lower-quality samples. Latent vectors are generated by sampling random uniform values within these predefined ranges.

The sampled latent vectors are input into the VAE classifier for the labeling process, and further into the decoder for generating pseudo-samples. Then, a filtering process is implemented. For larger coverage, it is only used with the boundary box strategy. The filtering process consists of selecting only samples with a classification confidence above a given threshold, p, from the VAE classifier. The performance of the model is evaluated both with and without filtering process.

When the data generation process is completed, the generated data is merged with the training data of the two new classes in the current task. After training, the classifier is then evaluated in the same way as presented in Sect. 4.1. The training process with generated data from VAE is displayed in Fig. 3.

4.4 Metrics

In CL context, the model is trained with a continually updating data stream of multiple tasks. Hence, it is necessary to conduct a comprehensive evaluation which not only assesses the model's capability to adapt to new information but also to retain past knowledge. In this experiment, we evaluate the performance of the model by focusing on the following metrics:

Accuracy by Tasks (ACT) is the accuracy of recognizing all classes trained so far in each task. This metric is used to indicate the overall performance of the model with both newly and previously learnt classes in all tasks.

New-Class Accuracy by Tasks (NCT) is the accuracy of recognizing new activities in the current task. This metric helps evaluating plasticity: the model's ability to learn new information.

Old-Class Accuracy by Tasks (OCT) is the accuracy of recognizing all old classes which have been learnt from the previous tasks. It is a measure of the model's stability: the model's ability to retain knowledge of previously learned classes when trained on new tasks.

Forgetting Score by Tasks (FS) [5] measures the degree to which a model's performance on previous tasks degrades as it learns new tasks. The forgetting score at task k, FS_k, is computed as:

$$FS_k = \frac{1}{k-1} \sum_{j=1}^{k-1} f_j^k$$

where $f_j^k = 1 - \frac{A_j^k}{\max_{i \in \{1,\ldots,k-1\}} A_j^i}$ and A_j^k is the accuracy on the classes learnt at task j with the model trained up to task k. Intuitively this metric gives the average performance loss across all tasks seen. A forgetting score of 1 thus indicates that all performance has been lost (the model entirely forgot) and a forgetting score of 0 indicates that the model is the best performing so far across all tasks seen (no forgetting).

5 Experimental Settings

5.1 Datasets

Our study was conducted using the open UCI HAR Dataset [28]. In our experiments, we use the raw data which is gathered from inertial sensors, including accelerometers and gyroscopes, across the x, y, and z axes. The specifications of the dataset are depicted in Table 1, and the frequency of each activity in the dataset is presented in Table 2.

5.2   Sampling Process from the Real Data

In CL tasks, due to limited storage capacity, it is very important to select the samples which are the good representatives of each class. With random sampling, the samples from each class are randomly selected based on the defined number of samples. This sample selection process is also applied in the case of EWC Replay. However, for iCaRL and LUCIR, following the methodology originally conducted in [26] and [12], herding sampling [37] is applied to select the samples for training the model.

Table 1. Specifications of UCI HAR Dataset

Number of participants	30
Device	Smartphone (Samsung Galaxy SII)
Collected data	3-axial linear data (x, y, z) from accelerometers and gyroscopes
Sampling rate	50 Hz
Year	2012
Number of classes	6

Table 2. Frequency of each activity in UCI HAR dataset

Description	Activity	# samples
Walking	0	1722
Walking Up	1	1544
Walking Down	2	1406
Sitting	3	1777
Standing	4	1906
Laying	5	1944

5.3   Implementation Details

Defining Exemplar Sizes for the Experiment. We use exemplar set sizes k of (10, 14, 17, 21, and 25) for the random sampling process. For iCaRL, that uses a fixed memory size [26], we determine the exemplar size by dividing the total memory by the current number of classes in each task. Table 3 indicates the memory footprint of real data and VAEs across all taks, yet we also explore performance with smaller real data sizes (10 and 14) for baseline comparison. This analysis aims to determine if VAE-generated data can match or outperform the use of more substantial real data in CL training, given the similar amount of space in each task. This provides insights into using generated data over real data, considering the trade-offs between sample quantity and quality in the training process.

Table 3. Size of real data as exemplars and VAE across all tasks in Kilobytes (KB). Total memory footprint after Task 3.

	Task 1	Task 2	Task 3
Real sample ($k = \mathbf{17}$)	206	410	614
Real sample ($k = \mathbf{21}$)	254	506	758
Real sample ($k = \mathbf{25}$)	301	602	901
VAE Model	392	794	1176

CL Training with Real Data and Generated Data as Exemplars. With real data, random sampling is used in EWC Replay while herding sampling is applied in iCaRL and LUCIR to follow the principle of each CL approach. With generated data from VAE, we align the generated data size per class to the average training data size for each new task, ensuring balanced training sets. For the filtering process, a threshold value p is used as the minimum probability criterion for sample selection. To choose this value, a number of experiments were previously conducted using p (the predicted probability from the VAE classifier) within the range $[0.75, 0.97]$. The results showed that the threshold of $p = 0.80$ yielded the best performance. The authors are aware that this result is dataset dependent and further experiments are necessary to assess the generality of this result.

Our experiments were run 30 times. More details on the training parameters of the implementation of CL training are described in Table 4.

Table 4. Parameter setting for the experiment

Parameters	Value
Learning Rate	0.0005
Batch Size	64
Number of Epochs	20
Latent Space Dimension (VAE)	64
Coefficient of Reconstruction Loss (VAE)	1
Coefficient of KL Divergence Loss (VAE)	0.001
Coefficient of Classification Loss (VAE)	1

6   Results

Figure 4 illustrates the all-class accuracy across tasks. The result reveals that random sampling, EWC Replay, and iCaRL have comparable accuracy, ranging from 53% to 60% in Task 2 and from 38% to 45% in Task 3. LUCIR demonstrates a lower accuracy in Task 2 with accuracies between 51% and 56%, but sees a notably higher accuracy in Task 3, increasing to the range of 42% and 45%. The VAE with boundary box technique outperforms others, maintaining around 62% accuracy in Task 2 and approximately 48% in Task 3. The filtering process of the VAE further enhancing accuracy by about 4% and 2% in Task 2 and Task 3 respectively. In contrast, VAE with the adaptive boundary approach exhibits a decrease in accuracy, falling from 57% to just under 40% by Task 3.

6.1   Plasticity of the CL Classifier

The new-class accuracy for each method is presented in Fig. 5. The data reveals that across all tasks, most sampling methods maintain a high accuracy rate, hovering from 92% to 97%. iCaRL shows a significant decline in the accuracy in Task 3, falling from roughly 92% in Task 2 to just around 84% in Task 3. Meanwhile, LUCIR, which has a lower accuracy of approximately 85% in Task 2, displays a significant improvement by reaching around 93% in Task 3.

6.2   Stability of the CL Classifier

The old-class accuracy is shown in Fig. 6. Despite a significant decline in the accuracy in all sampling methods from Task 2, VAE Boundary Box with filtering maintains the highest accuracy when transitioning to new tasks. Specifically, it achieves an accuracy of about 45% accuracy in Task 2 and nearly 30% in Task 3. This represents gains of approximately 12% and 3% in Task 2 and Task 3, respectively, compared to its non-filtered counterpart. Additionally, LUCIR has consistently outperformed iCaRL by approximately 2–4% in accuracy across each task. Moreover, it is also noticeable that the accuracy of the VAE with adaptive boundary sampling method is remarkably low, on par with the performance when using 10 and 14 real-data exemplars.

This is also explained by Fig. 7 where using adaptive boundary as a sampling method in VAE shows a higher forgetting score compared to other methods. In this measure, both the filtered and non-filtered versions of the VAE Boundary Box achieved significantly lower forgetting scores compared to other methods, at just 48% and 62% respectively. In Task 3, the filtered VAE Boundary Box outperforms all other methods with a significantly lower forgetting score of about 65%.

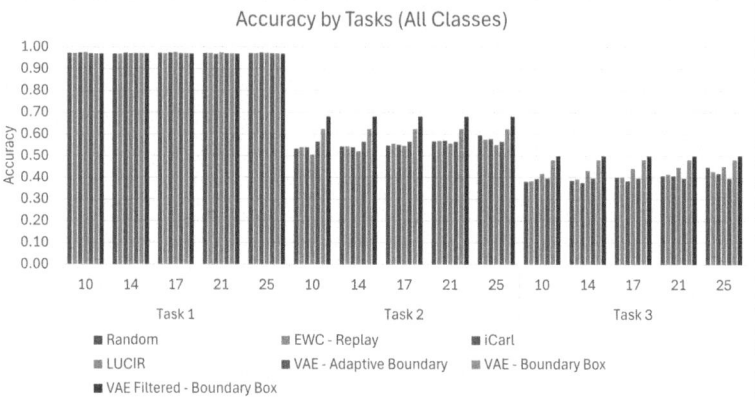

Fig. 4. All-class accuracy by tasks comparison between methods involving real data sampling (Random, EWC-Replay, iCaRL, and LUCIR) in different sample size k (10, 14, 17, 21, 25) and the methods using generated data from VAE (Adaptive boundary, boundary box with and without filtering process)

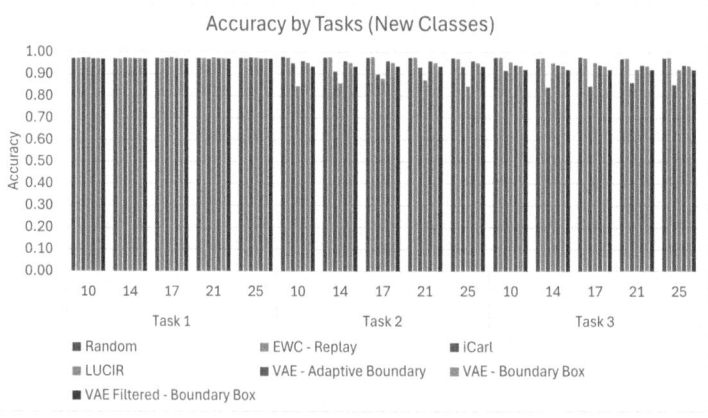

Fig. 5. New-class accuracy by tasks comparison between methods involving real data sampling (Random, EWC-Replay, iCaRL, and LUCIR) in different sample size k (10, 14, 17, 21, 25) and the methods using generated data from VAE (Adaptive boundary, boundary box with and without filtering process)

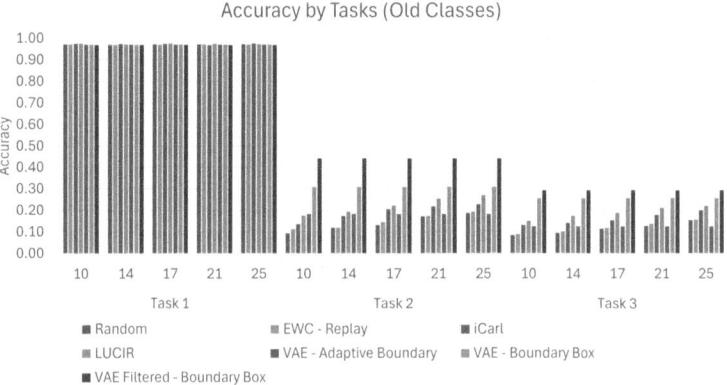

Fig. 6. Old-class accuracy by tasks comparison between methods involving real data sampling (Random, EWC-Replay, iCaRL, and LUCIR) in different sample size k (10, 14, 17, 21, 25) and the methods using generated data from VAE (Adaptive boundary, boundary box with and without filtering process)

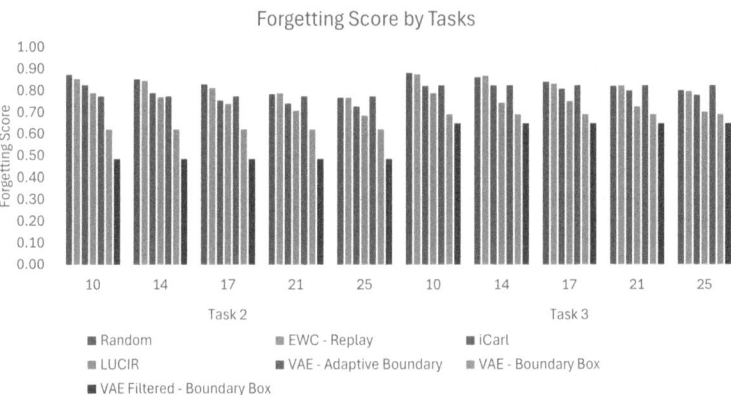

Fig. 7. Forgetting score by tasks (lower is better) comparison between methods involving real data sampling (Random, EWC-Replay, iCaRL, and LUCIR) in different sample size k (10, 14, 17, 21, 25) and the methods using generated data from VAE (Adaptive boundary, boundary box with and without filtering process)

6.3   Discussion

Our findings show that the choice of replay strategy for the CL classifier plays a crucial role in the plasticity and stability performance of the model. Our analysis across various tasks indicates that generative replay with VAE outperforms experience replay methods via exemplars. In addition, we see from Table 3 that the VAE has a comparable memory footprint, although slightly higher than $k = 25$. We can extrapolate that with our method we have a memory footprint equivalent to the holdout size of 33 samples. However, our VAE is capable of generating as many samples as needed.

The all-class accuracy depicted in Fig. 4 shows the VAE with boundary box sampling as a superior technique, consistently outperforming others across all tasks. This implies that VAE-generated samples can effectively complement real data, ensuring a diversified and representative training set that supports the classifier in learning new classes incrementally. Additionally, applying a filtering process based on the confidence of VAE classifiers refines model performance by supplying more reliable generated data.

Moreover, the new-class and old-class accuracy results from Fig. 5 and 6 demonstrate plasticity-stability performance of the model which addresses the critical balance between preserving old knowledge and acquiring new information in continual learning models. In the case of hybrid CL approaches such as iCaRL and LUCIR, despite being able to maintain a better old-class accuracy and forgetting score across tasks compared to most of the other techniques, they have lower accuracy in new-class accuracy in each task. This trend exemplifies the plasticity-stability trade-off inherent in both approaches, where the safeguarding of old information may be prioritized at the expense of optimally learning new data. From our experiments, VAE demonstrates its capability to deal with this issue by improving the knowledge retention of old tasks without having to sacrifice the learning of activities in new tasks.

Furthermore, our study highlights the role of sampling methods in the latent space of VAEs, revealing how boundary box sampling captures a broader diversity in the latent space than the adaptive boundary method, which has a higher forgetting score indicating a focus on dominant features over diversity. This diversity is crucial for smartphone sensor-based HAR, where individual variability is significant, influenced by health condition and age factors [34]. The boundary box sampling presents its potential by covering a wider range in the latent space, ensuring the generation of diverse samples. However, despite a notably low forgetting score in the second task, the VAE Boundary Box performance aligns with other methods by Task 3, indicating a potential area for improvement.

Our exploratory study is encouraging but broader validation on multiple datasets is necessary to generalize our findings. In addition, exploring other sampling methods (e.g. GMM) for the latent space of the VAE may allow to better capture the diversity of the sample and provide better exemplars.

7   Conclusion and Future Work

In conclusion, the findings from our exploratory study highlight the efficiency of using task-specific VAEs to support replay based CL methods using raw sensor data directly without the need for extensive preprocessing or feature engineering. The results show that using VAEs, particularly with boundary box sampling, to generate the samples significantly improves the performance of the CL model across tasks compared to exemplar-based hybrid methods, reflecting the quality of the generated data from the VAE.

Moreover, our plasticity-stability analysis illustrates the effectiveness of the VAE in maintaining a balance between preserving old knowledge and assimilating new information in each task, a crucial aspect of CL models. As demonstrated in our study, the improvement in model performance from the refining process applied to the generated data could be a good initiative for future research work, focusing on enhancing the quality of data produced by generative models.

Future work will include the validation of our methods on additional HAR datasets to enhance the generalisability of our findings, as well as exploring other sampling methods (e.g. GMM) for the latent space of the VAE that may better capture the diversity of the sample and provide better exemplars.

References

1. Aljundi, R., Babiloni, F., Elhoseiny, M., Rohrbach, M., Tuytelaars, T.: Memory aware synapses: learning what (not) to forget. In: Proceedings of the European Conference on Computer Vision (ECCV), pp. 139–154 (2018)
2. Bachlin, M., et al.: Potentials of enhanced context awareness in wearable assistants for Parkinson's disease patients with the freezing of gait syndrome. In: 2009 International Symposium on Wearable Computers. IEEE (2009)
3. Becker, C., Julien, C., Lalanda, P., Zambonelli, F.: Pervasive computing middleware: current trends and emerging challenges. CCF Trans. Pervasive Comput. Interact. **1**(1) (2019)
4. Bulling, A., Blanke, U., Schiele, B.: A tutorial on human activity recognition using body-worn inertial sensors. ACM Comput. Surv. (CSUR) **46**(3), 1–33 (2014)
5. Chaudhry, A., Dokania, P.K., Ajanthan, T., Torr, P.H.: Riemannian walk for incremental learning: understanding forgetting and intransigence. In: Proceedings of the European Conference on Computer Vision (ECCV), pp. 532–547 (2018)
6. Chavarriaga, R., et al.: The opportunity challenge: a benchmark database for on-body sensor-based activity recognition. Pattern Recognit. Lett. **34**(15) (2013)
7. Chen, T., Goodfellow, I., Shlens, J.: Net2net: accelerating learning via knowledge transfer. arXiv preprint arXiv:1511.05641 (2015)
8. Chua, S.L., Foo, L.K., Guesgen, H.W., Marsland, S.: Incremental learning of human activities in smart homes. Sensors **22**(21), 8458 (2022)
9. Goodfellow, I., et al.: Generative adversarial networks. Commun. ACM **63**(11), 139–144 (2020)
10. Hammerla, N.Y., Halloran, S., Plötz, T.: Deep, convolutional, and recurrent models for human activity recognition using wearables. arXiv preprint arXiv:1604.08880 (2016)
11. He, J., Mao, R., Shao, Z., Zhu, F.: Incremental learning in online scenario. In: Proceedings of the IEEE/CVF Conference on Computer Vision and Pattern Recognition, pp. 13926–13935 (2020)
12. Hou, S., Pan, X., Loy, C.C., Wang, Z., Lin, D.: Learning a unified classifier incrementally via rebalancing. In: Proceedings of the IEEE/CVF Conference on Computer Vision and Pattern Recognition, pp. 831–839 (2019)
13. Jha, S., Schiemer, M., Zambonelli, F., Ye, J.: Continual learning in sensor-based human activity recognition: an empirical benchmark analysis. Inf. Sci. **575**, 1–21 (2021)

14. Kann, B., Castellanos-Paez, S., Lalanda, P.: Evaluation of regularization-based continual learning approaches: application to HAR. In: 2023 IEEE International Conference on Pervasive Computing and Communications Workshops and other Affiliated Events (PerCom Workshops), pp. 460–465. IEEE (2023)
15. Kann, B., Castellanos-Paez, S., Lalanda, P.: Cross-dataset continual learning: assessing pre-trained models to enhance generalization in HAR. In: 2024 IEEE International Conference on Pervasive Computing and Communications Workshops and other Affiliated Events (PerCom Workshops), pp. 1–6. IEEE (2024)
16. Kemker, R., McClure, M., Abitino, A., Hayes, T., Kanan, C.: Measuring catastrophic forgetting in neural networks. In: Proceedings of the AAAI Conference on Artificial Intelligence, vol. 32 (2018)
17. Kingma, D.P., Welling, M.: Auto-encoding variational bayes. arXiv preprint arXiv:1312.6114 (2013)
18. Kirkpatrick, J., et al.: Overcoming catastrophic forgetting in neural networks. Proc. Natl. Acad. Sci. **114**(13), 3521–3526 (2017)
19. Lara, O.D., Labrador, M.A.: A survey on human activity recognition using wearable sensors. IEEE Commun. Surv. Tutor. **15**(3), 1192–1209 (2012)
20. Li, Z., Hoiem, D.: Learning without forgetting. IEEE Trans. Pattern Anal. Mach. Intell. **40**(12), 2935–2947 (2017)
21. Lopez-Paz, D., Ranzato, M.: Gradient episodic memory for continual learning. In: Advances in Neural Information Processing Systems, vol. 30 (2017)
22. Minhas, R., Mohammed, A.A., Wu, Q.J.: Incremental learning in human action recognition based on snippets. IEEE Trans. Circuits Syst. Video Technol. **22**(11), 1529–1541 (2011)
23. Nguyen, C.V., Li, Y., Bui, T.D., Turner, R.E.: Variational continual learning. arXiv preprint arXiv:1710.10628 (2017)
24. Ostapenko, O., Puscas, M., Klein, T., Jahnichen, P., Nabi, M.: Learning to remember: a synaptic plasticity driven framework for continual learning. In: Proceedings of the IEEE/CVF Conference on Computer Vision and Pattern Recognition (2019)
25. Rakaraddi, A., Siew Kei, L., Pratama, M., De Carvalho, M.: Reinforced continual learning for graphs. In: Proceedings of the 31st ACM International Conference on Information & Knowledge Management, pp. 1666–1674 (2022)
26. Rebuffi, S.A., Kolesnikov, A., Sperl, G., Lampert, C.H.: ICARL: incremental classifier and representation learning. In: Proceedings of the IEEE Conference on Computer Vision and Pattern Recognition, pp. 2001–2010 (2017)
27. Reiss, A., Stricker, D.: Introducing a new benchmarked dataset for activity monitoring. In: 2012 16th International Symposium on Wearable Computers, pp. 108–109. IEEE (2012)
28. Reyes-Ortiz, J., Anguita, D., Ghio, A., Oneto, L., Parra, X.: Human Activity Recognition Using Smartphones. UCI Machine Learning Repository (2012). https://doi.org/10.24432/C54S4K
29. Ros, M., Cuéllar, M.P., Delgado, M., Vila, A.: Online recognition of human activities and adaptation to habit changes by means of learning automata and fuzzy temporal windows. Inf. Sci. **220**, 86–101 (2013)
30. Roth, F., Becker, C., Vega, G., Lalanda, P.: Xware-a customizable interoperability framework for pervasive computing systems. Pervasive Mob. Comput. **47** (2018). https://doi.org/10.1016/j.pmcj.2018.03.005
31. Rusu, A.A., et al.: Progressive neural networks. arXiv preprint arXiv:1606.04671 (2016)
32. Shin, H., Lee, J.K., Kim, J., Kim, J.: Continual learning with deep generative replay. In: Advances in Neural Information Processing Systems, vol. 30 (2017)

33. Sun, L., Zhang, M., Wang, B., Tiwari, P.: Few-shot class-incremental learning for medical time series classification. IEEE J. Biomed. Health Inform. (2023)

34. Thu, N.T.H., Han, D.S.: Hihar: a hierarchical hybrid deep learning architecture for wearable sensor-based human activity recognition. IEEE Access **9** (2021)

35. Usmanova, A., Portet, F., Lalanda, P., Vega, G.: A distillation-based approach integrating continual learning and federated learning for pervasive services. arXiv preprint arXiv:2109.04197 (2021)

36. Van de Ven, G.M., Tolias, A.S.: Generative replay with feedback connections as a general strategy for continual learning. arXiv preprint arXiv:1809.10635 (2018)

37. Welling, M.: Herding dynamical weights to learn. In: Proceedings of the 26th Annual International Conference on Machine Learning, pp. 1121–1128 (2009)

38. Ye, J., Nakwijit, P., Schiemer, M., Jha, S., Zambonelli, F.: Continual activity recognition with generative adversarial networks. ACM Trans. Internet Things **2**(2), 1–25 (2021)

39. Ye, J., Stevenson, G., Dobson, S.: Detecting abnormal events on binary sensors in smart home environments. Pervasive Mob. Comput. **33**, 32–49 (2016)

The Role of Ethics in Smart Homes – A Workshop-Based Approach

Sally Bagheri[1,2,3]($\boxtimes$) and Andreas Jacobsson[1,2,3]

[1] Malmö University, Malmö, Sweden
`sally.bagheri@mau.se`
[2] Department of Computer Science and Media Technology, 21425 Malmö, Sweden
[3] Internet of Things and People Research Center, Malmö, Sweden

Abstract. Smart homes are increasingly popular and offer users multiple benefits, such as increased security, entertainment, health, and energy efficiency. But smart homes also raise ethical challenges. Analyzing ethical risks in smart homes requires an approach that can reveal and analyze the complex consequences of unethical IoT use. Such an analysis, however, is cumbersome and requires including many aspects and stakeholder perspectives. There is a lack of methods to analyze smart homes ethically and document such research results for continual evaluation over time as the smart home and our understanding of its ethics inevitably evolve and change. This work aims to design a workshop methodology to support systematic ethical analyses of smart homes. It builds on previous work considering smart homes as digital ecosystems to contextually examine ethical risks and challenges. A group of research participants were asked to undergo the workshop to evaluate its usefulness in supporting ethical discussions and documenting insights systematically. The results show the feasibility of the workshop design in conducting ethical analyses and eliciting system requirements for smart homes. Several unethical use cases are discussed, such as IoT gaslighting and surveillance concerns related to child users.

Keywords: Smart Homes · Ethics · Workshops · IoT · Digital Ecosystems

1 Introduction

When Internet of Things (IoT) technology is implemented in typical homes, it is commonly referred to as a smart home. The same logic can be applied to other IoT contexts, such as smart cities, hospitals, buildings, etc. The smart home sets itself apart from other smart contexts because it is commonly considered a private space, as opposed to the environments mentioned above, which are typically public and shared by several people. Data generated by smart homes can range from disclosing the most mundane activities that may take place in a home, such as cooking food or switching on and off the lamps, to the most private and intimate. Although smart Internet-connected systems can award users

© IFIP International Federation for Information Processing 2025
Published by Springer Nature Switzerland AG 2025
G. Rey et al. (Eds.): IFIPIoT 2024, IFIP AICT 737, pp. 226–242, 2025.
https://doi.org/10.1007/978-3-031-81900-1_14

many benefits and countless possibilities, they also introduce ethical challenges that must be addressed and carefully considered. Human-IoT interactions can, at best, have unintended or sub-optimal outcomes, such as using IoT devices for alternative purposes, such as using a security camera to spy on one's pets or neighbors. At worst, however, they can lead to highly unethical and even dangerous situations for their end-users and society at large. For example, smart locks can increase convenience while also increasing the risk of abusive control, such as locking someone in or out of the home. The smart home can pose particular ethical challenges, risking the safety and well-being of its users. Due to the contextual and complex nature of these ethical risks, their consideration and, ultimately, their mitigation is a cumbersome yet highly topical challenge.

The ethical impact of human-IoT interactions permeates all levels of society [17], and depending on who you ask, ensuring that smart homes are ethical can mean many different things. Within the broader scope of digital ethics, as explained by [2], the components of ethical considerations are commonly related to concerns of, for example, privacy, security, sustainability, fairness, and dignity [2]. While the vantage points overlap to some extent, each perspective is distinct and highlights different aspects and ethical risks of the IoT ecosystem. The all-encompassing nature of ethics will inevitably need to involve an increasingly diverse set of stakeholders to collaborate in addressing the complex concerns related to smart homes [19], a highly socio-technical system [13]. Methods for requirements engineering (RE) specifically aimed at including the many considerations of ethics in smart home design are currently lacking. Moreover, smart homes are used in several different arenas, such as health and elder care, energy monitoring, and child care, as well as general users interacting with IoT devices for convenience, leisure, or a more seamless living experience. This can lead to research results being siloed within different academic disciplines. A fragmented understanding of smart homes fails to recognize them as highly heterogeneous systems used in different ways by different users, all placed within the same smart home. In this sense, smart homes are complex environments with many interrelated parts, and the lack of techniques to analyze and document the results of ethical analyses risks losing valuable insights. Therefore, the ability to reiterate analyses, both with different stakeholder groups and also over time, is a necessary feature of ethical analyses as the smart home is a dynamic context and ever-changing in nature.

Previous research has approached smart homes as digital ecosystems (DE) [4] to ground ethical analyses in the details of specific smart home contexts. An ecosystem ontology has been proposed, shown in Fig. 1 [4], through which the results of such analyses can be documented systematically. This allows the process to be reiterated over time and for the insights to be developed and shared among different stakeholder groups. The research reported in the present paper builds upon the previous work approaching smart home contexts as DE to develop a method for eliciting ethical system requirements. DE, in this sense, can be defined as a counterpart to natural ecosystems [7], where biological species (BS) and digital species (DS) interact within a smart environment. Additional species, according to the ontology (Fig. 1), are economic species (ES) and organizational species (OS) and are differentiated based on incentives; ES are financial incentives and can represent the companies developing and offering IoT products and services intended for the home. OS are actors with other incentives, for example, governmental agencies such as tax agencies or police authorities, NGOs, or politically driven organizations [4]. The ecosystem approach is grounded in the understanding that privacy and other ethical concerns arise contextually [4]. Depending on the human users (BS), types and number of IoT devices (DS), companies (ES), and other data stakeholders present in the ecosystem (ES/OS), ethical considerations might differ. For example, the presence of children or IoT devices with certain functionalities (camera, microphone, motion, temperature, and other sorts of sensor) are relevant details of the smart home context when considering its ethics.

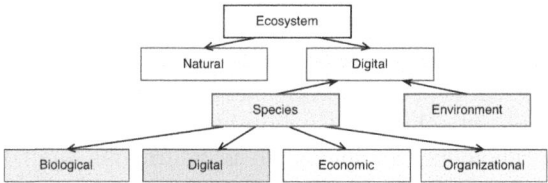

Fig. 1. Ecosystem Ontology

This work applies the Constructive Design Research process [12] and pilots the design of a Smart Home Ethics Workshop to conceptualize smart homes as DE, imagine unethical use cases, and suggest ethical system requirements. The artifacts include the workshop design, shown in Fig. 2, and the materials used to facilitate the workshop, shown in Fig. 3. The design artifacts can be considered a research contribution along with the insights and results gathered by deploying the workshops. Thus, this work contributes to smart home research through 1) a design rationale for ethical workshops, 2) insights into ethical concerns of smart homes, and 3) a discussion regarding the proposed method's value in analyzing and compiling ethical requirements for smart homes, where a lot of user interactions and thus personal information are in flux.

2   Previous Work

Our homes are commonly where we divulge the most honest accounts of our lived experience, and smart homes are no different. The range of activities occurring in the home can span from the most private and privacy-compromising to the most benign and commonplace. Our most intimate activities and the items on our grocery lists are examples of data that can be collected by smart home technology. Due to the wide range of data that smart homes might generate, process, and store, they have been described as socio-technical systems [13] constituted by its users, law and policymakers, and the smart home industry [18]. Additional stakeholders have been identified as different kinds of smart home bystanders [16], for example, domestic workers such as nannies [6], as well as society at large seen to how the *technical* and *social* typically intertwine in system engineering [14]. In this sense, analyzing the role of ethics in smart home systems can be understood as a holistic and all-encompassing consideration of the system and requires a wide range of stakeholders' perspectives to be included.

2.1 Ethical Requirements for Smart Homes

Requirements Engineering (RE) is the process of developing system requirements based on the needs and desires of a system's users [1]. RE has been described as the most crucial phase in software development [1] as system requirements act as a communication channel between stakeholders and developers [21]. RE is a complex technical, social, and cognitive process [15], and ethical RE is tedious due to the need to revisit and continuously adapt and update requirements over time [1] as well as the contextual nature of IoT ethics [20]. Ethical RE has been defined as the process of deriving ethical requirements from ethical principles and norms, akin to how legal requirements are derived from laws [9]. Eliciting ethical requirements for cyber-physical systems enabled by AI has been proposed by Guizzardi et al. [9], and although such systems are similar to IoT environments [8], methods for deriving ethical requirements for smart IoT homes are currently lacking within RE research. Due to the diversity of the stakeholders with "stakes" in the system [9], a common obstacle in RE is the communication between the groups "caused by the nature of different communities, societies, or individuals" [22]. The understanding of ethics and the smart home system may differ depending on who you ask. Bridging the communication gaps between stakeholder groups could be considered critical to successfully translating ethics into design requirements for smart home systems. Although ethical guidelines for developing digital technologies such as smart homes have been proposed [2], the challenge of developing system requirements informed by the smart home system's many stakeholders needs further inquiry.

As discussions across different stakeholder groups are imperative for eliciting requirements [3], system ontologies have been suggested to support the RE process in developing ethical requirements [9]. An ecosystem approach has shown promise in unifying stakeholder perspectives for RE [10]. The ecosystem ontology described in the previous section (Fig. 1) has been proposed to contextualize the exploration of ethical concerns and systematize the documentation of ethical discussions [4]. However, the DE approach [4] has yet to be explored as a method for ethical RE. Therefore, this work is exploratory and mainly concerned with operationalizing the DE approach for ethical analyses of smart homes. By applying prominent RE techniques, specifically conversational methods such as brainstorming and workshops [22], the aim is to elicit and document ethical requirements according to the ecosystem ontology. Applying the DE approach might mitigate the communication gaps amongst stakeholder groups, unify their understanding of the context, and document the discussions systematically.

3   Method

This work follows the Constructive Design Research (CDR) methodology [5,12]. CDR is a method described as research through design that emphasizes constructing new knowledge by imagining future worlds and considering how people engage with these worlds and each other. As design-driven research can sometimes entangle theory and practice, CDR is helpful in this intersection [11]. The study's central hypothesis (according to CDR [5]) was that by designing an ethical workshop, workshop participants could have meaningful ethical discussions by imagining smart home ecosystems and documenting their reflections. Following CDR instructions, the hypothesis was instantiated through creating artifacts [5], in this case, the Smart Home Ethics Workshop. Exploring artifacts through experimentation drives knowledge-creation [12], contributing to the realm of ethical smart home research.

4   Smart Home Ethics Workshop

This section outlines the workshop artifacts as they were initially designed, followed by an account of the rationale behind the design. The design of the artifacts maintains conversations and discussions as a central activity in ethical analyses and RE and adopts the DE approach proposed by [4]. In the subsequent sections, the research participants are presented, followed by a description of the three workshop sessions conducted, iterating the development and evaluation of the artifacts. The artifacts include the design of the workshop phases (Fig. 2) and the workshop kit (Fig. 3).

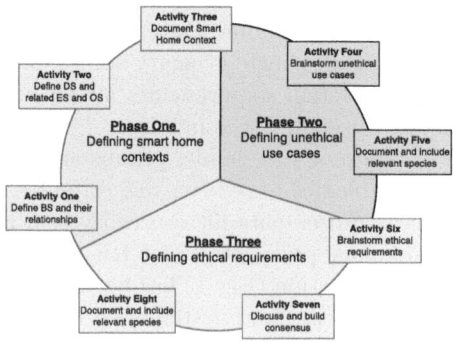

Fig. 2. Smart Home Ethics Workshop

Each workshop session was structured, including three distinct phases for brainstorming, discussion, and documentation, facilitating a comprehensive ethical analysis. Participants documented their discussions using a structured notation system, ensuring that the elicitation of ethical system requirements was both systematic and replicable. The outcome of undergoing the workshop was the documentation of ethical concerns related to the smart home context under analysis and system requirements to mitigate the identified concerns. Figure 3 shows the workshop kit, which included a notation system, a context card, use case cards, requirement cards, and color-coded species cards (according to the ecosystem ontology depicted in Fig. 1). Simply put, workshop participants were meant to fill out the context card using the species' cards and notation system to visualize the smart home context. Based on the context details, the participants brainstormed unethical use cases and mitigating system requirements, documenting their discussions on the remaining cards.

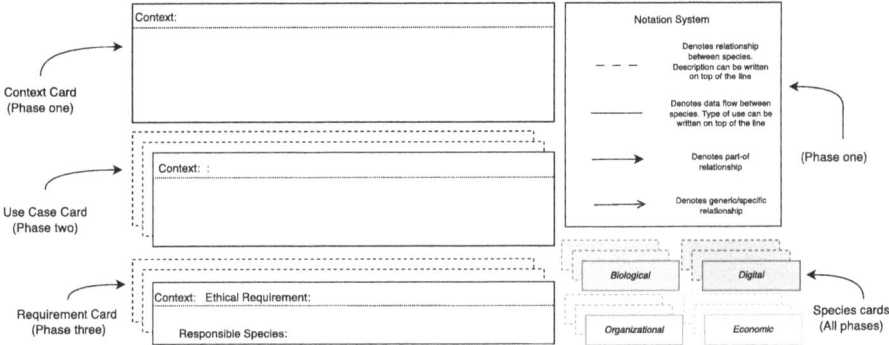

Fig. 3. Workshop Kit

4.1 Design Rationale

The workshop is meant to guide participants through three discussion-centered phases. According to the activities of phase one, participants are asked to define the smart home they will later analyze by considering the BS present in the context, their relationships to each other, the DS present, how BS are using them (for example, for convenience, security, health, or medical reasons), the ES developing the DS, and any other relationships between species such as contracts for IoT services or subscription-based products creating legal dependencies between BS and ES. These details are to be documented on the context card. The underlying rationale is to anchor the discussion in the specific details of the context and support upcoming workshop activities with a visual representation of the smart home. In the next phase, the focus shifts to imagining unethical use cases based on the specific context defined in the previous phase. Participants can be familiarized with ethical guidelines from previous research to promote idea generation or be encouraged to consider literature, movies/TV series, or other popular cultural references. As ideas dwindle, the next activity (activity five, see Fig. 2) is to document the use cases on their corresponding cards to tease out the details of each case, such as specifying the relevant species. This activity encourages participants to reflect deeply on ethical circumstances and include granularity, which might prompt new use cases as they define the details of the cases. In the third phase, an intermediary activity between brainstorming ethical requirements and documenting them on requirement cards, similar to phase two, is included: evaluating and building consensus (activity seven, see Fig. 2). The motivation behind including this activity is to emphasize discussions as a central activity in ethical analyses due to its complexity and all-encompassing nature and how ethical RE, i.e., defining what a system should and should not do from an ethical perspective, is understood differently depending on the stakeholders' perspective. The requirement cards task the participants with determining the species they deem ethically responsible for implementing the defined requirement. This, too, is meant to stress the understanding of ethical analyses as a discussion-centered process requiring the participants to exchange viewpoints, expertise, and opinions to build consensus and fill out the cards collaboratively. The rationale is not to reach conclusive appraisals regarding IoT ethics but to encourage ethical reflection and knowledge exchange. In summary, by undergoing the workshop activities, participants can imagine smart home contexts according to phase one, reflect on unethical use cases related to the specifics of the context according to phase two, and suggest ethical system requirements according to phase three.

4.2   Workshop Participants

Three workshops were deployed, each with 4–5 participants, for a total of 13 participants (see Table 1). All the workshops took place in the university's facilities and lasted around 1.5 h. All participants were bachelor students in computer science degree programs in Malmö, Sweden. Among the included participants, only three lived by themselves, while the majority lived with their parents, paving the way for an interesting detail in connection to the ethical use of smart homes – the participants are all young adults with various degrees of independence in terms of making decisions for themselves about their living conditions. Interestingly, only seven of the included participants had prior experience with IoT devices in the home environment, which sufficed for an abundance of perspectives with varying degrees of experience in terms of using smart home technology. As it turned out, the mix of people, living conditions, and experiences set the scene for a constructive process of ethical reflection and discussion-centered workshops on the ethics of smart homes.

Table 1. Workshop Participants

Participant	Workshop	Living Situation	IoT devices
#1	1	At home with parents	Smart TV
#2	1	At home with parents	Virtual Assistant, Smart TV, Smart Doorbell
#3	1	At home with parents	Smart Garage Door, Smart TV, Smart Thermostat
#4	1	Lives with partner	None
#5	1	Lives by themselves	None
#6	2	Student apartment	None
#7	2	Student apartment	None
#8	2	At home with parents	Virtual Assistant
#9	2	At home with parents	Virtual Assistant, Smart TV, Smart Lights, Smart Vacuum, Smart Lawn Mower
#10	3	At home with parents	None
#11	3	At home with parents	Virtual Assistant
#12	3	Student apartment	Virtual Assistant
#13	3	Student apartment	None

4.3 Iterating the Workshop Design

Each workshop began with an introduction to the DE approach and ecosystem ontology (Fig. 1) followed by a presentation of the workshop kit (Fig. 3) and the workshop method (Fig. 2). The description of the phases and corresponding activities were clear enough for the participants to follow without much influence from the workshop facilitator. Some instructions were given regarding using the workshop kit, but mostly, the authors remained in the background, taking observational notes. In the first iteration of the workshop, the participants opted to model a generic smart home with a nuclear family. The central insight gathered from the initial iteration was how time-consuming the first two phases of the workshop were. This informed the second iteration to specifically ask the participants to model contexts according to some instructions to limit the scope of the discussions. The authors decided to have the participants of the second workshop model a smart home context in which a child user was present as a BS. After sharing some personal experiences from their living situations, the participants asked to define two contexts, one including a child user below the age of 18 living with their parents and the other with an adult child above the age of 18 living with their parents, as this reflected many of their current living situations. Although pre-defining the context to some extent, by mandating a child user, was meant to focus the ethical analysis to save time, this format was engaging for the participants and therefore granted. It ultimately resulted in many comparative reflections analyzing the similarities and differences between the two contexts, which also took a long time.

Neither the first nor second iteration made it to phase three of the workshop. The participants spent an hour to an hour and a half conducting the activities in the first two phases, and keeping the workshop going for longer was not feasible due to the participants' time constraints. Therefore, in the third iteration of the workshop, yet another workshop format was explored; the participants were asked to familiarize themselves with the contexts and related use cases documented by the participants of the first and second workshop participants. This allowed the third iteration to start with activity six (see Fig. 2) and brainstorm ethical requirements based on the documentation of previous workshops. Therein, all phases of the workshop design were deployed and tested, albeit not consecutively.

5   Key Findings

This section documents the key findings of the three workshop iterations. A central theme emerged from each iteration and dominated the discussions; the first iteration dealt with what the participants referred to as "IoT gaslighting" (defined below). The second iteration mainly discussed the surveillance of children and, more specifically, how adult children, compared to under-aged children, negotiate their data rights with their parents. The third iteration reflected on some of the findings above and discussed the logic of surveillance at large and the responsibility of different species to ensure ethical smart home use.

5.1   IoT Gaslighting

In the first workshop, the participants explicitly decided to define the genders of the BS of the smart home ecosystem and coded the adult users as a heteronormative couple. One of the participants mentioned how male household members commonly drive IoT implementation. Therefore, it felt natural for the participants to assume that the male BS was responsible for the related upkeep of the smart home system as they were presumably the most knowledgeable. The participants reflected on how other family members (for example, the female spouse) might even avoid involving or educating themselves about the system as it is coded as a "male" task in the list of possible household chores. The participants also discussed how a male user might refrain or even disallow access to devices bordering on concerns of domestic abuse and other unethical surveillance practices. Participants identified the division of labor in the home as a personal matter, and the sentiment was that everyone should have the prerogative to run their household as they see fit. However, the participants also recognized how domestic labor is at times gendered, and as managing the IoT devices can be considered to be male-coded, this might increase the risk of coercive control. Smart home technology facilitating domestic abuse was identified as a use case for how such insidious behavior becomes increasingly unethical.

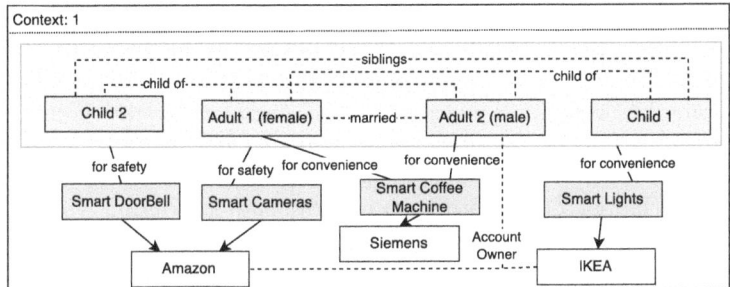

Fig. 4. Results from the first workshop iteration: context 1

One of the participants recalled a personal experience of having their sibling prank them by using the smart virtual assistant remotely and suddenly started playing loud music. The participants began considering at what point such a use case, using a smart device remotely to prank or tease other users, becomes unethical and bordering on domestic abuse. The following exchange was recorded:

Participant 1 My sister would like to check what I was listening to, and if it was like calm or study music or something, she would put up the volume and just blast like hard rock or something annoying.
Participant 2 I usually do that to my girlfriend (...) she gets so annoyed but its not like serious
Participant 3 You could probably do something like that with the lights too, like flickering them on and off
Participant 1 Yes, and if it has a dimmer you can make it like really bright suddenly
Participant 2 Isn't that what they did in that movie?

By referencing the movie *Gaslight*, the exchange above denotes the launch of a more extended discussion regarding what the participants came to refer to as IoT Gaslighting. They defined several use cases (see Fig. 5) to differentiate the different kinds of benign and playful versions of gaslighting, such as changing a song or flickering the lights, to more coercive forms of psychological abuse. According to the discussions, IoT gaslighting refers to using IoT devices duplicitously to manipulate someone into questioning themselves and their grasp of reality. DS, such as the smart coffee machine and smart lights, were mentioned as relevant to the use case as they could be used to distort reality and manipulate users by, for example, changing device settings or functions. Regarding the use case of unethical surveillance, the DS related to such use cases differed from those included for the IoT gaslighting use case (see Fig. 5). Related to surveillance concerns, OS such as the government surveilling BS and ES surveilling BS were exemplified. The latter was mainly discussed in relation to a specific ES, as the participants considered it to be the only ES defined in the context with the capability to realize the use case. Another surveillance concern was ES selling smart home-generated data to third parties with strong incentives to access such data, such as insurance companies, as this could lead to individualized insurance premiums. Lastly, the participants considered how governments might gaslight citizens. Some DS were given special mention, such as the state gaining control of countertop appliances, for example, to regulate food or caffeine intake. The thought process followed a dystopian path and was relatively short-lived, yet touched upon the risk of authoritarian governments interfering with what they currently consider personal matters.

Context: 1: IoT Gaslighting 1	Adult 1	Adult 2		Context: 1: Unethical Surveillance 1	Adult 1	Adult 2
adult users gaslighting each other	Coffee Machine	Smart Lights		adult users surveilling each other		all DS
Context: 1: IoT Gaslighting 2	Adult Users	Child Users		Context: 1: Unethical Surveillance 2	Adult Users	Child Users
adult users gaslighting child users		Smart Lights		adult users surveilling the child users	Smart Cameras	DoorBell
Context: 1: IoT Gaslighting 3	Child 1	Child 2		Context: 1: Unethical Surveillance 3	Amazon	All BS
child users gaslighting each other		Smart Lights		ES surveilling BS		All DS
Context: 1: IoT Gaslighting 4	Goverment	All BS		Context: 1: Unethical Surveillance 4	All BS	Third Party
goverment gaslighing citizens		Coffee Machine		ES selling BS's data	All ES	All DS
Context: 1: Domestic abuse	Male Adult	Female Adult		Context: 1: Surveillance 5	All BS	Goverment
male user restricting female users access device		All DS		goverment surveilling citizens		All DS

Fig. 5. Results from the first workshop iteration: use cases

5.2 Surveillance of Children

The most frequent use cases mentioned across all workshops were ethical concerns related to different forms of surveillance. In the second workshop, an in-depth discussion regarding the surveillance of children was analyzed. The participants defined two contexts, one with an underaged child living with their two parents and the other with an adult child. As the workshop participants were all students, many still lived at home with their parents, yet they were all of age. One concern that emerged from the discussion was related to collecting consent from children and at what age it would be conceivable for a child to advocate for themselves to exercise their data rights. The participants considered that as a child matures and inevitably reaches adulthood, the process of gaining access to one's data is opaque and unregulated. The participants agreed that children should not have to be 18 years old to gain control of their data, for example, to delete it. The child-parent relationship was referenced as to whether the child could successfully negotiate the exercising of such data rights. The participants also launched a broader discussion regarding the ethics of surveilling children for safety reasons. The process of incrementally pushing the boundaries of surveillance in the name of the safety and protection of the child was a central sentiment to the discussion. Many references to movies, series, and popular culture were made to exemplify these use cases. For example, one participant recounted the plot of a TV series episode where a parent implanted their child with a device recording all kinds of invasive data (location, heart rate, what they were seeing, what they were hearing, contents of their digestion, to name a few) to quench their parental anxieties, disregarding the best interest of the child and their developmental needs (Fig. 6).

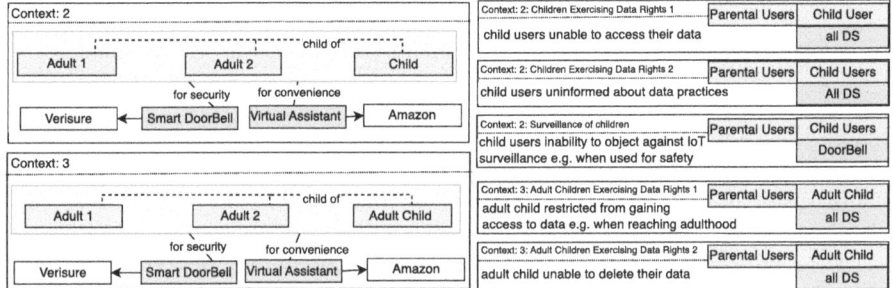

Fig. 6. Results from the second workshop iteration: context 2 and 3

5.3   Developing Ethical Requirements

The setup of the third iteration of the workshop allowed the participants to review the use cases developed by the previous iterations. Two use cases were discussed at length: surveillance of children and how to educate users appropriately regarding the ethical risks of smart home technology. The discussion mainly surrounded access to activity logs and how data is managed among household members. For example, the participants considered whether users should be able to delete or edit activity logs and whether viewing privileges should be granted to all smart home users. The participants considered whether restricting users' access to particular DS, especially concerning the lights and coffee machines, should be a device functionality. The participants agreed that such a requirement might even mitigate some of the ethical concerns related to surveillance and IoT gaslighting, as without such device features, the unethical use cases would be more difficult to actualize. In regards to the smart doorbell and smart camera, the participants discussed whether it was necessary to be able to restrict user access. This way, the participants argued, no single user would be able to monopolize the devices or the data it processes, allowing equal and full access to all DS of the context (see Fig. 4). The topic of educating users regarding the risks of smart homes was mentioned throughout all workshops as a central concern. Informing users about their data rights as well as including age-appropriate information (as the contexts included child users) was frequently brought up, as well as the poor design of the current process of granting "terms and agreements". The participants of the third workshop discussed this extensively and mentioned the inefficacy of such consent-collecting methods. The EU was often

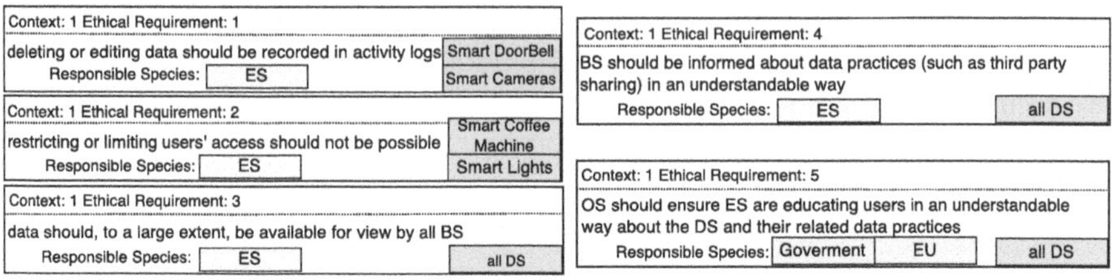

Fig. 7. Results from the third workshop iteration: ethical requirements

cited as the appropriate OS to retain responsibility for developing understandable information packages for users to educate themselves regarding the ethical risks of smart homes. The participants also consider whether it would be ethically sound to require ES to share data with OS if called upon, for example, by the EU or national police authorities. Although the details of the requirement and its implementation were left undefined, the participants seemed to agree that data collected by smart home devices should be disclosed if relevant to matters of criminal investigations, such as for evidence in domestic abuse cases.

6   Discussion

This section reflects on the workshop method and findings regarding the study's hypothesis - that workshop participants could have meaningful ethical discussions by designing and analyzing smart home ecosystems. In the first workshop, the participants drew upon their own experiences and popular culture to delve deep into concerns that piqued their interest (as in the case of IoT gaslighting). For example, they analyzed the broad spectrum of IoT gaslighting, ranging from pranking or teasing family members to abusive forms of manipulation and coercive control. As they were to document the species they considered relevant to the use cases, as per the instructions of activity five (see Fig. 2), they included the smart lights and countertop appliances. When discussing surveillance concerns at large, five additional kinds of surveillance use cases were discussed: both state and corporate surveillance, as well as unethical cases of domestic surveillance (BS species surveilling each other). By having the participants use the ecosystem ontology to specify the species of the use cases, a layer of granularity was added to the analysis, allowing the participants to systematically reflect on each concern. Documenting the use cases in this way also introduced the possibility of comparing smart home contexts with each other. The comparative analyses examined ethical nuances and tension points to consider how well-intentioned use cases can become ethically questionable under certain conditions. For example, parents might push for increasingly invasive surveillance practices, motivated by ensuring the safety of an (under-aged) child. Without the child's informed consent to the surveillance, it could be considered unethically invasive to the child's right to privacy. Similar ethical tensions can be observed in Ethical Requirement 5 (see Fig. 7); the participants reached a consensus in determining that they believed OS, such as the government and the EU, need to ensure that ES are in fact, explicitly and understandably informing users about risks related to smart home technology. Yet, if democracy were diluted, the use case for state surveillance and governments gaslighting citizens (see Fig. 5) would be increasingly probable.

6.1   Ethical Requirements for Smart Home Ecosystems

Many of the workshop discussions were typical of ethical analyses, in the sense that their inevitable conclusion was that there is no universal or general solution to mitigate all unethical smart homes concerns. Instead, the workshop encourages ethical reflection and offers a method to elicit system requirements aimed at safeguarding smart homes from specific unethical use cases. We argue that just undergoing the phases of the workshop was helpful as the activities allowed participants to design the unethical scenarios they have heard about, experienced themselves, are worried or concerned about, or have seen in movies or TV series. The three iterations of the workshops demonstrate different ways to analyze ethical concerns of smart home contexts. The first iteration showed how raw requirements can be elicited by imagining a smart home and the potentially unethical scenarios related to the context. The second took a more comparative form, facilitating specific analyses of common ethical concerns, such as children in smart homes. The third workshop showcased the benefit of the systematic nature of documenting discussion insights according to the workshop activities. By applying the ontology of DE, the analyses from previous workshops could be revisited and built upon by another group of participants. This allowed the scenarios and related requirements identified by one workshop group to be developed and reformulated by another. The last activities of the workshop had the participants identify the species they considered responsible for mitigating the ethical scenarios, which allowed the requirements to evolve and become more specific and well-defined. A general observation from conducting the workshop iterations is how time-consuming ethical analyses of smart homes can be. Due to the many examples of unethical smart home use, the participants of the first two iterations only had time to define the use cases, ending the workshops on phase two. Although the second iteration instructed the participants to focus on child users, with the ambition to limit the scope of the ethical analysis, the discussions were still lengthy. By allowing the participants to draw inspiration from TV, movies, and popular culture, there was no shortage of brainstorming use case ideas. Much of the inspiration in the discussions came from apparent examples in popular media, which, in a sense, include near-endless examples of unethical IoT use.

Although all the workshops resulted in rich discussions on smart home ethics, there is no evident way to evaluate or appraise the actual quality of the analyses themselves. As mentioned, ethics is all-encompassing, and there is no ultimate or universal solution to be uncovered. It is fair to conclude that this was reflected in the discussions. Thus, the main point of the proposed workshop method is not to ultimately determine whether smart home systems are indeed ethical or not.

Instead, it is to explore the lines between, on one end, the benign and harmless uses of smart home devices and, on the opposite end, more dangerous and, at times, illegal uses of the same technology. In other words, a lesson learned from the method design and its implementation in the workshops is that ethics is about the grey zones – by facilitating ethical discussions and revealing related concerns and system requirements in the process, the method design is indeed a contribution to itself. Moreover, as workshop participants documented their discussions systematically, the analyses could easily be revisited and reiterated, as shown by how participants of the third workshop iteration could pick up discussions from previous workshops, for instance, regarding the surveillance of children.

However, to ensure our findings' robustness, we acknowledge potential threats to validity arising from the specific participant group - undergraduate computer science students - whose limited experience with IoT devices may introduce biases. Future studies should include more diverse participant demographics to mitigate these biases and thus enhance the generalizability of our results. So, to further validate the findings beyond the immediate workshop sessions, follow-up studies will be conducted with different participant groups to test the consistency and applicability of the elicited ethical requirements. Additionally, longitudinal studies are planned to assess how these requirements evolve over time, reflecting the changes in technological and societal ethical standards. Findings regarding the participant's experiences of undergoing the workshop and their understanding of its usefulness were considered outside the scope of the research. Future work could make appropriate adaptations to adhere to different IoT contexts and larger participant pools and perhaps include the participants' views regarding the usefulness of the workshop approach. Scaling the workshop design and including an increasingly wide range of participants and stakeholder perspectives, the discussions regarding the role of ethics in smart homes can continue.

7 Conclusions

This paper outlines a workshop methodology to support a systematic ethical analysis of IoT-enabled smart homes. It is based on the approach to smart homes as digital ecosystems, which allows for considering multiple components, interactions, and stakeholders involved in the smart home environment. The methodology, which follows the Constructive Design Research approach, consists of three phases: (1) identifying the smart home ecosystem, (2) mapping the ethical challenges, and (3) proposing solutions and recommendations. We conducted workshops with a group of students as research participants. The results show that the workshop approach can help structure the process of identifying, discussing, and documenting ethical challenges in smart homes and propose context-specific requirements and recommendations. Scenarios revealed in the workshops include IoT gaslighting, surveillance shadowing, and ethics requirements elicitation. Although these scenarios provide valuable insights individually, it is necessary to consider the whole picture when handling ethical situations in the smart home. However, an inevitable conclusion from the workshops was that there appears to be no universal or general solution to mitigate all unethical smart home concerns. Another finding was that the workshop approach can facilitate the communication and dissemination of the research results, as it provides a clear and consistent format to present the ethical analysis of smart homes. This allows the analysis to be reiterated over time and with different stakeholder groups to identify additional ethical nuances. Thus, the workshop can be a valuable tool for researchers and practitioners interested in conducting ethical analyses of smart homes and other IoT domains with similar characteristics and challenges, mainly to understand ethics' complex role in smart Internet-connected living.

References

1. Ahmad, K., Abdelrazek, M., Arora, C., Bano, M., Grundy, J.: Requirements engineering for artificial intelligence systems: a systematic mapping study. Inf. Softw. Technol. **158**, 107176 (2023)
2. Ashok, M., Madan, R., Joha, A., Sivarajah, U.: Ethical framework for artificial intelligence and digital technologies. Int. J. Inf. Manage. **62**, 102433 (2022)
3. Azadegan, A., Papamichail, K.N., Sampaio, P.: Applying collaborative process design to user requirements elicitation: a case study. Comput. Ind. **64**(7), 798–812 (2013)
4. Bagheri, S., Jacobsson, A., Davidsson, P.: Smart homes as digital ecosystems: exploring privacy in IoT contexts. In: Proceedings of the 10th International Conference on Information Systems Security and Privacy - ICISSP, pp. 869–877. INSTICC, SciTePress (2024). https://doi.org/10.5220/0012458700003648
5. Bang, A.L., Krogh, P., Ludvigsen, M., Markussen, T.: The role of hypothesis in constructive design research. In: Proceedings of the Art of Research IV (2012)
6. Bernd, J., Abu-Salma, R., Frik, A.: {Bystanders'} privacy: the perspectives of nannies on smart home surveillance. In: 10th USENIX Workshop on Free and Open Communications on the Internet (FOCI 2020) (2020)
7. Briscoe, G., Sadedin, S., De Wilde, P.: Digital ecosystems: ecosystem-oriented architectures. Nat. Comput. **10**, 1143–1194 (2011)
8. Greer, C., Burns, M., Wollman, D., Griffor, E.: Cyber-physical systems and internet of things (2019). https://doi.org/10.6028/NIST.SP.1900-202
9. Guizzardi, R., Amaral, G., Guizzardi, G., Mylopoulos, J.: Eliciting ethicality requirements using the ontology-based requirements engineering method. In: International Conference on Business Process Modeling, Development and Support, pp. 221–236. Springer, Cham (2022)
10. Koch, M.: New re dimensions for digital ecosystems-initial results from an expert interview study. In: 2019 IEEE 27th International Requirements Engineering Conference (RE), pp. 398–403. IEEE (2019)
11. Koskinen, I., Krogh, P.G.: Design accountability: when design research entangles theory and practice. Int. J. Des. **9**(1) (2015)
12. Koskinen, I., Zimmerman, J., Binder, T., Redstrom, J., Wensveen, S.: Design research through practice: from the lab, field, and showroom. IEEE Trans. Prof. Commun. **56**(3), 262–263 (2013)
13. Maalsen, S.: Revising the smart home as assemblage. Hous. Stud. **35**(9), 1534–1549 (2020)

14. MacKenzie, D., Wajcman, J.: The Social Shaping of Technology. Open University Press (1999)
15. Maiden, N.A., Hare, M.: Problem domain categories in requirements engineering. Int. J. Hum. Comput. Stud. **49**(3), 281–304 (1998)
16. Marky, K., Voit, A., Stöver, A., Kunze, K., Schröder, S., Mühlhäuser, M.: "I don't know how to protect myself": understanding privacy perceptions resulting from the presence of bystanders in smart environments. In: Proceedings of the 11th Nordic Conference on Human-Computer Interaction: Shaping Experiences, Shaping Society, pp. 1–11 (2020)
17. Nehme, E., El Sibai, R., Bou Abdo, J., Taylor, A.R., Demerjian, J.: Converged AI, IoT, and blockchain technologies: a conceptual ethics framework. AI Ethics **2**(1), 129–143 (2022)
18. Rohde, F., Santarius, T.: Emerging sociotechnical imaginaries-how the smart home is legitimized in visions from industry, users in homes and policymakers in Germany. Futures **151**, 103194 (2023)
19. Shahraki, A., Haugen, Ø.: Social ethics in internet of things: an outline and review. In: 2018 IEEE Industrial Cyber-Physical Systems (ICPS), pp. 509–516 (2018)
20. Ustek-Spilda, F., Powell, A., Nemorin, S.: Engaging with ethics in internet of things: imaginaries in the social milieu of technology developers. Big Data Soc. **6**(2), 2053951719879468 (2019)
21. Wheatcraft, L.S., Ryan, M.J.: Communicating requirements–effectively! In: INCOSE International Symposium, vol. 28, pp. 716–732. Wiley Online Library (2018)
22. Zhang, Z.: Effective requirements development-a comparison of requirements elicitation techniques. In: Software Quality Management XV: Software Quality in the Knowledge Society, pp. 225–240 (2007)

Digital Twin-Based Security Orchestration, Automation and Response for IoT and CPS

Phu H. Nguyen[1]([⊠]) [iD], Ashish Rauniyar[1], and Toni Valtteri Niemi[2]

[1] SINTEF, Trondheim, Norway
{phu.nguyen,ashish.rauniyar}@sintef.no
[2] University of Oslo, Oslo, Norway
tonivn@ifi.uio.no

Abstract. The digitisation leveraging technologies in the Internet of Things (IoT) and Cyber-Physical Systems (CPS) has been largely adopted together with the Digital Twin (DT) paradigm. However, the distributed and heterogeneous nature of IoT or CPS poses significant challenges in safeguarding against diverse attack surfaces, including physical devices, network infrastructures, and third-party integration. Furthermore, the evolving security threats and potential cascading effects from cyber attacks add another layer of complexity to the security landscape. Therefore, in this paper, we propose a digital twin-based security orchestration automation and response framework, striving for the business continuity (SOAR4BC). Leveraging system contexts from the DT in combination with security intelligence from the security tools gives us a holistic context for SOAR, which has not been seen in the existing approaches. By subjecting tampered data and distributed denial of service (DDoS) detection to rigorous experimental evaluation, we substantiate the efficacy and reliability of the SOAR4BC framework in detecting and responding to security policy violations within simulated digital twin environments. This validation serves as a compelling proof of concept, highlighting the SOAR4BC framework's robustness in addressing cyber threats. Our work offers novel insights into the convergence of digital twin technology and cybersecurity, illuminating the unique challenges and opportunities inherent in DT-based IoT and CPS systems.

Keywords: IoT · CPS · Security · Digital Twin · Security Orchestration · SOAR · Critical Infrastructures · Machine Learning

1 Introduction

Our societies are relying on a vast array of services that are increasingly transitioning into digital ecosystems, and their susceptibility to cyber security threats becomes more pronounced [7, 21]. This digitization process involves the integration of advanced technologies such as the Internet of Things (IoT) and Cyber-Physical Systems (CPS), often accompanied by the adoption of the Digital Twin

G. Rey et al. (Eds.): IFIPIoT 2024, IFIP AICT 737, pp. 243–260, 2025.
https://doi.org/10.1007/978-3-031-81900-1_15

(DT) paradigm [1]. As systems become more interconnected and reliant on digital infrastructure, they become exposed to a myriad of security vulnerabilities. However, safeguarding these digitized systems presents a formidable challenge. The distributed and heterogeneous nature of CPS/IoT introduces complexities in defending against a wide array of attack surfaces [24]. These attack surfaces encompass not only traditional targets such as network infrastructures and physical devices but also extend to encompass third-party integration and supply chain dependencies. Moreover, the constantly evolving landscape of security threats, coupled with the potential cascading effects of cyber attacks, further exacerbates the challenge of ensuring the security and resilience of IoT/CPS systems.

According to Microsoft, "security orchestration, automation, and response (SOAR) refers to a set of services and tools that automate cyberattack prevention and response" [14]. Microsoft differentiates between security automation and security orchestration. Security automation refers to the use of information technology to replace manual processes for responding to cyber incidents and managing security events. In contrast, security orchestration involves integrating various security and IT tools to streamline processes, thereby enhancing security automation. According to Islam et al., security orchestration encompasses the planning, integration, cooperation, and coordination of activities among security tools and experts. This approach ensures that necessary actions in response to security incidents are automated across multiple technological environments [13].

Security orchestration has the potential to become an essential aspect of securing IoT ecosystems as the complexity and scale of IoT deployments continue to increase. Security orchestration involves automating and integrating security tools, processes, and technologies to provide a more cohesive and streamlined security process. By orchestrating security across different IoT devices and edge computing systems, organizations can reduce the risk of gaps or overlaps in security coverage [3]. Security orchestration is important for several reasons. First, it allows organizations to respond to security threats more quickly and efficiently. Automated security workflows can identify, triage, and respond to security incidents in real time, reducing the risk of data breaches or other cyber attacks. Second, security orchestration can help organizations achieve compliance with industry and government regulations. Many regulations require organizations to implement specific security measures, and security orchestration can help ensure that these measures are consistently applied across the IoT ecosystem. Finally, security orchestration can help organizations reduce the cost and complexity of security management. By automating security workflows and integrating security technologies, organizations can reduce the burden on security teams and achieve greater visibility into security operations [12].

Building on the state of the art in SOAR, this paper introduces a novel digital twin-based Security Orchestration Automation and Response framework for Business Continuity (SOAR4BC). This framework leverages the contextual insights provided by the DT, integrating them with security intelligence gleaned from various security tools. Context can be considered as a key for adapting to user need [26], including more automated security orchestration with human-in-the-loop. SOAR4BC aims to provide comprehensive protection for DT-based IoT/CPS systems by adopting a holistic approach to security orchestration.

Smart security orchestration for policy-based access control typically focuses on the edge layer. This includes implementing a Machine Learning agent (ML-agent) to detect and store threat patterns/data and to orchestrate and automate the control of deployment and (re)configuration of all the security requirements. The focus will be implementing orchestration on the edge layer and seeing how we can improve the flexibility and adaptability of access control policies. Emphasizing edge layer orchestration, SOAR4BC seeks to improve the flexibility and adaptability of access control policies, optimize resource utilization, and minimize latency by leveraging edge computing capabilities.

Through rigorous experimental evaluation, including the analysis of tampered data and distributed denial of service (DDoS) attack detection, this paper substantiates the efficacy and reliability of the SOAR4BC framework. The validation provided serves as a compelling proof of concept, demonstrating the SOAR4BC framework's ability to detect and respond to security policy violations within simulated DT environments. Moreover, this work offers valuable insights into the convergence of DT technology and cybersecurity, shedding light on the unique challenges and opportunities inherent in DT-based systems.

In principle, this paper presents novel contributions in leveraging DT within the SOAR framework specifically tailored for IoT/CPS systems. The primary contributions of this paper are outlined as follows:

- **Integration of DT**: We demonstrate the integration of DT within the security domain, mainly focusing on IoT/CPS systems. By harnessing the capabilities of digital twins, we establish a realistic and dynamic simulation environment mirroring the complexities of real-world systems.
- **Development of SOAR4BC Framework**: We introduce the SOAR4BC framework, uniquely designed to address security challenges within DT-based systems. This framework facilitates automated incident detection, analysis, and response orchestration, ensuring robust security measures are in place to safeguard the integrity of the system.
- **Experimental Evaluation and Validation**: Through rigorous data tampering and DDoS attack experimental evaluation and demonstration, we validate the efficacy and reliability of the SOAR4BC framework in detecting and responding to security policy violations within the simulated DT environment. Our experiments provide empirical evidence of the SOAR4BC framework's effectiveness in enhancing security posture and mitigating potential threats.
- **New Insights into DT Security**: Our research offers new insights into the intersection of DT technology and cybersecurity, shedding light on the unique challenges and opportunities presented by DT-based IoT/CPS systems. We contribute to the growing body of knowledge in this emerging field, paving the way for future advancements and innovations.

The remainder of this paper is structured as follows. We present a motivational example in Sect. 2. Our digital twin-based SOAR approach is presented in Sect. 3. We present our experiments in Sect. 4. Related works are discussed in Sect. 5. We conclude the paper in Sect. 6.

2   An Example Training Factory Industry 4.0

In this section, we present a training factory as a representative example of a CPS/IoT-based critical system. We used Fischertechnik ©Training Factory Industry 4.0 24V [9]. This factory replicates an ordering, manufacturing, and delivery process using several pieces of equipment like an automated High Bay warehouse. The Factory Industry 4.0 has been connected to a DT implemented as an instance of the DT platform called SINDIT[1]. SINDIT is synchronised in real-time with the physical assets and contains all pertinent data about the assets from the connected Factory Industry 4.0.

Within the SINDIT environment, we interface with six distinct components (h1–h6 in Fig. 1), each playing a pivotal role in the simulated industrial processes:

- **Highbay Warehouse (HBW)**: The HBW serves as a storage facility within the factory, housing raw materials and finished products.
- **Robot (VGR)**: This component embodies the automation aspect of the factory, executing tasks such as material handling and product assembly.
- **Sensor Unit (SSC)**: The SSC encompasses sensors dispersed throughout the factory, collecting real-time data on various parameters such as temperature, pressure, and machine statuses.
- **Delivery and Pickup (DPS)**: Responsible for managing the logistics of product transportation within the factory premises, the DPS ensures a seamless movement of goods between different stages of production.
- **Multi-Processing Station (MPO)**: The MPO represents a versatile processing unit capable of executing multiple tasks concurrently, enhancing production efficiency.
- **Sorting Line (SLD)**: This component oversees the sorting and categorization of products based on predefined criteria, streamlining the final stages of production.

The Training Factory Industry 4.0 provides many time-series outputs from the physical assets that are communicating using OPC-UA or MQTT via two corresponding gateways. Some representative security mechanisms have been deployed in the connected Factory Industry 4.0. We have utilized Mininet as a core component of our software-defined networking (SDN) infrastructure. This allowed us to create a virtual network environment mirroring the training factory's network, granting us extensive control over switch and firewall configurations at an application level for managing network security [15]. Ryu[2] is used as

---

[1] https://github.com/SINTEF-9012/SINDIT.

[2] https://ryu-sdn.org/.

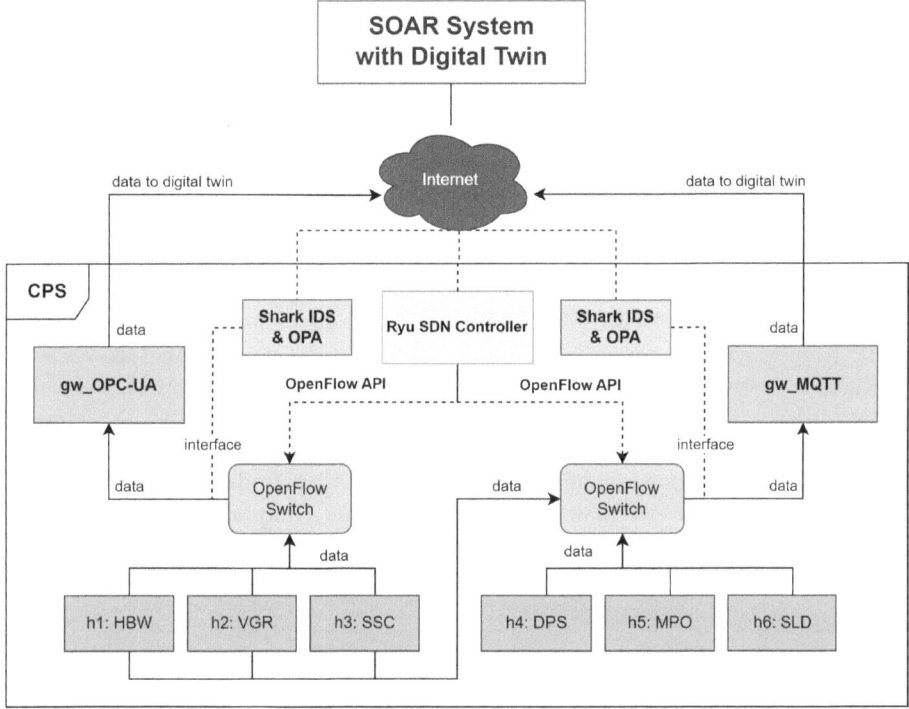

Fig. 1. The Factory Industry 4.0 connected to a SINTEF Digital Twin (SINDIT)

an SDN controller, which has a REST Firewall application. It is a Python script written by the Ryu developers that allows us to create, modify, and delete firewall policy rules remotely through REST calls. While the SDN controller allows us to manage flow control of the network, it does not report events that happen in the network. Therefore, a basic Intrusion Detection System (IDS) has been deployed to alert the SOAR system to security breach events. This system is named Shark IDS. To control the access policies that the Shark IDS will utilize, we deployed an Open Policy Agent (OPA)[3] server that will run alongside the Shark IDS. Instead of having hard-coded, custom rules written directly into the Shark IDS, it will request authorization from OPA and receive a response for handling policy access control. It can then forward any security breaches to the SOAR system, which can handle the incident response.

This Factory Industry 4.0 is a representative example of critical infrastructures in many different domains, such as manufacturing [11], energy [6], and healthcare, in which DT technology is widely used and security is of paramount importance [20]. Industry 4.0, characterized by the integration of CPS, IoT, and smart automation, faces unique and complex cyber-security challenges such as ransomware attacks, data tampering, supply chain attacks, distributed denial

---

[3] https://www.openpolicyagent.org/docs/latest/.

of service attacks, IoT device exploitation, man-in-the-middle attacks. It is vital that there is a systematic SOAR approach to leverage the DT as well as the security tools to enhance security automation with human-in-the-loop in addressing the threats and incidents.

3   Digital Twin-Based SOAR Approach

In this section, we present our SOAR4BC approach, which leverages the DT of physical systems to provide a holistic context for security orchestration, automation, and response. SOAR4BC is connected to other components of the DYN-ABIC framework [22], providing necessary information via a Kafka bus. As seen in Fig. 2, it receives inputs from AWARE4BC for incident details, MADT4BC for system information, RISK4BC for risk analysis data and CTI4BC for external incident information. SOAR4BC is also linked to AVATAR4BC to provide assistance to human operators. More details on these other modules can be found in [17,22]. In this paper, we mainly focus on the inner components of SOAR4BC, as presented in the following subsections.

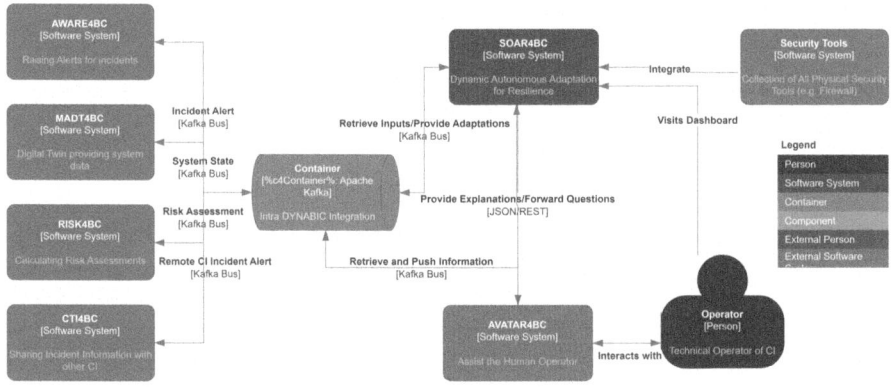

Fig. 2. High-level Component View

Figure 3 shows the inner components of the SOAR4BC solution. SOAR4BC finds the best possible security adaptations and orchestrates them. Adaptations can either be executed automatically, i.e. without human interference, or by following the human-in-the-loop paradigm. The degree of automation depends on the specific use case and action space. The playbook generation is needed by the Orchestration Unit, Tools Integration Unit and Action Automation Unit to streamline adaptations in response to incidents. For every incident, a new playbook is generated, which is compliant with the CACAO v2 standard[4]. It

---

[4] https://docs.oasis-open.org/cacao/security-playbooks/v2.0/security-playbooks-v2.0.html.

is represented in JSON format (see Listing 1.1) and has a similar structure independent of the incident: the leading preamble holds general data like ID, type, creation date and others.

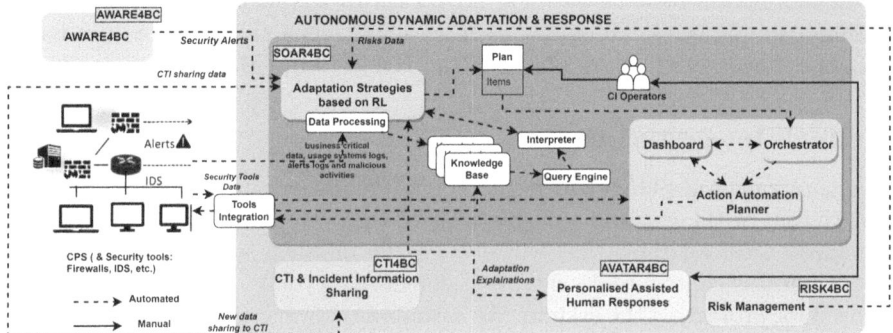

Fig. 3. Digital Twin based SOAR4BC Framework

Listing 1.1. An example playbook

```
1   {
2     "type": "playbook",
3     "spec_version": "cacao-2.0",
4     "id": "playbook--0392cbeb-bd2a-4b03-80f4-97e54be0c1a8",
5     "name": "SOAR4BC Playbook", ...
6     "workflow_start": "start--9339c898-3427-4da0-8b64-c3d761627cbf", ...
7       "action--a74d5427-5e97-42df-94e3-95923e49da16": {
8         "name": "Check Violation",
9         "description": "Check for violations in data packets of the SINDIT toy
               factory digital twin ",
10        "on_success": "if-condition--9c654f27-a3ff-4f12-8502-853e2c5c17a5", ...,
11        "type": "action",
12        "commands": [
13          {
14            "type": "http-api",
15            "description": "OPA checks for policy violation for data tampering",
16            "version": "1.0",
17            "playbook_activity": "analyze-collected-data"
18          }
19        ], ...
20      },
21      "if-condition--9c654f27-a3ff-4f12-8502-853e2c5c17a5": {
22        "name": "if_condition",
23        "step_extensions": {
24          "0": [
25            "extension-definition--418ee24c-9cb1-46d9-afa5-309e01aabc7f"
26          ],...
27        },
28        "type": "if-condition",
29        "condition": "No Value",
30        "on_true": "playbook-action--80dda560-21a0-4157-85e9-d93be5e6a1da",
31        "on_false": "action--a74d5427-5e97-42df-94e3-95923e49da16"
32      },
33      "playbook-action--80dda560-21a0-4157-85e9-d93be5e6a1da": {
34        "name": "Disable Communication",
35        "description": "Disable firewall so that the incoming data from that host
               will be blocked",
36        "on_success": "action--407f8ae0-d358-48f2-b6e0-7e734946189c",...
37      }
38   }
```

Generally, each playbook holds the id of the triggering incident alert (as its external reference) and its own id, which is structured as "playbook_"<incident_id>. After the preamble, workflows are defined. There are always multiple possible workflows with different rankings. The higher the ranking, the more preferred this workflow is over the others. Currently, we are implementing a simple version in which each workflow has a single adaptation based on a pre-defined action space stored in the **Knowledge Base** (see Sect. 3.3).

3.1   Tools Integration Unit

A key component of SOAR4BC is the Tools Integration unit, which harmonizes the activities of the existing security tools of the system. Security tools are our generalized term for tools that will protect the physical system. This could be firewalls, access control tools, intrusion detection systems, etc. They have been deployed for protecting the system. We assume that every security tool or service offers multiple security capabilities. When analysing a security operation or event occurring on an entity of a DT and triggered by a security service, several factors must be considered in specific runtime contexts.

- Tool-specific Context: The output (e.g., decision and metrics) within the specific context of the security tool, such as functionality, performance, configuration, input source, and input quality.
- Environment Context: The entity within the DT context, including its relationships with other entities, such as direct network connections to other entities or being operated by a specific user.
- Security Context: The operation/event within multiple security aspects, such as whether the entity is currently experiencing unauthorized access or has been detected with malware.

The Tools Integration acts as the end-point for tools in the SOAR component. This could, for instance, be an API gateway or other forms of end-points for tools to communicate via a connection from the physical system. When a security breach gets caught by a tool, it gets forwarded to the Tools Integration. The data then gets forwarded to the data processing unit, which processes it for orchestration.

3.2   Orchestration Unit

The Orchestrator is responsible for receiving data sent in and orchestrating security response. This implies that it should streamline the data it gets into streamline workflow and determine the appropriate course of action based on the information that it receives. In our architecture, it would be receiving processed data and communicating with the Action Automation Planner to trigger a response. Alongside the playbook, it should determine what kind of response should be orchestrated. The playbook is a set of rules about what to do regarding a certain type of incident based on configured rules, which are stored in the Knowledge Base.

3.3   Knowledge Base

The Knowledge Base unit is responsible for receiving data, processing, and structuring it. One of the main functionalities that the Knowledge Base unit provides is interoperability and interpretability. Information/data from both security tools and the digital twin can be heterogeneous structured and unstructured data. Processing this data in such a way that it can be forwarded to the orchestration system and be readable by the playbook is what the Knowledge Base is responsible for.

The Knowledge Base stores relevant information about the system being protected. Information that is relevant is the current state of the system, such as information about the IoT devices within the CPS, alongside information about the SOAR system itself. The database has a remote interface open for the SOAR system to update information to it. Depending on deployment, it can include a variety of information. In our approach, we are focusing on having the database as a middle-point between the orchestration/automation and the dashboard.

3.4   Action Automation Unit

The Action Automation Unit, an enterprise-level security orchestrator, will automate the execution of incident response processes and keep track of the tasks being executed.

The Action Automation Planner receives information from the Orchestrator and is responsible for automating the response. It has the simple job of automating responses forward to the relevant unit to which it is connected. In our architecture, this response would be sent out to Tools Integration, which will forward the response to the relevant security tools and services. The Action Automation Planner should have direct access to the units in the Tools Integration where responses to the relevant tool can be sent out.

The Dashboard acts as a visual platform for both the Orchestrator and the Action Automation Planner, as well as information about the IoT devices through the Digital Twin. The flow and state of data should be sent into the Dashboard by updating the database from these two units to view what is happening in the system visually. This is of great usefulness for maintainers of the system to get this information in an easy-to-digest manner. Using the digital twin solution, we can have a greater overview of the physical system.

4   Experimental Results

We have conducted experiments on two common security scenarios, i.e., data tampering (Sect. 4.1) and DDoS (Sect. 4.2), on the network behaviours and security protocols within the Training Factory Industry 4.0 presented in Sect. 2. Figure 4 shows the two representative playbooks, which adhere to the CACAO v2 standard, ensuring interoperability and adherence to industry best practices.

Data Tampering

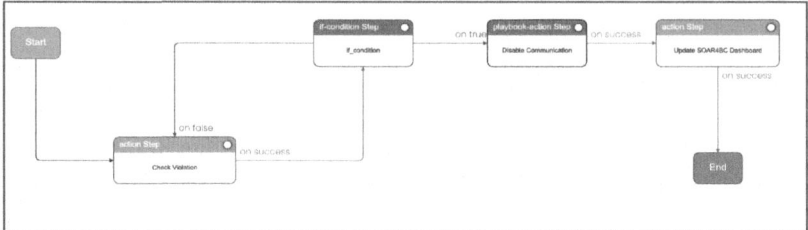

DDoS Detection

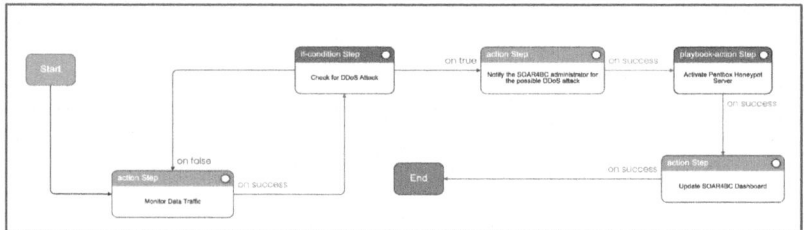

Fig. 4. SOAR4BC CACAO Playbooks for Data Tampering and DDoS Attack

4.1 Data Tampering Scenario

In this scenario, we delve into the ramifications of security policy breaches such as "Data Tampering". Specifically, we simulate instances where components in the factory environment transmit data violating established security protocols, prompting our SOAR4BC system to enact appropriate countermeasures.

To enable security policy violations in our experiments, we configured Mininet within VirtualBox 7.0. We integrated the Ryu controller with the firewall's API to establish firewall functionalities within the network environment. To detect security breaches, we incorporated a Shark-based IDS, which monitors network traffic, identifies policy violations, and communicates with our SOAR4BC system through a RESTful interface. SOAR4BC swiftly detects anomalies indicating potential data tampering because of the violation to the policy in OPA. Once an anomaly is flagged, the system verifies the integrity of the affected data and ensures any deviations are promptly assessed. Following verification, SOAR4BC orchestrates remediation steps, such as isolating the affected component within the DT environment to prevent further tampering and allow for a thorough investigation. Our SOAR4BC system assumes a crucial role in managing access control rules within OPA and orchestrating responses to detected security incidents. As shown in Fig. 5, upon detecting breaches, the SOAR system dynamically updates firewall policies managed by the Ryu SDN Controller to mitigate threats swiftly.

To visualize and analyze data from our experiments, we utilized Neodash as a dashboard solution, interfacing directly with the Neo4j database. Neodash

```
soar — python soar.py 192.168.56.6 — 80×24
[{"switch_id": "0000000000000001", "command_result": [{"result": "success", "det
ails": "Rule added. : rule_id=7"}]}]
[{"switch_id": "0000000000000001", "command_result": [{"result": "success", "det
ails": "Rule added. : rule_id=8"}]}]
[{"switch_id": "0000000000000001", "command_result": [{"result": "success", "det
ails": "Rule added. : rule_id=9"}]}]
[{"switch_id": "0000000000000001", "command_result": [{"result": "success", "det
ails": "Rule added. : rule_id=10"}]}]
[{"switch_id": "0000000000000001", "command_result": [{"result": "success", "det
ails": "Rule added. : rule_id=11"}]}]
[{"switch_id": "0000000000000001", "command_result": [{"result": "success", "det
ails": "Rule added. : rule_id=12"}]}]
{}

<Response [200]>
[EVENT HANDLER] New Data Captured
[ORCHESTRATOR] Getting Playbook Rule
[ACTION AUTOMATOR] Automating Response, Updating Dashboard
[FIREWALL SERVICE] Disabling Communication From Host 10.0.0.6
[{"switch_id": "0000000000000001", "command_result": [{"result": "success", "det
ails": "Rule deleted. : ruleID=7"}]}]
[{"switch_id": "0000000000000001", "command_result": [{"result": "success", "det
ails": "Rule deleted. : ruleID=8"}]}]
[]
```

Fig. 5. SOAR4BC inspecting for Data Tampering and orchestrating response

offers interactive visualization of toy factory components, switches, and gateways, enhancing visibility into network topology. The dashboard, as shown in Fig. 6, aggregates data from various sources, including SOAR responses, DT simulations, and host quarantine status, providing network and security operators with a comprehensive view of the network environment for informed decision-making and incident response.

4.2   DDoS Scenario

In our second experimental evaluation, we focus on a DDoS attack and show how SOAR4BC can orchestrate two different security mechanisms for responding.

Backup Gateway Strategy: Figure 7 shows the scenario of leveraging a backup gateway in the response. We have the HBW, VGR and SSC sending data to the OPC-UA gateway. At some point during the scenario the HBW and VGR gets infected by a botnet, which will initiate a DDOS attack towards the OPC-UA gateway. Using information about the packet count sent towards the gateway, we can create a response for the DDOS attack, isolating the infected hosts, and rerouting traffic from the SSC device towards a backup gateway, so that the non-infected device can continue sending data.

The result from this evaluation can be seen in Fig. 8, where we show the packet count per cycle on the OPC-UA gateway. At **point 1**, the HBW gets infected by the botnet and initiates a DDOS attack towards the gateway. We see that the traffic increases quite a lot, but it is still under the threshold we have put in place on the gateway. At **point 2**, the VGR initiates its DDOS attack

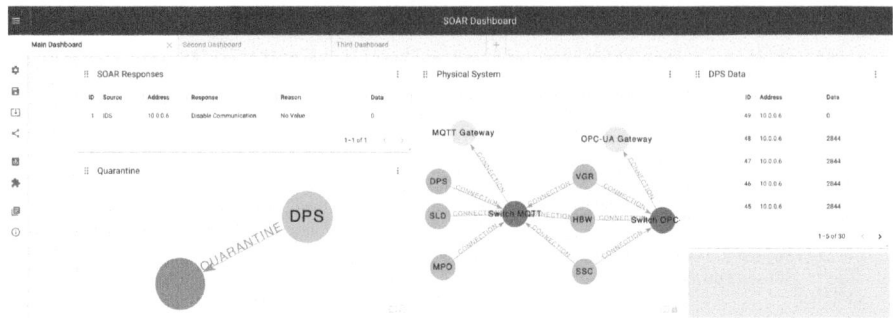

Fig. 6. SOAR4BC Dashboard for Data Tampering Incident Visualization and Response

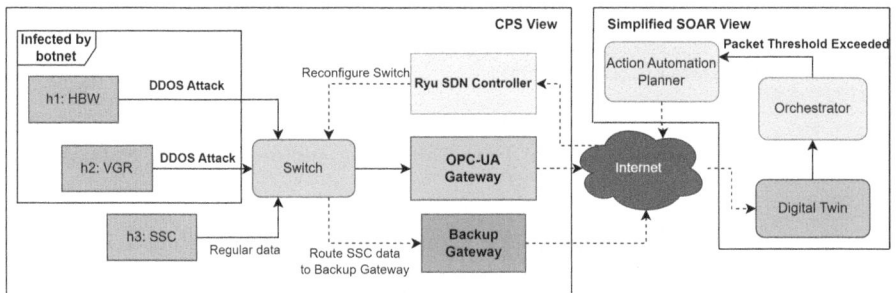

Fig. 7. Backup gateway strategy

towards the gateway, and a SOAR response gets triggered, where the infected devices get isolated, and the remaining device has its traffic rerouted to the backup gateway, meaning no new traffic will enter the old gateway.

We have a backup gateway in order to ensure business continuity. With a DDOS attack, there can often be lingering effects of the attack for a while as the system tries to recover from an unexpectedly large amount of packets going through it. By deploying a backup gateway as soon as the DDOS attack is detected, we can ensure that non-infected devices can continue their operations without getting halted.

Honeypot Strategy: For demonstrating the honeypot strategy, we integrated a honeypot server (HPS) alongside the existing components in the network topology of the Factory Industry 4.0 presented in Sect. 2. The HPS is logically integrated into the security toolbox of SOAR4BC via a custom Python script for the Ryu-SDN controller. This script empowers the Ryu controller to add new flow rules to switches, manage packet forwarding actions, and oversee communication between switches and the controller. This modification facilitates the redirection of DDoS traffic to the HPS for analysis upon detection of a DDoS

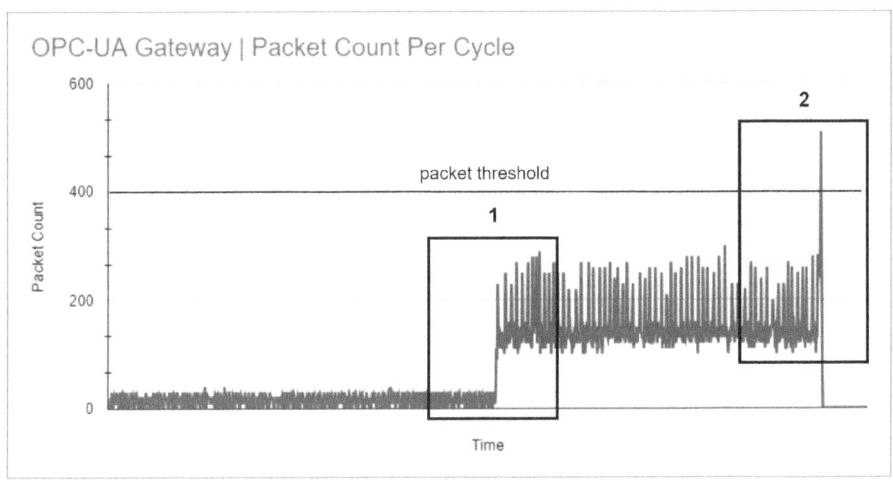

Fig. 8. Data traffic through OPC-UA Gateway

attack. The updated architecture enhances the SOAR4BC system's ability to detect and mitigate DDoS attacks.

Our experiment begins with the simulation of normal traffic within the Mininet environment to validate the detection capabilities of our SOAR4BC system. We ensure that normal traffic is accurately identified, with no false positives for DDoS attacks. Subsequently, we deliberately initiate a DDoS attack simulation from a designated host (DPS with IP 10.0.0.6) to the MQTT gateway (with IP 10.0.0.1) using hping3 network tool[5]. We adopt a classification-based approach to identify DDoS attacks by categorizing network traffic into normal and abnormal categories based on characteristic values extracted from data packets. These values, obtained at specific time intervals, form sequences labelled as either normal or abnormal. To build our detection model, we utilize ML algorithms such as SVM. SVM learns from labelled sequences to classify unlabeled samples, enabling the SOAR4BC system to discern whether incoming traffic signals a potential DDoS attack.

As expected, the inspection terminal in the SOAR4BC system promptly identified the DDoS attack, as shown in Fig. 9, triggering the redirection of traffic to the HPS for further analysis by security operation centres (SOC) with SOC personnel. In this case, the action space involves human-in-the-loop for the corresponding workflow in the security playbook. This means that the SOC personnel are alerted and can decide whether or not and when to trigger the honeypot strategy. For example, if the attacks impact has not reached a threshold, i.e., the revenue goal is still better than "spinning up a honeypot server".

When the threshold is reached, to scrutinize traffic redirected from detected DDoS attacks, the SOAR4BC system deploys a honeypot server within the net-

---

[5] https://www.kali.org/tools/hping3/.

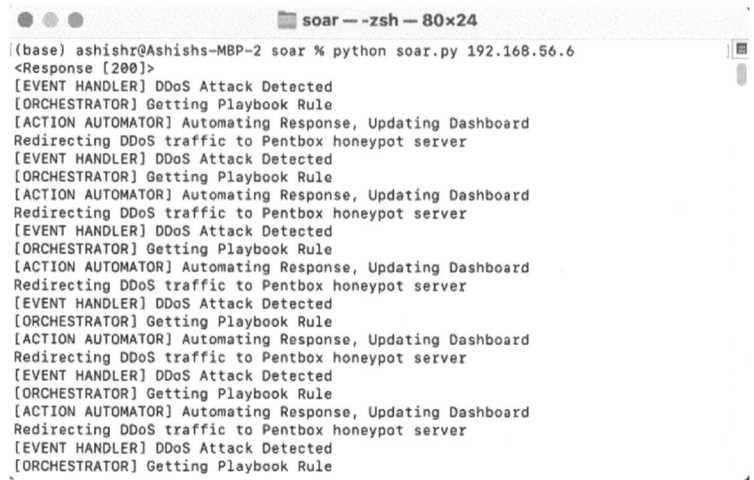

Fig. 9. Inspecting for DDoS Attack and Subsequent Response Orchestration

work architecture. The Pentbox honeypot serves as a decoy to attract and analyze potentially malicious traffic [25]. Redirecting DDoS traffic to the honeypot allows SOC personnel to observe attacker behaviour without endangering the actual network infrastructure.

Throughout these processes, SOAR4BC generates comprehensive incident reports, providing stakeholders with real-time insights into the scope, severity, and effectiveness of the response. These detailed reports support post-incident analysis and enhance future preparedness, demonstrating the framework's robustness in maintaining the integrity and resilience of critical infrastructure systems.

As shown in Fig. 10, this comprehensive experimental setup, evaluation and visualization on the dashboard demonstrate the effectiveness of our SOAR4BC framework in detecting and mitigating DDoS attacks within DT environments, offering robust security measures for DT-based CI systems.

5   Related Work

Bellavista et al. focus on reducing technological barriers by providing the IoTwins platform, which leverages the Digital Twin (DT) computing paradigm along with ICT technologies such as Cloud/Edge computing, Big Data, and Machine Learning [5]. The IoTwins platform facilitates the development and operation of industrial applications by offering a hybrid and distributed DT model. This model involves various industrial partners to validate and refine the DT, where SOAR functionality can be deployed and tested in real-world settings.

Islam et al. present an architecture-centric approach for designing a SOAR platform, highlighting key dimensions of the architecture design space [13]. Their

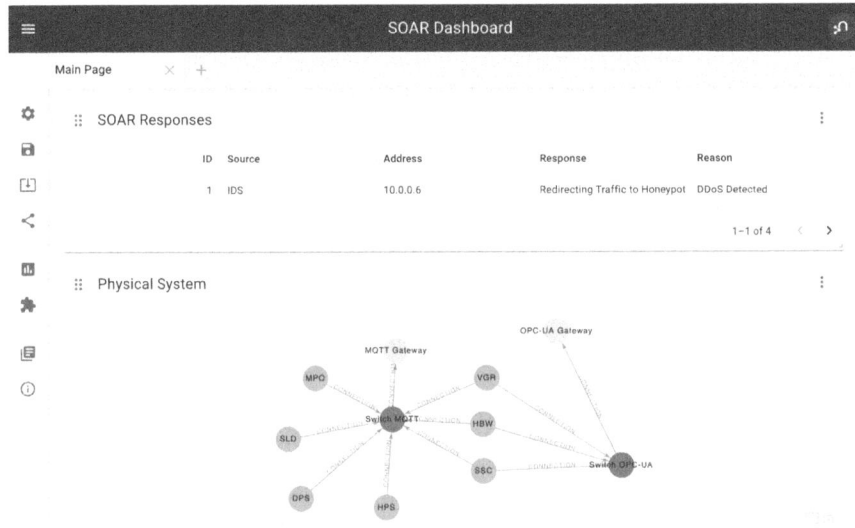

Fig. 10. SOAR4BC Dashboard for DDoS Attack Incident Visualisation and Response

work reduces the design complexity of a SOAR system by modularizing its functionalities and non-functional requirements. The architecture is divided into six layers: (1) security tool, (2) integration, (3) data processing, (4) semantic, (5) orchestration, and (6) User Interface (UI). This layered approach facilitates understanding and analyzing design choices. They conclude with a Proof of Concept (PoC) SOAR platform based on their architectural approach.

Empl et al. discuss SOAR4IoT, focusing on securing IoT assets using Digital Twins [8]. They address challenges in securing IoT devices due to their heterogeneity and inadequate security measures. Their work integrates the SOAR platform to benefit from tool integration, automation, streamlined workflows, and rapid responses. Digital twins are utilized for additional response measures, where live data from DT solutions enhance security measures for IoT devices.

Bartwal et al. introduce a SOAR Engine designed to enhance infrastructure security by dynamically deploying custom honeypots based on attacker behavior [4]. This approach engages attackers longer, conserves resources, and increases interaction with honeypots to gather organization-specific threat intelligence. Their system demonstrated improved attacker engagement, resource savings, and effective detection of malicious samples and DDoS traffic, showcasing its effectiveness in protecting internal networks.

Allison et al. explore the use of digital twins to support cybersecurity incident response in CPSs [2]. They discuss applying digital twins throughout the Incident Response (IR) Life Cycle, categorizing previous research based on IR phases and digital twin modes of operation. The authors propose integrating digital twins into IR playbooks to enhance the effectiveness and efficiency of incident response activities. By analyzing existing IR workflows and identifying the most suitable digital twin forms for different tasks, they highlight the potential of data-driven digital twins for anomaly detection and system monitoring, as well as the use of simulations for system intervention activities.

While these works contribute significantly to the fields of digital twins and SOAR, they highlight gaps and opportunities for further integration and enhancement. Current solutions often address specific aspects of security orchestration and response or focus on particular technologies. However, they do not fully leverage the combined potential of digital twins and SOAR capabilities.

To address these challenges, our proposed SOAR4BC framework integrates contextual insights from digital twins with security intelligence from various tools, adopting a holistic approach to security orchestration. The more AI-based automation supported, the more important it is to provide data quality [10,18, 23], and especially explainability for AI-based security tools as part of SOAR solutions [19]. SOAR4BC approach aims to provide comprehensive protection, enhance resource utilization, and minimize latency by leveraging edge computing capabilities [16], thereby advancing the state-of-the-art in securing CI systems.

6 Conclusions and Future Work

Our study underscores the critical importance of addressing cybersecurity concerns in the digitization of critical infrastructures (CI). As CI becomes increasingly interconnected through technologies such as the Internet of Things (IoT) and Cyber-Physical Systems (CPS), coupled with the adoption of the Digital Twin (DT) paradigm, the vulnerability to cyber threats escalates. The distributed and heterogeneous nature of CI presents formidable challenges in mitigating diverse attack surfaces, while the potential for cascading effects amplifies the complexity of the security landscape. In response to these challenges, we introduced the DT-based security orchestration automation and response (SOAR4BC) for business continuity framework. Designed to detect and orchestrate security responses and analyses, this framework ensures robust security measures for safeguarding the integrity of DT-based CI systems. Through rigorous experimental evaluation, focusing on tampered data and distributed denial of service (DDoS) detection, we demonstrated the efficacy and reliability of the SOAR4BC framework in identifying and responding to security policy violations within simulated DT environments. Our findings provide compelling evidence of the SOAR4BC framework's effectiveness, serving as a proof of concept for its practical application in addressing cyber threats in DT-based CI systems.

For future work, the application of AI solutions holds immense potential for enhancing the capabilities of the SOAR4BC framework. Leveraging deep reinforcement learning (DRL) can automate the smart generation of security playbooks by prioritizing security adaptations based on incident alerts, risk assessments, and system state observations. On the other hand, we can also support the continuous integration and continuous deployment (CI/CD) as part of SOAR4BC. This CI/CD support ensures that robust security measures are deployed throughout the lifecycle of DT-based CI systems, mitigating security risks at every stage of development and operation.

Acknowledgments. The research leading to this publication has received funding from the European Union's Horizon Europe research and innovation programme under Grant Agreement 101070455 (DYNABIC).

References

1. Alcaraz, C., Lopez, J.: Digital twin: a comprehensive survey of security threats. IEEE Commun. Surv. Tutor. **24**(3), 1475–1503 (2022)
2. Allison, D., Smith, P., Mclaughlin, K.: Digital twin-enhanced incident response for cyber-physical systems. In: Proceedings of the 18th International Conference on Availability, Reliability and Security, pp. 1–10 (2023)
3. Alwarafy, A., Al-Thelaya, K.A., Abdallah, M., Schneider, J., Hamdi, M.: A survey on security and privacy issues in edge-computing-assisted internet of things. IEEE Internet Things J. **8**(6), 4004–4022 (2020)
4. Bartwal, U., Mukhopadhyay, S., Negi, R., Shukla, S.: Security orchestration, automation, and response engine for deployment of behavioural honeypots. In: 2022 IEEE Conference on Dependable and Secure Computing (DSC), pp. 1–8 (2022)
5. Bellavista, P., Di Modica, G.: Iotwins: implementing distributed and hybrid digital twins in industrial manufacturing and facility management settings. Future Internet **16**(2), 65 (2024)
6. Bharatee, A., Ray, P.K., Subudhi, B., Ghosh, A.: Power management strategies in a hybrid energy storage system integrated AC/DC microgrid: a review. Energies **15**(19) (2022). https://doi.org/10.3390/en15197176. https://www.mdpi.com/1996-1073/15/19/7176
7. Chowdhury, N., Gkioulos, V.: Cyber security training for critical infrastructure protection: a literature review. Comput. Sci. Rev. **40**, 100361 (2021)
8. Empl, P., Schlette, D., Zupfer, D., Pernul, G.: Soar4iot: securing IoT assets with digital twins. In: Proceedings of the 17th International Conference on Availability, Reliability and Security, pp. 1–10 (2022)
9. Fischertechnik: Training Factory Industry 4.0 24V. https://www.fischertechnik.de/en/products/industry-and-universities/training-models/554868-training-factory-industry-4-0-24v. Accessed 16 June 2024
10. Goknil, A., et al.: A systematic review of data quality in CPS and IoT for industry 4.0. ACM Comput. Surv. **55**(14s) (2023). https://doi.org/10.1145/3593043
11. Isaja, M., et al.: A blockchain-based framework for trusted quality data sharing towards zero-defect manufacturing. Comput. Ind. **146**, 103853 (2023)
12. Islam, C., Babar, M.A., Nepal, S.: A multi-vocal review of security orchestration. ACM Comput. Surv. **52**(2) (2019). https://doi.org/10.1145/3305268
13. Islam, C., Babar, M.A., Nepal, S.: Architecture-centric support for integrating security tools in a security orchestration platform. In: Jansen, A., Malavolta, I., Muccini, H., Ozkaya, I., Zimmermann, O. (eds.) ECSA 2020. LNCS, vol. 12292, pp. 165–181. Springer, Cham (2020). https://doi.org/10.1007/978-3-030-58923-3_11
14. Microsoft Security: What is SOAR? https://www.microsoft.com/en-us/security/business/security-101/what-is-soar. Accessed 16 June 2024
15. Neupane, K., Haddad, R., Chen, L.: Next generation firewall for network security: a survey. In: SoutheastCon 2018, pp. 1–6 (2018). https://doi.org/10.1109/SECON.2018.8478973

16. Nguyen, H.H., Phung, P.H., Nguyen, P.H., Truong, H.L.: Context-driven policies enforcement for edge-based IoT data sharing-as-a-service. In: 2022 IEEE International Conference on Services Computing (SCC), pp. 221–230 (2022). https://doi.org/10.1109/SCC55611.2022.00041

17. Nguyen, P., et al.: Towards smarter security orchestration and automatic response for CPS and IoT. In: 2023 IEEE International Conference on Cloud Computing Technology and Science (CloudCom), pp. 298–302 (2023). https://doi.org/10.1109/CloudCom59040.2023.00055

18. Nguyen, P.H., et al.: Software engineering and AI for data quality in cyber- physical systems - sea4dq'21 workshop report. SIGSOFT Softw. Eng. Notes **47**(1), 26–29 (2022). https://doi.org/10.1145/3502771.3502781

19. Nguyen, T., Lam, A.N., Nguyen, P., Truong, L.: Security orchestration with explainability for digital twins-based smart systems. In: IEEE Annual Computer Software and Applications Conference (2024)

20. Rajmohan, T., Nguyen, P.H., Ferry, N.: A decade of research on patterns and architectures for IoT security. Cybersecurity **5**(1), 2 (2022)

21. Riggs, H., et al.: Impact, vulnerabilities, and mitigation strategies for cyber-secure critical infrastructure. Sensors **23**(8), 4060 (2023)

22. Rios, E., et al.: The dynabic approach to resilience of critical infrastructures. In: Proceedings of the 18th International Conference on Availability, Reliability and Security. ARES 2023. Association for Computing Machinery, New York (2023). https://doi.org/10.1145/3600160.3605055

23. Sen, S., Husom, E.J., Goknil, A., Tverdal, S., Nguyen, P., Mancisidor, I.: Taming data quality in AI-enabled industrial internet of things. IEEE Softw. **39**(6), 35–42 (2022). https://doi.org/10.1109/MS.2022.3193975

24. Sheikh, Z.A., Singh, Y., Singh, P.K., Ghafoor, K.Z.: Intelligent and secure framework for critical infrastructure (CPS): current trends, challenges, and future scope. Comput. Commun. **193**, 302–331 (2022)

25. Technicaldada: Pentbox. https://github.com/technicaldada/pentbox. Accessed 16 June 2024

26. Tigli, J.Y., Lavirotte, S., Rey, G., Hourdin, V., Riveill, M.: Context-aware authorization in highly dynamic environments. arXiv preprint arXiv:1102.5194 (2011)

GreenMov: A Fiware Based Interoperable Solution to Reduce the Environmental Impact of Mobility

Benoit Couraud[1,2](✉)(iD), Mehdi Nafkha[1], Franck Dechavanne[1],
Azeddine El Youssfi[1], and Paulo Moura[1](iD)

[1] Université Côte d'Azur, IMREDD, Nice, France
`benoit.couraud@glasgow.ac.uk`, `m.nafkha@cotedazurfrance.fr`
[2] James Watt School of Engineering, University of Glasgow, Glasgow, UK

Abstract. The recent advancements in the Internet of Things (IoT) have facilitated the deployment of numerous applications that enhance urban intelligence by improving the monitoring and control of city assets, such as lighting systems, traffic signals, and public transportation. However, these applications are often tailored to the specific needs of individual cities, limiting their replicability in other locations primarily due to the lack of interoperability in communication signals between assets. Despite various initiatives to establish standards for interoperability, real-world implementations frequently fall short of achieving fully interoperable systems that can be universally replicated, largely due to the absence of comprehensive solutions and implementation examples. This paper presents a fully interoperable use case for Green Mobility solutions in a smart city, utilizing air quality, traffic, and noise intensity data to provide transport recommendations to end-users. The implementation employs the NGSI-LD standard, Fiware data storage tools, and developed artificial intelligence-based algorithms to predict the transport situation for the following day and offer relevant traffic recommendations. This work has resulted in the development of several data models and standardized forecast algorithms with accuracy exceeding 75% on the noise and traffic datasets at our disposal, thereby enabling the potential for replication in other locations.

Keywords: Data models · forecasting services · green mobility · Fiware

1 Introduction

The deployment of IoT devices has enabled a variety of new use cases across sectors such as health, agriculture, energy, and industry [10]. Among these, mobility stands out as particularly significant due to its profound impact on daily life, economic growth, social inclusion, and the environment [8]. Consequently, numerous projects have emerged to enhance urban mobility by reducing environmental impacts, minimizing time spent in transit, and decreasing pollution (air

© IFIP International Federation for Information Processing 2025
Published by Springer Nature Switzerland AG 2025
G. Rey et al. (Eds.): IFIPIoT 2024, IFIP AICT 737, pp. 261–278, 2025.
https://doi.org/10.1007/978-3-031-81900-1_16

quality, noise, environment). IoT can address these challenges by monitoring air quality, enabling smart traffic management, and providing transport recommendations to end-users. Start-ups, companies, and municipalities have developed solutions aimed at mitigating the environmental and social impacts of transportation. However, these initiatives often remain as proof-of-concepts and are not easily replicable in other locations, primarily due to interoperability issues between solutions and differing local infrastructures [11]. The variability in sensor technologies necessitates customization to ensure compatibility with existing systems, and the lack of standardized data formats for communication between sensors and controllers further complicates integration. To tackle this interoperability challenge, the Fiware EU initiative advocates for the standardization of data storage through smart data models [4] that encompass various smart city domains, including energy, environment, and mobility. A data model provides a conceptual representation of the data structures required by a database or information system, defining how data is connected, stored, and processed. This blueprint facilitates the building of databases and enhances data management and analysis [7]. Adoption of standardized data models ensures interoperability between data-consuming services, such as decision-making tools, thereby promoting broader and more effective implementation of smart city solutions [9,12].

However, the adoption of a smart data model necessitates specific requirements and architectural considerations [6]. In this paper, we propose utilizing Fiware smart data models to design an end-to-end solution aimed at reducing the environmental impact of mobility in the city of Nice. This work is part of the GreenMov European project [1], which seeks to leverage Fiware Smart Data Models for green mobility solutions. By building on existing data models for mobility, this project extends these models and incorporates Artificial Intelligence (AI)-based services that utilize air quality, noise, and mobility data to provide relevant mobility recommendations to end-users and city councils for managing daily transport needs. The primary outcomes of this paper include a replicable architecture for green mobility solutions in urban environments, an extension of smart data models to facilitate green mobility services, and an example of an AI service designed to forecast the impact of mobility on noise annoyance.

Section 2 outlines the green mobility use case addressed in this work. Section 3 details the end-to-end architecture from sensors to end-users, while Sect. 4 describes one of the AI-based services developed for this use case.

2   Case Study Description: Green Mobility in Nice

Nice, the main city on the French Riviera, is significantly influenced by its transportation infrastructure, which is vital for both its bustling tourism industry and daily urban life. Meanwhile, the Nice Côte d'Azur Metropolis monitors air and noise pollution in specific areas along with traffic congestion. The Metropolis aims to enhance its existing data by collecting, consolidating, standardizing, and making it interoperable to allow a seamless integration of future use cases and services. The objective of Nice Metropolis and of the initiative described in this work is to improve residents' quality of life by reducing pollution, particularly from road traffic, through various strategies such as alternative routes, improved public transport options, and other solutions. The resulting solution could be replicated in other regions due to its standardized and high-quality data format, potentially becoming the standard for green mobility projects.

In the GreenMov project, the Nice Côte d'Azur Metropolis wants to leverage its sensors infrastructure to improve the quality of transport, and reduce its impact on the environment. The objectives are multifold:

- Reduce the impact of transport on the environment (air quality, climate change, noise)
- Reduce the traffic congestion in Nice
- Provide recommendations to citizens and city administration.

To accomplish these goals, the following use case is proposed: By monitoring air quality, noise levels, weather conditions, and traffic intensity, the Green-Mov project aims to predict environmental pollution and traffic conditions. This enables the project to offer recommendations to both the city and end-users, such as promoting increased use of public transportation or encouraging the use of shared bikes over personal vehicles. Two scenarios have been outlined to illustrate this use case more effectively.

2.1   Scenarios

Option 1. Antoine plans to drive to work from Cannes to Nice next Friday morning at 9 AM. On Thursday evening, he receives a notification from the Nice-Traffic App recommending that he use public transportation or bikes instead. The message indicates that air quality in Nice will be degraded on Friday morning and suggests using the public transportation or bikes available at that specific time, provided by the city of Nice.

Option 2. The city of Nice assesses Friday's Air Quality Index forecast alongside traffic predictions. Based on the forecasted conditions, additional electric buses and bicycles are deployed to accommodate commuters driving to Nice, and targeted messages are sent to regular Friday commuters.

Thus, this use case necessitates establishing an IoT infrastructure to monitor air quality, noise levels, and traffic patterns; ensuring data storage in an interoperable format using Fiware NGSI-LD (Next Generation Service Interface) data models standardized by ETSI; implementing AI-based forecasting services for traffic, noise, and air quality predictions; and offering recommendations based on anticipated future conditions.

An overview of the GreenMov's use case in Nice is depicted in Fig. 1, while Fig. 2 illustrates the deployment locations of all sensors.

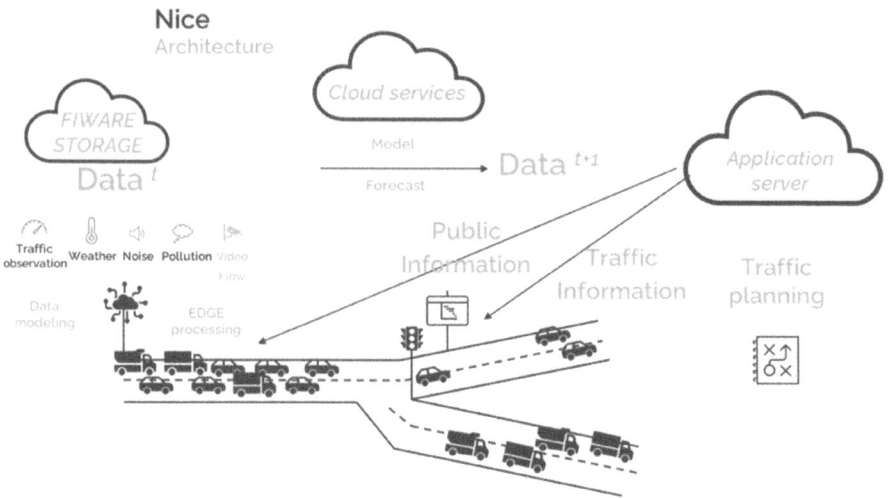

Fig. 1. General Architecture of GreenMov's Nice use case.

2.2 Data Sets

The data sets from Nice to be used in this use case implementation are available on the European Data Portal as well as various European, national, and local city portals. The use case requires data to evaluate air quality at specific locations, noise pollution, traffic activity, and real-time availability of alternative transportation solutions, such as buses, trams, or shared bikes. Consequently, six main categories of datasets are needed: air quality measurements, weather measurements, noise measurements, traffic measurements, public transportation availability, and bike availability. To enhance accuracy and coverage, multiple data sources were utilized for some of these datasets.

The primary Fiware NGSI-LD data models characterizing the collected data are: Traffic Flow Observed, Vehicle Emission Label, Air Quality Observed, Air Quality Monitoring, Weather Observed, Noise Level Observed, Noise Pollution, Public Transportation, and Bikes Availability.

The implementation of this use case also led to the development of new data models for green mobility, such as Noise Pollution, Traffic Environmental Impact, and several forecasting models specifying data forecasted for specific future times (e.g., Air Quality Forecast, Air Pollution Forecast), as well as Bikes and Public Transport Availability.

3 Interoperable IoT Architecture

Fiware and the GreenMov project have established a generic architecture that can serve as a foundational framework for various implementations. Figure 3 illustrates this architecture, which adopts a multi-layer structure.

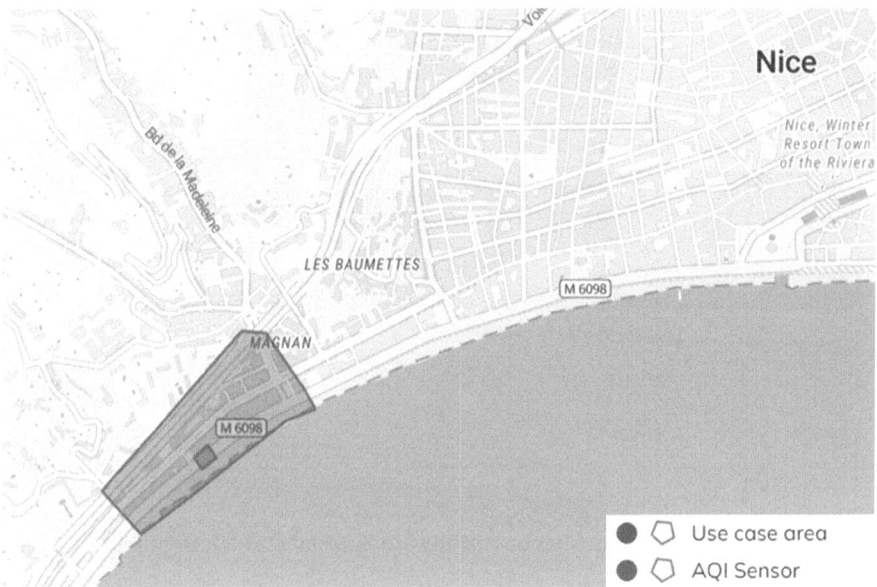

Fig. 2. GreenMov's Nice use case area.

At the base, the first layer comprises sensors that provide raw data. Parallel to the sensors, there are third-party and cloud services that supply relevant data for use cases, such as weather forecasts. The second layer consists of aggregation platforms, including proprietary platforms that directly gather data from the sensors, potentially using their own data models.

The third layer is composed of core Fiware solutions for data routing and storage. This layer includes the context broker, which ensures data consistency with existing data models and stores the data in appropriate databases. These databases can be real-time, such as those based on MongoDB, or historical, storing time-series data, such as PostgreSQL databases. API tools for historical databases include QuantumLeap (primarily for NGSI-v2), Cygnus, Draco, and Mintaka. The real-time brokers proposed in the generic architecture are OrionLD and Scorpio. Deployment can utilize container technology such as Docker or Kubernetes.

The application layer, next, encompasses all data analysis aspects, primarily based on historical data. This layer includes dashboards, data processing, and other analytical tools.

Finally, in parallel of these layers, we can find sub-services such as securing data access, using Keycloack and Keyrock identity and access management. Also, the addition of a LDES (Linked Data Event Stream) adapter can help in the supply of time series data by speeding up the process of data retrieval. Based on this generic architecture, the use cases described in Sect. 2 implemented their own specificities. The rest of this section describes these specificities.

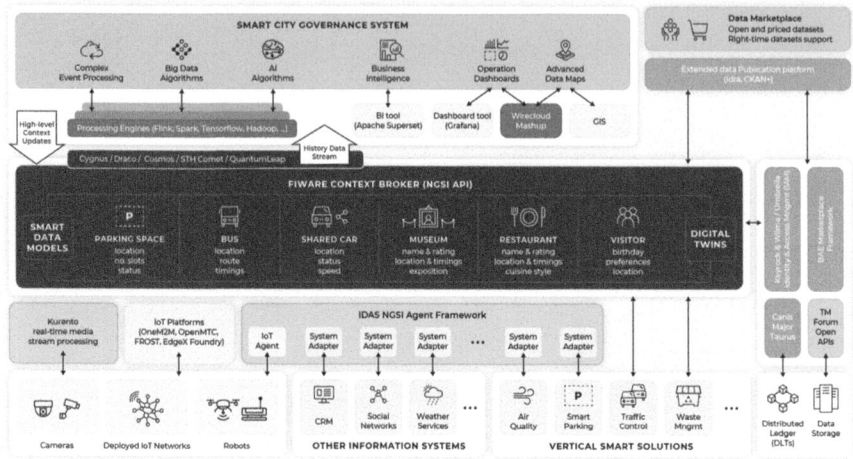

Fig. 3. General Architecture of Fiware implementation, from [3].

3.1 Adaptation to the Implementation of GreenMov Use Case in Nice

The architecture of Nice follows the architecture proposed in Fig. 4.

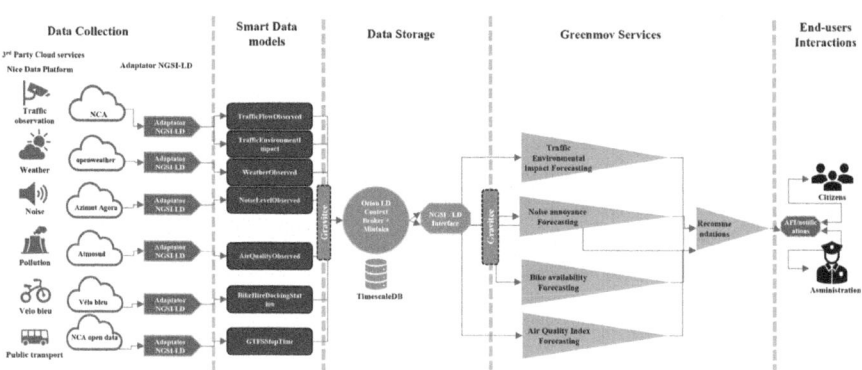

Fig. 4. Data Architecture of GreenMov's implementation in Nice.

The first layer, detailed on the left-hand side of Fig. 4, represents the data collection layer along with adapters that enable conversion to the NGSI-LD format. In the case of Nice, several sensors are utilized, including those for air quality monitoring, weather, noise, bike availability, transport availability, and traffic monitoring. Once this data has been translated into the appropriate data model, it is sent to the storage layer, which incorporates the Fiware context broker and storage technology. For the Nice use case, the context broker is Orion-LD, used in conjunction with Mintaka, and data storage is managed through PostgreSQL using TimescaleDB, an efficient time-series data storage solution. In addition to the APIs available in the generic architecture (Mintaka and Orion-LD), we implemented an API manager, named Gravitee, which provides several functionalities:

- Route renaming/routing, which allows clients (such as the services) to use different addresses than the standard context broker addresses to access the data.
- Also, it is worth noting that another benefit of Gravitee is the fact that the presence of one specific word (such as "temporal") in the URL of request sent by a third party can route the request to Mintaka instead of OrionLD. Everything is made transparent to the end-user who only need to know the URLs for data posting or retrieval.
- The last main advantage of Gravitee is the control of access to data. First, Gravitee implements a catalogue of available datasets to which any user can subscribe. But on top of this, it allows the data owners to grant access to some of the data, through the use of an API-Key specific to the end-users or to the application defined to access the dataset.

Data Collection. Several components were developed to collect the required data for the use case. These components were implemented in Node-RED and achieve the following tasks:

- Traffic observation: a component that collects and stores the traffic intensity directly from Nice metropolis measurements at specific locations. The software component implemented in Node-RED selects the last data, converts it into NGSI-LD format, and sends it to the context broker of the storage facility.
- Weather: a Node-RED flow leverages the European meteostat JSON API to retrieve weather forecast from Nice, converts it into NGSI-LD, and sends it to the context broker.
- Noise: For noise, using the API from Nice Côte d'Azur metropole, a nodered flow retrieves the noise data every day, extracts it, converts it into NGSI-LD, and sends it to the context broker.
- Air quality: Similar to the noise data, air quality is retrieved daily by a nodered flow that extracts the air quality information from the selected sensor, converts it into NGSI-LD, and sends it to the context broker.
- Bike availability: a Node-RED flow extracts bikes availability data available in the core of the veloblue stations website. From the webpage code, the nodered flow accesses the bikes availability data per stations, extracts the required bikes stations, converts the data into NGSI-LD, and sends it to the context broker.
- Public transport: a Node-RED flow retrieves the Nice Côte d'Azur metropole public transport GTFS data on a daily basis, convert it into NGSI-LD for the selected lines, and sends it to the context broker.

Data Storage. For data storage, the standard Orion-LD Docker image was employed to replicate the storage architecture, incorporating TimescaleDB and Mintaka. Additionally, several other components were integrated, including Gravitee as an API manager to offer a dataset catalog, enable re-routing (replacing standard Orion-LD URLs with custom URLs), and secure data access through API keys. An NGINX component was also added to serve as a proxy, directing different services based on the URL route.

Services. For the implementation of the services, several software components were designed and developed. These services were deployed in a container to facilitate replication in future use case locations. The services encompass the forecasting of air quality, traffic intensity, bike availability, and noise annoyance, as well as providing recommendations to citizens and the city council.

Figure 5 presents a generic architecture for most of the forecasting-related services. Each forecasting service includes an API to receive requests for the service's output, which is managed through kserve or FastAPI components. Most services incorporate an AI model that requires training, typically using the scikit-learn *fit* function. The trained model is then used to compute forecasts, which are processed by a *formula computation* component to generate actionable information. For instance, the air quality index forecasting service predicts future particle concentrations, which are then used by a computation service to calculate the future air quality index.

The services run on a Docker image, and the AI models are trained on a regular schedule (daily or weekly). An additional sub-service, MLFlow, operates in parallel to enable the service operator to monitor the machine learning components. Lastly, all services include HTTP client request components to retrieve the latest data from the storage facility's context broker, which is then used to generate short-term forecasts.

Front End Implementation. Front-end services are available to end-users of Nice. An interface was designed to facilitate user interaction with the services. Users can access and utilize the traffic recommendation services directly through the interface. Additionally, individual services outputs can still be retrieved through specific requests. Therefore, the interface for end-users is the WebApp that is displayed in Fig. 6. End users can use the slide in the middle of the interface to select the time for which they want a traffic recommendation. It goes up to one day ahead, although we could extend it to several days. Figure 6 shows an example of the interface when there is an event of high air quality pollution and high noise annoyance. In this case, a recommendation follows the logic of the traffic recommendation service and results in advices to use bikes and public transportation depending on the weather forecast.

The rest of the interface is constituted of graphs showing the accuracy of the forecasts along with the shape of future noise annoyance or traffic evolutions. Figure 6 shows these different visualisations proposed to the end-users, along with a map on which users can find where the bikes are available.

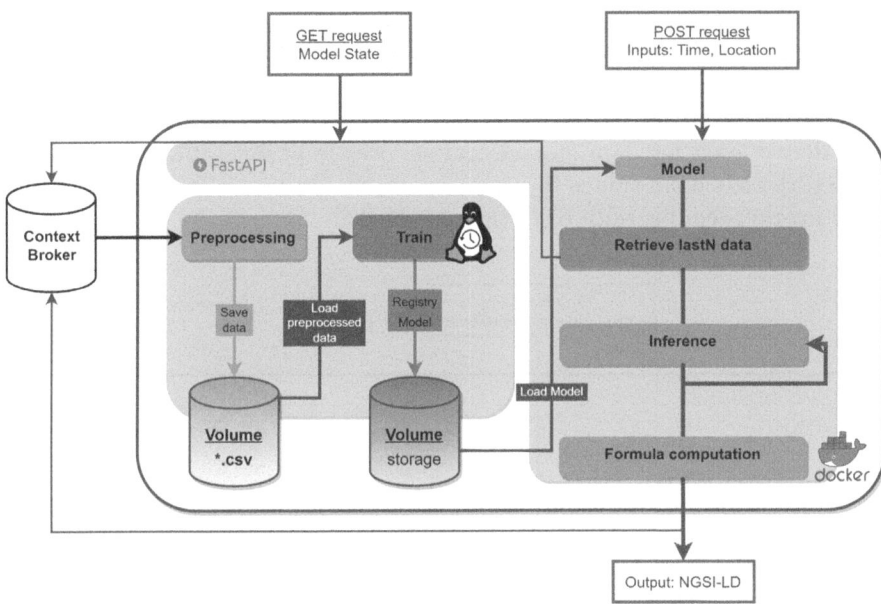

Fig. 5. General Architecture of Fiware & AI based Services.

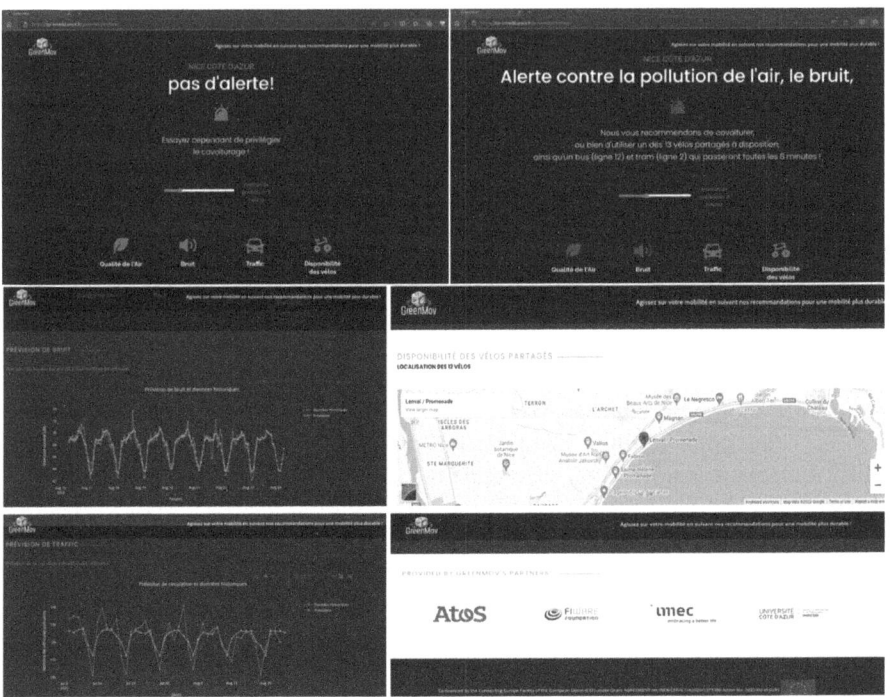

Fig. 6. Nice Use case front end.

Infrastructure. All the software components and storage facility were implemented in the University Côte d'Azur's owned servers located in IMREDD building's own data centre. This is depicted in Fig. 7 that highlights the two main components of the Nice use case architecture: on the right hand side, the main server that is used for data storage and services implementation, whereas the server on the left hand side is the one responsible for data collection, NGSI-LD formatting and sending data to the storage facility.

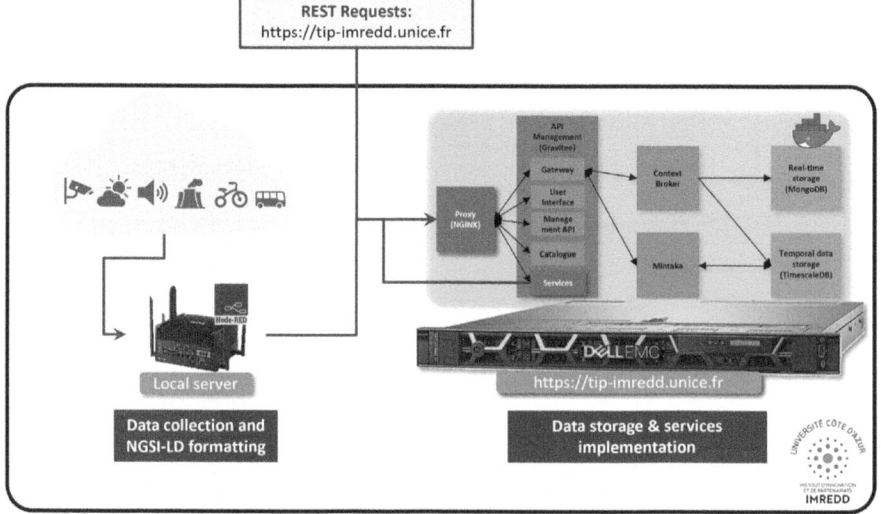

Fig. 7. Infrastructure of the Server implementation.

4   Forecasting Services

Services have been described shortly in the previous section. However, this section proposes to detail one specific forecasting service (noise annoyance forecasting) to showcase what can be done with city data and state of the art libraries. The same applies to other forecasting services, such as air quality, traffic, and bikes availability, although they might require other inputs such as weather forecasts. Noise annoyance forecasting is a service that predicts the level of noise disturbance in a specific location within a specified time frame. The aim of this service is to provide information about future noise intensity so it can be used to compute its expected impact. This noise intensity forecast is then sent to the noise annoyance calculation service for prediction of future noise annoyance, which will then be sent to the traffic recommendation generation service, as depicted in Fig. 8.

The rest of this section describes the process that was followed to provide accurate forecasts.

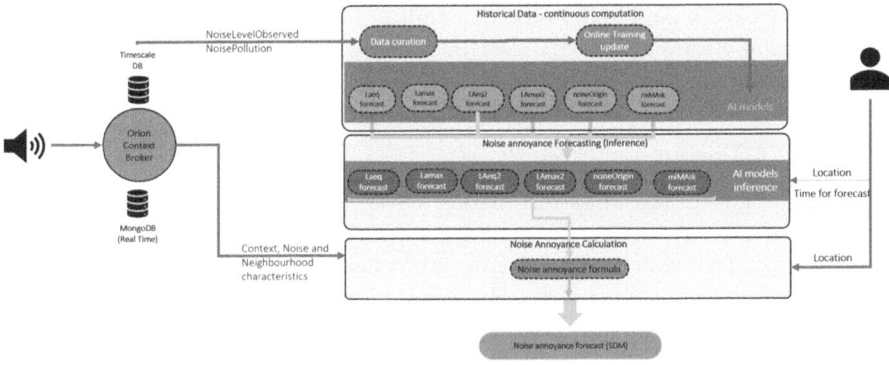

Fig. 8. Overview of the whole noise annoyance forecasting services.

4.1   Data Analysis

Historical Data. The historical data sets involved in the training of the AI model and the implementation of the noise annoyance forecasting service play a crucial role in its accuracy. In the case of Nice use case, the data set includes the noise levels in a specific location (Sensor with the following coordinates: 43°40'56.4"N 7°13'58.1"E) from 01/01/2020 until 2022. This data provides a comprehensive view of the noise situation in the area over a two-year period and can be used to train the AI model to make accurate predictions about future noise levels.

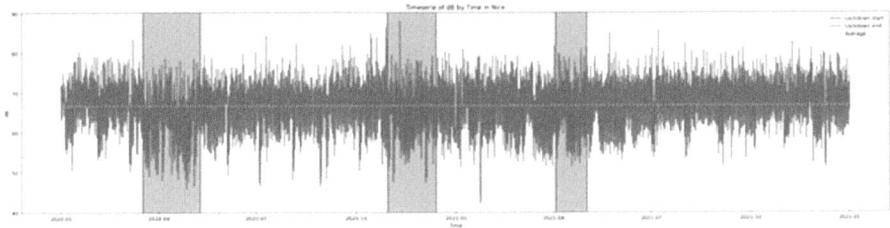

Fig. 9. Initial Noise dataset used in the use case of Nice.

Figure 9 shows the records used in the project, where Covid lockdown periods were highlighted in order to show that not all the available data can be used in the study. It shows that the training dataset of the forecasting models might require to be adjusted and benchmarked in order to avoid negative impacts from period of time that will never happen again.

Preprocessing. Before the data can be used in the calculation of noise annoyance, it is important to perform a thorough cleaning and pre-processing process to ensure accuracy and reliability of results. This process involves reviewing the data for any errors, discrepancies, or missing information, and correcting or removing these issues as necessary.

4.2   Model Design

The development of the noise forecasting service is essential to ensure its accuracy and effectiveness. The AI model must efficiently analyze historical traffic datasets, account for various factors influencing noise intensity, and predict future noise levels. To achieve this, the service must undertake several key steps, including data preparation, model selection, and model training. The appropriate AI model must handle the complexity of the data and the numerous factors affecting noise. This involves evaluating multiple AI models and selecting the one that delivers the most accurate predictions. In the case of traffic forecasting, models such as K-Nearest Neighbors (KNN), Decision Tree, and Random Forest were benchmarked. KNN outperformed the others, achieving an accuracy above 85%, which met the requirements of the GreenMov project. Consequently, further custom models were not explored.

Regarding features, a correlation study identified the following inputs for the model: type of day (weekday or weekend), hour of the day, and noise levels at various lags (1 h, 2 h, 3 h, 24 h, 72 h, and 168 h prior). Weather forecasts were found to be uncorrelated with noise values.

The model outputs a single noise intensity value for the next hour. This output can then be used iteratively to generate noise forecasts for subsequent hours by feeding the predicted noise intensity at h+1 as an input to predict the noise intensity at h+2.

In line with Green AI principles and to minimize data and computing power requirements, we conducted a study to analyze the necessity of large datasets. For our use case, the benchmarking results, as illustrated in Fig. 10, indicate that the size of the training dataset impacts forecast accuracy. A training dataset of two weeks provides sufficient accuracy for the GreenMov project's forecast accuracy requirements (>75% r^2).

Results. Figure 11 displays the r^2 scores for the different AI models used, and for different sizes of training dataset, with a maximum r^2 accuracy of 89%, and an average accuracy of 80.3%. These figures were obtained using a train/test split of 70%. Figures below show graphically the comparison between real measurements and predictions. We can see in Fig. 11 that there is a significant gap between forecast and measurements for the day before the last day, but these are due to a measurement error, given the fact that the recorded values were considerably low compared to all previous historic data.

4.3   Model Deployment

Once the model was designed, it was deployed within our infrastructure. This subsection outlines the process followed for service deployment.

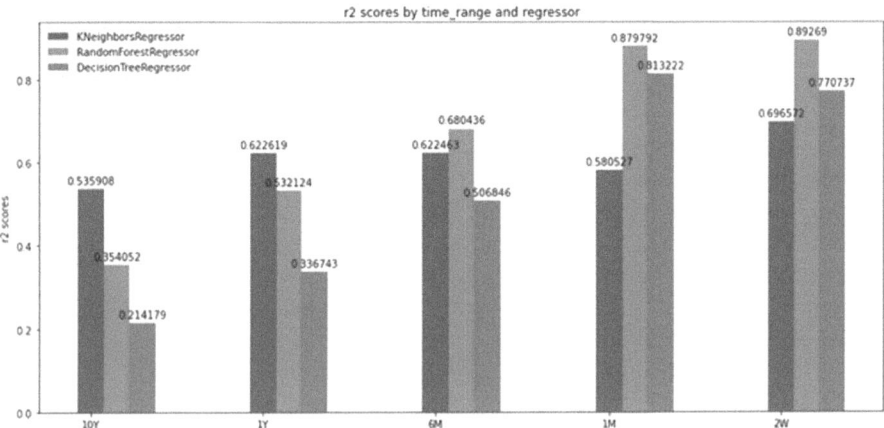

Fig. 10. Results of AI models benchmark for the use case of Nice.

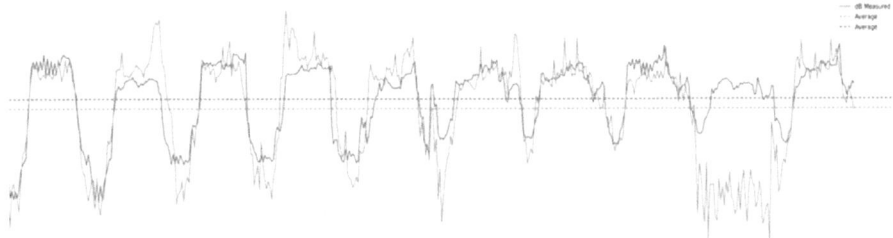

Fig. 11. Forecast (blue) vs Ground Truth (orange) for one week in 2022. (Color figure online)

The workflow leading to the final model is illustrated in Fig. 12. Initially, data was gathered for analysis to determine the noise forecasting model. This data was then cleaned (as detailed in the pre-processing section) and augmented with complementary information, such as data from the past few hours and the type of day.

During the model creation phase, various models, features, and training requirements were evaluated to identify the optimal combination. A separate model was designed for each location. Models tested included K-Nearest Neighbors (KNN), Decision Tree, Random Forest, and XGBoost. The selected features (inputs) included the type of day and previous noise levels (from the last hours up to 168 h ago). Training could use data spanning several years or be restricted to a few weeks or months to avoid capturing seasonal specificities, such as those from summer, when forecasting for winter. Consequently, a benchmark of training dataset sizes was conducted to determine the optimal size for the training dataset. This benchmarking led to a specific combination of model, training size, and features used in the final noise forecasting service.

In the rollout phase, we leveraged the architecture, inputs, and training requirements to provide a real-time solution that forecasts noise levels at the required times. The steps for computing a forecast are as follows:

- First, from the requested location of the forecast, the model that corresponds to the location is selected.
- Then, the last N data are requested to the context broker in order to retrieve the noise intensity at the previous times (last hour, last 2 h, last 24 h, ...).
- The noise level of the next hour is predicted.
- Using this forecast as an input of the next model's inference, the model is used to compute the noise intensity forecast in the next 2 h.
- This new forecast is used as an input to forecast the noise level in 3 h.
- And this process is repeated until the time of the requested forecast is reached. The result of the final forecast (for the requested time) is then formatted as NGSI-LD and fed back to the user.

Finally, at the end of each day, the daily data is retrieved from the context broker, and the model is retrained with the updated training dataset. This updated dataset comprises the previous training dataset with the data from the last day added and the oldest day's data removed. The updated model parameters are then stored using joblib for use in the following day's forecasts.

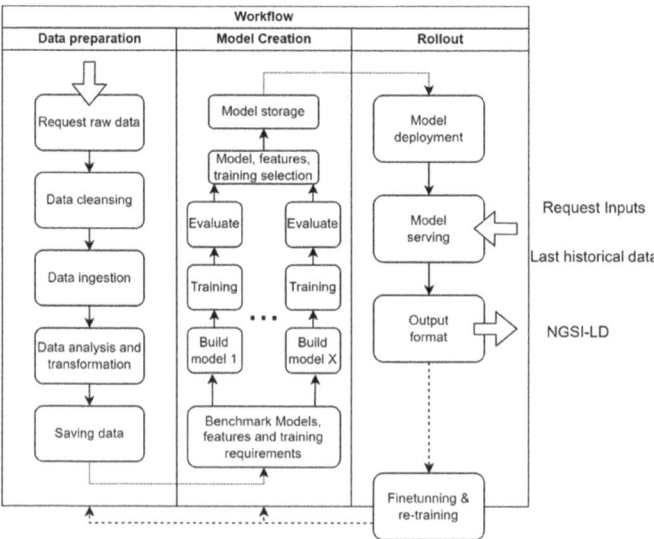

Fig. 12. Workflow for Noise forecasting service for each location.

In the next subsection all the technical aspects and selected technologies to accomplish the functions described are further discussed.

4.4   Noise Annoyance Calculation

The noise annoyance calculation service aims to provide a comprehensive assessment of the noise environment in a specific area, identifying when and where noise levels and sources are unacceptable. Key parameters include the type of noise source, which helps pinpoint contributors to noise pollution such as traffic, industrial activities, or construction sites. Another critical parameter is the average age of residents in the area, as different age groups exhibit varying sensitivities to noise. This information was collected for the locations of the sensors used in the Nice use case.

The noise intensity level is also essential, with the service calculating noise annoyance using various models, including the A-weighted equivalent continuous sound pressure level (LAeq). This calculation offers an assessment of the noise impact on residents, which can significantly affect their health, well-being, and quality of life.

To summarize, data requirements to compute the noise annoyance in an area involve the following: Area: The area of the calculation of the annoyance; Period of time: The measurement time; Type of area (residential, industrial, commercial); Noise level; Noise level classification; Average age level in the area; Dominant noise source in the area.

In order to make the calculations, values are aggregated from the data sets and a mathematical formula uses these values for the calculation of the noise annoyance index. This formula is inspired from the noise disturbance calculation tool developed within IKCEST - International Knowledge Centre for Engineering Sciences and Technology under the Auspices of UNESCO [2]. The formula used states that the annoyance level is the sum of the *Noise level value*, the *average age level value*, the *Noise source value* and the *Type of area value*. It requires to convert all the qualitative data (type of noise source) into quantitative data, using tables as shown in Fig. 13 and Fig. 14 for the output conversion. The outputs from the calculation are shown in the Figure below.

Noise sources (based on the area)	Value	Average age level	Value	Noise level	Value	Type of area	Value
Industrial and construction	2	0-35	1	40-50 dB	1	Residential	2
		35-50	1.5	50-60 dB	2	Commercial	1.5
Road and air traffic	2	50	2	60-65 dB	3	Mix	1.5
Enetrtainement and commercial	1.5			65-70 dB	4	Industrial	1
Domestic	1			70-80 dB	5		
				> 80 dB	6		

Fig. 13. Noise annoyance calculation parameters translation.

Using the values and the outputs from the Figures above, we can make a calculation example: For an industrial area with average age level of 40 and a noise level of 55 db the noise annoyance calculation is: $2 + 1.5 + 2 = 5.5$ Which corresponds to a moderate noise annoyance.

Noise annoyance	Value (from to)
Very calm	0-1
Calm	1-2
Good	2-3
Acceptable	3-4
Medium	4-5
Moderate	5-6
Annoying	6-7
Very annoying	7-8
Unsupportable	8-9
Dangerous	9-10
Very Dangerous	over 10

Enviromental impact	Value
Good	2
Medium	5
Moderate	6
Unhealthy	7
Dangerous	8
Extremely dangerous	Over 9

Fig. 14. Noise annoyance calculation outputs.

Finally, the internal architecture of the noise annoyance computation component is proposed in Fig. 15. A docker container enables an easy replication of the service. The architecture includes the application of the formula proposed in the previous section along with a local database to store the parameters of the formula.

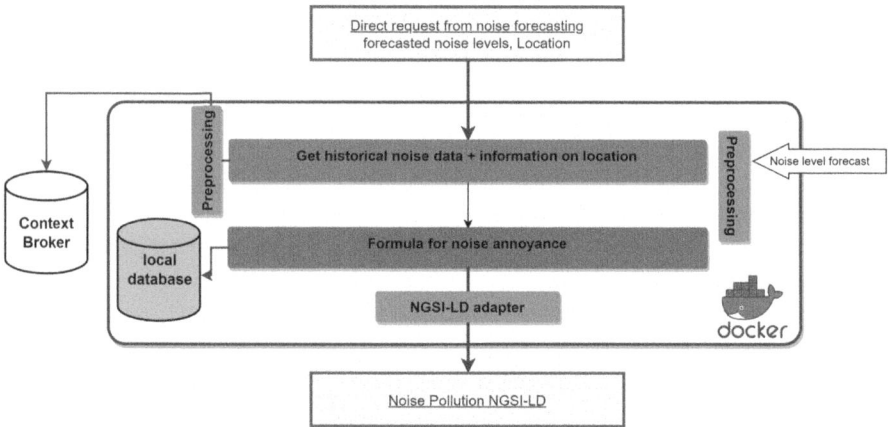

Fig. 15. Noise annoyance calculation architecture.

Following the workflow highlighted in Fig. 15, the noise annoyance calculation service receives the request directly from the noise forecasting service along with the location and the forecast for the future noise levels. Then, the service will request the context broker to get access to noise pollution information for the considered location. This provides information such as the building type, the noise origin, etc. Using this information, the formula described above is used to compute the noise annoyance index, that is then encapsulated into the NoisePollutionForecast smart data model and sent back to the noise forecasting service.

Although noise annoyance is a subjective variable, it can be computed based on local characteristics, such as the building types and source of noise, and based on the noise level. The output of this service is then converted into NGSI-LD format [5], and will then be used to automatically generate traffic recommendations that can help reducing the annoyance from traffic intensity.

5 Conclusion

The recent development of IoT has led to many applications that often use custom data models and fail to bring interoperability in a system that could be replicated at different locations if it was designed in an interoperable way. To address this issue, smart data models have been proposed and supported by the European commission through the NGSI-LD initiative standardized by ETSI. However, implementing an end-to-end use case based on Fiware smart data models still requires adaptation and development to extend data models to meet the use case requirements. In this work, we proposed an architecture to replicate an end-to-end NGSI-LD implementation that we applied to the GreenMov use case in Nice that aimed to provide recommendations to end-users and city council to reduce the environmental impact of mobility. Data from sensors had to be converted into the right NGSI-LD format before being stored in Fiware NGSI-LD compliant storage architecture. Then, several application services were proposed, among which forecast services that leverage NGSI-LD data to train machine learning models. An example was given with a noise annoyance forecasting model that manages to forecast day-ahead noise intensity levels with an accuracy greater than 75%. This use case and work demonstrates the relevance for interoperability solutions in order to provide replicable solutions that can be deployed in any country in the world.

Acknowledgments. This study was funded by the European GreenMov project, and this work was carried out on the technological platform "Smart City Innovation Center" funded with the support of the European Union through the European Regional Development Fund, the Metropolis Nice Côte d'Azur, the Department of Alpes Maritimes, the Region Sud Provence Alpes Côte d'Azur, and the State, particularly within the framework of the Initiative of Excellence of the Future Investments Program.

References

1. Green Mobility data models and services for smart ecosystems. https://green-mov.eu/
2. On-line calculation of noise pollution level (LNP) in impact assessment. https://www.gislite.com/app/sc444
3. Smart Data Models Reference. https://smartdatamodels.org/
4. The Fiware Smart Cities Reference Architecture. https://www.fiware.org/about-us/smart-cities/
5. Guidelines for modelling with NGSI-LD. Technical report, ETSI (2021). https://www.etsi.org/images/files/ETSIWhitePapers/etsi-wp-42-NGSI-LD.pdf

6. Carnevale, L., Galletta, A., Fazio, M., Celesti, A., Villari, M.: Designing a fiware cloud solution for making your travel smoother: the fliware experience. In: 2018 IEEE 4th International Conference on Collaboration and Internet Computing (CIC), pp. 392–398 (2018). https://doi.org/10.1109/CIC.2018.00059
7. Cirillo, F., Solmaz, G., Berz, E.L., Bauer, M., Cheng, B., Kovacs, E.: A standard-based open source IoT platform: fiware. IEEE Internet Things Mag. **2**(3), 12–18 (2019). https://doi.org/10.1109/IOTM.0001.1800022
8. Echeverría, L., Gimenez-Nadal, J.I., Molina, J.A.: Green mobility and well-being. Ecol. Econ. **195**, 107368 (2022). https://doi.org/10.1016/j.ecolecon.2022.107368. https://www.sciencedirect.com/science/article/pii/S0921800922000301
9. Pham, V.C., Makino, Y., Tan, Y.: A fiware IoT agent for echonet lite protocol. In: 2020 IEEE 9th Global Conference on Consumer Electronics (GCCE), pp. 235–239 (2020). https://doi.org/10.1109/GCCE50665.2020.9291983
10. Ramson, S.J., Vishnu, S., Shanmugam, M.: Applications of internet of things (IoT) - an overview. In: 2020 5th International Conference on Devices, Circuits and Systems (ICDCS), pp. 92–95 (2020). https://doi.org/10.1109/ICDCS48716.2020.243556
11. Santa, J., Bernal-Escobedo, L., Sanchez-Iborra, R.: On-board unit to connect personal mobility vehicles to the IoT. Procedia Comput. Sci. **175**, 173–180 (2020). https://doi.org/10.1016/j.procs.2020.07.027. https://www.sciencedirect.com/science/article/pii/S1877050920317063. The 17th International Conference on Mobile Systems and Pervasive Computing (MobiSPC),The 15th International Conference on Future Networks and Communications (FNC),The 10th International Conference on Sustainable Energy Information Technology
12. de la Vega, F., García-Martín, J.P., Santos, G.P., Torralba, A.: Implementation of a fiware-based integration platform and a web portal as aids to improve the control of ships navigation in a river. In: 2020 IEEE International Symposium on Systems Engineering (ISSE), pp. 1–3 (2020). https://doi.org/10.1109/ISSE49799.2020.9272242

Dynamic IoT Determination of Overall Heat Transfer Coefficient in a Portable Cabin in Kuwait

Ahmad Sedaghat[1](✉) [iD], Mohammad Nazififard[2] [iD],
and Mohamad Iyad Al-Khiami[3] [iD]

[1] Department of Mechanical Engineering, College of Engineering,
Australian University of Kuwait, 13015 Safat, West Mishref, Kuwait
a.sedaghat@au.edu.kw
[2] Polytech'Lab, Université Côte d'Azur, Nice, France
[3] Department of Civil Engineering, College of Engineering, Australian University of Kuwait,
13015 Safat, West Mishref, Kuwait

Abstract. Two portable cabins (size 2 m width, 2 m depth, 2.8 m height) were constructed using 75 mm Polyurethane sandwich panels (insulation walls) to simulate low energy buildings in Kuwait. Experimental measurements were conducted using eight K-type thermocouple probes on interior/exterior surfaces of the cabins' walls to dynamically evaluate overall heat transfer coefficient during the hot months of August and September 2023 using IoT data storage. The collected data was further curated to ensure quality by treating negative values, handling potential division by zero issues, and filtering out large numbers. The dynamic average overall heat transfer coefficients were found to be 0.186, 0.198, 0.203, and 0.206 W/m^{2}K for the East, North, West, and South facing walls, respectively. This is far better than the static (steady state) overall heat transfer coefficient of 0.2534 W/m^{2}K, indicating that the dynamic behavior of the insulation walls is very promising, particularly by saving 21.76% cooling energy demands in summertime in Kuwait.

Keywords: Insulation Sandwich Panels · Kuwait's Hot Climate · Low-Energy Building

1 Introduction

The building sector is one of the largest energy-consuming sectors in the world. In Kuwait, space heating and cooling account for about 70% of total residential energy consumption [1]. Krarti and Hajiah [2] stated that the building sector in Kuwait consumes 90% of the electricity for cooling, a figure also reported by Saber et al. [3]. There is enormous potential to increase the energy efficiency of buildings. However, a clear long-term government commitment, combined with well-designed packages of efficiency policies reinforced by adequate implementation capacity, is needed to improve energy efficiency in Kuwait's buildings.

Published by Springer Nature Switzerland AG 2025
G. Rey et al. (Eds.): IFIPIoT 2024, IFIP AICT 737, pp. 279–290, 2025.
https://doi.org/10.1007/978-3-031-81900-1_17

In Australia, space conditioning, or heating and cooling, accounts for an average of 40 to 50% of household energy use [4, 5]. It generates about 30% of the total CO_2 emissions [4]. The problem related to energy consumption and CO_2 emission in Australia is becoming more acute, as residential energy consumption increased from 402 PJ (Petajoules) in 2008 to 467 PJ in 2020, indicating an average increase of 15% [5]. With high projected space cooling requirements in buildings in both Kuwait and Australia, researchers need to develop a thermally efficient building for mainstream use. However, it is extremely difficult to overcome this challenge as further improvements of currently used conventional building envelopes, construction materials and methods have already been exhausted [6–9].

Some research suggested controlling solar radiation through windows. Our previous research in application of window films merely offered 1–3% energy saving, although it improved residential comfort to a high satisfaction level [10, 11]. Application of green roof top and bio-phase change materials (Bio-PCM) however, showed higher potential of up to 20% in Australia [12–14]. Potential options are to use alternative smart materials and techniques such as Bio-PCM and cool roof (CR) materials as house envelopes and adapt solar-assisted air-conditioning (SAC) systems. The main challenge is understanding the combined thermal behavior of such materials and technologies. Until the predictive thermal performance improvement of the aforementioned systems is scientifically proven, these materials and techniques will remain under-utilized by the stakeholders, including builders and regulatory authorities for mainstream building industries.

The importance of accurately calculating the convective heat transfer coefficient (CHTC) in sustainable buildings was highlighted [15]. An experimental and computational work was undertaken to assess the exterior convective heat transfer coefficient indicating that threefold discrepancies between the obtained values and standard static values that used in software tools like Design Builder. This had led to cooling load deviations of nearly 20% [15].

Another study investigated the impact of external wind conditions on the external convective heat transfer coefficient (CHTC) in high-rise buildings [16]. The study suggested the traditional methods underestimate the CHTC particularly in wintertime by up to 102%. The work highlighted the importance of dynamic evaluation of CHTC in different climates.

Uncertainties in CHTC in empirical methods that relied on steady-state methods were highlighted that had introduced a dynamic error [17]. A new dynamic model was introduced with suitable sampling frequency and dynamic measurement errors were evaluated.

The impact of balcony on the CHTC of building façade were computationally investigated and validated by wind tunnel tests [18]. The results indicated that the average CHTC was reduced by 17.5% and 35.2% at the windward and the leeward façades, respectively. The findings provided a better prediction of cooling and heating in buildings with balcony.

A thermometric (THM) was modified to predict the convective and radiative heat transfer for indirect heat flux measurements [19]. The developed methodology improved measurements of CHTC for buildings envelop using a low-cost experimental setup.

This paper addresses this challenge by investigating the thermal characteristics of a portable cabin to determine the dynamic overall heat transfer coefficient across different walls during the hot months of August and September in Kuwait.

2 Hot Climate of Kuwait

The State of Kuwait is a country in the West of Asia located at the northeast edge of the Arabian Peninsula. It borders Iraq in the north and the Kingdom of Saudi Arabia in the south (see Fig. 1). Kuwait has a coastal line of 500 km and shares water borders with Iran. Kuwait is located in latitudes between 28° and 31° N and longitudes between 46°, and 49° E. Kuwait includes ten islands and has flat geography with the highest elevation from sea level of 306 m [20].

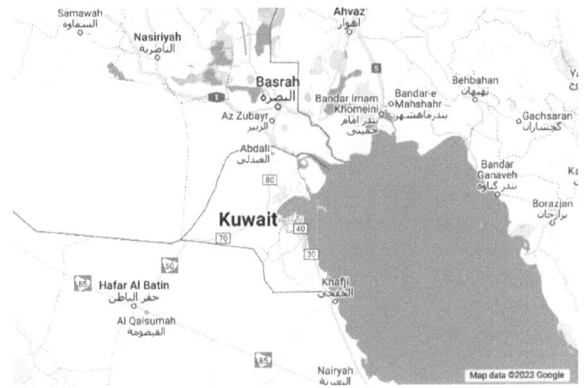

Fig. 1. Google map of the State of Kuwait in the Middle East of Asia.

The country's total area is 17,820 km^2, with a 4.67 million total population (in 2021). The largest island in Kuwait is Bubiyan which is connected to the mainland by a causeway consisting of two bridges with a combined length of 48.5 km. Most parts of the country are considered deserts with sparse vegetation. Kuwait's economy relies on oil, with the Burgan field having a proven oil capacity of 70 billion barrels, equivalent to 11 billion cubic meters [20]. This makes Kuwait the owner of the sixth-largest oil reserve in the world, supporting a strong economy with the Kuwaiti dinar rated as the strongest currency in the world.

Unlike UAE, Qatar, and Bahrain, Kuwait enjoys a colder winter season due to it being in the vicinity of Iraq and Iran and being influenced by similar weather conditions of these countries. Although the Kuwaiti climate is classified as a subtropical desert climate according to the Köppen climate classification [21], Kuwait is less humid, particularly during the year's warm months. Kuwait has scorching summers and mild winters.

3 Methodology

Two identical portable cabins are designed with external dimensions of 2 m × 2 m and
2.99 m height with a slope to 2.94 m, whilst the internal height up to the false ceiling is
2.8 m. Hence, the interior space of each room is exactly 2 m width, 2m depth, and 2.8 m
height (see Fig. 2). The rooms are fabricated of steel frame by using 120 mm I-beam
at bottom and 40 mm × 40 mm square hollow section for frame support at bottom.
Columns are made from 50 mm × 50 mm × 2 mm (thickness) hollow sections with
angles. The leg height is 300 mm from the ground. Lifting lugs are provided for lifting
and handling. Entrance steps are also provided separately [22, 23].

Fig. 2. The portable cabin for low-energy research in Kuwait.

Purlins in the roof are made from 50 mm × 50 mm × 2 mm (thickness) hollow
sections. PVC Skirting of 3 mm thick & 100 mm height is used. Wall and Roof are made
from 75 mm Polyurethane sandwich panel. The slope roof is covered with gypsum
ceiling. The flooring is made from 18 mm thick plywood finished with Vinyl sheet.
One aluminum external door is used, which is a single leaf of size 2 m × 1 m with a
heavy-duty door closer. The door is installed in the middle of one side of the cabin. One
aluminum window with a size of 1 m × 1 m double leaf is used with weather proofed
glass. The window is 50 cm below the roof and located in the middle of the wall [22,
23].

All wirings for electrical power sockets and switch sockets run through PVC conduits
fixed in the wall sandwich panels. The main distribution board (MDB) is fixed. Three
multiple plugs are positioned on 3 sides of the room. An LED light is installed on the
back wall with an electric switch near door wall, according to the company standards.
The air conditioner system is a split A/C 1.5 ton (18000BTU) [22, 23].

3.1 Measuring Equipment

Eight K-type thermocouples were installed on interior and exterior wall surfaces of the portable cabin as depicted in Fig. 3. Two 4 Channel Data Logger were employed with the technical specification provided in Table 1. Four K-type temperature sensors were installed on the interior surfaces of the North, East, South, and West walls, assigned to channels 1, 2, 3, and 4 of the data loggers, respectively. Similarly, four K-type temperature sensors were installed on exterior surfaces (see Fig. 3).

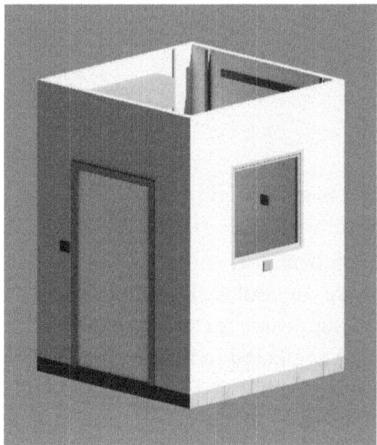 

Fig. 3. The K-type thermocouple installed on interior/exterior wall surfaces.

The data logger device has the capability to measure temperatures from four channels. Over 6300 recorded data was stored in iCloud for each channel adding up more than 50,000 data points for the months of August to September 2023 in Kuwait. The data logger device has a temperature measurement accuracy within 1 °C and a resolution of 0.1 °C, as detailed in Table 1.

Additionally, an indoor preset temperature of 20 °C was maintained throughout the experiment by the AC system's controller. Indoor temperatures were also recorded using an IoT system provided by a weather monitoring device [24]. This device provides real-time readings of various parameters including AQI (air quality index), PM of three different sizes, temperature, humidity, and HI (heat index) at one-minute intervals. An outdoor weather station was also installed to record outdoor weather conditions [24].

3.2 Heat Transfer Coefficient

By measuring the transient surface temperature of the walls, and neglecting heat generation or storage within the walls, the rate of heat transfer across the sandwich walls can be calculated using the Fourier's law of heat conduction as follows [26]:

$$\frac{dQ}{dt} = \frac{kA}{L}(T_o(t) - T_i(t)) \quad [W] \tag{1}$$

Table 1. Technical specification of the data logger [25].

Parameters	Range
K-type Thermocouple range	−200 to 1370 °C,
Temperature Resolution	0.1 °C
Accuracy level (within 18–28 °C)	±(0.3%rdg + 1 °C)
Sampling Rate:	Start from 1 s up
Operating Temperature:	0–50 °C
Operating Humidity:	<80%
Storage Temperature:	−20–50 °C
Storage Humidity:	<90%

In Eq. (1), the rate of heat transfer, (dQ/dt), is measured in the unit of watt (W), k is the thermal conductivity of the sandwich panel wall ($k = 0.0201 \frac{W}{m.K}$), A is the area of the walls approximated by ($A = 2 \times 2.8 = 5.6\,m^2$), L is the thickness of the wall ($L = 0.075\,m$), $T_i(t)$ is the temporal temperature on cooler side (interior) of the wall surface, and $T_o(t)$ is the temporal temperature on hotter side (exterior) of the wall surface. The effects of door and window surface sizes are neglected in the present analysis.

Using Newton's Law of Cooling on convective heat transfer, the calculated rate of heat transfer (dQ/dt) from Eq. (1), is used to determine the convective heat transfer coefficient for interior/exterior walls as follows [26]:

$$h_i = \frac{dQ/dt}{A(T_i(t) - T_{indoor}(t))} \quad \left[\frac{W}{m^2K}\right] \tag{2}$$

$$h_o = \frac{dQ/dt}{A(T_o(t) - T_{outdoor}(t))} \quad \left[\frac{W}{m^2K}\right] \tag{3}$$

In Eqs. (2) and (3), h_i and h_o are the convective heat transfer coefficients $\left(\frac{W}{m^2K}\right)$ for indoor and outdoor wall surfaces, respectively. T_{indoor} is the indoor ambient temperature. Here, it is fixed to 20 °C inside the portable cabin using the AC controller. $T_{outdoor}$ is the outdoor ambient temperature which changes dynamically during the studied months.

Having determined the convective heat transfer coefficient for interior/exterior walls, the R-values (thermal resistance) for each wall and the interior/exterior surfaces are determined as follows [26]:

$$R_{wall} = \frac{L}{k} \quad \left[\frac{m^2K}{W}\right]$$

$$R_{inside} = \frac{1}{h_i} \quad \left[\frac{m^2K}{W}\right]$$

$$R_{outside} = \frac{1}{h_o} \quad \left[\frac{m^2K}{W}\right] \tag{4}$$

The total thermal resistance and the overall heat transfer coefficient is calculated (including effects of solar irradiations) as follows:

$$R_{total} = R_{wall} + R_{inside} + R_{outside} \left[\frac{m^2 K}{W} \right]$$

$$U = \frac{1}{R_{total}} \qquad \left[\frac{W}{m^2 K} \right] \qquad (5)$$

4 Results

This research aims to determine the dynamic overall heat transfer coefficient of different walls of the portable cabin in real-time measurements to better understand the thermal characteristics of insulation walls in hot summertime of Kuwait.

Eight temperature sensors were installed on interior and exterior walls of the portable cabin in total, from 8th August to 21st September 2023. Data was collected in 10 min intervals and stored in iCloud using IoT. The results of temperature variations on interior and exterior surfaces with over 6350 data readings are illustrated for wall surfaces facing East, North, West, and South in Fig. 4.

The accuracy of temperature measurements was 1 °C. The average temperature on exterior East, North, West, and South walls was 40.5, 37.8, 39.6, and 39.7 °C introducing an uncertainty for standard deviation values of ± 8.1, 5.1, 8.1, and 7.8 °C, respectively. For the interior East, North, West, and South walls, these values were 23.2, 22.5, 21.1, and 21.5 °C, and an uncertainty for standard deviation values of ± 2.7, 1.4, 1.5, and 1.5 °C, respectively. Therefore, the interior walls' CHTC are more accurate compared to exterior walls' values according to these statistics.

In Fig. 4a, the interior wall surface's temperature is shown varied between a minimum of 12 °C and a maximum of 35.8 °C on the East wall by maintaining the indoor temperature at 20 °C (see Table 2). The exterior surface of the South wall however experienced much higher temperatures with a minimum of 20.9 °C and a maximum of 81.7 °C on hotter days in August 2023. The average temperature was higher in the East wall with 40.49 °C on exterior and 23.18 °C on interior side (see Table 2).

The rate of heat transfer was calculated using Eq. (1). As shown in Fig. 5 and Table 2, the minimum rate of heat transfer of 0.9 W and a maximum value of 86.30 W was observed on the South wall. The West wall with the value of 27.77 W had the highest average value among all walls.

Using the absolute values of the calculated convective heat transfer coefficient for interior wall surfaces, the results are demonstrated in Fig. 6a. The West wall interior surface has the highest cooling effect with the values of 0.0, 89.24, and 4.58 (W/m^{2}K), as the minimum, maximum, and the average, respectively (see Table 2).

As shown in Fig. 6b and Table 2, the exterior convective heat transfer coefficients are much smaller compared with the cooler interior values. The North wall exterior surface has the highest cooling values with 0.0, 9.98, and 1.18 (W/m^{2}K), as the minimum, maximum, and the average, respectively.

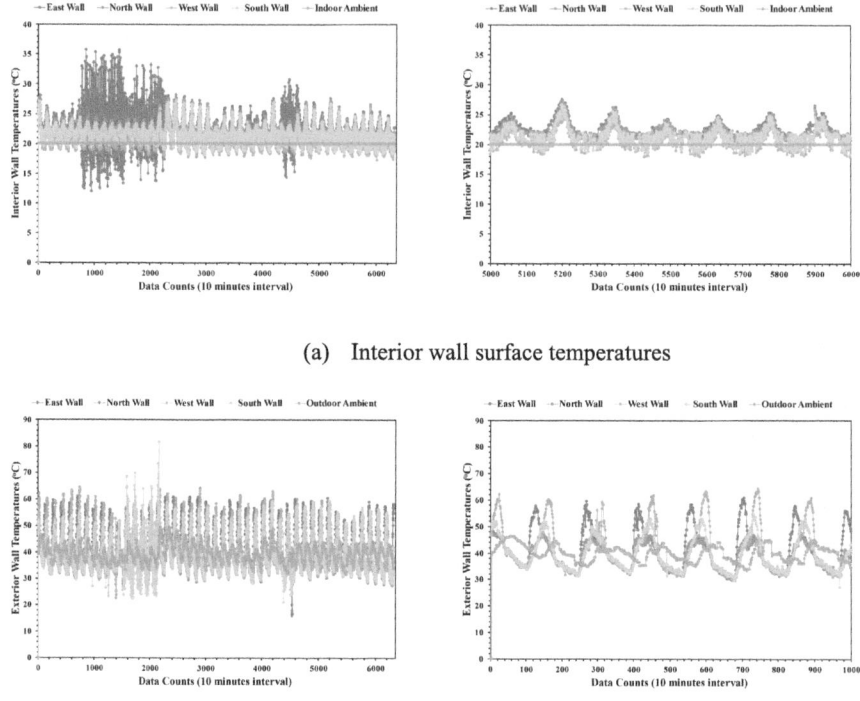

(a)   Interior wall surface temperatures

(b)   Exterior wall surface temperatures

Fig. 4. Temperature measurements on (a) interior wall surfaces and (b) exterior wall surfaces during August to September 2023 in Kuwait.

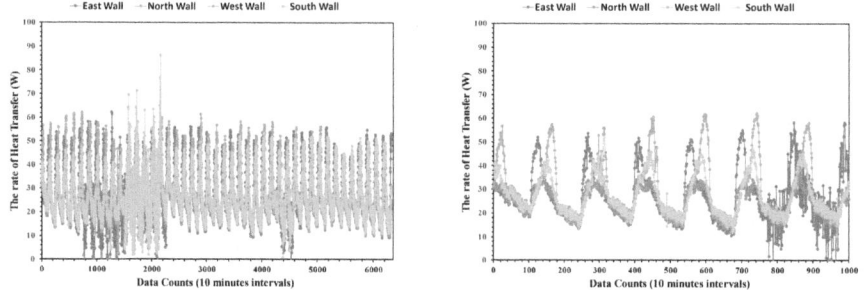

Fig. 5. The rate of heat transfer through the walls during August to September 2023 in Kuwait.

The indoor temperature remained at 20 °C throughout the study period and the outdoor temperature, however, varied from minimum temperature of 31.7 °C to maximum temperature of 44.2 °C, and the average temperature of 38.47 °C during the months of August to September 2023 in Kuwait (see Fig. 4).

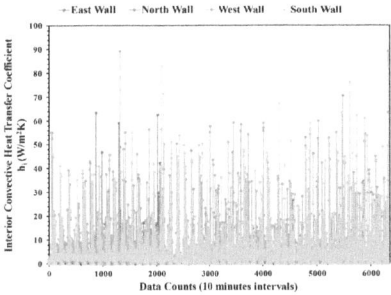 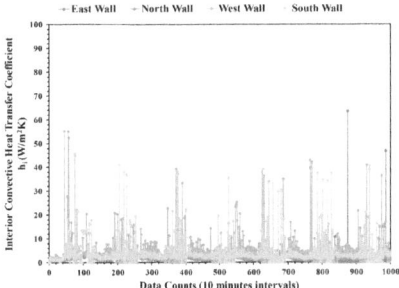

(a)   Interior wall surface values for the convective heat transfer coefficient

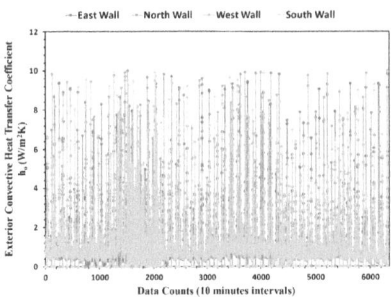 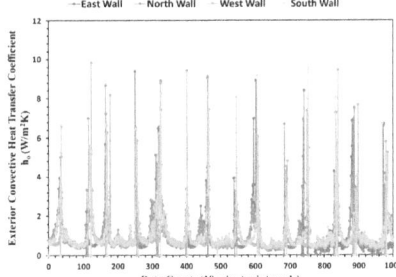

(b)   Exterior wall surface values for the convective heat transfer coefficient

Fig. 6. The convective heat transfer coefficients on (a) interior wall surfaces and (b) exterior wall surfaces during August to September 2023 in Kuwait.

Calculating $R_{wall} = \frac{0.075}{0.0201} = 3.73\left(\frac{m^2 K}{W}\right)$ and using the Eqs. (4) and (5), the average thermal resistance values and the average overall heat transfer coefficient were calculated. The overall findings of this study are summarized in Table 2. As observed in Table 2, the dynamic overall heat transfer coefficient of the walls is lower than the statically (steady state) standard value of 0.2534 (W/m^{2}K) [17, 18], indicating that the insulation sandwich panel walls perform even better than it was anticipated, particularly, in the hottest months of the year in Kuwait.

Table 2. Summary of findings of this research.

Location	Parameter	East Wall	North Wall	West Wall	South Wall
Interior Wall Surface	Max. Temp. (°C)	35.8	28.2	27.1	27.2
	Min. Temp. (°C)	12	19.9	17.3	18.2
	Avg. Temp. (°C)	23.18	22.50	21.14	21.53
	Max. $h_i \left(\frac{W}{m^2K} \right)$	63.52	34.57	89.24	82.81
	Min. $h_i \left(\frac{W}{m^2K} \right)$	0.00	0.00	0.00	0.00
	Avg. $h_i \left(\frac{W}{m^2K} \right)$	1.78	2.11	4.58	4.56
	Avg. $R_{inside} \left(\frac{m^2K}{W} \right)$	0.56	0.47	0.22	0.22
Exterior Wall Surface	Max. Temp. (°C)	60.9	50.2	64.4	81.7
	Min. Temp. (°C)	15.9	27.6	22.6	20.9
	Avg. Temp. (°C)	40.49	37.82	39.64	39.72
	Max. $h_o \left(\frac{W}{m^2K} \right)$	9.83	9.98	9.92	9.92
	Min. $h_o \left(\frac{W}{m^2K} \right)$	0.00	0.00	0.00	0.00
	Avg. $h_o \left(\frac{W}{m^2K} \right)$	0.92	1.18	1.03	1.11
	Avg. $R_{outside} \left(\frac{m^2K}{W} \right)$	1.08	0.85	0.97	0.90
Overall Wall Values	Max. Heat Rate (W)	62.13	37.22	61.98	86.30
	Min. Heat Rate (W)	0.15	9.00	2.70	0.90
	Avg. Heat Rate (W)	26.00	22.98	27.77	27.29
	Avg. $R_{total} \left(\frac{m^2K}{W} \right)$	5.38	5.05	4.92	4.85
	Dynamic U-value $\left(\frac{W}{m^2K} \right)$	0.186	0.198	0.203	0.206
	Static U-value $\left(\frac{W}{m^2K} \right)$	0.2534	0.2534	0.2534	0.2534

5   Conclusions

The thermal performance of polyurethane sandwich panel walls was investigated in a portable cabin in Kuwait. Eight K-type thermocouple probes were installed on the interior and exterior surfaces of the cabins' walls during the hot months of August and September 2023. The data was recorded using IoT and stored in iCloud. The results showed that the dynamic average overall heat transfer coefficients were 0.186, 0.198, 0.203, and 0.206 W/m²K for the East, North, West, and South facing walls, respectively. These values are significantly lower than the static overall heat transfer coefficient of

$0.2534\ \mathrm{W/m^2K}$, indicating superior thermal performance under dynamic conditions, particularly, during the hot summer months of Kuwait. This indicates that for the average dynamic U-value of 0.1983 for all walls, the cooling loads can be reduced by 21.76% in summer months of Kuwait. The results improved our understanding of thermal behavior of insulation walls in hot climates. The findings will contribute to development of low-energy buildings in Kuwait and countries with similar climatic conditions. Future research should continue to explore these findings across different seasons and conditions to fully establish the benefits and applicability of advanced insulation materials in energy-efficient building design.

Acknowledgments. This study is fully funded by the Kuwait Foundation for the Advancement of Sciences (KFAS) under grant no. CN19-35EM-06, which is gratefully acknowledged. The Australian University (AU) of Kuwait is also greatly acknowledged for its support throughout the KFAS project.

Disclosure of Interests. The authors have no competing interests to declare that are relevant to the content of this article.

References

1. 2019 Kuwait Energy Outlook, Sustaining prosperity through strategic energy management. https://www.kisr.edu.kw/media/filer_public/a7/d7/a7d7ecfa-242e-4c5f-a9bc-f971295b0a41/keo_report_english.pdf. Accessed 21 June 2024
2. Krarti, M., Hajiah, A.: Analysis of impact of daylight time savings on energy use of buildings in Kuwait. Energy Policy 39(5), 2319–2329 (2011)
3. Saber, H.H., Maref, W.: Energy performance of cool roofs followed by development of practical design tool. Front. Energy Res. 7, 122 (2019)
4. Canberra, A.C.T.: Energy use in the Australian residential sector 1986–2020. Department of the Environment, Water, Heritage and the Arts, Australia (2008)
5. Energy Data Homepage. https://www.energy.gov.au/energy-data/australian-energy-statistics/energy-consumption. Accessed 21 June 2024
6. Aldawi, F., et al.: A new house wall system for residential buildings. Energy Build. 67, 403–418 (2013)
7. Howard, B., et al.: Spatial distribution of urban building energy consumption by end use. Energy Build. 45, 141–151 (2012)
8. Zhao, H.X., Magoulès, F.: A review on the prediction of building energy consumption. Renew. Sustain. Energy Rev. 16(6), 3586–3592 (2012)
9. Panayiotou, G., Kalogirou, S.A., Tassou, S.A.: Evaluation of the application of Phase Change Materials (PCM) on the envelope of a typical dwelling in the Mediterranean region. Renew. Energy 97, 24–32 (2016)
10. Sedaghat, A., et al.: Effects of window films in thermo-solar properties of office buildings in hot-arid climates. Front. Energy Res. 9, 173 (2021)
11. Sedaghat, A., et al.: Climate change and thermo-solar patterns of office buildings with/without window films in extreme hot-arid climate of Kuwait. Sol. Energy 217, 354–374 (2021)
12. Sharma, A., et al.: Review on thermal energy storage with phase change materials and applications. Renew. Sustain. Energy Rev. 13(2), 318–345 (2009)
13. Bruno, F., Tay, N., Belusko, M.: Minimising energy usage for domestic cooling with off-peak PCM storage. Energy Build. 76, 347–353 (2014)

14. de Gracia, A.: Dynamic building envelope with PCM for cooling purposes–proof of concept. Appl. Energy **235**, 1245–1253 (2019)
15. Zheng, L., Chong, A., Poh, H.J., Sekhar, C.: Impact of building porosity on exterior convective heat transfer coefficients: an experimental and computational parametric study. Build. Environ. **247**, 111023 (2024)
16. Ding, K., Calautit, J.K., Jimenez-Bescos, C.: Significance of external wind conditions on the convective heat transfer coefficients (CHTC) and energy performance in multi-zone high-rise buildings. Energy Build 114570 (2024)
17. Ohlsson, K.A., Östin, R., Grundberg, S., Olofsson, T.: Dynamic model for measurement of convective heat transfer coefficient at external building surfaces. J. Build. Eng. **7**, 239–245 (2016)
18. Tao, S., Yu, N., Ai, Z., Zhao, K., Jiang, F.: Investigation of convective heat transfer at the facade with balconies for a multi-story building. J. Build. Eng. **63**, 105420 (2023)
19. Evangelisti, L., Barbaro, L., De Cristo, E., Guattari, C., D'Orazio, T.: Towards an improved thermometric method: Convective and radiative heat transfer for heat flux measurement through an indirect approach. Thermal Sci. Eng. Progress **49**, 102479 (2024)
20. Wikipedia Kuwait Homepage. https://en.wikipedia.org/wiki/Kuwait#cite_note-10. Accessed 21 June 2024
21. Middle East Political Map Homepage. https://www.mapsnworld.com/middle-east-political-map.html. Accessed 21 June 2024
22. Sedaghat, A., et al.: Implementing cool roof and bio-pcm in portable cabins to create low-energy buildings suitable for different climates. Sustainability **15**, 14700 (2023). https://doi.org/10.3390/su152014700
23. Sedaghat, A., et al.: Exploring energy-efficient building solutions in hot regions: a study on bio-phase change materials and cool roof coatings. J. Build. Eng. **76**, 107258 (2023)
24. Sedaghat, A., et al.: Case studies on energy performance of walling materials in various regions. International Journal of Environmental Science and Technology, 1–28 (2024)
25. Sedaghat, A., et al.: A new approach for selecting and implementing phase change materials in Kuwaiti Buildings: practical considerations. J. Energy Storage **88**, 111477 (2024)
26. Venkateshan, S.P.: Heat transfer. Springer Nature (2021)

Author Index

© IFIP International Federation for Information Processing 2025
Published by Springer Nature Switzerland AG 2025
G. Rey et al. (Eds.): IFIPIoT 2024, IFIP AICT 737, pp. 291–292, 2025.
https://doi.org/10.1007/978-3-031-81900-1

The manufacturer's authorised representative in the EU is Springer
Nature Customer Service Centre GmbH, Europaplatz 3, 69115 Heidelberg,
Germany. If you have any concerns regarding our products, please
contact ProductSafety@springernature.com

Printed and bound by CPI Group (UK) Ltd, Croydon, CR0 4YY
29/04/2026
02099538-0007